# LEGAL AND ETHICAL REGULATION OF BIOMEDICAL RESEARCH IN DEVELOPING COUNTRIES

*Nkasi, Chinemere, Ogemdi, and Nnamdi, Jr,*
*for their love and stimulus*

# Legal and Ethical Regulation of Biomedical Research in Developing Countries

REMIGIUS N. NWABUEZE
*University of Southampton, UK*

Routledge
Taylor & Francis Group
LONDON AND NEW YORK

First published 2013 by Ashgate Publishing

Published 2016 by Routledge
2 Park Square, Milton Park, Abingdon, Oxfordshire OX14 4RN
711 Third Avenue, New York, NY 10017, USA

First issued in paperback 2016

*Routledge is an imprint of the Taylor & Francis Group, an informa business*



**British Library Cataloguing in Publication Data**
Nwabueze, Remigius N., 1968–
Legal and ethical regulation of biomedical research in developing countries.
1. Medicine – Research – Law and legislation – Developing countries. 2. Medicine – Research – Moral and ethical aspects – Developing countries. 3. Medicine – Research – Law and legislation – Africa – Case studies.
I. Title
344.1'24041-dc23

**The Library of Congress has cataloged the printed edition as follows:**
Nwabueze, Remigius N., 1968–
Legal and ethical regulation of biomedical research in developing countries / by Remigius N. Nwabueze.
pages cm
Includes bibliographical references and index.
ISBN 978-1-4094-6610-9 (hardback)
1. Human experimentation in medicine–Law and legislation–Africa, English-speaking. I. Title.
KQC698.5.N88 2013
344.6704'196–dc23

2012043463

ISBN 13: 978-1-138-27930-8 (pbk)
ISBN 13: 978-1-4094-6610-9 (hbk)

# Contents

# Table of Cases

*Abdullahi v Pfizer, Inc.*, 2002 WL 31082956 (S.D.N.Y).
*Abdullahi v Pfizer*, 399 F. Supp. 2d 495 (2005).
*Abdullahi v Pfizer*, 77 Fed. Appx. 28 (C.A. 2nd Cir., 2003).
*Abdullahi v Pfizer, Inc.*, F.3d 163 (2nd Cir., 2009).
*African Continental Bank v A-G* (Northern Nigeria) [1967] 1 All N.L.R. 76 (SCN).
*African Newspapers Ltd. v Coker* [1973] 1 NMLR 386.
*African Press Ltd. v Ikejiani* [1953] 14 WACA 386.
*Agoaka v Ejiofor* [1972] 2 ESCLR 109.
*Allen v Flood* [1898] AC 1 (HL).
*American Cyanamid Co. v Ethicon* [1975] A.C. 396 (HL).
*Anns v Merton London Borough* [1978] A.C. 728 (HL).
*Attorney General v Guardian Newspapers Ltd. (No. 2)* [990] 1 A.C. 109.
*Attorney-General of the Federation v Pfizer Inc. & Others*, FHC/ABJ/CR/27/07.
*Baby Kasozi v Pope John's Hospital* [1974] EA 221 (Uganda).
*Bailey v Lally*, 481 F. Supp. 203 (US Dist. Ct. ML., 1979).
*Bailey v Lally*, 481 F. Supp. 203 at 205 (US Dist. Ct. ML., 1979).
*Bakare v Oluwide* [1962] 2 All NLR 324.
*Baker v Willoughby* [1970] A.C. 467 9HL; *Jobling v Associated Dairies Ltd.* [1982]
A.C. 794 (HL).
*Barnett v Chelsea & Kensington Hospital Management Committee* [1969] 1 Q.B. 428.
*Baxendale-Walker v Law Society* [2007] 3 All ER 330 (CA).
*Biakanja v Irving*, 320 P.2d 16 (Sup. Ct. Cal., 1958).
*Blyth v Birmingham Waterworks Co.* [1856] 11 Ex 781.
*Bolam v Friern HMC* [1957] 1 WLR 582.
*Sidaway v Royal Bethlem Hospital* [1986] A.C. 871 (HL).
*Bolam v Friern Hospital Management Committee* [1957] 1 W.L.R. 582.
*Bonsor v Musicians Union* [1956] A.C. 104.
*Bow Valley Husky (Bermuda) Ltd. v Saint John Shipbuilding Ltd.* [1997] 3 S.C.R. 1210.
*Boys v Chaplin* [1971] A.C. 356.
*British Industrial Plastics Ltd v Ferguson* [1940] 1 All ER 479 (HL).
*Burton v Brooklyn Doctors Hospital*, 88 A.D. 2d 217 (N.Y. S. Ct., 1982).
*C.B.S. Songs Ltd. v Amstrad Consumer Electric plc* [1988] A.C. 1013 (HL).
*Campbell v MGN Ltd* [2004] 2 A.C. 457.
*Candler v Crane Christmas & Co. Ltd.* [1951] 2 K.B. 164 (C.A.).
*Cann v Wilson* [1888] 39 Ch. D 39.

*Caparo Industries plc v Dickman* [1990] 2 A.C. 605 (HL).
*Catalona v Washington University* 128 S. Ct 1122 (2008).
*Chatterton v Gerson* [1981] Q.B. 432.
*Coco v A.N. Clark (Engineers) Ltd.* [1969] RPC 41.
*Cole v Turner* [1704] 6 Mod. 149.
*Cooper v Hobart* [2001] 206 D.L.R. ($4^{th}$) 193 (S.C.C.).
*Council of Civil Service Unions v Minister for Civil Service* [1985] 1 A.C. 374 (GCHQ).
*Cox v College of Optometrists of Ontario* [1988] 65 O.R. 2d 461 (Ont. Div. Ct.).
*Customs and Excise Commissioners v Barclays Bank plc* [2007] 1 A.C. 181 (HL).
*D v United Kingdom* [1997] 24 EHRR 423.
*Dimes v Grand Junction Canal* [1852] 10 E.R. 301
*Doe v Illinois Masonic Medical Centre*, 696 N.E.2d 707 (App. Ct. Ill., 1998).
*Doe v Sullivan* 938 F.2d 1370 (1991).
*Donoghue v Stevenson* [1932] A.C. 562.
*Emerald Construction Co. v Lowthian* [1966] 1 WLR 691 at700701.
*Fagan v Metropolitan Police Commissioner* [1969] 1 Q.B. 439.
*Fawehinmi v NBA (No. 2)* [1989] 2 NWLR 558 (SCN).
*Filartiga v Pena-Irala*, 630 F.2d 876 at 887 ($2^{nd}$ Cir., 1980).
*Foskett v McKeown* [2000] 2 WLR 1299.
*Garret v Taylor* [1620] Cro Jac 567.
*Gelsinger v University of Pennsylvania* (Complaint filed on 18 September 2000, Philadelphia County Court of Common Pleas Trial Division.).
*Glass v UK* [2004] 1 FLR 1019.
*Gold v Haringey Health Authority* [1988] 1 Q.B. 481.
*Goodwill v British Pregnancy Advisory Service* [1996] 1 W.L.R. 1397.
*Greenberg v Miami Children's Hospital*, 264 F. Supp. 2d 1064 at 1070 (S.D. Fla. 2003).
*Gregg v Kane*, 1997 WL 570909 (E.D. Pa.).
*Grimes v Kennedy Krieger Institute* [2001] 366 Md. 29, 782 A.2d 807.
*Halikas v The University of Minnesota*, 856 F. Supp. 1331 (US Dist. Ct. $4^{th}$ Div., 1994).
*Halushka v University of Saskatchewan* [1965] 53 D.L.R. (2d) 436 (Sask. Ct. App.).
*Harding v Wealands* [2005] 1 W.L.R. 1539.
*Head v Colloton*, 331 N.W.2d 870 (Sup. Ct. Iowa, 1983).
*Hedley Byrne & Co. Ltd. v Heller & Partners Ltd.* [1964] A.C. 465 (HL).
*Henley v Wise*, 303 F. Supp. 62 (N.D. Ind. 1969).
*Hill v Chief Constable of West Yorkshire* [1989] A.C. 53 (HL).
*Hoffman-La Roche v Sec. State, Trade and Industry* [1975] AC 295.
*Holly v Auld*, 450 So.2d 217 (S. Ct. Florida, 1984).
*Hoover v West Virginia Department of Health and Human Services*, 129 F. 3d 1259 ($11^{th}$ Cir. 1997).
*Howe v Lees* [1910] 11 C.L.R. 361.

*Hyman v Jewish Chronic Disease Hospital, 206 N.E. 2d 338 (*1965).
*In re Cincinnati Radiation Litigation*, 874 F. Supp 796 (1995).
*In re Popkin*, 460 F.2d 328 (1st Cir. 1972).
*Ireland v UK* [1978] 2 EHRR 25 (ECtHR).
*Jackson v Bishop*, 404 F.2d 571 (CA, 8th Cir. 1968).
*Kadic v Karadzi*, 70 F.3d 232 (2nd Cir. 1996).
*Kalu v State* [1998] 13 NWLR (Pt. 583) 531 (SCN).
*Kavuma v Hotel International Ltd.* [1993]11 KALR 73 (SCU).
*Kaye v Robertson* [1991] F.S.R. 52.
*Keenan v United Kingdom* [2001] 33 EHRR 913.
*Kelly v Solari* (1841) 152 ER 24.
*Kenedi v Hungary* (Application no. 31475/05), European Court of Human Rights (Second Section), 26 May 2009.
*King v University of Saskatchewan* [1969] 6 D.L.R. (3d) 120 at 125 (SCC).
*Knight & Searle v Dove* [1964] 2 All ER 307.
*Konrady v Oesterling*, 149 F.R.D. 592 (US Dist. Ct., 1993).
*Kpebimoh v The Board of Governors Western Ijaw Teachers Training College* [1966] N.M.L.R. 130 (HC).
*Kus v Sherman Hospital*, 644 N.E.2d 1214 (App. Ct. Ill., 1995).
*Lamb v Camden London Borough* [1981] Q.B. 625 (C.A.).
*Ward v Cannock Chase District Council* [1986] Ch. 546.
*Lardner v The Sketch Publishing Co. Ltd.* [1979] 3 LRN 276.
*Law v National Greyhound Racing Club Ltd.* [1983] 1 W.L.R. 1302 (C.A.).
*Lawal v Northern Spirit* [2003] UKHL 35 (HL).
*Locabail (UK) Ltd. v Bayfield Properties Ltd.* [2000] Q.B. 451.
*Lubbe v Cape Plc* [2000] 1 W.L.R. 1545.
*Lumley v Gye* (1853) 2 E & B 216.
*Mainstream Properties Ltd. v Young* [2008] 1 AC 1(HL).
*Marten v Royal College of Veterinary Surgeons' Disciplinary Committee* [1966] 1 QB 1 (CA).
*Matviuw v Johnson*, 70 Ill.App.3d 481 (App. Ct. Ill., 1979).
*Maynard v West Midlands Regional Health Authority* [1984] 1 W.L.R. 634.
*McDonald v Coys of Kesington* [2004] 1 W.L.R. 2775.
*McKinney v University of Guelph* [1990] 76 D.L.R. (4th) 545.
*McWilliams v Sir William Arrol & Co. Ltd* [1962] 1 W.L. R. 295.
*Meadow v General Medical Council* [2007] 1 All ER 1 (CA).
*Medical and Dental Practitioners Disciplinary Tribunal v Okonkwo* [2001] 7 NWLR 206 (SCN).
*Merkur Island Shipping Corporation v Laughton* [1983] 2 AC 570 (HL).
*Millar v Bassey* [1994] EMLR 44 (CA).
*Moore v Regents of the University of California*, 793 P.2d 479 (Cal. S. Ct. 1990).
*Moses v Macferlan* [1760] 97 ER 676.
*Murphy v Brentwood DC* [1991] 1 AC 398 (HL).
*Nettleship v Weston* [1971] 2 Q.B. 691 (C.A.).

*Njereketa v Director of Medical Services* [1950] 17 EACA 60 (C. A. for E. Afri.).
*Nthenda v Alade* [1974] 4 ESCLR 109.
*Obeya M. S. Hosp. v A-G.* [1987] 7 SCNJ 42 (SCN).
*Okekearu v Tanko* [2002] 9 S.C.N.J 1 (SCN).
*Omo-Osagie v Okutubo* [1969] 2 All NLR 175.
*Osman v United Kingdom* [1998] 29 EHRR 245.
*Palsgraf v Long Island Ry. Co.*, 248 N.Y. 339 (1928, C.A.).
*Peter Walker Ltd. v Hodgson* [1909] 1 K.B. 239.
*Phillips v Eyre* [1870] 6 L.R.Q.B. 1.
*Pope John's Hospital v Kasozi* [1974] E.A. 221.
*Port Arthur Shipbuilding Co. v Arthurs* [1968] 70 D.L.R. (2d) 693 (Sup. Ct. Can.).
*Porter v Magill* [2001] UKHL 67 (HL).
*R (on the application of Purdy) v DPP* [2009] UKHL 45.
*R v Bow Street Metropolitan Stipendiary Magistrate ex p. Pinochet Ugarte (No. 2)* [2000] 1 A.C. 119 (HL).
*R v Brown* [1994] 1 A.C. 212 (HL).
*R v Dept. of Health, ex p. Source Informatics Ltd.* [2000] 1 All ER 786 (CA).
*R v Ethical Committee of St Mary's Hospital (Manchester) ex p. H.* [1988] 1 FLR 512.
*R v Gough* [1993] A.C. 646 (HL).
*R v Inland Revenue Commissioners, ex p. National Federation of Self Employed and Small Business Ltd.* [1982] A.C. 617 (HL).
*R v Rand* [1865–66] L.R. 1 Q.B. 230.
*R v Altrincham Justices, ex p. N. Pennington* [1975] Q.B. 549.
*R(Pretty) v DPP* [2002] 1 AC 800.
R *v Advertising Standards Ltd. ex p. Direct Line Financial Services* [1998] C.O.D. 20.
*Re BHT (UK) Ltd* (2004) EWHC 201 (Ch).
*Re F (Mental Patient: Sterilisation)* [1990] 2 A.C. 1 (HL).
*Re T* [1992] 3 W.L.R. 782.
*Re Vanek and Governors of the University of Alberta* [1975] 57 D.L.R. (3d) 595 (Alberta Sup. Ct. App. Div.).
*Reg. v Bar Council, ex p. Percival* [1991] 1 Q.B. 212 (DC).
*Reg. v Chief Rabbi, ex p. Wachmann* [1992] 1 W.L.R. 1036 (Q.B.D.).
*Reg. v Criminal Injuries Compensation Board, ex p. Lain* [1967] 2 Q.B. 864.
*Reg. v Jockey Club, ex p. Aga Khan* [1993] 1 W.L.R. 909 (C.A.).
*Regina v Panel on Take-Overs and Mergers, ex p. Datafin Plc* [1986] 1 Q.B. 815 (CA).
*Reibl v Hughes* [1980] 114 D.L.R. (3d) 1.
*Report of the European Commission of Human Rights on the Greek Case*, 1969 Y.B. Eur. Conv. On H.R.
*Reynolds v Times Newspapers Ltd* [2001] 2 A.C. 127 (HL).
*Richards of Rockford, Inc. v Pacific Gas & Electric Co.*, 71 F.R.D. 388 (N.D. Cal. 1976).

*Robertson v McGee*, 202 WL 535045 (N.D. Okla).
*Rochin v California*, 342 U.S. 165 (S. Ct. 1952).
*Roe v Minister of Health* [1954] 2 Q.B. 66 (CA).
*Ross v Caunters* [1980] 1 Ch. 297.
*Rowe v Vale of White Horse DC* (2003) EWHC 388.
*Rowland v Divall* [1923] 2 K.B. 500.
*Samuelson v Susen,* 576 F.2d 546 (US Ct. App. 3rd Cir., 1978).
*Schloendorff v Society of New York Hospital*, 211 N.Y. 125 (1914).
*Series 5 Software Ltd. v Clarke* [1996] 1 All ER 853.
*Sidaway v Board of Governors of the Bethlem Royal Hospital and the Maudsley Hospital* [1985] A.C. 871.
*Sim v Stretch* [1936] 52 T.L.R. 669.
*Skidmore v Dartford and Gravesham NHS Trust* [2003] T.L.R. 1 (HL).
*Smith v Bush* [1990] 1 A.C. 831 (HL).
*Sosa v Alvarez-Machin*, 542 U.S. 692 (2004).
*State v Pfizer Inc. & Ors., Charge No. K/21c/07.*
*Stephens v Avery* [1988] Ch. 449.
*Stewart v Cleveland Clinic Foundation*, 736 N.E.2d 491 (Ct. App. Ohio, 1999).
*Stovin v Wise* [1996] A.C. 923 (HL).
*Stuart v Bell* [1891] 2 Q.B. 341.
*Sutherland Shire Council v Heyman* [1985] 60 ALR 1.
*Taff Vale Railway Co. v Amalgamated Society of Railway Servants* [1901] A.C. 426.
*Tarasoff v The Regents of the University of California*, 551 P.2d 334 (Cal. Sup. Ct., 1976).
*Tarleton v M'Gawley* [1794] Peake 270.
*The Solicitor-General Western Nigeria v Adedoyin* [1973] 3 U.I.L.R. 143 (CAW).
*Thomas v Local Government Service Board* [1965] 1 All N.L.R. 168 (SCN).
*Trachtman v Anker*, 563 F.2d 512 (2nd Cir., 1977).
*Trop v Dulles*, 356 U.S. 86 (S. Ct. 1958).
*Ukpoma v Daily Times Nig. Ltd.* [1979] 2 LRN 357.
*US v Stanley*, 283 U.S. 669 (US S. Ct. 1987).
*Vine v National Dock Labour Board* [1957] A.C. 488.
*Vu v Singer Co.*, 538 F. Supp. 26 at 29 (N.D. California, 1981).
*W v Egdell* [1889] 2 WLR 689 (CA).
*Washington University v Catalona* 437 F. Supp.2d 985 (Dist. Ct. Missouri, 2006).
*Washington University v Catalona* 490 F.3d 667 (Eight Cir., 2007).
*Watt v Longsdon* [1930] 1 K.B. 130.
*Webb v The Queen* [1994] 181 C.L.R. 41.
*Weiss v Solomon* [1989] R.J.Q. 731 (C.S. civ.).
*White v Jones* [1995] 2 A.C. 207 (HL).
*White v Paulsen*, 997 F. Supp. 1380 (E.D. Wash. 1998).
*Whittingham v Crease & Co.* [1978] 5 W.W.R. 45 (B.C. Sup. Ct.).
*Willis v Association of Universities of the British Commonwealth* [1964] 2 All ER 39.
*Wilson v Pringle* [1987] QB 237.

*Winnipeg Condominium Corp. No. 36 v Bird Construction Co.* [1995] 1 S.C.R. 85.
*X v Germany* [1984] 7 EHRR 152.
*Yearworth v North Bristol NHS Trust* [2010] Q.B. 1 (CA).
*Youssopoff v MGM* [1934] 50 T.L.R. 581.
*Yueun Kun Yeu v Attorney-General of Hong Kong* [1988] A.C. 175 (PC).
*Zango v Pfizer*, No. FHC/K/CS/204/2001 (Kano Federal High Court, Nigeria).
*Zimmer v Ringrose* [1981] 124 D.L.R. (3d) 215 (Albt. Ct. App).

# Acknowledgements

The author gratefully acknowledges a two-year (2007–2009) Leverhulme Research Fellowship granted to the author by the Leverhulme Trust that made the research and writing of this book possible. The author is also grateful to colleagues who read the whole or parts of the manuscript of this book; these include the late Professor David Price, De Montfort University; Professor Penny Lewis, Centre of Medical Law and Ethics, King's College London; Professor Hazel Biggs, University of Southampton; Dr Caroline Jones, University of Southampton; and Dr Alun Gibbs, University of Southampton. Many thanks to Dr Henry Ojambo, Faculty of Law, Makerere University, Uganda; Dr Godwin Ndossi, Director of Food Science and Nutrition, Tanzania Food and Nutrition Centre; and Dr Paul Ndebele, then of College of Medicine, University of Malawi, for respectively assisting the author during his research visits to Uganda, Tanzania and Malawi. As always, the author is grateful for the friendship and support of Mr James Ezike, a Lagos-based legal practitioner in Nigeria, and Dr DeLloyd J. Guth, Professor of Law and History, Faculty of Law, University of Manitoba, Winnipeg, Canada.

Finally, the author wishes to acknowledge the support and encouragement given to him by the publishing editor, Ms Alison Kirk, the Assistant Editor for Law, Ms Sarah Horsley, and the insightful and helpful comments from the two anonymous referees.

# Introduction

In the last 15 years, there has been some fermentation in bioethical scholarship relating to research involving human subjects in developing countries,[1] especially international collaborative research in Africa; this has led to the production of two major reports in the US and the UK.[2] Why has this global focus on research involving human subjects in developing countries analysed? Does research in developing countries raise regulatory, ethical and legal issues different from those that occur in developed countries? Are legal and ethical regulatory systems in Africa and other developing countries able to respond effectively to the ethical and legal liability issues that arise from the conduct of international collaborative research in their territories? In short, why have developing countries become an important location for the conduct of international collaborative research, especially clinical trials? While the focus of this book is to engage with these questions, this introductory chapter provides an overview of international collaborative research in developing countries, as well as a summary of the chapters that follow.

## The Growth of Externally-Sponsored Research in Developing Countries

Both the pace and scope of international collaborative research in developing countries have increased in recent years. A recent report estimated that 40 per cent to 50 per cent of new drug applications submitted in the EU and US are tested in developing countries, especially countries in Latin America, India, China, Eastern Europe and Russia.[3] Clinical trials are increasingly outsourced to Contract Research Organizations operating in offshoring countries.[4] While 'outsourcing' refers to the engagement of third parties, like Contract Research Organizations (CROs), to conduct clinical trials for another entity, such as pharmaceutical companies,

---

1 In this book, the terms 'developed' and 'developing' countries are not used in any technical sense, but colloquially to refer, respectively, to resource-rich countries in the North and resource-poor countries in the South.

2 For USA: National Bioethics Advisory Commission, *Ethical and Policy Issues in International Research: Clinical Trials in Developing Countries, vols. 1 and 2* (Bethesda, Maryland: NBAC, 2001); and for the UK: Nuffield Council on Bioethics, *The Ethics of Research Related to Healthcare in Developing Countries* (London, NCB, 2002 and 2005).

3 M. Huijstee and I. Schipper (eds), *Putting Contract Research Organisations on the Radar* (Amsterdam: SOMO, 2011) at 12.

4 For a good discussion of the strategies, operations and dynamics of CROs: Jane E. Winter and Jane Baguley (eds), *Outsourcing Clinical Development: Strategies for Working with CROs and Other Partners* (Aldershot: Gower Publishing Ltd., 2006).

'offshoring' is the conduct of clinical trials in non-traditional trial regions, such as developing countries.[5] The changing landscape of international collaborative research, favouring the location of clinical trial sites in developing countries, has given rise to a phenomenon characterized as the globalization of clinical trials.[6] Some factors account for the recent increase in the pace and scope of international collaborative research in developing countries; these include the HIV/AIDS pandemic that plagued many parts of the developing world, especially the east and southern African countries. In the wake of the HIV/AIDS pandemic, there was a huge influx of foreign research fund, medical devices, laboratory equipment and investigators into many parts of Africa. While this significantly increased HIV/AIDS-related research in Africa, access to antiretroviral therapies for most HIV/AIDS patients in Africa was very limited or non-existent. Although access has improved significantly over the years, it helps to explain why participation in clinical research was highly valued by most HIV/AIDS patients in Africa, as it was often their only means of getting direly needed healthcare. Thus, many HIV/AIDS patients in Africa were desperate to participate in HIV/AIDS-related research. The reality that participation in research offered the only chance of therapeutic benefits for some African patients led to a shift away from understanding research as a burden to understanding it as an opportunity for a benefit.[7] As desperation potentially leads to exploitation, HIV/AIDS-related research in Africa raised significant concerns about the safety, welfare and rights of research participants. While this will be addressed in the substantive chapters, it underscores the point that the pace and scope of international collaborative research in Africa gained some momentum with the HIV/AIDS pandemic.

Furthermore, the US National Bioethics Advisory Commission (NBAC) and the Office of Inspector General have identified additional factors underpinning the globalization of biomedical research.[8] First, international collaborative research in developing countries might be driven by the abundance of disease, huge population of research subjects, poverty, illiteracy, and inadequate healthcare infrastructures in developing countries. However, the NBAC emphasised that such research might be purely altruistic, and aimed at helping a developing country to

5 M. Huijstee and I. Schipper, supra, note 3, at 12.

6 For in-depth analysis of this concept: Department of Health and Human Services, Office of the Inspector General, *The Globalization of Clinical Trials: A Growing Challenge in Protecting Human Subjects* (DHHS, 2001).

7 Bernard Dickens, et al., 'Research on Human Populations: National and Internal Ethical Guidelines' (1991), 19 Law, Medicine & Health Care 157; Larry Gostin, 'Ethical Principles for the Conduct of Human Subject Research: Population-Based Research and Ethics' (1991), 19 Law, Medicine & Health Care 191 at 196.

8 National Bioethics Advisory Commission, *Ethical and Policy Issues in International Research: Clinical Trials in Developing Countries, vol. 1* (Bethesda, Maryland: NBAC, 2001) at 1–7; Department of Health and Human Services, Office of the Inspector General, *The Globalization of Clinical Trials: A Growing Challenge in Protecting Human Subjects* (DHHS, 2001) at 8–9.

overcome a peculiar health problem; for instance, the collaboration of US and developing countries' researchers to combat diseases that rarely occur in the US such as malaria, dengue fever and tuberculosis. Similarly, the Nuffield Council on Bioethics observed that research 'related to healthcare carried out in developing countries, often sponsored by developed countries, has made many outstanding contributions to the understanding, prevention and treatment of disease',[9] and noted that such altruistic contributions to the healthcare of developing countries was not a recent phenomenon because 'research on diseases such as malaria, yellow fever and sleeping sickness has been carried out in what are now regarded as developing countries for more than a century'.[10] Second, the choice of developing countries for the conduct of externally-sponsored research might be motivated by low regulatory visibility in most developing countries. Simply put, pharmaceutical companies and CROs 'escaping tighter regulations' on clinical trials in developed countries have found regulatory succour in developing countries where oversight mechanisms for research involving human subjects are not fully developed.[11] For instance, a recent report on the ethics of Phase 3 clinical trials conducted in developing countries to secure the registration and marketing rights of major psychotherapeutic drugs in Europe and North America observed that psychotherapeutic agents were tested against placebos in developing countries, even when similar trials are prohibited by regulations in developed countries. A representative of AstraZeneca was said to have explained the use of placebos in offshored trials of psychotherapeutic agents on the basis that 'almost all Western European Research Ethics Committees (RECs) no longer approve this kind of trials because of the ethical concerns and AstraZeneca is therefore compelled to look for locations outside Western Europe'.[12] Until 2007, Nigeria exemplified such a state of low regulatory visibility; unsurprisingly, Pfizer's clinical trial of trovan (an antibiotics drug) in Nigeria in 1996 raised serious ethical and legal controversies (these are explored in chapter one).

Third, clinical research in a developing country might be conducted to achieve some marketing objectives. For instance, drugs approved by regulatory agencies in developed countries might not be licensed for marketing in a developing country without the approval of the developing country's drug regulatory authority. To grant such approval, regulatory authorities in developing countries usually require a domestic testing of the drug, although it had already been approved for use in developed countries. Thus, externally-sponsored clinical trials in developing countries might be conducted just to secure marketing rights for new drugs.

---

9 Nuffield Council on Bioethics, *The Ethics of Research Related to Healthcare in Developing Countries* (London, NCB, 2002) at 6.

10 Ibid., at 6.

11 Huijstee and Schipper, supra, note 3, at 34.

12 Irene Schipper and Francis Weyzig, *Ethics for Drug Testing in Low and Middle Income Countries: Considerations for European Market Authorisation* (Amsterdam: SOMO, 2008) at 58.

African countries, however, do not represent a significant percentage of the global pharmaceutical market. While developing countries constitute only 20 per cent of the global pharmaceutical market, Africa represents only 1.1 per cent of that market.[13] As the globalization of clinical research intensifies, Africa's share of the global pharmaceutical market is likely to rise; the point, however, is that domestic testing of pharmaceuticals for marketing in developing countries has contributed to the rise in the volume of international collaborative research in developing countries. Fourth, since trials are most efficiently undertaken in sites where the condition being studied is most prevalent, the abundance of infectious and non-communicable diseases in developing countries makes them natural and appropriate locations for clinical trials. One of the reasons given by Pfizer, for conducting the trovan trial in Nigeria, was that epidemic meningitis occurs only in tropical regions, and that similar trials were not feasible in cold regions like the US. Furthermore, the Report of the Office of Inspector General observed that sponsors use 'emerging sites for their research to gain access to large numbers of subjects with a particular disease, especially those that are "naïve subjects" (i.e., have not been treated for the disease being studied), and to obtain data on different racial or ethnic groups'.[14] Fifth, arguably the most important reason for the growth of externally-sponsored research in developing countries is that it is cheaper and faster to conduct biomedical research in developing countries than in developed countries. It has been observed that in developing countries, sponsors 'recruit subjects quickly and, therefore, bring drugs to the market faster', and that sponsors were able 'to recruit subjects more quickly in certain countries, particularly Russia and those in Eastern Europe, than in Western sites'.[15] Similarly, the Nuffield Council on Bioethics observed that while 'some forms of sponsorship have been altruistic, others have been driven by academic interests which may not reflect national priorities for research in the country in which the research is being conducted or by economic considerations related to the marketing of healthcare products'.[16] Thus, the need to reduce cost in pharmaceutical R&D has been one of the main drivers of both the outsourcing and offshoring of clinical trials. In 2008, for instance, it was estimated that US-based pharmaceutical companies spent US$47.4 billion on R&D, and out of this sum, US$32.2 billion (or 68 per cent of the total R&D cost) was spent on clinical trials.[17] Outsourcing of clinical trials to contract research organizations operating in offshoring countries presents

---

13 Remigius N. Nwabueze, 'What Can Genomics and Health Biotechnology Do for Developing Countries' (2005), 15 Albany Law Journal of Science and Technology, 369 at 388.

14 Department of Health and Human Services, Office of the Inspector General, *The Globalization of Clinical Trials: A Growing Challenge in Protecting Human Subjects* (DHHS, 2001), at 8.

15 Ibid., at 8.

16 Nuffield Council on Bioethics, supra, note 9, at 6.

17 Huijstee and Schipper, supra, note 3, at 25.

pharmaceutical companies with a significant opportunity to reduce the R&D cost above, as well as improving their efficiency.[18]

## Externally-Sponsored Research as Foreign Direct Investment: The Indian Example

The increase in the pace and scope of international collaborative research in developing countries is a reflection of developing countries' domestic economic policy. In other words, developing countries conceive externally-sponsored research as a form of foreign direct investment (FDI); thus, externally-sponsored research in their territories is actively promoted as a strategic economic policy. Externally-sponsored research brings foreign capital and skilled manpower into developing countries; it also offers great opportunities for the transfer of technology to developing countries, and contributes immensely to capacity building for biomedical research in developing countries. Thus, the Nuffield Council on Bioethics emphasized how important it is 'that research in developing countries, particularly when sponsored by developed countries, is used as a platform for enhancing the skills of scientists in those developing countries', and that 'collaborative research projects generate opportunities for training and for developing human resources'.[19] All this means that some developing countries have deliberately set out to encourage and attract international collaborative research as a means of boosting their economy and furthering their developmental agenda. Unsurprisingly, therefore, some developing countries operate relatively weak regulatory frameworks in order to facilitate the outsourcing and offshoring of clinical trials into their territories.

In the last decade, clinical trials have been increasingly offshored to India and other developing countries like Brazil, Argentina and Peru, from many parts of the developed world.[20] There are currently more than 150 CROs operating in India.[21] India participates in 7 per cent of global Phase 3 clinical trials, and the growth rate of the Indian clinical trial sector is more than twice that of the global market.[22] Almost 90 per cent of all clinical trials in India are conducted by CROs.[23] India, therefore, presents a quintessential example of a developing country with such strategic economic policy in relation to externally-sponsored clinical trials. Patralekha Chatterjee observed that India is one of the world's 'preferred

18 Ibid., at 30.

19 Nuffield Council on Bioethics, supra, note 9, at 126.

20 P. Sree Sudha, 'How Ethical are Clinical Trials in India' (2007), Indian L.J. 9.

21 The Associated Chambers of Commerce and Industry of India, *Workshop on Clinical Trials*: http://www.assocham.org/events/showevent (last accessed on 17 September 2011).

22 Huijstee and Schipper, supra, note 3, at 51.

23 Radhieka Pandeya, 'New Code for Inspecting Human Drug Trials Mint', New Delhi, 10 November 2010.

destinations for clinical trials' and that '[D]rug companies are drawn to India for several reasons, including a technically competent workforce, patient availability, low costs and a friendly drug-control system'.[24] The booming clinical trial industry has been good for India's economy. In 2007, for instance, clinical trials business in India was valued at US$200 million and was estimated to reach US$1 billion by 2010.[25] But lax regulation, inadequate subject protection measures and 'high-profile cases in which pharmaceutical companies were shown to be withholding information from regulators'[26] in India have led to concerns about the potential exploitation of Indian research subjects.

Sudha highlighted some scandalous cases in India in which clinical trials were either not subjected to regulatory controls or failed to obtain the informed consent of research participants; one of such cases was a placebo-controlled clinical trial of an experimental oral cancer drug in which the patients were neither told that they were involved in research rather than therapy, nor that an established effective treatment was available for their condition.[27] Also, Rathod discussed an ethically questionable randomized controlled trial of a cervical cancer screening programme in India;[28] while women in the experimental group were screened by either human papilloma virus (HPV) testing, cytologic testing or visual inspection with acetic acid (VIA), and appropriate treatment provided for those with confirmed positive screening results, women in the control group did not receive any screening or treatment even though the aforementioned screening categories are widely accepted to be effective.[29] Thus, Rathod suggested that the HPV screening for cervical cancer in rural India was unethical because it lacked equipoise.[30]

Despite the availability of research guidelines published by the Indian Council of Medical Research,[31] research scandals in India have taken place against a backdrop of weak regulation, for as Nair and Martin observed, '[I]nstitutional mechanisms for ethical reviewing of research involving human participants in

24 Patralekha Chatterjee, 'Clinical Trials in India: Ethical Concerns' (2008), 86 Bulletin of the World Health Organisation 581 at 581.

25 Ibid., at 581.

26 Ibid., at 581.

27 P. Sree Sudha, 'How Ethical are Clinical Trials in India' (2007), Indian L.J. 9.

28 Sujit D. Rathod, 'Commentary on HPV screening for cervical cancer in rural India' (2011), 8 Ind. J. Med. Ethics 180.

29 But, see R. Sankaranarayanan, et al., 'Reply to S.D. Rathod's Commentary on HPV screening for cervical cancer in rural India' (2011), 8 Ind. J. Med. Ethics 182–183, suggesting that the non-provision of screening to the control group was consistent with the standard of care for cervical cancer control in India, that is, 'clinical diagnosis and treatment of invasive cancer only when symptomatic women seek medical attention' (at 182).

30 Rathod, supra, note 28.

31 Indian Council of Medical Research, Ethical Guidelines for Biomedical Research on Human Subjects (New Delhi: Indian Council of Medical Research, 2006).

India are weak and vulnerable'.[32] To worsen matters, the Indian drug regulatory authority (the Drug Controller General of India – DCGI) is perceived to be pro-pharmaceutical industry and lacks the oversight ability to manage the booming clinical trial sector in the country.[33] Furthermore, Nundy and colleagues observed that the DCGI was 'understaffed and lacks expertise to evaluate protocols. Currently, the technical staff consists of just three pharmacists, including the controller, and not one medically qualified doctor', and that the sorry state of Indian regulatory apparatus contributed to research scandals in which 'trials took place without regulatory approval'.[34] As in many African countries, the protective function of some research ethics committees in India is undermined by budgetary constraints, inadequate secretarial services and other relevant infrastructure, lack of ethical review capacity, and lack of expertise by some members of Institutional Ethics Committees.[35] In addition, most research ethics committees in India lack independence and thus face serious problems of conflict of interest.[36] Interestingly, Chandra Gulhati, editor of a medical periodical in India, was quoted as saying that: 'Fewer than 40 Ethics Committees in India are properly constituted and functioning, which means that the safety of the subjects of clinical trials is on the back burner'.[37]

In response to these concerns, the influential Indian Council of Medical Research (ICMR) launched its Clinical Trials Registry in 2007. The Indian Clinical Trials Registry is consistent with and based on the World Health Organisation's International Clinical Trials Registry Platform (ICTRP), launched by the WHO in 2005.[38] Registration of clinical trials at the relevant registry is intended to promote transparency; and the registry can serve as a clearing house for all clinical trials conducted in a country. With the Registry, duplication of clinical trials can be avoided; also, information relating to interventions that proved ineffective in a trial would be easily available in a searchable database. In this way, a Clinical Trials Registry helps to enhance the protection of research subjects, as well as promoting sound ethics in clinical trials. However, the Indian Clinical Trials Registry had some drawbacks. The first was that registration was not mandatory – not required by law; hence, drug companies and investigators who registered their clinical

---

32 V.M. Nair and D.K. Martin, 'Concerns about ethical review of health research in India' (2004), 1 Ind. J. Med. Ethics 119 at 120.

33 Huijstee and Schipper, supra, note 3, at 51 and 58–62.

34 Samiran Nundy, et al., 'A New Colonialism? – Conducting Clinical Trials in India' (2005), 352 New Eng. J. Med. 1633 at 1634.

35 Nair and Martin, supra, note 32, at 119. Also, generally, N.Madhiwalla, 'The NBC and the Bioethics Movement in India' (2011), 8 Ind. J. Med. Ethics 3–5.

36 A recent survey suggests that significant improvements have been made in the composition and functioning of research ethics committees in India: Pratibha Nadig, et al., 'Competence of ethics committees in patient protection in clinical research' (2011), 8 Ind. J. Med. Ethics 151–154.

37 Quoted in Chatterjee, supra, note 24, at 582.

38 http://www.who.int/ictrp/en/ (last accessed on 17 September 2011).

trials did so voluntarily. There was no legal sanction for the failure to register an approved trial at the Indian Clinical Trials Registry. This gap began to be closed in 2008 when the editors of 12 Indian biomedical journals, in conjunction with the Indian Clinical Trials Registry, issued a publication policy to the effect that their journals would not accept or publish the results of clinical trials unless such trials were registered with the Clinical Trials Registry.[39] This 'informal' mechanism to encourage registration was followed by a formal legal requirement to register each new trial, issued by the Drugs Controller General of India (DCGI) in 2009.[40] Within the first six months of the enactment of the DCGI's order, more clinical trials were registered in India than had been done voluntarily since the inception of the registry in 2007.[41] Currently, more than one thousand and eight hundred trials have been registered in the Indian Clinical Trials Registry.[42] In sum, India is not only the hub of clinical research in the developing world, but also it promotes externally-sponsored research as a form of foreign direct investment.

## Concerns About Exploitation: Ethical and Statutory Regulation

As can be surmised from the discussion above, international collaborative research involving human subjects in Africa and other developing countries raises significant concerns about the potential exploitation of research participants.[43] While these concerns are partly due to the low-regulatory visibility under which research involving human beings is conducted in many developing countries, they are exacerbated by the dominance of the private sector in the global research industry.[44] Unlike half a century ago, when biomedical research was funded mainly by the public sector, the current landscape of international research reflects a greater funding of biomedical research activities by private entities, such as the pharmaceutical, biotechnology and medical device companies.[45] For instance, the US National Bioethics Advisory Commission observed that while the US

39 Chatterjee, supra, note 24, at 581.

40 S. Nikarge and D. Pamnani, 'Clinical Trials Watch' (2009), 6 Ind. J. Med. Ethics 228-231; S. Nikarge, 'The Clinical Contours of Clinical Research in India' (2010), 7 Ind. J. Med. Ethics 178.

41 S. Nikarge, 'The Clinical Contours of Clinical Research in India' (2010), 7 Ind. J. Med. Ethics 178.

42 Arvind Pandey, et al., 'The upgraded Clinical Trials Registry India: a summary of changes' (2011), 8 Ind. J. Med. Ethics 186.

43 Jeremy Sugarman, et al., 'Ethical oversight of multinational collaborative research: lessons from Africa for building capacity and for policy' (2007), 3 Research Ethics Review 84–86.

44 See, Sanjay Nagral, 'Ethics, equity and justice: a view from the belly of the beast' (2011), 8 Ind. J. Med. Ethics 9–12, noting that the rise of private medicine has posed significant challenges to ethical conduct in medical practice and research.

45 NBAC, supra, note 8.

government 'has continued to increase its investment in biomedical research, private industry funding has increased much more rapidly', and that over 'the last 40 years, US funding of all research and development has seen a dramatic shift in its primary source from the public to private sector'.[46] The US National Bioethics Advisory Commission further observed that this development has led to the belief 'that market forces have pressured private organizations to become more efficient in the conduct of research, which may – absent vigilance – compromise the protection of research participants'.[47]

The fear that research subjects in Africa and other developing countries might be exploited or be needlessly injured in unethical research has been heightened by recent research scandals in Africa and other parts of the world; some of these scandals are explored in chapter one. Historically, however, the most notorious of modern research scandals dates back to the atrocious and unethical medical experiments carried out on captive subjects by Nazi scientists.[48] While the trial of the Nazi doctors was the basis for the promulgation of the Nuremberg Code in 1947, formal regulation of biomedical research, however, dates back to the Prussian era.[49] More research scandals in the US and other parts of the western world in the 1960s and 1970s prompted the development of research guidelines and a more systematic approach to research governance.[50] In 1966, for instance, Henry Beecher published an influential journal article in which he documented twenty-two examples of unethical research conducted in various US institutions. [51] This was followed by a more egregious scandal in which researchers at a US government's department (US Public Health Service) conducted a study on the natural course of syphilis involving poor African American men who did not provide consent for the study; indeed, the men were actively deceived, by being told that they were enrolled in the study for the treatment of their syphilis. Although penicillin was available for the treatment of syphilis at that time, none of the men received this therapy.[52] Echoes of the racist slant in the Tuskegee study could be heard in more recent

46 Ibid., at 3

47 Ibid., at 3.

48 M. Grodin, 'Historical Origins of the Nuremberg Code' in G.J. Annas and M. Grodin (eds), *The Nazi Doctors and the Nuremberg Code: Human Rights in Human Experimentation* (New York: Oxford University Press, 1992), 121–144.

49 Directive of the Prussian Minister of Religious, Educational and Medical Affairs 1900. See, generally, Sev S. Fluss, 'The Regulation of Human Experimentation: Historical and Contemporary Perspectives', in David N. Weisstub, *Research on Human Subjects: Ethics, Law and Social Policy* (Oxford, Elsevier Science Ltd., 1998) 222–242.

50 David J. Rothman, 'Ethical and Social Issues in the Development of New Drugs' (1987), 63 Bull. N.Y. Acad. Med. 557–568.

51 H. Beecher, 'Ethics and Clinical Research' (1966), New Eng. J. Med. 1354–60.

52 James H. Jones, *Bad Blood: The Tuskegee Syphilis Experiment* (New York: Free Press, 1993).

condemnations of similar biomedical studies.[53] The dominance of the Tuskegee scandal in the imagination of modern bioethical discourse is such that Peter Laurie and Sidney Wolfe, and Marcia Angell, analogized the short-course AZT placebo-controlled trial (for prevention of perinatal transmission of HIV/AIDS) in many developing countries to the Tuskegee study.[54] These sorts of scandals triggered formal oversight mechanisms and research governance in the US and most parts of the western world; as Rothman observed, 'human experimentation incidents illustrate the power of scandal to effect political and social change'.[55]

In the US, the Belmont Report provides the foundation for the substantive ethical principles that govern research involving human subjects.[56] These principles are organized around the tripartite requirements of autonomy or respect for persons, beneficence and justice.[57] However, Mary Simmerling and colleagues have argued that while the Belmont Report's influence has attained a sort of hegemonic character, the substantive principle that it established 'distorts the philosophical requirements of the ethical principles of beneficence, respect for persons, and justice in both their conceptual specification and practical application',[58] and, furthermore, that '*Belmont*'s model relies on a simplistic accounting of the concepts of beneficence, respect for persons, and justice'.[59] In addition to the substantive ethical requirements in the Belmont Report, 'ethically sound research must comply with an important *procedural requirement* – prior ethical review by a body that is competent to assess compliance with these substantive ethical principles'.[60] This type of independent and competent ethical review bodies are known as Institutional Review Boards (IRB) in the US, Research Ethics Board (REB) in Canada, Research Ethics Committees (REC) in England and Wales, Institutional Review Committees (IRC) in Uganda, and Health Research Ethics Committees (HREC) in Nigeria; the core responsibility of research ethics committees is the protection of the rights and welfare of research

---

53 For instance, P. Farmer and N.G. Campos, 'New malaise: Bioethics and Human Rights in the Global Era' (2004), 32 J.L. Med. & Ethics 243–251, compared an international collaborative biomedical study in Uganda, on the behavioural and biologic risk factors associated with the spread of HIV/AIDS (discussed in chapter two), with the US Tuskegee study.

54 Peter Lurie and Sidney M. Wolfe, 'Unethical Trials of Interventions to Reduce Perinatal Transmission of the Human Immunodeficiency Virus in Developing Countries' [1997], 337 New Eng. J. Med. 853–856; Marcia Angell, 'The Ethics of Clinical Research in the Third World' [1997], 337 New Eng. J. Med. 847–849.

55 Rothman, supra, note 50, at 557.

56 National Commission, *Belmont Report: Ethical Principles and Guidelines for the Protection of Human Subjects of Research* (National Commission, 1979).

57 Ibid., at 4–10.

58 Mary Simmerling, et al., 'Introducing A New Paradigm For Ethical Research In The Social Sciences: Part 1' (2007), 101 Northwestern University Law Review 837 at 859.

59 Ibid., at 839.

60 NBAC, supra, note 8, at 5 (Italics in the original).

subjects. More recently, the legitimacy, utility and constitutionality of the system of regulation through research ethics committees have come under serious academic scrutiny. For instance, Bledsoe and colleagues have questioned the social utility and fundamental role of research ethics committees, noting that the upsurge in regulation has produced an overwhelmingly negative result, and that University 'IRB offices, terrified at the spectre of their institutions losing all federal funds, opted overwhelmingly for conservatism'.[61]

Bledsoe and colleagues further argued that since IRBs took the role of 'protecting the institution from both lawsuits and the suspension of federal funding', they 'proceeded to develop a number of related responses that the iron cage model might predict', as well as defined 'their most fundamental task not as that of anticipating risk to the subject, the original object, but to the institution from noncompliance, no matter how trivial'.[62] From a legal perspective, however, Hamburger argued that ethics committees regulate research by licensing speech and press, contrary to the prohibition of the First Amendment of the US Constitution which protects against the licensing of speech and press.[63] In a sustained rebuttal of Hamburger's argument, James Weinstein opined that the regulation of research through the framework of ethics committees does not constitute an impermissible constitutional restraint on speech because biomedical research, for instance, involves more conduct than speech, does not contain significant communicative elements, nor is it a precondition for speech necessary for the functioning of democracy.[64] Thus, biomedical research would not be able to trigger the First Amendment protection of speech and press because of the fundamental distinction in American constitutional law between speech and conduct. Regarding social science research, which involves more communicative elements, such as interviews, surveys, conversations, or written and oral directions connected with experiments or tests, all of which are analogous to speech for the purposes of the First Amendment, Weinstein argued that the First Amendment protection is not implicated because regulations establishing research ethics committees belong to the category of rules of general applicability which, on the face of it, do not violate the First Amendment, although such rules of general applicability might burden speech incidentally.[65] In any event, Jonathan Moss has

61 Caroline H Bledsoe, 'Regulating Creativity: Research and Survival in the IRB Iron Cage' (2007), 101 Northwestern University Law Review, 593 at 612.

62 Ibid., at 612.

63 Phillip Hamburger, 'Getting Permission' (2007), 101 Northwestern University law Review 405–492.

64 James Weinstein, 'Institutional Review Boards and the Constitution' (2007), 101 Northwestern University Law Review 493–561.

65 Similarly, Menikoff observed that 'individual researchers are not subject to a regulatory burden rising to the level of constitutional concern': Jerry Menikoff, 'Where's The Law? Uncovering The Truth About IRBs And Censorship' (2007), 101 Northwestern University Law Review 791 at 799.

argued that research ethics committees' functions are so great and so critical that even if research ethics committees were declared unconstitutional there would be a need to reinvent them, although the alternative or replacement body might not be as efficient as current research ethics committees.[66]

Famously, Beauchamp and Childress expanded the substantive ethical principles enshrined in the Belmont Report into four separate elements: autonomy, beneficence, nonmalficence and justice.[67] Beauchamp and Childress' principled approach to ethical reasoning is popularly known as principlism.[68] But, as highlighted in chapter four, significant criticisms have been levelled against principlism, one of which is that it lacks specification.[69] This might explain Claire Foster's laudable attempts to use actual case studies to give practical meaning to normative principles analogous to principlism.[70] More recently, Charles Foster has criticized principlism and its ethically pluralistic approach, arguing that principlism relies on external sources for the infusion of its substantive content, is not extensive enough to manage all bioethical problems, suffers from the hegemony of autonomy, and does not take dignity into account.[71] Foster, therefore, suggested that 'dignity ought to be the foundational principle of bioethics'.[72] In the context of international research, however, it has been suggested that ethical appraisal of research should be based on broader principles of development, social justice and human rights, all of which go beyond principlism.[73] Similarly, Farmer and Campos advocated a human rights approach to bioethics, suggesting that bioethics should be embedded in a social context, and that more attention should be focused on discussing the overlay of social justice onto bioethics;[74] thus, they opined that with

66 Jonathan Moss, 'If Institutional Review Boards Were Declared Unconstitutional, They Would Have To Be Reinvented' (2007), 101 Northwestern University Law Review 801–807.

67 T.L. Beauchamp and J.F. Childress, *Principles of Biomedical Ethics, 6th edn* (New York: Oxford University Press, 2009).

68 R. Gillon, 'Four Scenarios' (2003), 29 J. Med. Ethics 267–268; Marvin J.H. Lee, 'The problem of "thick in status, thin in content" in Beauchamp and Childress' principlism' (2010), 36 J. Med. Ethics 525.

69 E. Meslin, et al., 'Principlism and the ethical appraisal of clinical trials' (1995), 9 Bioethics 399–418.

70 Claire Foster, *The Ethics of Medical Research on Humans* (Cambridge: Cambridge University Press, 2001).

71 Charles Foster, *Human Dignity in Bioethics and Law* (Oxford: Hart Publishing, 2011), at 113–114.

72 Ibid., at 111.

73 S.R. Benatar and P.A. Singer, 'A New Look at International Research Ethics' (2000), 321 BMJ 824–826; S.A. Benatar and P.A. Singer, 'Responsibilities in International Research: A New Look Revisited' (2010), 36 J. Med. Ethics 194–197.

74 P. Farmer and N.G. Campos, 'New malaise: Bioethics and Human Rights in the Global Era' (2004), 32 J.L. Med. & Ethics 243–251.

'a new focus on human rights, bioethics can engage other disciplines to ensure that social and economic rights for the poor are realized'.[75]

Despite the criticisms above, the substantive ethical principles in the Belmont Report, expounded by Beauchamp and Childress as principlism, and the procedural ethical requirement, grounded in ethical review of research protocols by independent and competent ethics committees, have been embraced by international research guidelines; of which the two best known are the Declaration of Helsinki and Council for International Organizations of Medical Sciences guidelines.[76] There are also two well-known specialist guidelines underpinned by the substantive and procedural ethical principles above; one of them is the UNAIDS/WHO Guidance Document, which regulates HIV/AIDS vaccine research. [77] The other is the ICH Harmonised Tripartite Guideline: Guideline for Good Clinical Practice, which regulates the conduct of clinical trials;[78] it was promulgated for the adoption of regulatory bodies in the European Union, Japan and USA. While these international guidelines provide an excellent model for regulatory emulation, the need for local or national domestic guidelines in African countries has never been greater; not least because international guidelines have not taken the peculiar local circumstances of Africa into consideration – only local guidelines can achieve that end. Also, the provisions of international guidelines often conflict, thereby confusing African countries and their researchers as to which guideline should provide the rule of action. For instance, chapter two highlighted the divergent positions of major international guidelines regarding the use of placebo-controlled trials when an effective therapy exists for the condition being studied.[79] More importantly, and following from the conflicting provisions of international guidelines, sponsors and investigators from developed countries undertaking externally-sponsored research in developing countries often make strategic use of international guidelines. Thus, they only adhere to a guideline that supports their objectives or national interests; for this reason, international guidelines that are perceived to be inconvenient,

75 Ibid., at 245.

76 World Medical Association. *Declaration of Helsinki, Ethical Principles for Medical Research Involving Human Subjects* (59th WMA General Assembly, Seoul, 2008); Council for International Organisations of Medical Sciences (CIOMS), *International Ethical Guidelines for Biomedical Research Involving Human Subjects* (Geneva: CIOMS, 2002.

77 Joint United Nations Programme on HIV/AIDS and World Health Organisation, *Ethical Considerations in Biomedical HIV Prevention Trials: UNAIDS/WHO Guidance Document* (Geneva: UNAIDS/WHO, 2007).

78 International Conference on Harmonisation of Technical Requirements for Registration of Pharmaceuticals for Human Use, *ICH Harmonised Tripartite Guideline: Guideline for Good Clinical Practice* (1996).

79 For a detailed criticism of European drug regulatory authorities, regarding the acceptance of data for drug registration generated from placebo-controlled studies conducted in developing countries contrary to the Declaration of Helsinki, see Irene Schipper and Francis Weyzing, *Ethics for Drug Testing in Low and Middle Income Countries: Considerations for European Market Authorisation* (Amsterdam: SOMO, 2008), 15–19.

or whose provisions are thought to impose burdensome duties on investigators and sponsors, are often ignored.[80] Furthermore, the strategic and tendentious use of international research guidelines in developing countries, by sponsors and investigators from developed countries, is made possible by the ambiguity of the guidelines themselves; such ambiguities create a need for their interpretation. This means that an international guideline whose requirements are perceived to be burdensome could be interpreted into irrelevance.

Much of the criticism above is underscored by the controversy surrounding the placebo-controlled trial of a short-course AZT treatment regimen in developing countries, to determine the efficacy of a short-course AZT treatment regimen in the prevention of perinatal transmission of HIV/AIDS (this is examined fully in chapter one). At the time of the short-course AZT trial, the Helsinki Declaration provided for the use of the 'best current diagnostic and therapeutic methods' for the control group, a requirement that is largely retained by the current 2008 version, which meant the provision of a full-course AZT treatment to the poor pregnant women in the control group; but the full course AZT treatment was expensive and unaffordable in the developing countries where the trials took place. In order to justify the placebo-controlled short-course AZT trial, however, the US researchers and sponsors of the study took the view that the 'best current diagnostic and therapeutic methods' meant treatment that was locally available (practically meaning 'no treatment' in the developing countries where the trial was conducted because AZT treatment was too expensive and locally unaffordable), and not treatment that was available anywhere in the world. This triggered one of the most remarkable debates in the history of biomedical research, a debate often identified by epithets such as 'standard of care in research', 'universal versus local standards of care', and 'double standards' in biomedical research.[81] Also, the debate led to the revision of major international research guidelines in the early 2000s, although in the end, the very issue at stake was left largely unresolved. Regarding the use of placebo-controls when an effective (but unaffordable) treatment exists, for instance, chapter two shows that there is currently a clear difference of opinion between the provisions of CIOMS (largely favouring such trials) and the Helsinki Declaration, which maintains its opposition to such trials except in very limited circumstances; for example, where the study entails no serious risk of harm to subjects. The US National Bioethics Advisory Commission has polarized the debate further by recommending that placebo-controlled trials in developing countries are permissible despite the availability of effective treatments, provided that the placebo design is justified by the investigators and sponsors: 'Researchers and sponsors should design clinical trials that provide members of any control

80 P. Laurie and D.B. Greco, 'US exceptionalism comes to research ethics' (2005), 365 Lancet 1111; Sylvester C, Chima, 'Regulation of biomedical research in Africa' (2006), 332 BMJ 848 at 848.

81 Ruth Macklin, *Double Standards in Medical Research in Developing Countries* (Cambridge: Cambridge University Press, 2004).

group with an established effective treatment, whether or not such treatment is available in the host country. Any study that would not provide the control group with an established effective treatment should include a justification for using an alternative design'.[82] Thus, there is a dire need for local guidelines in Africa that reconcile, contextualize and adapt these international research guidelines to the peculiar circumstances of Africa.

In Africa, happily, regulation has moved to the front burner of bioethical discourse. As chapters one and three suggest, a good number of African countries have developed guidelines based on well-known international biomedical research guidelines; these African guidelines have, however, taken local circumstances and conditions into consideration. African countries that do not have local or domestic research guidelines apply one or more of the popular international research guidelines mentioned above. It has even been suggested that the African Union should show strong and responsible leadership by promulgating a detailed Directive or regulation regarding the conduct of research involving human beings in Africa, and that the Directive should be domesticated in a legally binding form by member states of the African Union.[83] The conclusion of this book will address how that proposal can be implemented by the African Union. Although the debate on the regulation of international collaborative research in developing countries has raged for many years, there is hardly any comparable analytical focus on the existence, substance and operation of domestic research guidelines in individual African countries.

Interestingly, the US Office of Inspector General identified this gap in its 2001 Report, observing that the 'FDA's informational void concerning the performance of foreign institutional review boards is of particular concern for emerging sites with little experience in conducting clinical research'.[84] For many years, it was assumed that research guidelines in Africa were either non-existent or poorly developed, and that ethical review procedures in Africa were rudimentary at best. While some of these assumptions remain valid, especially with regard to the independence, competence and performance of ethics committees in some African countries, on the whole, however, these assumptions lack solid foundation and do not reflect the reality of current research governance in Africa. In an empirical study conducted by Nancy Kass and colleagues, for instance, they observed that 'research ethics review is increasingly routine in Africa'.[85] Based on a survey of the experiences of developing countries' researchers, Hyder and colleagues also opined that 'ethical

82 NBAC, supra, note 8, at 28.

83 Sylvester C. Chima, 'Regulation of biomedical research in Africa' (2006), 332 BMJ 848–851.

84 Department of Health and Human Services, Office of the Inspector General, *The Globalization of Clinical Trials: A Growing Challenge in Protecting Human Subjects* (DHHS, 2001), at 18.

85 Nancy Kass, et al., 'The Structure and Function of Research Ethics Committees in Africa: A Case Study' (2007), 4 PLoS Medicine 26 at 29.

guidelines in developing countries exist and are able to offer some protection to research subjects, which is different from the hypothesis that such local guidelines are either non-existent or entirely worthless'.[86] More interestingly, the debate on the regulation of biomedical research in Africa has moved from ethical and self/professional regulation to legal and statutory regulation.[87] In light of research scandals in Africa that took place under a climate of low-regulatory visibility, it is understandable that African commentators mostly support the use of statutory and enforceable regulatory frameworks for the oversight of research involving human beings in Africa.[88] Chapter one articulates the reasons why statutory regulation should be the norm in Africa.

Even in developed countries, enforceable guidelines are beginning to pervade the regulatory firmament. In Europe, for instance, two examples could be highlighted. The first is the Council of Europe Convention on Human Rights and Biomedicine, which adopts a human rights approach to the ethical and legal difficulties raised by modern applications of biology and medicine;[89] the Convention is enforceable in member states of the Council of Europe that have signed and ratified the Convention.[90] While the Convention does not give a private right of action, and a member state, qua government, can only get an advisory opinion from the European Court of Human Rights concerning issues involved in the interpretation of the Convention, Plomer however opined that the provisions of the Convention are indirectly enforceable.[91] In an action to enforce the right of privacy (Art. 8) under the European Convention on Human Rights, for example, the European Court of Human Rights could deploy the Council of Europe's Convention on Human Rights and Biomedicine to expound the right of privacy

86 A.A. Hyder, 'Ethical Review of Health Research: A Perspective from Developing Country Researchers' (2004), 30 J. Med. Ethics 68 at 71.

87 Dominique Sprumont, 'Legal Protection of Human Research Subjects in Europe' (1999), 6 European Journal of Health Law 25 at 41.

88 For instance, Cheluchi Onyemelukwe, 'Research Involving Humans in African Countries: A Case for Domestic Legal Frameworks' (2008), 16 Afr. J. Int'l & Comp. L. 152–177; Chima, supra, note 83.

89 Council of Europe, Convention on Human Rights and Biomedicine, Oviedo, 4. IV. 1997. The Convention's use of human rights and human dignity to mediate modern applications of biology and genetic engineering echoes Annas' suggestion for a moratorium on human cloning, and other similar applications of genetic engineering techniques, based on human dignity and human rights: George J. Annas, 'The Man on the Moon, Immortality, and other Millennial Myths: The Prospects and Perils of Human Genetic Engineering' (2000), 49 Emory L.J. 753–782.

90 For extended analysis of the Convention, see P. Zilgalvis, 'The European Convention on Human Rights and Biomedicine: its past, present and future', in A. Garwood-Gowers, *Healthcare Law: The Impact of the Human Rights Act 1998* (London: Cavendish Publishing, 2001).

91 Aurora Plomer, *The Law and Ethics of Medical Research: International Bioethics and Human Rights* (London: Cavendish Publishing Ltd., 2005) at 18.

under the European Convention on Human Rights.[92] The second example of enforceable regulation in Europe is the EU Clinical Trials Directive;[93] this directive was transposed into UK law in 2004.[94] It is an enforceable statutory framework for the conduct of clinical trials in the UK, and other European countries that have domesticated the EU Clinical Trials Directive.

Even in the US, the patchwork of research governance includes statutory frameworks such as those represented by the National Research Act 1974[95], the Common Rule,[96] and the US Food and Drug Administration regulation.[97] More globally, it has been suggested that legally enforceable research guidelines should be the norm. For instance, Annas argued that the 'Nuremberg Code, the Helsinki Declaration, and the WHO/CIOMS guidelines are almost universally seen as advisory and ethical only',[98] and that they have 'no legal status in most countries, and they provide no mechanism for accountability or sanction of researchers who disregard their concepts'.[99] For this reason, Annas suggested that it has become necessary to 'seek more definitive action or international research rules from the United Nations'.[100] Practically, this meant that the United Nations should develop an international Covenant on Human Experimentation based on the Nuremberg Code but, unlike the Nuremberg Code, the Covenant should extend to both therapeutic and non-therapeutic research, as well as research on vulnerable populations or groups, such as the terminally ill.[101] Annas suggested that the proposed Covenant on Human Experimentation should be enforced by an international tribunal for human experimentation, which should be established for that purpose; the jurisdiction of the tribunal should be initially limited to civil sanctions.[102] Realising, however, that the 'competing political agendas of the member states' of the United Nations was bound to frustrate the suggestion, Annas and Grodin called on lawyers and physicians to join a new organization, Global Lawyers and Physicians (GLP), which should be able to put the 'establishment of such an International Medical Tribunal … on the agenda

92 This approach is evident in *Glass v UK* [2004] 1 FLR 1019.

93 The European Clinical Trials Directive 2001/20/EC.

94 Medicines for Human Use (Clinical Trials) Regulations 2004 (SI 2004/1031).

95 National Research Service Award Act. Pub. L. No. 93–348, 88 Stat. 342 (1974).

96 Health and Human Services (Common Rule) Title 45 Code of Federal Regulations, Part 46 (2005).

97 Department of Health and Human Services, Code of Federal Regulations (CFR), Title 21 Part 50 (Food and Drugs Administration).

98 George J. Annas, 'The Changing Landscape of Human Experimentation: Nuremberg, Helsinki, and Beyond' (1992), 2 Health Matrix 119 at 135.

99 Ibid, at 135.

100 Ibid.

101 Ibid., at 137.

102 Ibid.

as an advocacy effort of all medical and legal associations around the world';[103] lawyers and physicians were also asked to work collaboratively toward the global implementation of international documents relating to human rights, medical research and experimentation.[104] The proposals by Annas came in the wake of a draft Criminal Covenant on Human Experimentation developed by Bassiouni and colleagues for adoption by the United Nations.[105] In addition to being enforceable and binding among member states of the United Nations, Bassiouni and colleagues argued that a specialized Convention on human experimentation was necessary to remove the ambiguity surrounding the status of the Nuremberg Code and the Declaration of Helsinki as customary rules of international law. Thus, the adoption of 'a convention would mean removal of such ambiguities by creating clearly recognizable rights and unmistakably binding duties'.[106] The draft code developed by Bassiouni and colleagues was, however, rejected by the United Nations, out of fear that it might implicate the practices of pharmaceutical industries in some member states of the United Nations.[107] In sum, therefore, there is a global trend towards enforceable regulatory frameworks.

## Issues of Legal Liability and African Law

In addition to the argument above for enforceable research regulations, analytical attention has just begun to be focused on the legal liability issues that arise from research involving human participants. The importance of legal liability issues is highlighted by the local (Nigeria) and transnational (US) litigation instituted against Pfizer by parents and representatives of the children involved in Pfizer's clinical trial of trovan in Nigeria in 1996. As chapters one and seven will show, the United States Court of Appeal decided in favour of the claimants on the issue of subject-matter jurisdiction;[108] a further appeal to the US Supreme Court was dismissed in 2010, prompting Pfizer to settle the suit out of court.[109] Although anecdotal, this judicial victory suggests that litigation offers a real chance of remedy to aggrieved research subjects. While a flood of similar litigation is not expected in Africa, due to the poverty of most research subjects, the threat of

103 George J. Annas and Michael A. Grodin, 'Medical Ethics and Human Rights: Legacies of Nuremberg' (1999), 3 Hofstra L. & Pol'y Symp. 111 at 119.

104 Ibid., at 122.

105 M.C. Bassiouni, et al., 'An Appraisal of Human Experimentation in International Law and Practice' (1981) 72 J. Crim. Law and Criminology 1597–1655.

106 Ibid., at 1662.

107 Sharon Perley, et al., The Nuremberg Code: An International Overview', in Annas and Grodin, supra, note 48, at 166.

108 *Abdullahi v Pfizer, Inc.*, F.3d 163 (2nd Cir., 2009).

109 Washington Legal Foundation, 'Court Allows Suit to Proceed Alleging Human Rights Violations', Press Release on 29 June 2010 (on file with author).

legal actions has become a potential force of deterrence against unethical conduct in international collaborative research undertaken in developing countries. The litigation against Pfizer shows that, in the future, African courts might be asked to decide more cases relating to research related injuries.

Africa presents an interesting mix of legal systems.[110] Some are bi-jural in nature, that is, they operate local customary law and received English law, including English-type of law, such as statutes and Constitution. Common law African countries, like Nigeria and Uganda, represent the bi-jural systems. Other bi-jural systems in Africa, especially some Francophone African countries, operate local customary law alongside the received French civil law. Some African countries, however, operate a tri-jural system, such as South Africa, where local customary law operates alongside some received English common law rules and the received Roman-Dutch civil law.[111] Another African tri-jural system is Cameroon, where customary law, local legislation and received French law operate in East Cameroon, and customary law, local legislation, and received English law operate in West Cameroon.[112] All this is a relic of colonization. Because of limitations in training and language, the legal analysis in this book concentrates on the jurisprudence of *common law* African countries; thus the legal liability issues that arise from research involving human beings in Africa are examined in the light of legal categories drawn from common law African countries. While all the common law African countries received the same English common law in their territories,[113] there are differences in terms of the date of reception – for instance, Nigeria received only common law rules in operation in England as at 1 January 1900[114] – and also differences in the way in which each African common law country settled the problem of internal conflict of law, that is, conflict arising from the dual application of customary law and received English law.[115] While these differences

---

110 For an excellent overview of legal systems in countries of West Africa, East Africa, Central and Southern Africa, see A.N. Allott, *Judicial and Legal Systems in Africa, 2nd edn* (London: Butterworths African Law Series, 1970).

111 See, generally, F. Du Bois (ed.), *Wille's Principles of South African Law, 9th edn* (Cape Town: Juta & Co., 2007).

112 J.A. Clarence, et al., 'The Federal Republic of Cameroon', in Allott, supra, note 110, at 108–121.

113 For excellent analysis: A. Allott, *New Essays in African Law* (London: Butterworths – African Law Series, No. 13, 1970).

114 B.O. Nwabueze, *The Machinery of Justice in Nigeria* (London: Butterworths – African Law Series, 1963) at 127. A.O. Obilade, *The Nigerian Legal System* (London: Sweet and Maxwell, 1979) at 69–82. The reception date for Uganda is 11 August 1902: Christopher Mubirumusoke, 'Application of the Received Law of Torts in East Africa and the Problem of Transplanting Legal Norms', in Thomas W. Bechtler (ed.), *Law in a Social Context: Liber Amicorum Honouring Professor Lon L. Fuller* (The Netherlands: Kluwer, 1987) at 136.

115 Remigius N. Nwabueze, 'The Dynamics and Genius of Nigeria's Indigenous Legal Order' (2002), 1 Indigenous Law Journal 153 at 174–191; Nwabueze (BO), supra,

should be borne in mind, in addition to differences in local legislation and judicial inclinations which might affect the outcome of a suit, it is likely, however, that the outcome of a case subject to the application of received English common law will be the same in most common law African countries.[116] In her commentary regarding the uncritical application of the received English law of torts in Africa, Cottrell captured this possibility (of unified judicial outcome) when she observed that the 'common law seems to have a homogenizing effect, and what happens in the High Court of socialist Tanzania is very much what happens in the High Court of essentially capitalist Nigeria'.[117] Although dated, this observation generally reflects the current state of the received English common law in Africa. In an essay in honour of Professor Lon Fuller, Mubirumusoke attributed the influence and dominance of English jurisprudence in common Law Africa, especially in the law of torts, to the unimaginative and unquestioning application of reception clauses through which the common law was transplanted into Africa.[118] In this book, therefore, the author implies that common law African countries, especially those used as cases studies in chapter three, would give a common answer to the legal liability issues examined in chapters five, six and seven; in so doing, the author has proceeded on the assumption, noted by Cottrell above, that the received English common law has a 'homogenizing effect' in Africa. Where necessary, however, the author has given attention to distinctive local materials and case law which might make the outcome of a case different for a particular common law African country.

In the eventuality that African courts begin to engage with more cases relating to research injuries, as suggested above, questions would arise as to the appropriate legal categories that should underpin such suits. Potential suits are likely to cover a wide range of legal categories, such as the law of tort, administrative law, contract law, unjust enrichment, constitutional law, and human rights. These forms of actions need more analytical exposure in the context of African law.[119] Even in developed countries, legal analysis of research involving human subjects is sparse,

note 114, at 39–43.

116 This is even truer for common law African countries located within the same region, as demonstrated by Veitch for East Africa: E. Veitch, *East African Cases on the Law of Tort* (London: Sweet and Maxwell, 1972) at 1–24.

117 Jill Cottrell, 'The Functions of the Law of Torts in Africa' (1987), 31 J. Afr. L. 161 at 183. Earlier, she observed that for 'practical purposes, therefore, one may treat the Nigerian law of tort as being identical with that of England except where the latter has been modified by statute': Jill Cottrell, 'The Tort of Negligence in Nigeria' (1973), 17 J. Afr. L. 30 at 30.

118 Christopher Mubirumusoke, 'Application of the Received Law of Torts in East Africa and the Problem of Transplanting Legal Norms', in Thomas W Bechtler (ed.), *Law in a Social Context: Liber Amicorum Honouring Professor Lon L Fuller* (The Netherlands: Kluwer, 1987) 127–188.

119 Technically, there is no such thing as 'African Law'. In this book, however, the phrase is used colloquially to refer to the law applicable in common law African countries.

compared to the voluminous ethical, policy and philosophical literature on the subject; attention in the Western world has only recently begun to be focused on the legal liability issues that arise from research involving human subjects.[120] In the context of administrative law, for instance, Hadskis and Carver expressed their surprise that administrative law has not been used more often to interrogate the exercise of powers by ethics committees, despite the fact that 'administrative law principles can play a pivotal role in defining the rights of research stakeholders and the procedural responsibilities of REBS (Research Ethics Boards)'; also, 'administrative law offers the potential for judicial oversight of the exercise of REB decision-making power in some circumstances'.[121] Arguably, the law of torts is the single most important legal category for the regulation of research involving human subjects. Interestingly, the concepts of tort law contributed significantly to the analytical frameworks underpinning chapters five, six and seven, where the legal analyses are concentrated. The important regulatory role that the law of torts could assume in this area is beginning to be recognized. Charrow, for instance, observed that instead of expanding the regulatory scheme for research involving human subjects, it might 'make more sense to rely on the tort system to correct any problems'.[122]

The definition of 'tort' is, however, not free from difficulty. Generally, 'tort' means a 'wrong'. Fleming defined 'tort' in general terms to mean 'an injury other than a breach of contract, which the law will redress with damages', although he quickly added that the definition he gave was far from informative, 'nor even strictly accurate in view of other remedies, like self-help and equitable relief by injunction, which are sometimes available against a tort, actual or threatened'.[123] The law of torts is a potentially ubiquitous regulator; its jurisdiction covers virtually every human activity, including research involving human subjects. For this reason, Linden observed that the 'law of torts hovers over virtually every activity of modern society'.[124] Although some commentators refute an instrumentalist or teleological role for the law of torts,[125] it is arguable that the

---

120 Examples of recent works in this regard include: Hazel Biggs, *Healthcare Research Ethics and Law: Regulation, Review and Responsibility* (London: Routledge-Cavendish, 2010); T. Lemmens and D.R. Waring (eds), *Law and Ethics in Biomedical Research* (Toronto: University of Toronto Press, 2006); Plomer, supra, note.

121 M. Hadskis and P. Carver, 'The Long Arm of Administrative Law: Applying Administrative Law Principles to Research Ethics Boards' (2005), 13 Health Law Review 19 at 28.

122 Robert Charrow, 'Protection of Human Subjects: Is Expansive Regulation Counter-Productive?' (2007), 101 Northwestern University Law Review 707 at 718.

123 John G. Fleming, *The Law of Torts, 9th edn* (Sydney: LBC Information Services, 1998) at 3.

124 Allen M. Linden, *Canadian Tort Law, 7th edn* (Markham, Ontario: Butterworths, 2001) at 1.

125 For instance, Ernest Weinrib, 'Understanding Tort Law' (1989), 23 Valp. L.J. 485.

law of torts is generally compensatory in nature. Equally, the law of torts deters substandard conduct, is educative, provides psychological comfort to the injured, and functions as an ombudsman.[126] Wade emphasized the function of the law of torts as an ombudsman, observing that the law of torts has the potential to be a bulwark against abuse of power or mistreatment of citizens by government officials.[127] In Tanzania, Pande highlighted the potentiality of the law of torts as an ombudsman by deploying the tort action of false imprisonment as a mechanism to challenge the abuse of power and excesses of public officials in Tanzania.[128]

The law of torts can play a similar role in externally-sponsored research in Africa. International collaborative research in Africa and other developing countries is sponsored by developed countries or powerful multinational corporations that are richer than some underdeveloped countries in Africa; these multinational corporations can also easily influence governments in developing countries. This sort of power-dependent relationship is ideal for the intervention of the law of torts as an ombudsman. Thus, where an African subject suffers injury from participation in externally-sponsored research due to lack of regulatory oversight, and the government is unable or unwilling to call the sponsor to account, the law of tort (as an ombudsman) can fill the gap by providing a means of complaint and compensation for the injured subject. In essence, the law of torts is capable of performing all its potential functions in Africa. Cottrell even observed that some of the functions mentioned above are already being performed in Africa by the law of torts, particularly by 'making some contribution to the compensation of road accident victims, and to the victims of official abuse of power'.[129] Thus, the law of torts could be brought into the service of claimants who suffered injury from participation in research or clinical trials.

The rapid commercial and industrial growth attained by most African countries in the wake of political independence from Britain in the 1960s greatly increased the occasions for causing tort damage.[130] In turn, the rise in tort litigation catalysed the growth of African tort scholarship.[131] Unfortunately, tort scholarship in Africa has lost the momentum that it gained in the 1970s and 1980s.[132] So, has the law of

126 Linden, supra, note 124, at 4–29.

127 John W. Wade, 'Tort Law as Ombudsman' (1986), 65 Or. L. Rev. 309–325.

128 B.B. Pande, 'Protecting the Individual Against the State Through False Imprisonment Actions: The Tanzanian Experience' (1983), 32 Int'l & Com. L. Q. 506–515.

129 Jill Cottrell, 'The Functions of the Law of Torts in Africa' (1987), 31 J. Afr. L. 161 at 182.

130 Mauro Bussani, 'Tort Law and Development: Insights Into The Case of Ethiopia and Eritrea' (1996), 40 J. Afri. L. 43 at 45, observing that Western countries faced the same phenomenon with the rise of industrial revolution.

131 For instance, see Jill Cottrell, 'The Tort of Negligence in Nigeria' (1973), 17 J. Afr. L. 30, exploring the huge influx of negligence cases into Nigerian courts up to the decade following its political independence in 1960.

132 Tort literature in common law Africa at this period include: G. Kodilinye, *The Nigerian Law of Torts* (London: Sweet and Maxwell, 1982); E. Veitch, *East African*

torts become irrelevant in Africa? Internet and electronic searches of relevant legal databases (for example, Westlaw, LexisLibrary, HeinOnline, and Google) hardly reveal any decent and quality Afrocentric tort scholarship that is comparable to the African tort literature of the 1970s and 1980s.[133] The author personally searched some university libraries, bookshops, markets and malls in Uganda, Nigeria, Tanzania, and Malawi between 2008 and 2009 but nothing in the nature of quality and substantial tort scholarship turned up. The dearth of African tort scholarship contrasts sharply with the voluminous literature on human rights in Africa. Undoubtedly, African human rights scholarship was buoyed by the adoption and ratification of the African Charter on Human and Peoples' Rights in the mid-1980s by member states of African Union, then Organisation of African Unity.[134] The African Charter was developed as a regional response to the egregious human rights abuses perpetrated by some post-independent African political leaders;[135] it was also intended to mainstream human rights within the Charter of the African Union.[136] Since 1990s, there is hardly any volume of the Journal of African Law (the flagship journal on African law) that does not contain an article on human rights in Africa. Compared to human rights, therefore, the law of torts in Africa has taken the back burner position, but that might speak to the greater advantage of human rights as a more suitable platform of resistance against political oppression and economic exploitation by African political leaders. In the face of oppressive African governments, social activists might consider that human rights frameworks, which impose clear restraints on excessive and arbitrary exercise of State power, offer a better platform for social mobilization than the law torts. In her analysis of the functions of the law of torts in Africa, Cottrell alluded to this insight when she observed that there was 'one striking absence from the roll of defendants in Nigeria: there are no actions in tort against the state'.[137] In sum, therefore, while

---

*Cases on the Law of Tort* (London: Sweet and Maxwell, 1972); Jill Cottrell, 'The Tort of Negligence in Nigeria' (1973), 17 J. Afr. L. 30–39; B.B. Pande, 'Protecting the Individual against the State through False Imprisonment Actions: The Tanzanian Experience' (1983), 32 Int'l & Comp. L.Q. 506–515; Jill Cottrell, 'The Functions of the Law of Torts in Africa' (1987), 31 J. Afr. L. 161–184.

133 Exceptions include: Remigius N. Nwabueze and Polycarp Okorie, 'Flexibility of Damages for Conversion and Detinue' (2009), 17 African Journal of International and Comparative Law 102–117; Mauro Bussani, 'Tort Law and Development: Insights Into The Case of Ethiopia and Eritrea' (1996), 40 J. Afri. L. 43–52.

134 African Charter on Human and Peoples' Rights, 21 I.L.M. 58 (1982).

135 Generally, U.O. Umozurike, *The African Charter on Human and Peoples' Rights* (The Hague: Martins Nijhoff, 1997).

136 Gino I. Naldi, 'Future Trends in Human Rights in Africa: The Increased Role of OAU?', in R.A. Murray and D. Malcolm (eds), *African Charter on Human and Peoples' Rights: The System in Practice, 1986–2000* (Cambridge: Cambridge University Press, 2002) at 1–35.

137 Jill Cottrell, 'The Functions of the Law of Torts in Africa' (1987), 31 J. Afr. L. 161 at 174.

human rights and constitutional law frameworks are useful legal categories and, in conjunction with other legal categories, might be deployed to analyse some of the legal issues that arise from research involving human subjects, tort law, however, has the potential to play a greater role in the regulation of research involving human subjects; for instance, in terms of the width and reach of its claims and the likelihood of success for claimants.

## Summary of Chapters

The analysis above suggests that while ethical regulation of biomedical research in Africa and other developing countries has attracted global attention in the last decade, and should continue to do so, equal attention should also begin to be bestowed on the legal liability issues, such as the application of common law rules, and the development of legally enforceable regulations. Consequently, this book explores not only the important ethical issues that arise from research involving human subjects in Africa, but also the potential legal liability issues that are involved. Thus, chapter one explores the national and international regulatory contexts of research involving human subjects in Africa by examining some of the major research scandals that mark the history of biomedical research in Africa and other parts of the world. The scandals provide a historical background to major research regulations in Africa and the developed world. Also, chapter one deploys these scandals as a factual matrix for applying the theory of equipoise analysed in chapter two. In light of the abuses involved in those scandals, chapter one suggests the development of legally enforceable research guidelines in Africa, and the strengthening of ethics review capacity in Africa. Chapter two examines the concept of equipoise, by interrogating its utility as a normative or fundamental ethical criterion for the justification of clinical research in Africa and other developing countries. A clinical trial that lacks equipoise is not only unethical, but it might also cause harm to research subjects. Equipoise is a state of genuine uncertainty regarding the therapeutic merits of a set of interventions; it must exist before a trial commences and must remain throughout the duration of the trial. A crucial objective of drug trials is to resolve equipoise by eliminating doubt in the clinical community regarding a set of therapeutic interventions. Equipoise, however, entails or implies certain duties, such as the duty not to give subjects a known inferior treatment, and the corollary duty not to use a placebo design when an effective treatment exists for the condition being studied. These requirements make the application of equipoise very controversial, especially in developing countries where basic treatments are not available and the healthcare infrastructures are in a perennial state of dilapidation. Thus, chapter two examines the meaning of equipoise, the criticisms leveled against it, its relevance in Africa, and how the duties implied by equipoise affect the ethics of clinical research in Africa. Moreover, chapter two deploys equipoise as a conceptual and normative framework that could be used to analyse the research scandals examined in chapter one.

Chapter three, however, focuses on the development of research guidelines in three selected African countries, that is, Uganda, Malawi and Nigeria. Chapter three examines the history of the guidelines in these countries, the impetus for their development, their contents, the ethics review process established by the guidelines, and research governance infrastructures in the selected countries. Chapter three not only articulates the regulatory responses of Uganda, Malawi and Nigeria to research scandals that occurred in their territories; it also impugns the popular assumption that most African countries lack regulatory mechanisms for the oversight of research involving human subjects. On the contrary, chapter three suggests that research regulation in most African countries has attained a level of sophistication comparable to the regulations in developed countries, although ethics review capacity still needs to be strengthened.

Chapter four focuses on the functions, scope, nature and machinery of ethics review in Africa. It explores various functions of ethics committees and the philosophical bases of ethics review. Chapter four also examines the debate on whether the duties of ethics committees include the scientific and legal reviews of protocols. Furthermore, chapter four explores special problems that arise from the ethics review of international collaborative research; it also examines the critical question of ethical review capacity in Africa, and explores the emerging institutional trends towards the establishment of bioethical capacity and training of ethics committee members in Africa. Chapter four also addressed the problem of funding ethics committees in Africa, and the question of whether ethics committees in Africa should charge fees for their services. Finally, chapter four explores the problems raised by the existence and operation of commercial review boards; thus, it examines the nature and mode of operation of commercial review boards, and the serious questions of conflict of interests inherent in their operation.

Obviously, the conduct of research involving human subjects is not a totally harmless activity; research subjects might suffer harm caused negligently or intentionally. Similarly, investigators might have a cause for complaint, for instance, against the decision or conduct of ethics committees and their members. Thus, research involving human subjects raises legal liability issues. Chapter five begins the legal analysis by examining potential causes of action that might be brought against ethics committees and their members by research subjects. Chapter five embarks on this inquiry by examining the question of whether ethics committees have a corporate legal personality that is separate from their members; this helps to determine whether ethics committees could be sued as a corporate body. Chapter five identifies actions in negligence as the most important legal mechanisms available to research subjects against ethics committees and their members. Consequently, chapter five provides a detailed analysis of the law of negligence, and its application to research ethics committees and their members. Finally, chapter five examines professional disciplinary actions that might be instigated by research subjects against professional members of ethics committees. Chapter six focuses on legal claims that are available to investigators/researchers against ethics committees and their members. The decision of an ethics committee to reject a protocol, or recommend a substantial modification, might adversely affect an investigator's economic and social interests, or interests in their reputation. For instance, in the course of the proceedings of an ethics committee, a member of the committee might make imputations of incompetence against an investigator, which lower the investigator in the estimation of right-thinking members of the society. Also, such defamatory remarks might be embodied in the rejection letter written by the committee to the investigator and copied to the sponsor. Similarly, the denial of ethics approval might cause the investigator to lose a potentially lucrative (research) contract with a sponsor. Most uncommonly, however, an ethics committee and its members might intentionally procure a breach of an investigator's research contract or, otherwise, inflict economic loss on the investigator by behaving unlawfully towards a third party. In these situations, the investigator would be happy to seek legal remedies. An investigator's principal legal remedy against an ethics committee and its members lies in the administrative law action of judicial review. Other remedies include an action for injunction; the torts of procuring a breach of contract, and causing loss by unlawful means; an action for negligent economic loss; and an action for defamation. An investigator might also claim for a legal and constitutional right to research. Chapter six examines these familiar common law and constitutional forms of action in the unique and novel contexts of research ethics committees and their members.

Finally, chapter seven examines the liability of investigators in actions brought by research subjects. As already noted, research is not a harmless activity, and might expose subjects to significant harm or injury. In some circumstances, therefore, research participants could institute legal proceedings against investigators (and sponsors) to redress injuries suffered as a result of their participation in research. Chapter seven examines the potential causes of action available to research subjects against their investigators; these include claims in negligence; battery; constitutional law; unjust enrichment; breach of confidence; and claims brought in foreign (non-African) courts. Chapter seven highlights the procedural and substantive frameworks for extraterritorial claims brought in English and American courts by African claimants injured in international collaborative research. The conclusion reflects on the themes of this book and the author's suggestions.

# Chapter 1
# Regulatory Contexts of Biomedical Research in Developing Countries

## Introduction

The Nuremberg Code was the direct outcome of the trial of Nazi doctors and scientists for the atrocious biomedical experiments they conducted on captive and vulnerable subjects; this is generally known as the Medical Case. As a regulatory framework, therefore, the Nuremberg Code came in the wake of scandals that gave rise to the Medical Case; since then, this pattern or timing of regulation has marked the history of research involving human subjects. Thus, the general trend is that regulations come after scandals in biomedical research activities. Rothman observed that 'human experimentation incidents illustrate the power of scandal to effect political and social change'.[1] Similarly, Curran opined that the 'Drug Law of 1962 … probably would never have been enacted … without the vast public outcry for stronger drug control laws that resulted from the terrible outbreak of infantile deformity … by the drug Thalidomide'.[2] In the same vein, Robert Charrow observed that the US Congress responded to the Tuskegee research scandal by enacting the National Research Service Award Act in 1974; the 1974 Act made prior ethical review, by an Institutional Review Board, a condition for research funded under the Public Health Service Act.[3] In essence, regulation in the field of biomedicine has been reactive (and not proactive) to scandals;[4] much of this is evident in chapters one and three. Therefore, to understand the detailed regulation of research in Africa explored in chapter three, this chapter begins with analysis of some of the international, regional and national biomedical research scandals which furnish a solid background and context for current research regulations. In addition, these scandals, particularly those that took place within the African

---

1 David J. Rothman, 'Ethical and Social Issues in the Development of New Drugs and Vaccines' (1987), 63 Bull. N.Y. Acad. Med. 557–568, at 557.

2 W.J. Curran, 'Governmental regulation of the use of human subjects in medical research: The approach of two federal agencies' (1969), 98 Daedalus 409.

3 Robert Charrow, 'Protection of Human Subjects: Is Expansive Regulation Counter-Productive' (2007), 102 Northwestern University law Review 707–722.

4 For analysis of some of the most influential pieces of regulation and their historical contexts: Sev S. Fluss, 'The Regulation of Human Experimentation: Historical and Contemporary Perspectives', in David N. Weisstub (ed.), *Research on Human Subjects: Ethics, Law and Social Policy* (Oxford: Elsevier Science Ltd., 1998) 222–242.

continent, provide a factual and legal matrix for applying the normative framework of equipoise analysed in chapter two. Furthermore, this chapter interrogates the regulatory models of research in Africa; the scope of research guidelines in Africa; and the enforceability of African research guidelines. In the concluding section, this chapter suggests that African countries should promulgate clear, comprehensive and legally enforceable research guidelines.

## International Regulatory Contexts

Recent research scandals in some African countries raise ethical concerns that are better understood in their historical and international contexts. As examined in more detail below, some of the African biomedical research scandals include the clinical trial of a short-course zidovudine to test its efficacy in the reduction of perinatal or vertical transmission of HIV/AIDS (mother-to-child transmission of HIV/AIDS); the clinical trial of trovan to determine its efficacy in the treatment of epidemic meningitis; the first HIV-1 candidate vaccine trial; the ethically questionable studies on the biologic and behavioural risk factors associated with the transmission of HIV/AIDS; and the tenofovir (HIV/AIDS) vaccine trials. The analysis that follows shows that these African research scandals have some interesting international and historical parallels.

In the early nineteenth century, for instance, gonorrhoea and syphilis studies were undertaken by medical scientists, who were characterized by Vikenty Veressayev as 'bizarre disciples of science', and 'zealots of science', in Germany, France, Russia, Ireland, and the United States of America.[5] The gonorrhoea study involved the inoculation of gonorrhoea-free (healthy) patients without their consent with pure cultures of gonococcus to prove that it was the agent responsible for gonorrhoea.[6] Similar inoculations were undertaken with respect to syphilis to demonstrate that it was contagious in its secondary stage.[7] The syphilis study was so outrageous that even after Ricord, the greatest opponent of the hypothesis that secondary syphilis was contagious, had accepted his error, unethical and unconsented inoculations with the disease were still carried out by some investigators, despite the abundant scientific proof contrary to their hypothesis, thus rendering more victims to science.[8] More detailed and specific instances of research scandals at the international level are provided below in order to highlight the historical background and contexts for those that occurred in Africa.

5 Vikenty Veressayev, *The Memoirs of a Physician* (New York: Alfred A. Knopf, 1916; translated from Russian by Simeon Linden), at 332–366.

6 Ibid.

7 Ibid.

8 Ibid.

*The Tuskegee Syphilis Study*

Between 1930 and 1973, the United States Department of Public Health Services (USPHS) conducted research on the natural progression of syphilis in Tuskegee, Macon County, Alabama.[9] The research subjects in the Tuskegee study were mainly poor African Americans, many of whom suffered from syphilis but were denied treatment as part of the study design despite the availability of penicillin in the 1950s as an effective therapy for the treatment of the disease.[10] Even before penicillin became standard care for syphilis, arsenotherapy was available during the study as an effective treatment for the disease. Nonetheless, the subjects were denied that intervention because of the study's predication on non-treatment.[11] Moreover, participants in the Tuskegee study were prevented from obtaining private treatment for the disease even though medical and health services were available.[12] When some of the Tuskegee study subjects died, the USPHS induced family members to give consent for anatomical examination for the last stage of the study. The subjects of the Tuskegee study were told that the objective of the study was to treat them, so instead of obtaining their informed consent, the USPHS deliberately deceived them.[13] The study was not submitted to nor approved by an ethics committee,[14] as ethics review procedures did not come into existence until the 1960s.[15] For the USPHS, it is arguable that since ethics review procedures are not retrospective, the USPHS was justified in believing that the Tuskegee study, which began in the 1930s, was excluded from review. Though this argument offers some vindication, the USPHS remains morally responsible for that ethically problematic research.

In the early 1970s, the Tuskegee study was made public, necessitating the empanelling of an ad hoc advisory committee. The committee presented a report to the Assistant Secretary for Health in 1973 with scathing findings that the Tuskegee study was not undertaken with the informed consent of research subjects and that the subjects were unjustifiably denied penicillin when it became available in the

9 James H. Jones, *Bad Blood: The Tuskegee Syphilis Experiment* (New York: The Free Press, 1993).

10 'The 40-Year Death Watch', Medical World News, 18 August 1972, pp. 15–17; Doleres Katz, 'Why 430 Blacks with Syphilis Went Uncured for 40 Years', Detroit Free Press, 5 November 1972.

11 Allan M. Brandt, 'Racism and Research: The Case of the Tuskegee Syphilis Study' (1978), Hastings Center Report 21, at 26–27.

12 Ibid., at 25.

13 Ibid. Also, Amy L. Fairchild and Ronald Bayer, 'Uses and Abuses of Tuskegee' (1999), 284 Science 919.

14 Jones, supra, note 9, at 1.

15 P. Ferguson, 'Do Researchers Feel an LREC Hinders Research?' (2001), 165 Bull. of Med. Ethics, 17 at 19; Joanne Roman, 'U.S. Medical Research in the Developing World: Ignoring Nuremberg' (2002), 11 Cornell J.L. & Pub. Pol'y 441.

1950s.[16] Civil litigation brought by surviving research subjects and the estates of deceased ones followed, but ended in monetary settlements. More troubling for the Tuskegee study was that, despite the 1940's enunciation of the Nuremberg Code on the ethics of Medical research and the wide public uproar ignited by the publicizing of the unethical research at the Jewish Chronic Disease Hospital in the 1960s,[17] the Tuskegee study continued without alteration. The unjustifiable continuation of the Tuskegee study may be with some racist undertones.[18] Brandt strongly argued that the historical context of the study captured the racist prejudice against African Americans, and the then prevailing medical attitude towards blacks, disease and sex. Furthermore, it underpinned the dismissive and lackadaisical attitude of the medical community and US government, until horrors of the study were brought to the peoples' conscience by the US press.[19] A contemporary consequence of the Tuskegee study is the current distrust of medical experimentation and medical researchers that most African-Americans hold.[20]

*The Nuremberg Medical Case*

It was the trial of Karl Brandt and others (now called the Medical Case) between 1946 and 1947 by the Nuremberg Military Tribunal that shook the confidence of the international community in the propriety of leaving research subject protection and welfare to the sole judgment and conscience of an investigator.[21] The Karl Brandt trial revealed horrendous experiments conducted by some Nazi scientists and physicians on prisoners in concentration camps without their consent or any form of ethics or institutional review. Such unethical experiments included

---

16 Department of Health, Education, and Welfare, *Final Report of the Tuskegee Syphilis Study Ad Hoc Advisory Panel* (Washington, D.C.: GPO, 1973).

17 Jay Katz, *Experimentation with Human Beings: The Authority of the Investigator, Subject, Professions, and State in the Human Experimentation Process* (New York: Russell Sage Foundation, 1972), at 10–11

18 Some authors have argued that there is a connection between racism and certain experimentation with human subjects; for instance, see, Annette Dula, 'Yes, There Are African-American Perspectives on Bioethics', in Nancy S. Jecker, et al. (eds), *Bioethics: An Introduction to the History, Methods, and Practice* (Boston: Jones and Bartlett Publishers, 1997), 252–254; Herbert Aptheker, 'Racism and Human Experimentation' (1974), 53 Political Affairs, 27–60; Brandt, supra, note 39.

19 Brandt, supra, note 11.

20 The Human Radiation Experiments, *Final Report of the President's Advisory Committee* (New York: Oxford University Press, 1996). Also, Fairchild and Bayer, supra, note 13.

21 M. Grodin, 'Historical Origins of the Nuremberg Code', in G.J. Annas and M. Grodin (eds), *The Nazi Doctors and the Nuremberg Code: Human Rights in Human Experimentation* (New York: Oxford University Press, 1992), 121–144; Matthew Lippman, 'The Nazi Doctors Trial and the International Prohibition on Medical Involvement in Torture' (1993 ), 15 Loy. L.A. Int'l Comp. L.J. 410.

the following: deliberate infection with typhus, malaria, and epidemic jaundice, yellow fever, smallpox, paratyphoid, cholera, and diphtheria to test the efficacy of experimental vaccines and drugs; high-altitude experiments in which non-consenting subjects were locked in low pressure chambers that mimicked the atmospheric conditions and pressures prevailing at high altitude up to 68,000 feet; freezing experiments in which victims were denuded and exposed for long hours to temperatures below freezing point or placed inside a tank of ice water; deliberate infliction of battle-like wounds and aggravated infection thereof to test the efficacy of sulfanilamide and other drugs; deliberate poisoning of the food of victims to determine the effects of certain poisons and bullets on human beings; sexual sterilization experiments using surgery, high-dose x-rays, and pharmacological techniques; and the deliberate killing of some Jewish prisoners to provide skulls and skeletons for cranial and racial research at the Reich University of Strasbourg.[22]

Though the defendants at the Nuremberg Military Tribunal claimed that their actions were justifiable under the existing domestic law and were not condemned by then prevailing international law, the Tribunal presented ten basic principles of ethical, moral and legal complexion that provided the measure of the defendants' actions.[23] These principles crystallized into what is known as the Nuremberg Code,[24] and they set minimum standard for the ethical conduct of biomedical research. Normatively, the Nuremberg Code is at least part of customary international law[25]

---

22 *United States v Karl Brandt*, reprinted in Katz, supra, note 17, at 292–294.

23 Excerpt of the judgement of the Nuremberg Military Tribunal is reproduced in Irving Ladimer and Roger W. Newman (eds), *Clinical Investigation in Medicine: Legal, Ethical, and Moral Aspects* (Boston: Law-Medicine Research Institute, Boston University, 1963), at 116–119.

24 For the early attempts at the international level to codify the principles enunciated by the Nuremberg Military Tribunal, see Robert K. Woetzel, *The Nuremberg Trials in International Law* (London: Stevens & Sons Ltd., 1962), at 232–244

25 Pascal Arnold and Dominique Sprumont, 'The "Nuremberg Code": Rules of Public International Law', in Ulrich Tröhler and Stella Reiter-Theil (eds), *Ethics Codes in Medicine: Foundations and Achievements of Codification Since 1947* (Sydney: Ashgate Publishing Co., 1998), at 90: 'Due to its (Nuremberg Code) continuing and uniformed applications (*usus*) by a majority of countries, as well as the general recognition of its binding nature (*opinio juris*), these basic principles have become rules of customary international law. In fact, they are applied in the common interest of all nations and are so deeply rooted in the international legal consciousness that they constitute peremptory public international law (*ius cogens*). This means that they cannot be modified by any State or professional organization, either by statute or ethical guidelines.' See also, Jonathan Todres, 'Can Research Subjects of Clinical Trials In Developing Countries Sue Physician-Investigators For Human Rights Violations?' (2000), 16 N.Y.L. Sch. J. Hum. Rts. 737, at 750–752.

and binds member states of the United Nation.[26] However, its existence has not prevented subsequent research scandals.

*Jewish Chronic Disease Hospital Study*

In 1963, twenty-two chronically ill and debilitated patients at the Jewish Chronic Disease Hospital (JCDH) in Brooklyn were given injections of live cancer cells to study their immunologic status, or their rejection responses. The study was a non-therapeutic clinical research project and was funded by the United States Public Health Service, and the American Cancer Society.[27] The patients' consent was not obtained and the study was not submitted for institutional review. The litigation that followed exposure of this unethical research, brought by one of the directors of JCDH, gives useful insights into the mood of the public concerning human subject experimentation. Despite investigation by the State Department of Education and Kings County District into the JCDH scandal, a director of the JCDH brought an action in court seeking access to medical records of the hospital to investigate facts concerning the alleged unethical and improper experiments on some of the hospital's patients. In *Hyman v Jewish Chronic Disease Hospital*,[28] the defendants argued that the hospital records were confidential and that the plaintiff was not personally liable for the wrongdoing and unethical research conducted by the hospital. The court held that as a director, the plaintiff was entitled to know the facts upon which the potential liability of the hospital rested. It further held that the plaintiff was entitled to inspect records that reveal improper and unethical research by the hospital and any confidentiality would be protected by an appropriate order of the court as to concealment of the names of individual patients. In addition, the Attorney General of New York, pursuant to the applicable Education Law, brought a petition in the Board of Regents Grievance Committee (BRGC) for the revocation of the licences of the principal investigators (Drs Southam and Mandel) in the cancer study. The BRGC found the investigators guilty of the allegations in the petition and recommended their censure and reprimand. While accepting the findings of the BRGC, the Board of Regents of the University of the State of New York modified the sentences by suspending the licences of the investigators for a year but stayed execution of the suspension.

---

26 Christine V.D. Wyngaert and Guy Stessens, *International Criminal Law: A Collection of International and European Instruments* (The Hague: Kluwer Law International, 1996), at 501.

27 See, letter from Chester M. Southam, MD to Emmanuel Mandel, MD on 5 July 1963; reproduced in Jay Katz, *Experimentation with Human Beings: The Authority of the Investigator, Subject, Professions, and State in the Human Experimentation Process* (New York: Russell Sage Foundation, 1972), at 10–11.

28 *Hyman v Jewish Chronic Disease Hospital, 206 N.E. 2d 338* [1965].

*Other Research Scandals in Industrialized Countries*

The Western world has witnessed other historic medical research scandals. For instance, the cold war motivated unethical radiation experiments conducted or sponsored by USA governmental agencies.[29] In the litigation that followed, Beckwith J. observed:

> The allegations in this case indicate that the government of the United States, aided by officials of the City of Cincinnati, treated at least eighty-seven of its citizens as though they were laboratory animals. If the Constitution has not clearly established a right under which these plaintiffs may attempt to prove their case, then a gaping hole in that document has been exposed. The subject of experimentation who has not volunteered is merely an object.[30]

Others include the controversial experimental drug trials on US soldiers during the 1991 Gulf War,[31] and research on deceased persons and their parts in Canada,[32]

29 Trudo Lemmens, 'In the Name of National Security: Lessons from the Final Report on the Human Radiation Experiments' (1996), 6 European Journal of Health Law 7–23; George J. Annas, *Some Choice: Law Medicine, and the Market* (New York: Oxford University Press, 1998), 157–160; Welsome, E., 'The Plutonium Experiment', Albuquerque Tribune, 15, 16 and 17 November 1993; The Human Radiation Experiments, *Final Report of the President's Advisory Committee* (New York: Oxford University Press, 1996).

30 *In re Cincinnati Radiation Litigation*, 874 F. Supp 796 (1995).

31 Though use of the experimental drugs (pyridostigmine bromide 30 mg tablets and pentavalent botulinum toxoid vaccine) without prior consent of soldiers was allowed by the USA Food and Drug Administration (FDA), and subsequently by the court, the ethics of that incident remain controversial. See, George J. Annas, 'Changing the Consent Rules for Desert Storm' (1992), 326 New England Journal of Medicine 770–773; Annas, supra, note 29, at 132–139; Schuchardt, E.J., 'Walking a Thin Line: Distinguishing Between Research and Medical Practice During Operation Desert Storm' (1992), 26 Columbia J. Law Soc. Prob. 77–115; G.J. Annas and M.A. Grodin, 'Treating the Troops: Commentary' (1991), 21 Hastings Center Report 24; *Informed Consent for Human Drugs and Biologics; Determination That Informed Consent Is Not Feasible, Fed. Reg. 1990; 55: 52813-52817; 21 C.F.R. Section 50.23(d)*; *Doe v Sullivan,* 756 F. Supp 12 (1991); *Doe v Sullivan* 938 F.2d 1370 (1991).

32 Charlie Gillis, 'Doctor Left Autopsies Unfinished in Halifax: Children's Organs Found in Warehouse', National Post, 3 October 2000, at A8.

USA.,[33] UK,[34] and Australia,[35] without family members' consent.[36] However, contemporary research scandals in the West mainly concern conflict of interest issues.[37] Interestingly, a recent medical research scandal in Nigeria exhibits patterns of the historic genre. This may excuse any effort to sensitize developing countries to the ethically problematic aspects of medical research by drawing their attention to the unhappy historical moments of experimentation with human subjects.[38]

## Frameworks of Response to International Research Scandals

As part of the international and domestic response to some of the scandals above, many current research guidelines embody an important procedural ethics

---

33 Paul Wildie, 'Husband Sues After Brain Tissue Taken From Dead Wife', National Post, 29 January 2000, at A13; Peter Gorner, 'Parents Suing Over Patenting of Genetic Test: They Say Researchers They Assisted are Trying to Profit From a Test for a Rare Disease', Chicago Tribune, 19 November 2000, at A1.

34 Stephen White, 'The Law Relating to Dealing with Dead Bodies' (2000), 4 Medical Law International 145.

35 Michael Perry, '"Body-Parts Supermarket" Causes Uproar in Australia: No consent for Research', National Post, 20 March 2001, at A13.

36 See generally, Remigius N. Nwabueze, 'Biotechnology and the New Property Regime in Human Bodies and Body Parts' (2002), 24 Loy. L.A. Int'l & Comp. L. Rev., pp. 19–64, at 19–21.

37 There is a growing literature on conflict of interest in biomedical research. See, David Blumenthal, 'Conflict of interest in Biomedical Research' (2002), 12 Health Matrix: Journal of Law-Medicine 377–392; J.A. Goldner, 'Dealing with Conflicts of Interest in Biomedical Research: IRB Oversight as the Next Best Solution to the Abolitionist Approach' (2000), 28 J.L. Med. & Ethics 379; K.C. Glass and T. Lemmens, 'Conflict of Interest and Commerciliazation of Biomedical Research: What Is the Role of Research Ethics Review?', in T. Caulfied and B. Williams-Jones (eds), *The Commercialization of Genetic Research: Ethical, Legal and Policy Issues* (New York: Kluwer, 1999), at 79; R.G. Spece, et al. (eds), *Conflicts of Interest in Clinical Practice and Research* (New York: Oxford University Press, 1996); M. Little, 'Research, Ethics and Conflicts of Interest' (1999), 25 J. Med. Ethics 259; R.A. Phillips and J. Hoey, 'Constraints of Interest: Lessons at the Hospital for Sick Children' (1998), 159 C.M.A.J. 955; The Lancet (editorial), 'A Curious Stopping Rule from Hoechst Marion Roussel' (1997), 350 Lancet 155; The Lancet (editorial), 'Good Manners for the Pharmaceutical Industry' (1997), 349 Lancet 1635; E.J. Emmanuel and D. Steiner, 'Institutional Conflict of Interest' (1995), 332 New Eng. J. Med. 262; K.C. Glass and T. Lemmens, 'Research Involving Humans', in J. Downie, et al. (eds), *Canadian Health Law and Policy* (Markham: Butterworths, 2002, 2nd edn), at 459–500, particularly at 466–475; *Grimes v Kennedy Krieger Institute*, 366 Md. 29; 782 A.2d 807 (2001).

38 Henry K. Beecher, 'Medical Ethics and Medical History: Experimentation in Man', in Ladimer and Newman (eds), supra, note 23, at 2–39.

requirement.[39] This means that a research protocol must receive the prior approval of an ethics committee before its execution.[40] As the US National Bioethics Advisory Commission observed, 'ethically sound research must comply with an important *procedural requirement* – prior ethical review by a body that is competent to assess compliance with … substantive ethical principles'.[41] (Italics in the original) Guideline 2 of the Council for International Organization of Medical Sciences (CIOMS), for instance, provides that every research proposal involving human beings must be 'submitted for review of their scientific merit and ethical acceptability to one or more scientific review and ethical review committees'.[42] In weaker terms, the World Medical Association research guideline (the Declaration of Helsinki, 2000) stipulates that experimental protocol involving human subjects 'should be submitted for consideration, comment, guidance, and where appropriate, approval to a specially appointed ethical review committee'.[43] However, the latest version of the Declaration of Helsinki rejects a non-mandatory and discretionary formulation of the obligation for ethical review: 'The research protocol must be submitted for consideration, comment, guidance and approval to a research ethics committee before the study begins'.[44] The guideline by the International Conference on Harmonization (ICH-GCP)[45] and many domestic or national guidelines make similar provisions. Research on identifiable human

---

39 World Health Organisation (WHO), *Operational Guidelines for Ethics Committees that Review Biomedical Research* (Geneva: World Health Organisation, 2000); the NBAC observed that 'ethically sound research must comply with an important *procedural requirement* – prior ethical review by a body that is competent to assess compliance with these substantive ethical principles' (italics in the original), National Bioethics Advisory Commission (NBAC), *Ethical Issues in International Research: Clinical Trials in Developing Countries: Report and Recommendations of the National Bioethics Advisory Commission* (Bethesda, Maryland: NBAC, 2001) at 5.

40 Generally, see, Bowen Hosford, *Bioethics Committees: The Health Care Provider's Guide* (Maryland: An Aspen Publication, 1986), particularly, at 8–16.

41 NBAC, supra, note 39, at 5.

42 Council for International Organization of Medical Sciences, *International Ethical Guidelines for Biomedical Research Involving Human Subjects* (CIOMS, 2002), Guideline 2.

43 World Medical Association (Declaration of Helsinki), *Ethical Principles for Medical Research Involving Human Subjects* (WMA: 52nd WMA General Assembly, Edinburgh, Scotland, October 2000), Article 13.

44 World Medical Association (Declaration of Helsinki), *Ethical Principles for Medical Research Involving Human Subjects* (WMA: 59th WMA General Assembly, Seoul, October 2008), Article 14.

45 International Conference on Harmonization of Technical Requirements for Registration of Pharmaceuticals for Human Use – Good Clinical Practice: Consolidated Guideline (ICH, May 1996). Also see, World Health Organisation (WHO), *Guidelines for Good Clinical Practice (GCP) for Trials on Pharmaceutical Products* (WHO Technical Series, No 850, 1995); Directive 2001/20/EC of the European Parliament and of the Council of 4 April 2001 (the Clinical Trials Directive).

tissues or data is included within the rubric of 'research involving human beings' or 'human experimentation'.[46]

Generally, the normative character of some of the guidelines above makes them legally and judicially unenforceable,[47] although other means of enforcement, such as discipline by a professional group or denial of funding by a grant agency, might be available. Institutional or ethics review of clinical research, or any research involving human subjects, has generally become the gold standard for determining the ethics of human experimentation.[48] The framework of institutional review is intended to protect the rights, safety, and welfare of research subjects,[49] and to promote public confidence and trust in biomedical investigation and integrity of the process.[50] Institutional review has also become the cornerstone of biomedical research funding and its emergence was suggested to have been partly responsible for the progressive increase in biomedical research budget and funding in the United States of America.[51] Though the mere existence of an ethics review committee neither guarantees the complete absence of unethical researches[52] nor necessarily facilitates societal confidence in the integrity and responsibility of scientific researchers, it does promise to be a veritable framework for curbing the excesses of protocols that pay scant attention to other overriding societal values.[53]

46 Ladimer and Newman, supra, note 23, at 18; CIOMS, supra, note 42, Guideline 1, commentary; Declaration of Helsinki, supra, note 44, Article 1. Also, P.A. Andanda, 'Human-tissue-related inventions: ownership and intellectual property rights in international collaborative research in developing countries' (2008), 34 J. Med. Ethics 171–179.

47 Angela Campbell and Kathleen C. Glass, 'The Legal Status of Clinical and Ethics Policies, Codes, and Guidelines in Medical Practice and Research' (2000–2001), 46 McGill L.J. 473–89. For a similar criticism of UNESCO's *Universal Declaration on the Human Genome and Human Rights* (1997): Allyn L. Taylor, 'Globalisation and Biotechnology: UNESCO and an International Strategy to Advance Human Rights and Public Health' (1999), 25 American Journal of Law & Medicine 479–541. But in the USA, the guideline on human subjects' protection and the ethical review of research involving human participants is statutory and judicially enforceable: The Common Rule, 45 CFR 46; the United States Food and Drug Administration, 21 CFR 50, 21 CFR 56, 21 CFR 312; and the United States Agency for International Development, 22 CFR 225.

48 Nuffield Council on Bioethics, *The Ethics of Research Related to Healthcare in Developing Countries* (London: Nuffield Council on Bioethics, 2002) at 101.

49 WHO, supra, note 39, at 1.

50 Robert A. Pearlman, 'Introduction to the Practice of Bioethics', in Jecker, et al. (eds), supra, note 18, at 260–261.

51 Nathan Hershey and Robert D. Miller, *Human Experimentation and the Law* (Maryland: Aspen Systems Corporation, 1976), at 1–2.

52 Nuffield Council on Bioethics, supra, note 48, at 103; Henry Beecher documented examples of unethical biomedical research conducted in the USA despite the existing Nuremberg Code, enunciated by USA judges in the Medical Case: Henry K. Beecher, 'Ethics and Clinical Research' (1966), 274 New Eng. J. Med. 1354–1360.

53 A.M. Capron, 'Human Experimentation', in Robert M. Veatch (ed.), *Medical Ethics* (Boston: Jones & Bartlett Publishers, 1997, 2nd edn), at 156.

As Pope Pius XII once said, 'science is not the highest value to which all other orders of values … should be subordinated'.[54] Thus, the existence of ethics review reaffirms society's conviction that social or moral considerations should be infused into scientific enterprise.[55] More detailed analysis of the constitution, dynamics and mechanisms of ethics review committees are provided in chapter four.

## Impetus for the Regulation of Biomedical Research in Africa

The regulation of biomedical research in Africa is a response to several factors. These include research scandals that occurred within the continent, increasing biomedical research activities in Africa, the glaring need to protect the rights and welfare of research participants, and the insistence by international sponsors and organizations that research they support in Africa must comply with standards set out in international regulatory instruments, such as CIOMS, and the research guidelines of the sponsoring country or entity. Although it is not clear which of these factors is preponderant, research scandals have certainly played a pivotal role. Rwabihama and colleagues, however, suggest that ethics review requirements, as a condition for research funding, in the guidance documents of developed countries that sponsor research in Africa are mainly responsible for the proliferation of research regulation and the establishment of ethics committees in Africa.[56] Chapter three, however, suggests that, as in the international contexts where research regulations came in the wake of scandals, some African countries developed their regulations in response to (biomedical research) scandals that occurred within their territories. Those without such experiences have simply regulated anticipatorily or in response to the requirements of international funding bodies and institutions. The analysis below provides only a summary of the major research scandals that occurred in Africa.

### *AZT Placebo-Controlled Trial in Africa*

In 1997, a shocking research scandal involving some African countries, such as Cote d'Ivoire, Burkina Faso, Ethiopia, Kenya, Malawi, South Africa, Tanzania, Uganda, and Zimbabwe, was bought to public attention by The Public Citizen, a health public advocacy group. The scandal concerned placebo-controlled trials that

54 Pope Pius XII, *The Moral Limits of medical Research and Treatment* (Rome, Italy: Address Presented at First International Congress on Histopathology of Nervous System, 14 September 1952). Posted on: www.ewtn.com/library/PAPALDOC/P12PSYCH.HTM [Last visited on 19 March 2011].

55 Ibid.

56 Jean-Paul Rwabihama, et al., 'Ethics committees for biomedical research in some African emerging countries; which establishment for which independence? A comparison with the USA and Canada' (2010), 36 J. Med. Ethics 243 at 246.

tested the efficacy of a short-course zidovudine (AZT) in the reduction of perinatal transmission of HIV/AIDS. These trials raised the ethical issue of whether an ethically unacceptable research in a developed country (for instance the USA) could be ethically appropriate in a developing country; in other words, whether the standard of care in research is universal or dependent on local circumstance.[57] The trial was ethically controversial because an effective treatment (known as 076 regimen) to prevent the transmission of HIV/AIDS from infected pregnant women to their unborn children already existed in the USA and many European countries. As such, a similar trial in these Western countries could not have secured ethical approval. From the outset, therefore, the short-course zidovudine trials in Africa and other developing countries raised the critical issue of equipoise examined in chapter two. In particular, the trials engaged the issue of whether the fundamental ethical conditions of equipoise were satisfied absent the provision of a full-course zidovudine regime to the control group. As chapter two highlights, equipoise implies the idea that a known inferior treatment should not be given to participants in clinical research; thus, equipoise mandates a duty to provide the best treatment to research participants which, in the case of the short-course zidovudine trials, was the 076 (full-course zidovudine) regimen. The trials also raised the allied question of whether the placebo-controlled design for the trials was ethically justifiable in view of the serious nature of the disease under study, the resource-

57 The huge literature on the debate include: P. Fidler, 'Geographical Morality Revisited: International Relations, International Law, and the Controversy over Placebo-Controlled HIV Clinical Trials in Developing Countries' (2001), 42 Harv. Int'l L.J. 299; Leonard H. Glantz, et al., 'Research in Developing Countries: Taking "Benefit" Seriously' (1998), Hastings Center Rep., Nov–Dec. 1998, 38; Jonathan Todres, 'Can Research Subjects of Clinical Trials in Developing Countries Sue Physician-Investigators for Human Rights Violations?' (2000), 16 N.Y.L. Sch. J. Hum. Rts. 337; Ronald Bayer, 'The Debate Over Maternal-Fetal HIV Transmission Prevention Trials in Africa, Asia, and the Caribbean: Racist Exploitation or Exploitation of Racism?' (1998), 88 Am. J. Pub. Health 567; David Orentlicher, 'Universality and its Limits: When Research Ethics can Reflect Local Circumstances' (2002), 30 J.L. Med. & Ethics 403; Eldryd Parry, 'The Ethics of Clinical Research in Developing Countries' (2000), 34 J. Royal C. Physicians Lon. 328; Joanne Roman, 'U.S. Medical Research in the Developing World: Ignoring Nuremberg' (2002), 11 Cornell J.L. & Pub. Pol'y 441; Robert Levine, 'International Codes of Research Ethics: Current Controversies and the Future' (2002), 35 Indiana L. Rev. 557; Harold Varmer and David Satcher, 'Ethical Complexities of Conducting Research in Developing Countries' (1997), 337 New Eng. J. Med. 1003; Peter Lurie and Sidney M. Wolfe, 'Unethical Trials of Interventions to Reduce Perinatal Transmission of the Human Immunodeficiency Virus in Developing Countries' (1997), 337 New Eng. J. Med. 853–856; Marcia Angell, 'The Ethics of Clinical Research in the Third World' (1997), 337 New Eng. J. Med. 847–849; George Annas and Michael Grodin, 'Research Forum: Ethics and Studies of HIV; Human Rights and Maternal-Fetal HIV Transmission Prevention Trials in Africa' (1998), 88(4) American Journal of Public Health 560; Robert A. Crouch and John D. Arras, 'AZT Trials and Tribulations' (November–December 1998) Hastings Center Report 26; Levine Carol, 'Placebos and HIV: Lessons Learned' (November–December 1998) Hastings Center Report 43.

poor settings of the trials and the availability of a proven, though unaffordable, treatment for the condition under study.[58]

Critics of the trial argued that it was unfair, and tantamount to double standards in biomedical research, to conduct trials in Africa that would not pass regulatory muster in industrialized countries.[59] Proponents of the trial, including many African scholars and researchers,[60] argued that the trial properly responded to the realities of the health care situation in Africa, generally characterized by poor medical facilities, low per capital expenditure on health, and inaccessibility to the 076 regimen due to resource constraints. Furthermore, a Ugandan researcher, Dr Edward Mbidde,[61] argued that the complex administration of the 076 regimen presented practical problems that militated against its use as a control arm in Africa. In the USA, for instance, the 076 regimen was started in a hospital setting very early in the pregnancy, between 14 and 34 weeks, and continued through delivery to about 6 weeks after birth. It was also administered intravenously. Practical realities of health care delivery in Africa can hardly meet the requirements of such complex drug administration. For instance, most pregnant women in Africa obtain prenatal care for the first time only in their third trimester when it would be too late to commence treatment with the 076 regime. It was, therefore, argued that a trial in Africa that sought to test the efficacy of a cheaper and affordable (in Africa) short-course AZT treatment, capable of oral administration and much later in pregnancy, in line with the health infrastructures in Africa, was ethical. In the end, the short-course zidovudine trials were halted in 1998 when sufficient evidence in Thailand made its continuation unnecessary.[62]

In response to the AZT Placebo-Controlled Trials above, some African countries developed their guidelines in a manner that clearly tailor the standard of care in research to the treatment and health standards available in their countries. For instance, the Ugandan guidelines provide that: 'Research participants in a control group of a research project of a diagnostic, therapeutic, or preventive intervention should receive an established effective intervention or as may be determined with

58 For analysis of the controversy relating to the use of placebo-controlled design to conduct foreign sponsored research in Africa, see Andrew Kitua, et al., 'The use of placebo in a trial of rectal artesunate as initial treatment for severe malaria patients en route to referral clinics: ethical issues' (2010), 36 J. Med. Ethics 116–120.

59 For instance: Ruth Macklin, *Double Standards in Medical Research in Developing Countries* (Cambridge: Cambridge University Press, 2004).

60 Edward Mbidde, 'Bioethics and Local Circumstances' (1998), 279 Science 155; Sylvester C. Chima, 'Regulation of Biomedical Research in Africa' (2006), 332 BMJ 848–850; S.R. Benatar and P.A. Singer, 'A New Look at International Research Ethics' (2000), 321 BMJ 824–26; K. Shapiro and S.R. Benatar, 'HIV Prevention Research and Global Inequality: Steps Towards Improved Standards of Care' (2005), 1 J. Med. Ethics 39–47. But see Richard Baraza, 'Kenyan Statutory Body was Unaware of Study' (2001) 1 BMJ 625.

61 Supra, note 60.

62 Stolberg, Sheryl Gay, 'Placebo Use Is Suspended in Overseas AIDS Trials', New York Times, 19 February 1998, p. A16.

reference to the applicable national health standards'.[63] Arguably, this is a pragmatic adaptation of the theoretical requirements of equipoise, such as the duty to provide the best proven treatment, to the peculiar circumstances of Uganda.

*Vaccine and Transmission Studies in Uganda*

Uganda experienced further biomedical research scandals; these relate to the trial of HIV-1 vaccine, and studies that examined the risk factors which contribute significantly to the transmission of HIV/AIDS. In 1999, Uganda became the first country in Africa to conduct the trial of a candidate vaccine for HIV/AIDS. However, the HIV-1 vaccine trial was almost marred by socio-political and cultural controversies that surrounded its inception. In the course of the investigator-community dialogue that preceded the trial, it became obvious that the trial participants and local communities were unsettled by serious rumours that volunteers would be deliberately exposed to, or injected with, HIV/AIDS virus. Conflicting media reports, confusion of the vaccine with treatment for HIV/AIDS, and sheer political opportunism raised such public concern that warranted an open debate in the Ugandan Parliament relating to the ethics and propriety of the trial. For instance, an influential politician in Uganda was said to have organized a widely-publicized rally accusing the Ugandan president of sanctioning the vaccine trial in return for foreign financial assistance to prosecute his war agenda in the neighbouring country of Congo.[64] The immediate impact of these rumours was the disruption of an on-going campaign by the Ugandan Ministry of Health to increase polio vaccination in Uganda.[65] This is not unlike the reaction to the trial of trovan in Nigeria (examined below).

Furthermore, studies in Uganda on the behavioural and biologic risk factors associated with the transmission of HIV/AIDS sparked ethical debate in 2000. The retrospective study of about 415 couples, some of whom were HIV-1 discordant, found that the serum viral load was a significant factor in the heterosexual transmission of HIV-1.[66] The study was, however, criticized for being ethically questionable, because the Ugandan volunteers were not given treatment for HIV infection. Nor were the uninfected individuals told that their partners were HIV-positive.[67] The investigators defended the ethics of the study on the grounds that

---

63 Ugandan National Council for Science and Technology, *National Guidelines for Research Involving Humans as Research Participants* (Kampala: UNCST, 2007), Section 7.2.

64 R.D. Mugerwa, et al., 'First Trial of the HIV-1 Vaccine in Africa: Ugandan Experience' (2002), 324 BMJ 226–29.

65 Ibid.

66 T.C. Quinn, et al., 'Viral Load and Heterosexual Transmission of Human Immunodeficiency Virus Type 1' (2000), 342 New Eng. J. Med. 921–929.

67 M. Angell, 'Investigators' Responsibilities for Human Subjects in Developing Countries' (2000), 342 New Eng. J. Med. 324; Gretchen Vogel, 'Study of HIV Transmission

antiretroviral treatments were not available in the rural district of Rakai where the study was conducted, and that under the prevailing Ugandan national policy on HIV/AIDS, health workers were prohibited from disclosing the HIV-status of an individual to a third party. Thus, in addition to issues of post-trial treatment or benefits raised by this study, a topic examined more fully in chapter four, the Ugandan study on the behavioural and biologic risk factors associated with the transmission of HIV/AIDS also raised the issue of standard of care for research participants; in that sense, the Ugandan study above implicates the theory of equipoise examined in chapter two. If equipoise's duty on investigators to provide the best treatment to research participants were to be taken seriously in Africa, as argued in chapter two, then the Ugandan study above appears morally indefensible. The explanation that antiretroviral treatments were not available in the rural district of Rakai, the location of the trial, would not be acceptable because such treatments were available elsewhere. For similar reasons, Farmer and Campos dismissed the approval of the Ugandan study by four ethics review committees in the US and Uganda, observing that 'ethical codes and review boards are not always helpful .... They set their sights on compliance with the law, not pragmatic ethical engagement with the interests of the study subjects'.[68] Farmer and Campos further observed that, by denying treatments to the participants in the Ugandan study and failing to inform the uninfected individuals that their partners were HIV-positive, the investigators and sponsors of the study should be taken to 'endorse an unacknowledged consensus that in fact all humans are not created equal and that this inequality accounts for both differential distribution of disease and differential standards of care, making it acceptable to perform research in some parts of the world that would be unethical in the United States'.[69]

### *Trovan Clinical Trial in Nigeria by Pfizer*

During the first quarter of 1996, there was an epidemic outbreak of meningitis in Kano, a northern Nigerian city. The epidemic was acute in nature, recording about two-hundred-and-fifty-thousand cases and twenty-five-thousand deaths.[70] It was even said to be the worst outbreak of epidemic meningitis in medical history. The meningitis epidemic was compounded by the simultaneous epidemic outbreak of measles and cholera.[71] Doctors Without Borders (a medical non-governmental

Sparks Ethics Debate' (2000), 288 Science 22–23.

68 P. Farmer and N.G. Campos, 'New Malaise: Bioethics and Human Rights in the Global Era' (2004), 32 J.L. Med. & Ethics 243 at 244.

69 Ibid., at 244.

70 Emmanuel R. Ezeome and Christian Simon, 'Ethical Problems in Conducting Research in Acute Epidemics: The Pfizer Meningitis Study in Nigeria as an Illustration' (2010), 10 Developing World Bioethics 1–10.

71 Idris Mohammed, *Academics, Epidemics & Politics* (Ibadan, Nigeria: Bookcraft, 2007), at 171–176.

organization) rushed to Kano to provide treatment with a cheap and internationally recommended antibiotics, chloramphenicol. Within weeks of the epidemics, Pfizer also learned about it from an Internet site and quickly mobilized its research team to fly into the Nigerian city of Kano and conduct a clinical trial of its new drug, trovafloxacin (hereafter, trovan). It seemed that the objections from Dr Juan Walterspiel, a Pfizer medical scientist, regarding the ethics of the trial could not deter Pfizer, which later dismissed Dr. Walterspiel from its employment.[72] Ezeome and Simon have examined the circumstances in which it is ethically permissible to conduct clinical research during an epidemic outbreak of a disease, such as the one that occurred in Kano in 1996. The authors observed that an acute epidemic characteristically combines three distinct health challenges, being all at once a public health problem, a health emergency and a disaster situation. This atrocious combination makes it extremely necessary to justify the ethics of research conducted during a period of (epidemic) emergency when treatment is desperately needed by the research participants. In the trovan case, Ezeome and Simon concluded that the trial lacked the 'anticipatory planning and prior policies … needed to promote the protection of subjects when an acute epidemic strikes'.[73] The clinical trial of trovan started on or about the 22 March 1996, and was to determine the efficacy of trovan in the treatment of meningococcal meningitis, and also, to compare it to ceftriaxone, the gold standard for treating the disease. The trial was conducted in Kano Infectious Disease Hospital, part of the hospital complex of Aminu Kano University Teaching Hospital. Two hundred Nigerian children were enrolled in the study; one hundred of them were assigned to the trovan arm, while the other one hundred were used as active controls and were given ceftriaxone, though it was alleged that some of the children in the control group were not given the proper dosage of ceftriaxone.[74] At the end of the trial, five children on the trovan arm died and six children on the control arm died. Many others were alleged to have suffered brain damage, paralysis, or became deaf. Pfizer did not make any follow-up visit to the Nigerian research participants. A sort of official conspiracy of silence in Nigeria kept the trovan tragedy out of public purview until the US Washington Post published the scandal in 2000 and 2001.[75]

Pfizer was accused of not obtaining informed consent from parents of the children enrolled in the study. The parents of the research participants could not speak English (Hausa is the local language) and believed that their children were getting effective treatment rather than being enrolled in a clinical research.[76] Pfizer

72 Tamar Lewin, 'Families Sue Pfizer on Test of Antibiotic', posted on www.dr-rath-research.org [last visited on 26 Feb. 2011]; Marisa Anne Pagnattaro, 'International Legal and Ethical Consideration at Pfizer, Inc.' (2005), 22 J. Legal Stud. 169–77.

73 Ezeome and Simon, supra, note 70, at 10.

74 Mohammed, supra, note 71, at 200–201.

75 'Compensation for Trovan test victims' (Editorial) Daily Sun (Nigeria), 12 February 2010 at 1.

76 Lewin, supra, note 72.

denied the claims made against it, alleging that nurses at the hospital explained the study in lay terms to the parents and obtained their verbal consent. Pfizer further alleged that those parents were informed that alternative treatment, offered by Doctors Without Borders (operating in the same hospital), was available, and that in terms of percentage, the death toll from the study was lower than that of the disease. But Pfizer's claim of adherence to the informed consent process was vehemently denied by Prof. Idris Mohammed, chairman of the Task Force on the control of the epidemic, who avowed that no 'consent of any kind – informed or not; written or verbal; in English or in Hausa – was obtained from the children or their parents'.[77] The trovan trial exemplifies the problem of consent to research in a resource-poor and largely illiterate community. As argued in chapter two, this challenge makes it highly undesirable to substitute equipoise with consent as the foundational framework for evaluating the ethics of clinical research. Furthermore, Pfizer claimed that the study was primarily a humanitarian effort that saved about one-hundred-and-eighty-nine lives, and made drugs and equipment available to the hospital. However, a commentator questioned Pfizer's humanitarian claims and asked: 'But why … did it (Pfizer) not fly in substantial supplies of the rather more expensive drug it was using as a comparison to Trovan so that every sick child could have a better chance of life?'[78] Similarly, Prof. Mohammed observed that it was not true, as Pfizer implied, 'that they provided facilities for diagnosis or treatment of patients with meningitis during the epidemic'; nor did Pfizer fly in a complete laboratory to Kano as it claimed.[79] These rebuttals have left a gaping hole in Pfizer's claim of ethical propriety in the trovan trial.

Another disturbing aspect of the trial was the allegation that ethical approval for the trovan study was not given by Nigerian authorities, contrary to Pfizer's contention.[80] Interestingly, Prof. Mohammed, chairman of the Federal Task Force appointed by the Nigerian government at the inception of the epidemic to lead national and international efforts to control the epidemic, had written to Pfizer (at the outset of the trial) instructing it to terminate the trial for want of ethical justification and necessary approvals. Bizarrely, however, the trial continued, despite Mohammed's letter of termination, obviously with the permission of 'higher' authorities in the Nigerian federal government. Later, Prof. Mohammed was blackmailed and accused of demanding bribes from Pfizer; he was also accused of terminating the trial out of ill motives. Prof. Mohammed was, however, fully vindicated by a Probe Panel set up by the Nigerian government to investigate

77 Mohammed, supra, note 71, at 204–205.

78 Sarah Boseley, 'Ailing Ethics: A clinical trial raises disturbing questions about drug companies' activities in Africa', the Guardian (UK), 20 January 2001, page unknown.

79 Mohammed, supra, note 71, at 200.

80 However, the Nigerian National Agency for Food and Drug Administration and Control (NAFDAC) approved the importation of trovan into Nigeria: Sam Eferaro, 'NAFDAC Okayed Pfizer's Trovan Trials', Vanguard (Lagos), 8 January 2001, page unknown.

the trial after the disclosures by the Washington Post in 2000-2001.[81] In 1997, when Pfizer submitted its application to the US Food and Drug Administration for the use of trovan in the treatment of meningitis epidemic, it included a document purporting to have approval of the Nigerian study given by the Kano Infectious Disease Hospital's ethics committee. As a representative of the Nigerian Federal Government at the time of the trial, however, Prof. Mohammed has affirmed 'categorically that Pfizer did not receive government's approval for the trial',[82] and that it was 'obvious that there was no clearance from the Nigerian drug control agency NAFDAC, just as there was no approval from a duly constituted ethics committee since none was in existence at the time of the trial of Trovan'.[83] In a recent telephone interview by the Washington Post with some of the Nigerian doctors who participated in the study (and those alleged to have been members of the ethics committee),[84] it was revealed that the ethical approval letter for the trovan trial was written one year after the study had taken place but was backdated. The telephone interview further confirmed Mohammed's allegation that the Kano Infectious Disease Hospital did not have an ethics committee at the time of the trovan trial.[85] What is often not clear in some of the materials on the Nigerian trovan trial is whether Pfizer also obtained ethical review and approval of the Nigerian study in the USA, as required by international guidelines and US domestic legislation. If the Washington Post's position on the lack of ethical approval for the trovan study was accepted, then it is arguable that the omission contributed to the death of some of the Nigerian children in the study, though it is not clear that if there had been a proper and effective ethics committee, it would have stopped the study or made it achieve positive results.

Trovan reached the market in the USA in 1998, and made about $160 million in the first year, but its use was not approved for children, and not for epidemic meningitis.[86] In 1999, following complaints of liver damage, the FDA further restricted its use.[87] The trovan study was the subject of administrative inquiry in Nigeria,[88] and litigated in Nigerian and the US courts.[89] In *Abdullahi v Pfizer, Inc.*, the US Court of Appeals, Second Circuit, reversed a ruling of the lower court which upheld an objection to strike out the suit initiated by the claimants, who were participants in the trovan trial.[90] Recently (29 June 2010), the US Supreme

---

81 Mohammed, supra, note 71, at 171–196.

82 Ibid., at 197.

83 Ibid., 203.

84 Joe Stephens, 'Doctors Say Trial's Approval Was Backdated', Washington Post, 16 January 2001, page A01.

85 Ibid.

86 Marcia Angell, *The Truth About the Drug Companies* (New York: Random House, 2005).

87 Lewin, supra, note 72.

88 'Pfizer drug trial in Nigeria being investigated' (2001), 357 Lancet 9250.

89 Lewin, supra, note 72.

90 *Abdullahi v Pfizer, Inc.*, 562 F.3d 163 (US Ct. App., 2$^{nd}$ Cir., 2009).

Court refused to allow a review of the Court of Appeal's decision above.[91] Detailed analysis of these and similar cases is undertaken in chapters six and seven. The Nigerian litigation was settled out of court in 2010, with Pfizer agreeing to pay a total compensation package of US$75m through the Meningitis Trust Fund established for that purpose by Pfizer in conjunction with the Nigerian authorities. Out of that amount, US$30m was to be paid to the victims or participants in the trial. Each participant in the trial or, in case of a dead victim, their family was to receive US$75,000, an equivalent of about twenty-six million naira (N26m) in local currency. US$30m was earmarked for establishing a pediatric health facility in Kano, the site of the trial, and US$15m was set aside for legal fees and sundry expenses.[92] To qualify for compensation, the participants in the trial or their families must produce evidence of their identity, proof of death or permanent incapacity as a result of participation in the trovan trial.[93] These requirements, in addition to a DNA test to be undergone by the claimants for compensation at Pfizer's expense, have proved daunting for some of the claimants and a fresh litigation is already underway. Pfizer has already handed over the medical records and relevant documents concerning the two hundred participants in the trial to the Meningitis Trust Fund, chaired by a retired Nigerian Supreme Court Justice, A.B. Wali. So far, the Meningitis Trust Fund has received about six hundred applications for compensation from alleged victims in the trial, a figure that far exceeds the two hundred children that actually participated in the trial.[94] While some of the claimants for compensation have already undergone a DNA test administered in Nigeria by a combined team of Nigerian and US forensic experts, the Trovan Victims Forum (TVF), an umbrella organization of the participants in the trovan trial, has objected to the requirement for a DNA test, alleging that it was a ploy by Pfizer to refuse payments to the victims, and that a new DNA test to be compared with tissue samples taken more than fourteen years previously was likely to be unreliable.[95] Pfizer insists, however, that it would only deal with individual claimants and not organizations like the TVF. As a result of these difficulties in the payment of the compensation, a fresh litigation has been commenced by some of the claimants for compensation; an Abuja Federal High Court judge hearing the new suit has issued a temporary injunction prohibiting both the disbursement of

---

91 Washington Legal Foundation, 'Court Allows Suit to Proceed Alleging Human Rights Violations', Press Release on 29 June 2010 (on file with author).

92 'Compensation for Trovan test victims' (Editorial) Daily Sun (Nigeria), 12 February 2010 at 1.

93 Ibid.

94 Joe Nwankwo, 'Pfizer compensates Trovan victims with N26m each', Daily Independent, 26 January 2010, page unknown.

95 Adamu Abuh, 'The Trovan debacle comes to a close', The Guardian (Nigeria), 20 May 2010, at 13.

the compensation fund by the Meningitis Trust Fund and the conducting of DNA testing on the claimants.[96]

The trovan trial has helped to draw attention to the unacceptable consequences of ethically suspicious biomedical studies sponsored by external agencies and corporations in developing countries. More importantly, it has helped to highlight the importance of and need for ethics review of research in many developing countries. The trovan scandal led to an erosion of public trust in the ability of the Nigerian government to protect its citizens against unjustifiable research risks. Many Nigerians were understandably upset that their government not only permitted such unethical trials, but it also participated actively in the trial through (undisclosed) approvals granted by the Federal Ministry of Health and other governmental agencies. Thus, in 2004, when rumours that polio vaccines in Nigeria were deliberately contaminated and posed harm to children made the rounds, many states in Nigeria (especially in northern Nigeria) refused to take part in the polio immunization programme despite the assurances of the Nigerian Federal government that the vaccines were safe.[97] As Dr Ibrahim D Ahmed, the secretary general of the Supreme Council of Sharia, poignantly observed: 'The Council harbours strong reservations on the safety of our population not least because of our recent experience in the Pfizer scandal, when our people were used as guinea pigs with the approval of the federal ministry of health and the approval of all the relevant UN agencies'.[98] Thus, the aftermath of the trovan scandal was a temporary suspension of the polio eradication programme in Nigeria.

### *Tenofovir Trials in Cameroon, Ghana, Nigeria and Malawi*

In 2004, four African countries (Cameroon, Ghana, Nigeria and Malawi) were chosen as research sites for a placebo-controlled and randomized study sponsored by the Family Health International (FHI) to test the efficacy of tenofovir (Viread) in the prevention of HIV infection. Funding for the study was provided by Bill and Melinda Gates Foundation, and the drugs (including the placebo) were supplied

96 Paul Ohia, 'More Woes for Pfizer, Loses Appeal in US Supreme Court', THIS DAY, 30 June 2010, page unknown.

97 As poignantly observed by Mohammed: 'The Trovan trial has done enormous long-term damage to immunisation in Nigeria. Again, I should know because it was my rotten luck that I served as chairman of the National Programme on Immunisation between 2000 and 2004. The people of Kano in particular, and northern Nigeria in general have become highly suspicious of any medicines or vaccines offered them for free, particularly if foreign – read European or American – aid is involved. All immunisation was rejected by parents at some stage, including routine immunisation against measles, tuberculosis, tetanus, diphtheria, poliomyelitis and meningitis. Despite attempts to reassure them, the people of many states of northern Nigeria still resist immunisation of any kind': Mohammed, supra, note 71, at 210.

98 Abiodun Raufu, 'Nigeria postpones programme of polio immunisation' (2004), 328 BMJ 1278.

by the manufacturer, Gilead Inc. free of charge. The Nigerian arm of the trial was cancelled by the FHI due to failure of the local researchers to meet the 'necessary scientific standards'.[99] Soon afterwards, the trials became muddled in ethical controversy.[100] The scandal was brought to public attention in July 2004 by an HIV/AIDS lobby and advocacy group, Act Up Paris.[101] The group alleged that the trial was unethical and should be stopped immediately. Furthermore, Act Up Paris alleged that the Tenofovir trials exploited the vulnerability of female participants and commercial sex workers, and that their recruitment was motivated by financial considerations, particularly, to minimize the cost of the trials. In addition, Act Up Paris argued that the participants were given inadequate prevention counselling because there were only five counsellors and one doctor for four hundred prostitutes/participants. Inadequate counselling in the Tenofovir trials arguably violates the important regulatory requirement that the '(P)articipants in both the control arm and the intervention arm should receive all established effective HIV risk reduction measures'.[102] Moreover, the prostitutes in the Tenofovir trials were given male condoms instead of female condoms. But the most serious accusation was that the trial sponsors and investigators failed to provide treatment for those who seroconverted during the study.[103] Non-provision of health care (antiretroviral treatment) after the study became the focal point of debate that ensued.[104] Due to these concerns, the Cameroonian authorities suspended the trial in early February 2005, though the suspension was lifted later and the FHI was allowed to follow-up currently enrolled participants after it agreed to implement the recommendations

99 'FHI Cancels Nigerian Arm of Clinical Trial Testing Tenofovir for HIV Prevention', Kaiser Daily HIV/AIDS Report, 16 March 2005 (page unknown).

100 Lancet Editorial, 'The Trials of Tenofovir Trials' (2005), 365 Lancet 1111. Also, Ariana E. Cha, 'AIDS Drug Trial Turned Away: Protests by Prostitutes in Cambodia Ended Tenofovir Testing', The Washington Post, 23 May 2006, page unknown.

101 Act Up Paris, 'Tenefovir: Inethical Trial', http://www.actupparis.org.

102 UNAIDS/WHO, *Ethical Considerations in Biomedical HIV Prevention Trials* (Geneva: UNAIDS/WHO, 2007), Guidance Point 15.

103 In another context, it was argued that the provision of such a treatment was obligated by African moral theory because the participants and the researcher are taken to 'share a way of life that imposes special obligations to care for one another's quality of life that can go beyond those listed in a contract': Thaddeus Metz, 'African and Western Moral Theories in a Bioethical Context' (2010), 10 Developing World Bioethics 49 at 56. For a detailed analysis of the problem of ancillary care: Henry S. Richardson and Leah Belsky, 'The Ancillary-care Responsibilities of Medical Researchers: An Ethical Framework for Thinking about the Clinical Care That Researchers Owe their Subjects' (2004), 34 The Hastings Center Report 25; Henry S. Richardson, 'Incidental Findings and Ancillary-Care Obligations' (2008), 36 J.L. Med. & Ethics 256.

104 J.A. Singh and E.J. Mills, 'The Abandoned Trials of Pre-Exposure Prophylaxis for HIV: What Went Wrong' (2005), 2 PLoS Medicine 824–827.

made by the Cameroon's Ministry of Health.[105] Some commentators have, however, blamed the Tenofovir scandal on the ignorance of activists and protestors due to miscommunication among stakeholders, as well as irresponsible reporting by the media based on speculation and overreaction, and with intent to sensationalize the facts of the trial.[106] Other commentators, however, justified the actions of activists and protestors against the trial; they blamed the investigators and sponsors of the Tenofovir trials for excluding, or insufficiently communicating with, the key community groups regarding the design of the trials.[107]

As in the Ugandan study on the behavioural and biologic risk factors associated with the transmission of HIV/AIDS, the Tenofovir trial raised not only issues of post-trial obligations and justice (examined further in chapter four), ancillary care, fair subject recruitment, and exploitation; it also raised the critical issues of standard of care and ethics of placebo-controlled trials which, as highlighted in chapter two, are all splinters of the concept of equipoise.[108] For instance, in responding to arguments that non-provision of sterile needles and syringes to participants in the Tenofovir trial in Thailand was consistent with the policy of government in Thailand, Chua and colleagues observed that 'whether a needle exchange exists in Thailand, or what the policies of the trial's funders are regarding needles and syringes, investigators have a duty to respect the Helsinki Declaration's requirement' that new interventions should be tested against the best current prophylactic, diagnostic and therapeutic methods.[109] While the placebo-controlled design for the Tenofovir vaccine trials could not be impugned ethically because there was no effective HIV/AIDS vaccine that could have been used as the control,[110] the alleged failure to provide antiretroviral treatment to participants who seroconverted during the study breached the duty, imposed by equipoise on

105 'Cameroon Health Ministry Agrees to Allow Follow-Up in Viread Trial; FHI to Help Participants Infected During Study Access Treatment', Medical News Today, 26 Feb. 2005 (page unknown).

106 Singh and Mills, supra, note 104, at 0824–0827; J. Lange, 'We must not let protestors derail trials of pre-exposure prophylaxis for HIV' (2005), 2 PLoS Medicine e248.

107 Arlene Chua, et al., 'The Tenofovir Pre-Exposure Prophylaxis Trial in Thailand: Researchers Should Show More Openness in Their Engagement with the Community' (2005), 2 PLoS Medicine 1044; Melissa Ditmore, 'Response to Joep M.A. Lange' (2005), 2 PLoS Medicine 1045.

108 Singh and Mills acknowledged that the issue of standard of care permeated the debate on the Tenofovir trials: Singh and Mills, supra, note 104.

109 Arlene Chua, et al., 'The Tenofovir Pre-Exposure Prophylaxis Trial in Thailand: Researchers Should Show More Openness in Their Engagement with the Community' (2005), 2 PLoS Medicine 1044 at 1045.

110 For instance, Guidance Point 15 of UNAIDS/WHO, *Ethical Considerations in Biomedical HIV Prevention Trials* (Geneva: UNAIDS/WHO, 2007) provides in part: 'The use of a placebo control arm is ethically acceptable in a biomedical HIV prevention trial only when there is no HIV prevention modality of the type being studied that has been scientifically validated in comparable populations or approved by relevant authorities'.

investigators and sponsors, to provide the best treatment to participants. Similarly, the lack of appropriate care for the participants who seroconverted during the Tenofovir study violated Guidance Point 14 of UNAIDS/WHO Guidance Document to the effect that '(P)articipants who acquire HIV infection during the conduct of a biomedical HIV prevention trial should be provided access to treatment regimens from among those internationally recognized as optimal'.[111]

## Regulatory Models in Africa

It is apparent that research scandals in Africa occurred under a climate of low regulatory visibility. This would seem to suggest three things. First, African countries should develop clear and comprehensive guidelines that should regulate the conduct of research involving human subjects. The Nuffield Council on Bioethics has supported this approach for African countries, noting that the multiplicity of existing international research guidelines and their often-conflicting provisions create a situation in which 'the formulation of national guidance assumes particular importance. By developing its own national guidance, a developing country is able to take account of its particular needs and cultural context'.[112] Otherwise, African countries (or, in particular, ethics review committees in Africa) would continue to go through the hard and painful process of interpreting and applying international research guidelines against the background and cultural contexts of Africa, a process that is not free from controversy, as ably adumbrated by Godfrey Tangwa.[113] Equally, Marshall pointedly observed that there is a 'disconnect between ideal ethical standards (embodied in international guidelines) and how they are applied in a world of structural imperfections and social, political, and economic inequities'.[114] Also interesting is the case study explored by Mfutso-Bengu and Taylor in relation to malaria research in Malawi involving autopsies on paediatric cadavers; the research had to be approved by ethics committees in Malawi and another country but the two committees, while agreeing on the principle of informed consent as enshrined in international guidelines, disagreed

111 UNAIDS/WHO, *Ethical Considerations in Biomedical HIV Prevention Trials* (Geneva: UNAIDS/WHO, 2007). Similar, but less stringent, duty was imposed by Guidance Point 16 of the 2000 version of the UNAIDS Guidance Document which was in force at the time of the Tenofovir trials.

112 Nuffield Council on Bioethics, *The Ethics of Research Related to Healthcare in Developing Countries* (London: Nuffield Council on Bioethics, 2005), at 66.

113 G.B. Tangwa, 'Between universalism and relativism: a conceptual exploration of problems in formulating and applying international biomedical ethical guidelines' (2004), 30 J. Med. Ethics 63–67.

114 Patricia A. Marshall, 'Human Rights, Cultural Pluralism, and International Health Research' (2005), 26 Theoretical Medicine and Bioethics 529 at 535.

on its correct application to the research in question conducted in Malawi.[115] The issue, therefore, was the correct interpretation, specification and application of international guidelines in the light of cultural and local circumstances. Furthermore, research guidelines developed in affluent parts of the world and adopted (or sought to be adopted) in African countries might create imperceptibly external influences that disregard or deepen social vulnerabilities in Africa. Thus, Garrafa and colleagues suggested that 'the most appropriate way forward … is for poor and low-income countries to create their own autonomous regulatory systems, with transparent social control mechanisms that are operated democratically at all levels'.[116] Second, research guidelines in Africa should have the primary aim of protecting the rights and welfare of research participants, as well as facilitating the conduct of scientifically valid and useful research. This is stating the obvious since the pre-eminent aim of regulation is the protection of research participants, and the facilitation of any scientific activity that is consistent with that protection.[117] The dynamics of this protection are further explored in chapter four. Third, research guidelines in Africa should be legally enforceable, with penal sanctions for the breach of their provisions.[118] As Starkman poignantly observed:

> There have been enough examples of both therapeutic and non-therapeutic research which was ethically or legally offensive to demonstrate the need for a legislative approach, which would enable us to prohibit or control research that is or has the potential to be ethically offensive. Prevention is preferable to legislating after the fact.[119]

Currently, however, some African countries rely entirely on international research guidelines. Ghana and Sudan are paradigmatic examples as they do not at present have any officially recognized national regulation or guideline.[120] Reliance on international guidelines is not problematic per se, only that they do not have

---

115 Joseph M. Mfutso-Bengu and T.E. Taylor, 'Ethical Jurisdictions in Biomedical Research' (2002), 18 Trends in Parasitology 231–234.

116 V. Garrafa, et al., 'Between the needy and the greedy: the quest for a just and fair ethics of clinical research' (2010), 36 J. Med. Ethics 500 at 503.

117 Paul M. McNeill, 'International Trends in Research Regulation: Science as Negotiation', in David N. Weisstub (ed.), *Research on Human Subjects: Ethics, Law and Social Policy* (Oxford: Elsevier Science Ltd., 1998) 243–263.

118 Research subject protection based on formal legal mechanisms has also been advocated for developed countries as well: D.R. Waring and T. Lemmens, 'Integrating Values in Risk Analysis of Biomedical Research: The Case for Regulatory and Law Reform' (2004), University of Toronto Law Journal 249.

119 B. Starkman, 'Models for Regulating Research; The Council of Europe and International Trends', in David N. Weisstub (ed.), *Research on Human Subjects: Ethics, Law and Social Policy* (Oxford: Elsevier Science Ltd., 1998) at 281.

120 Dya E.M. Elsayed and Nancy E. Kass, 'Assessment of the Ethical Review Process in Sudan' (2007), 7 Developing World Bioethics 143–148.

the force of law (being neither treaties nor conventions); nor do they take local and cultural contexts into consideration, as already mentioned above. Nevertheless, non-binding guidelines could be useful in a number of ways.[121] For instance, a defendant whose conduct is consistent with standards set out in a guideline might be able to establish a defence against malpractice actions. Moreover, guidelines help the courts to develop legal standards of care where the (legal) rules are unclear or non-existent on a particular issue. Furthermore, guidelines could be a rich source of information for research subjects on the level of professional conduct expected of their investigators. While an enforceable regulatory model is the best for Africa on account of its binding character and in light of the legal analyses developed in chapters five, six and seven, it is better seen in the context of alternative models of regulation available internationally.

Regulation may take the form of professional or industry self-regulation;[122] this generally involves the constitution of an ethics review committee composed of professional associates or colleagues of the researcher or investigator and, as such, raises strong issues of bias and potential for inadequate review.[123] For instance, can professional colleagues be trusted to review objectively, and if appropriate reject, the research proposal of one of their own? McNeill highlights some of the problems inherent in professional or industry self-regulation by referring to a New Zealand case in which an ethics committee, that reviewed and approved a cervical cancer study, was composed of only the professional peers of the investigator; an official inquiry indicted the committee for approving unethical research that led to the deaths of women with cervical cancer.[124] McNeill observed that the deaths 'could have been prevented with adequate review'.[125] Subsequently, the chairman

121 Angela Campbell and Kathleen C. Glass, 'The Legal Status of Clinical and Ethics Policies, Codes, and Guidelines in Medical Practice and Research' (2000–2001), 46 McGill L.J. 473 at 477.

122 South Africa offers good example of professional self-regulation: Medical Research Council (South Africa), *Guidelines on Ethics for Medical Research* (2001–2002). For national guidelines in South Africa: Department of Health, *Ethics in Health Research: Principles, Structures and Processes* (Pretoria, DoH, 2004); Department of Health, *Guidelines for Good Clinical Practice in the Conduct of Clinical Trials in Human Participants in South Africa* (Pretoria, DoH, 2000). South Africa, however, currently makes prior ethics review of research a mandatory legal requirement: National Health Act 2004, Act No. 61 of 2003.

123 Keymanthri Moodley and Landon Myer, 'Health Research Ethics Committees in South Africa 12 Years into Democracy' (2007), 8 BMC Medical Ethics.

124 P.M. McNeill, 'The Implications for Australia of the New Zealand Report of the Cervical Cancer Inquiry: No Cause for Complacency' (1989), 150 Medical Journal of Australia 264; Paul M. McNeill, 'International Trends in Research Regulation: Science as Negotiation', in David N. Weisstub (ed.), *Research on Human Subjects: Ethics, Law and Social Policy* (Oxford: Elsevier Science Ltd., 1998) at 245.

125 Paul M. McNeill, 'International Trends in Research Regulation: Science as Negotiation', in David N. Weisstub (ed.), *Research on Human Subjects: Ethics, Law and Social Policy* (Oxford: Elsevier Science Ltd., 1998), 245.

of the committee, Prof. Bonham, was charged and found guilty of professional misconduct.[126] Apart from professional or industry self-regulation, there are at least four models of research regulation.[127] Thus, a valid statute or legislation could make ethics review and compliance with other guidance for research a legal requirement for the conducting of research involving human beings.[128] This is the position in Finland, Germany, France, and to some extent, USA and England and Wales. Penal sanctions could accompany non-compliance.[129] Less specifically, formal legislation may compulsorily require biomedical research institutions to devise their own ethics review system. Furthermore, governmental research agencies may develop guidelines that make ethics review a pre-requisite for funding.[130] Lastly, ethics review may be incorporated by a cross-reference national legislation.[131] It is surprising that despite the value of enforceable research guidelines, and lessons learned from regional and international research scandals, most African countries have either opted for the third regulatory option above or professional regulation.[132] For instance, some research guidelines in Africa are developed by semi-autonomous governmental agencies (some of) whose remits go beyond bioethical issues. These include the Ugandan National Council for Science and Technology,[133] the Kenyan National Council for Science and Technology,[134] the National Research Council of Malawi, the National Health Science and Technology Council of Ethiopia, the Tanzanian National Institute for Medical Research, and the Health Research and Development Committee of Botswana. Since some African countries currently do not have any local or national research guidelines, and others have just recently developed theirs or are in the process of doing so, there is an opportunity to adopt a regulatory framework that reflects the lessons learned from their own experiences and those of other countries. It is suggested that a legally binding and enforceable guideline would meet that need.[135]

126 Ibid.

127 Marie Hirtle, Trudo Lemmens, and Dominique Sprumont, 'A Comparative Analysis of Research Ethics Review Mechanisms and the ICH Good Clinical Practice Guideline' (2000), 7 European Journal of Health Law, at 267.

128 See statutes cited supra, note 47; Simon Verdun-Jones and David N. Weisstub, 'The Regulation of Biomedical Research Experimentation in Canada: Developing an Effective Apparatus for the Implementation of Ethical Principles in a Scientific Milieu' (1996–97), 28 Ottawa Law Review 297–341, at 340.

129 Hirtle and Lemmens, and Sprumont, supra, note 127, at 268.

130 Ibid.

131 Ibid.

132 Legally enforceable guidelines were also recommended for Canada: Verdun-Jones and Weisstub, supra, note 132.

133 Ugandan National Council for Science and Technology Act 1990, c. 209.

134 Science and Technology Repeal Act, Cap 205, Laws of Kenya, 1979.

135 A similar suggestion was made in the context of an appraisal of the national resources for health research in selected African countries: Joses M. Kiriga and Charles Wambebe, 'Status of National Health Research Systems in Ten Countries of the

African countries with voluntary guidelines appear to have already missed this opportunity. In a powerful critique of voluntary (non-legally binding) guidelines, Starkman provides an interesting argument in favour of legally binding guidelines and bemoans the 'reluctance to consider that legislative regulation of research might be more efficient and effective than ethical guidelines revised from time to time'.[136] Starkman proceeds to summarize the advantages that make legislative regulation preferable to regulation through legally unenforceable guidelines:

> Briefly, legislation would apply to all biomedical research. It is debated openly, its provisions are made public, and the process of legislation provides accountability. It promotes uniformity and certainty. It is more readily enforceable. It can offer protection against liability. It is consistent with other fundamental law – for example, in Canada, the Charter of Rights and Freedoms. It makes it possible to clarify the conditions under which vulnerable persons can legally be the subjects of research. It provides the same powerful protection that countries are now choosing for regulating embryo research and in vitro fertilization. Legislation has all the advantages that have been claimed for guidelines, and none of the disadvantages.[137]

Happily, a few African countries have legally binding research guidelines as advocated by Starkman above. For instance, research guidelines in Nigeria[138] are legally enforceable as they have the force of a statute. Another feature is that Nigeria's guidelines incorporated some international guidelines. For instance, the Nigerian National Code of Health Research Ethics promulgated under the Nigerian Health Act incorporates the ICH-GCP for clinical trials.[139] Although prior ethics review has become a statutory requirement in Nigeria the legislation in Nigeria fails to specify a sanction for non-compliance with its provisions, other than the suspension or termination of research, report to other appropriate authorities, or the instigation of professional disciplinary action.[140] This situation contrasts sharply with the Finnish Medical Research Act which criminalizes a violation

---

WHO African Region' (2006), 6 BMC Health Services Research 135. More recently, Onyemelukwe made a good case for the legislative underpinning of research governance in Africa: Cheluchi Onyemelukwe, 'Research Involving Humans in African Countries: A Case for Domestic Legal Frameworks' (2008), 16 Afr. J. Int'l & Comp. L. 152–177.

136 B. Starkman, 'Models for Regulating Research; The Council of Europe and International Trends', in David N. Weisstub (ed.), *Research on Human Subjects: Ethics, Law and Social Policy* (Oxford: Elsevier Science Ltd., 1998) at 272.

137 Ibid., at 274.

138 The National Health Act 2011.

139 National Code of Health Research Ethics 2007 (Nigeria), at 26 and 42.

140 For similar observation on Nigeria: Cheluchi Onyemelukwe, 'Regulating Research Involving Humans in Nigeria: Some Recent Improvements' (2008), 16 Health Law Review 36 at 40.

of its provisions.[141] The threat of criminal sanctions is not to deter legitimate biomedical research activity but to ensure that procedural and substantive ethical requirements are satisfied. A legally operative guideline without a penal sanction is just a paper tiger. This gap needs to be plugged by other African countries in the process of developing enforceable guidelines. Interestingly, South Africa has moved to legislative regulation of research, and ethics review of protocols has become a mandatory legal requirement since 2004.[142] For instance, section 71 of the South African National Health Act 2004 provides that notwithstanding 'anything to the contrary in any other law, research or experimentation on a living person may only be conducted – (a) in the prescribed manner; and (b) with the written consent of the person …'; the Act then proceeds to establish the conditions under which research might be performed on vulnerable persons, such as minors.[143] Furthermore, section 72 of the (South African) National Health Act 2004 established the National Health Research Ethics Council (NHREC) whose remit includes the promulgation of 'guidelines for the functioning of health research ethics committees'.[144] NHREC is also empowered to register and audit health research ethics committees; set norms and standards for conducting research on humans and animals, including the conduct of clinical trials; adjudicate complaints about the functioning of health research ethics committees and hear any complaint by a researcher; refer violation or potential violation of an ethical or professional rule by a researcher or health care provider to the relevant statutory health professional council; and institute disciplinary actions against any person found to be in violation of any norms and standards, or guidelines, set for the conducting of research.[145] With NHREC as the national regulatory body in South Africa, section 73 of the National Health Act 2004 establishes institutional ethics committees, and provides that every 'institution, health agency and health establishment at which health research is conducted, must establish or have access to a health research ethics committee, which is registered with the National Health Research Ethics Council'. Accordingly, institutional health research ethics committees in South Africa are generally empowered to review protocols for research intended to be conducted within their institutions and, in particular, to 'grant approval for research by the relevant institution, agency or establishment in instances where research proposals and protocol meet the ethical standards of that health research ethics committee'.[146]

---

141 Medical Research Act (Finland), No. 488/ 1999 (amended in 2004), section 27.

142 National Health Act 2004 (South Africa), Act No. 61 of 2003. Generally: Jerome A. Singh, 'Health Research and Human Rights in South Africa' (2004), 363 The Lancet 1393.

143 National Health Act 2004 (South Africa), Act No. 61 of 2003, section 71(2) and (3).

144 Ibid., section 72(20(a).

145 Ibid., section 72(6).

146 Ibid., section 73(2)(b).

In sum, therefore, although most guidelines in Africa are voluntary and promulgated by governmental bodies, the totality of research guidelines in Africa generally reflect the entire spectrum of regulatory models mentioned above, including legislative regulation.

## Scope of Research Guidelines in Africa

Research guidelines vary in their scope of coverage. Some are comprehensive and cover all aspects of research involving human subjects, while others are much more limited in scope and apply to only one or more aspects of research, such as clinical trials. Research involving human subjects goes beyond the limits of biomedical studies. It encompasses any systematic investigation directed to the advancement and generalization of knowledge through a physical or psychological intervention on human beings or analysis of records of identifiable persons. Some research guidelines in Africa are quite comprehensive. For instance, the Ugandan guideline applies to all research involving human participants in Uganda, including 'research in social sciences and humanities, conventional and alternative medicines and research conducted in or by public institutions, private, inter-governmental and non-governmental organizations, and research conducted in a foreign country on human biological materials collected from Uganda'.[147] The provisions of the Cameroonian guideline arguably entail a similar coverage.[148] This is consistent with the increasing international trend to extend ethics review to all research involving human subjects whatever be the field of study, whether in the biomedical, behavioural, social or anthropological disciplines.[149] There are, however, guidelines in Africa that restrict research to health research. These include research guidelines in Nigeria,[150] Tanzania,[151] Ethiopia,[152] Zambia,[153] and Botswana.[154] It is not clear why these guidelines focus entirely on health research, thereby leaving much room for an unregulated area of research activity (non-

---

147 UNCST, Guidelines, supra, note 63, s. 1.5.

148 Ministerial Decree N0 079/A/MPH/DS of October 22, 1987 on the Creation and Organisation of an Ethics Committee Regulating all Research Involving Human Beings, articles 2 and 3. Many thanks to Prof. Godfrey Tangwa for making a copy of this legislation available to me and to Ghislain Mbessa for translating it from French to English.

149 Paul M. McNeill, 'International Trends in Research Regulation: Science as Negotiation', in David N. Weisstub (ed.), *Research on Human Subjects: Ethics, Law and Social Policy* (Oxford: Elsevier Science Ltd., 1998) 257–262.

150 National Code of Health Research, supra, note 140.

151 TANHER & NHREC, Guidelines on Ethics for Health Research in Tanzania (2001).

152 Ethiopian Science and Technology Commission, National Health Research Ethics (Addis Ababa, 2005).

153 Grateful to Bornwell for this information.

154 HRDC, Health Research Guidelines (2005).

health research). Arguably, the majority of research involving human beings is likely to be health-related, directly or indirectly. However, it is suggested that African countries should develop guidelines that encompass every field of research activity, whether health-related or not.

### Enforceability of Guidelines in Africa

The enforceability of research guidelines in Africa depends on the source of a particular guideline or its mode of promulgation. In other words, whether the guideline is issued by a professional body or backed by legal sanctions. As mentioned above, voluntary guidelines issued by professional bodies and associations do not generally have a direct legal force, though some legal and non-legal consequences may accompany a breach of their provisions. For instance, Dickens argued that the breach of a voluntary guideline could constitute a breach of funding contract in relation to protocols funded by the government; such a breach might also amount to a breach of the investigator's contract of employment with their university or hospital and, therefore, attracts both public and private law remedies.[155] Furthermore, research studies involving human subjects cannot be undertaken in some African countries without the permit or authorization of a central governmental agency (or Ministry) such as the Ugandan National Council for Science and Technology, the Tanzania Commission for Science and Technology (COSTECH),[156] and the National Institute for Medical Research (NIMR),[157] and the Kenyan Ministry of Education, Science and Technology. These statutory bodies grant research permits (or ethics clearance in the case of NIMR) only after a protocol has secured an ethics approval. The ethics procedure ensures compliance with the applicable guidelines. To that extent, voluntary guidelines are indirectly enforced in practice. Similarly, research permits may be withdrawn for non-compliance with the terms of approval or for harm or injury to research participants.[158] More importantly, it is an offence to conduct (or continue) research involving human subjects without the required permit. Foreign researchers who did so or remained in the country after their research permits had been cancelled might be charged with an immigration offence. Moreover, a researcher may be liable to professional disciplinary actions for breach of professionally applicable research guidelines. In contrast, African countries with legally enforceable guidelines do have clear provisions that make compliance mandatory. As pointed out in the case of Nigeria, however, the appropriate legislation failed to specify a penal sanction for the breach of their provisions.

155 B.M. Dickens, 'Conflicts of Interest in Canadian Health Care Law' (1995), 21 American Journal of Law & Medicine 259.

156 Tanzania Commission for Science and Technology Act 1986 (No. 7 of 1986).

157 National Institute of Medical Research Act No. 23 of 1979.

158 For instance, UNCST Guidelines, supra, note 63, at s. 13.

## Conclusion

While research scandals constitute a dark spot in the history of research involving human subjects, biomedical research is undeniably a very useful and beneficial activity; for this reason, it has been suggested that every person has a moral duty to participate in research.[159] Interestingly, research scandals do often catalyse research regulation. For instance, the horrendous research on captive subjects by Nazi doctors and scientists, exposed in the Nuremberg trial, formed the basis of the Nuremberg Code enunciated during the trial. Similar research scandals triggered a flurry of (biomedical research) regulations by States and international organisations, such as the World Health Organisation, the World Medical Association, and the Council of International Organisation of Medical Sciences. The regulatory response has taken both procedural and substantive approaches. Thus, a procedural requirement that prior ethics review is mandatory for the conduct of research involving human subjects has become the cornerstone of research subjects' protection and funding; this complements substantive ethical requirements, meaning that the research must be socially useful, scientifically valid and ethically justifiable.

As this chapter suggested, research scandals in Africa took place under a climate of low regulatory visibility, heavy burden of preventable diseases, high rates of illiteracy and widespread poverty among research participants.[160] The chapter also evaluated the relevance of equipoise, analysed in chapter two, by deploying research scandals in Africa as the factual and legal matrix for examining the application of equipoise in Africa. Furthermore, this chapter examined the factors which incentivize research regulation in Africa. While a good number of African countries have national research guidelines, and others simply apply one or more of the available international research guidelines, only very few countries in Africa operate legally enforceable guidelines. Even in those cases, as in Nigeria, some of the legally enforceable guidelines do not specify a legal sanction that goes beyond professional and administrative disciplinary actions. In light of the advantages of a legally enforceable guideline examined above, this chapter suggested that enforceable guidelines should be the norm in Africa.

---

159 John Harris, 'Scientific research is a moral duty' (2005), 31 J. Med. Ethics 242–248

160 Generally, Colleen C. Denny and Christine Grady, 'Clinical research with economically disadvantaged populations' (2007), 33 J. Med. Ethics 382–385; R.R. Kishore, 'Biomedical Research and Mining of the Poor: The Need for their Exclusion' (2006), 12 Science and Engineering Ethics 175–183.

# Chapter 2
# Equipoise and the Normative Framework for Biomedical Research in Africa

## Introduction

Equipoise is a foundational requirement for the ethical justification of clinical research. At the risk of oversimplification, equipoise is a state of genuine uncertainty regarding the comparative merits of two (or more) treatments for a disease. In order to consider a clinical trial ethically justifiable, equipoise must exist before it is commenced and must remain throughout the duration of the trial. Put differently, the existence of equipoise is a precondition for the commencement, and continuation, of a clinical trial, which must be designed in such a manner that the results of the trial should be able to eliminate the therapeutic uncertainty, and thus disturb equipoise. As Drews observed, '[C]linical trials are, after all, conducted because doubt exists, and they can be justified only if they are structured in a way that will bring more clarity to an open therapeutic question'.[1] Where one of the treatments in a clinical trial is already known to be effective and superior to the other arms of the trial, equipoise does not exist and the resultant trial is morally indefensible. As Freedman observed, 'equipoise is an ethically necessary condition in all cases of clinical research'.[2] Although the principle of equipoise and its implications for clinical research were identified by Fried in the 1970s,[3] it was Freedman's re-conceptualization of equipoise in the late 1980s that has proved to be the most influential.[4] Thus, this chapter begins with analysis of the concept of equipoise, its various strands and manifestations, and the criticisms that have been made against equipoise. Next, the chapter interrogates the version of equipoise that should be applicable to clinical research in Africa. Finally, this chapter considers the impact of equipoise on the physician's duty to provide the best treatment (therapeutic obligation), on the use of placebo-controlled trial designs, and the interface between

---

1 Jügen Drews, 'Between Ethical Demands and Economic Constraints', in M.A. Santoro and T.M. Gorrie (eds), *Ethics and the Pharmaceutical Industry* (Cambridge: Cambridge University Press, 2005) at 24.

2 Benjamin Freedman, 'Equipoise and the Ethics of Clinical Research' (1987), 317 New Eng. J. Med. 141–145; reproduced in Helga Kuhse and Peter Singer, *Bioethics: An Anthology* (Oxford: Blackwell Publishing, 2006) at 513.

3 C. Fried, *Medical Experimentation, Personal Integrity and Social Policy* (Amsterdam: North-Holland Publishing, 1974).

4 Freedman in Kuhse and Singer, supra, note 2, 513–519.

equipoise and research subjects' informed consent. The aim of this chapter, as the sub-sections indicate, is to project equipoise not only as the normative framework for evaluating the ethics of clinical trial research in Africa and other developing countries, but also as a prism for examining biomedical research scandals in Africa; some of those scandals were analysed in the chapter one.

## Theoretical Equipoise

As noted above, equipoise is a state of genuine uncertainty regarding the comparative merits of therapeutic regimens; the task, however, is to determine whose certainty is necessary for the disturbance of equipoise. In other words, whose knowledge or belief is relevant;[5] is it that of the clinical investigator or the clinical community? Arguably, the viability of clinical research depends on the answer to this important question. Until Freedman's influential analysis, equipoise was understood in a restrictive and subjective sense to indicate the clinical investigator's individual sense of therapeutic uncertainty. Thus, Freedman observed that in the simplest model of equipoise 'testing a new treatment B on a defined population P for which the current accepted treatment is A, it is necessary that the clinical investigator be in a state of genuine uncertainty regarding the comparative merits of treatments A and B for population P', and that if 'a physician knows that these treatments are not equivalent, ethics requires that the superior treatment be recommended'.[6] Because this type of equipoise relies heavily on the investigator's subjective knowledge, which could come from a great array of sources, equipoise is potentially easily disturbed and, thus, poses a threat to the commencement or continuation of the clinical trial of a new drug against standard therapies. Freedman characterized this subjective understanding of equipoise as 'theoretical equipoise[7] and observed that it produced three problems for clinical research.

First, the study or reasoning preceding the trial, or the preliminary results that prompted the trial, might have actually influenced the investigator to prefer one of the treatments in the proposed trial; consequently, the investigator could not be said to be in equipoise, with the result that equipoise would have been disturbed even before the commencement of the trial. As a matter of ethical necessity, therefore, the proposed trial would have to be abandoned. There are many sources of evidence likely to upset theoretical equipoise 'including data from the literature, uncontrolled experience, considerations of basic science and fundamental physiologic processes, and perhaps a "gut feeling" or "instinct" resulting from

5 As Ashcroft observed: 'Equipoise is about beliefs, and beliefs that are held or not held, or held to be false, by given subjects. Equipoise, in other words, is a propositional attitude', R. Ashcroft, 'Equipoise, Knowledge and Ethics in Clinical Research and Practice' (1999), 13 Bioethics 314 at 320.

6 Freedman in Kuhse and Singer, supra, note 2, at 513.

7 Ibid., at 515.

(or superimposed on) other considerations'.[8] Furthermore, Christian Mormont observed that while the 'conviction of a clinician can, certainly, be grounded on rational proofs or intuitions generated by his practice',[9] it can also be 'grounded on the need to reassure himself, to protect his narcissism, or to expand his clientele, all of which sow the needs of behaviours based on superstition or magic'.[10] This sort of evidence projects theoretical equipoise as highly sensitive, precarious and 'balanced on a knife's edge'.[11] Chalmers suggested that the problems of equipoise at the onset of clinical trial could be solved with randomization beginning with the first subject.[12] In other words, to obviate experiential knowledge of the therapeutic merits of an intervention sought to be investigated in a clinical trial, the first patients to receive the intervention should be randomized to the investigational arm of the trial. In essence, Chalmers approach, as observed by Brody, amounts to a plea for earlier commencement of clinical trials, so that if the first patient to receive a new intervention did so in the context of a randomized controlled trial, the problem of prior knowledge of the comparative merit of the new intervention gained from practical (clinical) experience would be avoided.[13] Freedman, however, opined that Chalmers' solution was largely ineffective since equipoise might be disturbed even before the enrolment of research subjects and gaining of practical experience on the therapeutic merits of an investigational drug. In other words, therapeutic evidence or knowledge obtained by the investigators (probably from the scientific literature) at the very earliest stage of formulating the hypothesis and preparing the protocol might be sufficient to disturb equipoise.

Second, even when theoretical equipoise is not disturbed at the onset of clinical trial (as examined above), it might nevertheless be disturbed late or early in the study when preliminary comparative results show that one arm of the trial is more effective than the other. In such a case, equipoise, as theoretically understood, is disturbed and the trial would have to be terminated even if, in the end, the preliminary results turn out to be of no statistical significance. Ian Kennedy's analysis of the law and ethics of randomized clinical trials confirms the impact of preliminary data on the existence of theoretical equipoise. Thus, he observed that when preliminary results concretize a doctor's treatment preference, it becomes

8 Ibid., at 516.

9 Christian Mormont, 'Ethical Questions Pertaining to the Use of Placebos', in David N. Weisstub (ed.), *Research on Human Subjects: Ethics, Law and Social Policy* (Oxford: Elsevier Science Ltd., 1998) at 538.

10 Ibid., at 538.

11 Freedman in Kuhse and Singer, supra, note 2, at 516.

12 T. Chalmers, 'The Ethics of Randomisation as a Decision-Making Technique and the Problem of Informed Consent', in T.L. Beauchamp and L. Walters (eds), *Contemporary Issues in Bioethics* (Encino, C.A.: Dickenson, 1978) 426–429.

13 Baruch A. Brody, 'When are Placebo-Controlled Trials No Longer Appropriate?' (1997), 18 Control Clinical Trials 602 at 604–605 (reproduced in George F. Tomossy and David N. Weisstub, *Human Experimentation and Research* (Aldershot: Ashgate Publishing, 2003) at 457.

difficult to justify their patient's continued participation in clinical research in a way that is consistent with the doctor's unyielding fidelity to their patient's best interest. As Kennedy observed, this remains the case notwithstanding that the preliminary results turned out to be statistically insignificant or incapable of validating or invalidating the research hypothesis.[14] What the above means is that preliminary results of a trial are likely to lead to the premature termination of such trials in a manner that is both scientifically and ethically questionable.[15] In order to solve this problem of theoretical equipoise, which arises during the course of a trial, Chalmers suggested the use of data-monitoring committees.[16] As envisaged by Chalmers, the committee members would operate independently of the investigators and would be the only ones to know the preliminary results. In essence, the investigators' ignorance of ongoing results helps to keep their equipoise intact. Freedman attacked this solution, arguing that it is unethical for an investigator to keep themselves in ignorance of information which might be relevant for a patient's treatment: a 'clinician is not merely obliged to treat a patient on the basis of the information that he or she currently has, but is also required to discover information that would be relevant to treatment decisions. If interim results would disturb equipoise, the investigators are obliged to gather and use that information'.[17] Similarly, Ian Kennedy rejected an approach involving the interposition of 'an independent review committee' (Chalmers' Data Monitoring Committee) on the ground that it 'shifts the responsibility of decision-making, but does not resolve the dilemma which the doctor is faced with, since the doctor is still bound by his duty to put his patient first'.[18] Finally, the third problem posed by theoretical equipoise relates to its negative impact on patients' recruitment for clinical research. For instance, enrolment of subjects must stop upon the disturbance of equipoise. Freedman illustrated this particular problem of theoretical equipoise with Taylor and colleagues' analysis of the termination of a study on alternative treatments for breast cancer due to the investigators' difficulty in recruiting patients after their equipoise had been disturbed.[19]

On account of the problems above, Freedman observed that theoretical equipoise is 'both conceptually odd and ethically irrelevant';[20] he suggested that equipoise should be understood in a clinical sense (clinical equipoise) to indicate

---

14 Ian Kennedy, *Treat Me Right: Essays in Medical Law and Ethics* (Oxford: Oxford University Press, 1988) at 219–220.

15 Arguably it is unethical to terminate a trial without scientific justification and, thereby, inhibit the acquisition of relevant knowledge.

16 T.C. Chalmers, 'Invited Remarks' (1979), 25 Clinical and Pharmacological Therapy 649–650.

17 Freeman in Kuhse and Singer, supra, note 2, at 514.

18 Kennedy, supra, note 14, at 220.

19 K.M. Taylor, et al., 'Physicians' Reasons For Not Entering Eligible Patients in a Randomised Clinical Trial of Surgery for Breast Cancer' (1984), 310 New Eng. J. Med. 1363–1367.

20 Freedman in Kuhse and Singer, supra, note 2, at 515.

a state of uncertainty in the clinical community regarding the comparative merits of a set of therapeutic interventions. Freedman's analysis projects clinical equipoise (examined below) as a robust and better explanatory model for the ethics of clinical research. In North America, Freedman's clinical equipoise is the dominant conceptual framework for appraising the ethics of clinical research.[21] In contrast, theoretical equipoise is the normative standard for the ethical evaluation of randomized clinical trials in the UK, although the concept is best known in the UK as the 'uncertainty principle'.[22] As with theoretical equipoise, the uncertainty principle is balanced on the edge and easily disturbed. Similarly, the fragility of the uncertainty principle is engendered by its susceptibility to the physician's 'hunch' or 'gut feeling'.[23] To address this problem, Collins, Doll and Peto sought to introduce an objective criteria to the uncertainty principle and observed that 'no patient should be entered [in a trial] if the responsible physician … [is] for any medical or non-medical reason(s) *reasonably certain* that one of the treatments that might be allocated would be inappropriate' (italics in the original) or, putting it differently, 'patients can be entered only if the responsible physician is *substantially uncertain* as to which of the treatments would be most appropriate for this particular patient'.[24] Arguably, the standards of reasonableness and substantiality are objectively decipherable standards in private law, and they imply that not every hunch of the physician would count for the uncertainty principle. Nonetheless, Weijer, Shapiro and Glass observed that the objective criterion incorporated into the uncertainty principle by Collins, Doll and Peto was of marginal utility because it is the individual physician who still has to decide what counts as reasonable or substantially uncertain.[25] Furthermore, they observed that the uncertainty principle, unlike clinical equipoise, makes it 'difficult, if not impossible, to conclude that a physician ever errs in enrolling a patient in a trial. So long as the physician claims he or she was uncertain, even if madly or incompetently so, he or she cannot be said to be wrong'.[26]

21 C. Weijer, S. Shapiro and K. Glass, 'For and against: clinical equipoise and not the uncertainty principle is the moral underpinning of the randomised controlled trial' (2000), 321 BMJ 756–757.

22 Richard Peto and Colin Baigent, 'Trials: the next 50 years: Large scale randomised evidence of moderate benefits' (1998), 317 BMJ 1170.

23 A Schafer, 'The Randomized Clinical Trial: For Whose Benefit? (1985), 7 IRB: A Review of Human Subjects Research 4–6, noting that a physician's preference might be labelled as a bias or hunch or based on mere intuition.

24 R. Collins, R. Doll and R. Peto, 'Ethics of Clinical Trials', in C.J. Williams (ed.), *Introducing New Treatments for Cancer: Practical, Ethical and Legal Problems* (Chichester, England: John Wiley & Sons, 1992) at 50 (Italics in the original). For a similar definition: Sally Stenning, '"The Uncertainty Principle": Selection of Patients for Cancer Clinical Trials', in Williams (ed.), ibid., at 161.

25 C. Weijer, S. Shapiro and K. Glass, supra, note 21, at 756.

26 Ibid., at 756.

Notwithstanding the criticism above, the uncertainty principle carries the advantage that a patient enrolled in a randomized treatment comparison receives no less standard of care than would have been available had there been no trial. This underpins Collins, Doll and Peto's observation that as 'long as trials are governed by the "uncertainty principle", there is an approximate parallelism between good science and good ethics, *so there is no pressure to be any more unethical than ordinary medical practice is*'. (Italics in the original) Furthermore, in a recent debate regarding the relative values and moral defensibility of clinical equipoise and the uncertainty principle (theoretical equipoise), Murray Enkin offered a robust defence of the uncertainty principle, observing that a physician 'cannot participate in a controlled trial if she is certain that one arm is superior to the others and that some of her patients will receive an inferior treatment by participating in the trial'.[27] For Enkin, it is immaterial that the physician's preference was based on a hunch, and it 'does not matter whether her certainty is based on formal scientific studies, on personal experience, on anecdote, on tacit understanding, or rules of thumb. Whether her certainty is in accord with or diverges from the view of the medical community is irrelevant'.[28] This normative cleavage in the approach to clinical research between the UK and North America runs deep and appears to find no middle ground. One of the sub-sections below examines the impact of this normative bifurcation on Africa and other developing countries.

## Clinical Equipoise

Unlike theoretical equipoise, 'clinical equipoise' is shaped by consensus in the medical or clinical community. It refers to the absence of a 'consensus within the expert clinical community about the comparative merits of alternatives to be tested'.[29] In such a case, the clinical trial must be designed in a way that the outcome should be able to resolve the disputes among clinicians one way or another. Freedman argued that grounding equipoise on the knowledge of a professional or expert community, rather than the individual investigator's knowledge, is consistent with the basic rationale of clinical trials which are conducted because 'there is a current or imminent conflict in the clinical community over what treatment is preferred for patients in a defined population P. The standard treatment is A, but some evidence suggests that B will be superior .... Or there is a split in the clinical community, with some favouring A and others favouring B'.[30] Clinical trials are meant to resolve such conflicts.

---

27 Murray E. Enkin, 'For and against: clinical equipoise and not the uncertainty principle is the moral underpinning of the randomised controlled trial' (2000), 321 BMJ 756 at 758.

28 Ibid., at 758.

29 Freedman in Kuhse and Singer, supra, note 2, at 516–517.

30 Ibid., at 516.

Furthermore, clinical equipoise resonates with the professional standards that underpin malpractice litigation where the question is not whether a medical professional evinced superior treatment preferences, but rather, whether they acted in conformity with the standard prevailing in the medical community. Accordingly, Freedman observed that persons are 'licensed as physicians after they demonstrate the acquisition of this professionally validated knowledge, not after they reveal a superior capacity for guessing. Normative judgements of their behaviour, e.g., malpractice actions, rely on a comparison with what is done by the community of medical practitioners'.[31] Freedman, therefore, suggested that clinical equipoise offers a more robust normative framework for clinical research and avoids the three problems noted for theoretical equipoise above. For instance, an individual investigator's treatment preference does not disturb (clinical) equipoise provided that their responsible and competent colleagues prefer the investigator's less-favoured treatment. This would not have been possible with theoretical equipoise where therapeutic subjectivity and individual treatment preferences play a much stronger role. Thus, in clinical equipoise, an investigator can enrol their patient in clinical research notwithstanding the existence of a treatment preference which is not generally shared in the clinical community. In this sense, clinical equipoise is consistent with a physician's therapeutic obligation to their individual patients. Weijer and Miller captured this resonance in their observation that clinical equipoise carries the advantage that 'therapeutic procedures in a clinical trial are consistent with competent medical care'.[32] Furthermore, unlike theoretical equipoise, interim results of a clinical trial too weak to influence the judgement of the clinical community would not be able to disturb clinical equipoise attained at the beginning of that trial. Partly for these reasons, Freedman concluded that 'clinical equipoise is far weaker – and more common – condition than theoretical equipoise'[33] and is the 'alternative, preferable interpretation of equipoise'.[34] Freedman's clinical equipoise has not, however, been accepted without significant criticism.

### *Criticism of Clinical Equipoise*

In an interesting textual and epistemological critique of Freedman's clinical equipoise, Fred Gifford observed that Freedman conflated community equipoise with clinical equipoise.[35] Gifford argued that although Freedman explicitly employed 'clinical equipoise' as his criterion for the moral legitimacy of a randomized clinical trial, yet a textual analysis showed that Freedman actually

31 Ibid., at 517.

32 C. Weijer and P.B. Miller, 'When are research risks reasonable in relation to anticipated benefits?' (2004), 10 Nature Medicine 570 at 571.

33 Freeman in Kuhse and Singer, supra, note 2, at 517.

34 Ibid., at 516.

35 Fred Gifford, 'Freedman's "Clinical Equipoise" and "Sliding-Scale All-Dimensions-Considered Equipoise"' (2000), 25 Journal of Medicine and Philosophy 399–426.

meant 'community equipoise'.[36] Even at that, Gifford argued, community equipoise, as the proper referent of Freedman's equipoise, suffers from ambiguities and complications.[37] For instance, the notion of community equipoise elides different versions of equipoise and fails to answer important questions, such as whether the relevant community includes patients and whether equipoise refers to the judgement of patients or physicians or both; also, there is no indication of how the relevant community is to be constructed, and whether equipoise is dependent on the unanimous judgement of the community or just a majority of them.[38] Since clinical equipoise, in the sense of 'clinical relevance',[39] connotes something different from 'community equipoise', in the sense of 'community agreement',[40] Gifford argued that Freedman's epistemological confusion went beyond mere error in nomenclature. In essence, Gifford implied that Freedman's clinical equipoise was no different from the theoretical equipoise that Freedman roundly rejected. More significantly, Gifford opined that clinical equipoise, as conceived by Freedman and clarified above, does not provide a robust conceptual framework for determining when trials should be continued despite the emergence of preliminary data affecting an investigator's equipoise. Gifford partly attributed this problem to the one-dimensional nature of clinical equipoise and submitted that the problem could be obviated by adopting a framework he identified as the multi-dimensional or all-dimensions-considered equipoise (ADC equipoise). The ADC equipoise is based on patients' values and takes the different and variable outcomes of a set of interventions into account in determining whether equipoise has been reached or disturbed.[41] While Gifford acknowledged the difficulties involved in the application of the ADC equipoise, he considered it a better framework for evaluating the ethics of clinical research than Freedman's clinical equipoise.

Similarly, Karlawish and Lantos argued that Freedman's clinical equipoise was flawed as a conceptual architecture for the ethical justification of clinical research because it privileged physicians' judgement about medical evidence necessary to justify clinical trial over patients' values.[42] Accordingly, the authors suggested a reconceptualization of clinical equipoise to 'community equipoise' in order to evince the shared decision-making that characterizes the doctor-patient relationship and to emphasize the need for both patients and investigators to be in equipoise before clinical trial can be ethically justified. Furthermore, Karlawish and Lantos

36 Ibid., at 403. Also, F. Gifford, 'Community Equipoise and the Ethics of Randomized Clinical Trials' (1995), 9 Bioethics 127–148.

37 Fred Gifford, 'So-Called "Clinical Equipoise" and the Argument from Design' (2007), 32 Journal of Medicine and Philosophy 135–150.

38 Ibid., at 137.

39 Gifford (2000), supra, note 35, at 404.

40 Ibid., at 404.

41 Ibid., at 413–418.

42 J.H.T. Karlawish and J. Lantos, 'Community Equipoise and the Architecture of Clinical Research (1997), 6 Cambridge Quarterly of Healthcare Ethics 385–396.

argued that clinical research is not a field exclusive to physicians since it involves both questions of science (that is scientific and technical aspects of a protocol) and value (that is, a broader set of considerations on the moral worth of a decision which go beyond matters of science).[43] By taking the values of patients into consideration in clinical research, Karlawish and Lantos argued that community equipoise might be justified on three grounds.[44] First, the role of patients in clinical research has increased in recent years through patients' advocacy groups and the widespread use of information technologies. The case of HIV/AIDS research, where patients played a significant role in determining the HIV/AIDS research agenda, illustrates patients' participation in the design of clinical research. Thus, modern patients are much more informed and knowledgeable about the scientific aspects of their medical condition than was the case in the past. Second, clinical decision-making takes place in the context of physician-patient relationship; this sort of partnership should also govern research decision-making. Third, medical knowledge is sociological in nature and, therefore, not confined to physicians. Thus, Karlawish and Lantos opined that equipoise should be based on the collective uncertainty of the community of physicians and patients;[45] this they called 'community equipoise' and, therefore, suggested 'a revision of Freedman's concept of clinical equipoise to a broader sense of community that includes physicians and patients. Community equipoise is an essential condition for physicians and patients to answer these questions: should there be a trial? If so, what kind?'.[46]

While the criticisms above implicitly accept the criterion of equipoise, but argue for its reformulation, there are, however, commentators who argue for the rejection of the concept altogether. For instance, Veatch had in 2002 argued that what was necessary to justify clinical trials was not the uncertainty of the researcher or the research community but, rather, a patient's indifference between two treatment options and their willingness to be randomized after having enough information on the alternatives.[47] Thus, the relevant criterion is *patient's* equipoise, not clinical equipoise as conceived by Freedman. Veatch observed that clinicians' and patients' equipoise might be at variance (physicians being in equipoise when their patients are not) and that this 'clarifies the lack of relevance of clinical community equipoise in justifying a randomization. The mere fact that a particular clinician or even a community of clinicians is in equipoise does not imply that a potential subject should be'.[48] Randomization, Veatch submitted, should therefore be on the basis of a potential subject's indifference between two treatment options

43 Ibid., at 390–391.

44 Ibid., at 386–387.

45 Ibid., at 387.

46 Ibid., at 394.

47 Robert Veatch, 'Indifference of Subjects: An alternative to equipoise in randomized clinical trials' (2002), 19 Social Philosophy and Policy 295–323.

48 Robert Veatch, 'The Irrelevance of Equipoise' (2007), 32 Journal of Medicine and Philosophy 167 at 176.

or willingness to take the risk of receiving the less attractive treatment for the good of science.[49] From this, Veatch argued that since randomizations are justified by a potential patient's informed consent, irrespective of their equipoise, equipoise was therefore logically irrelevant.[50] In the end, Veatch concluded that 'it is not anyone's equipoise that is morally critical; it is whether the potential subjects consent to be randomized without being unduly coerced, manipulated, or exploited'.[51] Below, however, one of the subsections offers a criticism of the bigger role assigned to consent by Veatch in the justification of clinical trials. On their part, Miller and Brody argued that clinical trial was different from clinical care and, therefore, both should respond to different criteria of ethical and moral justification.[52] Thus, they submitted that while the duty to provide patients with the best proven therapy was justified in clinical care (within the context of doctor-patient relationship), such a duty was, however, not necessary for the moral justification of clinical research where the important concern is non-exploitation (rather than equipoise).[53] As they observed: 'Requiring that all research interventions are governed by a standard of not compromising the health or medical care of research participants applies the ethical standards of therapeutic medicine to the fundamentally different activity of clinical research'.[54] The (alternative) non-exploitation framework suggested by Miller and Brody entails a duty to ensure: that risks to subjects are reasonable; that the research has social value, and is scientifically valid; that subjects give free and informed consent; that there is fair subject selection; that there is independent review of the research; and respect for persons.[55] Accordingly, Miller and Brody rejected clinical equipoise for entangling two significant principles that should be kept separate, that is (a) the scientific principle that an honest null hypothesis is the epistemic prerequisite for conducting clinical trials, and (b) the ethical

49 Ibid., at 177.

50 Ibid., at 167–183.

51 Ibid., at 182.

52 Franklin G. Miller and Howard Brody, 'A Critique of Clinical Equipoise' (2003), 33 The Hastings Center Report 19–28.

53 The non-exploitation framework of Miller and Brody was criticized for being inadequately developed and incoherently articulated: L.A. Jenson, 'A closer look at the bad deal trial: Beyond clinical equipoise' (2005), 35 Hastings Center Report 29–36; Paul B. Miller and Charles Weijer, 'Equipoise and the Duty of Care in Clinical Research: A Philosophical Response to Our Critics' (2007), 32 Journal of Medicine and Philosophy 117–133.

54 Franklin G. Miller and Howard Brody, 'Clinical Equipoise and the Incoherence of Research Ethics' (2007), 32 Journal of Medicine and Philosophy 151 at 158–159. Also: P. Litton and F.G. Miller, 'A normative justification for distinguishing the ethics of clinical research from the ethics of medical care' (2005), 33 J.L. Med. & Ethics 566–574.

55 Miller and Brody (2007), supra, note 54; Alex J. London, 'Two Dogmas of Research Ethics and the Integrative Approach to Human-Subjects Research' (2007), 32 Journal of Medicine and Philosophy 99 at 102; Ezekiel J. Emmanuel, et al., 'What Makes Clinical Research in Developing Countries Ethical? The Benchmarks of Ethical Research' (2004), 189 Journal of Infectious Disease 930–937.

principle that no patient should be given an inferior treatment in a randomized trial.[56] They submitted that while equipoise was relevant for the first principle only, it was generally and mistakenly understood to cover the second principle as well. If equipoise actually included the second principle (no inferior treatment principle), they argued, it would be contradictory for some commentators to affirm a consensus that equipoise governs clinical trials while, at the same time, accept the existence of a controversy over the legitimacy of placebo-controlled trials;[57] in other words, a consensus on clinical equipoise, impliedly prohibiting the withholding of effective or standard therapy, should result in the uncontroversial and logical rejection of placebo-controlled trials, yet this is not the case in practice. Thus, Miller and Brody observed that the dissonance between the general acceptance of clinical equipoise and the (conflicting) common practice of research ethics boards in approving placebo-controlled trials evinced an incoherence that undermined clinical equipoise.[58]

Some of the criticisms above prompted a philosophical re-visitation of the concept of equipoise by Miller and Weijer, who argued that equipoise is susceptible to conceptual rehabilitation and improvement through the reconciliation of the formulations adduced by its most prominent exponents – Fried and Freedman.[59] At the risk of oversimplification, Miller and Weijer argued that the individual (theoretical) and clinical equipoise are complementary concepts, serve different purposes and should be considered at two different levels of analysis. Thus, while *individual* or *theoretical* equipoise is relevant to a physician's judgement concerning the question of whether or not it is morally permissible to enrol their patient in a randomized clinical trial, *clinical* equipoise, on the other hand, underpins the decision of research ethics boards regarding the ethical acceptability of a protocol involving the randomization of patients to different trial arms. In this way, Miller and Weijer submitted, the two versions of equipoise are not contradictory as they operate at two distinct levels and avoid the dilemma of having to choose between the two of them. In other words (and contrary to Freedman), both versions of equipoise are relevant to the ethical assessment of clinical research. Gifford has, however, dismissed Miller and Weijer's attempts at rehabilitating equipoise.[60] In part, Gifford argued that the prominent role given to individual (theoretical) equipoise by Miller and Weijer, as opposed to Freedman's

56 Franklin G. Miller and Howard Brody, 'Clinical Equipoise and the Incoherence of Research Ethics' (2007), 32 Journal of Medicine and Philosophy 151 at 153.

57 For instance: B.A. Brody, L.P. McCullough and R.R. Sharp, 'Consensus and Controversy in Clinical Research Ethics' (2005), 294 Journal of the American Medical Association 1411–1414.

58 Miller and Brody (2007), supra, note 54, at 155.

59 Paul B. Miller and Charles Weijer, 'Rehabilitating Equipoise' (2003), 13 Kennedy Institute of Ethics Journal 93–118.

60 Fred Gifford, 'Pulling the Plug on Clinical Equipoise: A Critique of Miller and Weijer' (2007), 17 Kennedy Institute of Ethics Journal 203–226.

rejection of its relevance, brought with it those disadvantages that led Freedman to reject the concept in the first place, especially its fragility and vulnerability to early disturbance. Notwithstanding the criticisms above, equipoise has continued to retain its popularity as a foundational framework for the ethical evaluation of clinical research; this is in part evidenced by the ongoing debate on the meaning and justifications of the concept and the fascination it holds on commentators.[61]

## Which Way Africa? Clinical Equipoise or the Uncertainty Principle?

It is not clear from the bioethical literature whether African countries subscribe to one or the other of the two main schools of equipoise, or to both of them. Whichever way they choose, however, equipoise is bound to impact significantly on the conduct of clinical research in Africa. It might be asked, however, whether the concept of equipoise is even relevant to or applies in Africa. In a recent article, Oricha and Yauri considered the applicability of equipoise and the uncertainty principle in the design and conduct of randomized clinical trials in Africa.[62] They observed that the best treatments are often unavailable or too expensive in Africa, a situation that compels African physicians to provide their patients with whatever treatment that is available although 'the clinician is reasonably certain there is a better treatment'.[63] Thus, the authors argued that it is difficult for physicians in Africa to comply with the requirements of the uncertainty principle since it requires physicians to provide their patients with what they personally know or believe to be the best treatment. In other words, the uncertainty principle would prohibit physicians in Africa from enrolling their patients in clinical trials involving randomization to a known inferior arm of the trial notwithstanding that the better or preferable treatment is generally unavailable or too expensive in Africa. An unintended consequence of this approach is the prohibition of all desperately needed research in Africa and other developing countries into sustainable, less expensive (probably less efficacious) and easy to implement treatments.[64] Furthermore, Oricha and Yauri argued that the only 'justification for pushing an "uncertainty" agenda' in Africa would be to enable African patients

---

61 Indeed, an entire volume of the Journal of Medicine and Philosophy was recently devoted to a symposium on equipoise; for a summary of the symposium: Franklin G. Miller and Robert M. Veatch, 'Symposium on Equipoise and the Ethics of Clinical Trials' (2007), 32 Journal of Medicine and Philosophy 77–78.

62 Bello S. Oricha and Muhammad B. Yauri, 'Uncertainty Principle Versus Clinical Equipoise in Clinical Trials in Sub-Saharan Africa: Are They Really Tenable? (2003), 2 Annals of African Medicine 99–100.

63 Ibid., at 100.

64 Winston Chiong, 'The Real Problem with Equipoise' (2006), 6 American Journal of Bioethics 37 at 40.

to benefit from free trial drugs.[65] Arguably, this means that a physician in Africa could pretend to be uncertain as to the relative merits of therapeutic regimens just to enable his patients to access a treatment that would otherwise be unavailable; but the authors condemned this practice of falsehood for being paternalistic in nature and capable of betraying the trust underlying the doctor-patient relationship in Africa. Thus, they concluded that the 'uncertainty principle' would be difficult to justify in Africa.

Regarding clinical equipoise, Oricha and Yauri argued that its viability in Africa is undermined by what they identified as 'patient's equipoise', a version of clinical equipoise that is based on the uncertainty of well-informed group of patients regarding the comparative merits of a set of therapeutic interventions (relevant to their medical condition).[66] In other words, informed patients' uncertainty determines the state of equipoise.[67] The implication, Oricha and Yauri argued, is that only patients in equipoise should be randomly assigned to the trial arms, while those with a treatment preference should be given the preferred treatment.[68] They further observed that while 'patient's equipoise is the true equipoise of clinical trials because clinical equipoise demands beneficence',[69] its applicability in Africa, relying as it does on a literate and well-informed patient population, is impaired by high rates of illiteracy and role allocations under which decisions might be made on behalf of competent adult patients. Concluding, therefore, that both the uncertainty principle and clinical equipoise are not viable in Africa, Oricha and Yauri suggested an alternative explanatory model based on the notions of 'social contract', under which clinical research might be done in Africa provided there is a 'guaranteed supply of subsidized test and treatment(s) and obvious relevance of the trial to the test community's disease pattern'.[70] But the notion of social contract in the research setting, implying that research subjects should give up some of their protection for the benefit of the society as a whole, should not be accepted in Africa without further analysis and development. Potentially, the social contract alluded to by Oricha and Yauri requires African patients to participate in trials that might not benefit them (or, indeed, might harm them) provided that their community benefits from the research. As it were, once this prospect of benefit exists, equipoise should be irrelevant for the ethical justification of such research. Arguably, this might be seen as a short step to the conscription of subjects for research in Africa contrary

65 Oricha and Yauri, supra, note 62, at 100.

66 Generally: D. Halpern, et al., 'Informing Patients of Uncertainty in Clinical Trials' (2001), 285 JAMA 2713–2714.

67 Ashcroft has argued that it is possible to construct a range of equipoise, including patient equipoise, collective or professional equipoise, community equipoise and industry equipoise: R Ashcroft, 'Equipoise, Knowledge and Ethics in Clinical Research and Practice' (1999), 13 Bioethics 314 at 320–322.

68 Oricha and Yauri, supra, note 62, at 99.

69 Ibid., at 100.

70 Ibid., at 100.

to the fundamental bioethical principle that no individual should be sacrificed for the benefit of the society as a whole.[71]

For different reasons, however, Alex London argued that clinical equipoise, as widely understood based on Freedman's conceptualization, might not be relevant for research in developing countries.[72] In essence, London's analysis resonates with the question of whose doubt or uncertainty is relevant for the determination of equipoise. London observed that clinical equipoise as traditionally conceived presupposes a universal clinical community, thus making certainty as to the effectiveness of treatment developed in a particular clinical context relevant for gauging the state of equipoise in another, but different, clinical context. Yet, as the author observed, treatment developed in one clinical context, say developed countries, might not, without more, be effectively administered or implemented in another clinical context, say developing countries.[73] In other words, the absence of uncertainty as to the relative merits of a set of interventions in the US, for example, does not (or should not) necessarily preclude a state of equipoise in Africa with respect to a similar set of therapeutic interventions. As the author observed, factors that might render an intervention established for one setting clinically irrelevant in another setting include the economic profile of the intervention, level of infrastructure required for the implementation of the intervention, availability of facilities and appropriate technology, and skilled staff.[74] Thus, London implies that clinical equipoise as traditionally conceived pays little attention to the different clinical contexts of a treatment's development and implementation and, accordingly, clinical equipoise is irrelevant to international research conducted in developing countries where it is extremely difficult to implement some of the standard treatments established for developed countries. For international clinical trials to flourish in developing countries where they are desperately needed for the development of cheap and easy to implement therapeutic interventions, London suggested a liberal approach to equipoise where the relative therapeutic merits of a set of interventions are not merely based on their biological effectiveness, but also on their overall therapeutic profile or net therapeutic advantages, including the sustainability of their implementation in the relevant population, ease of administration, economic cost of the intervention, and side effects; in this way, London argued, an inferior treatment, as in the placebo-controlled short-course zidovudine trials in Africa in the mid-1990s, might be ethically employed in the design of clinical trials in developing countries. London, therefore, advocated for a broad conception of equipoise that avoids the problems above through a

71 The Helsinki Declaration 2008 captured this in Guideline A6: 'In medical research involving human subjects, the well-being of the individual research subject must take precedence over all other interests'.

72 Alex J. London, 'Equipoise and International Human-Subjects Research' (2001), 15 Bioethics 312–332.

73 Ibid., at 317.

74 Ibid., at 325.

careful resolution of the tension between, on the one hand, finding effective and employable interventions in developing countries and, on the other hand, the requirement of moral boundaries for the ethical conduct of clinical research.[75] London's approach, however, is vulnerable to the criticism that he abandoned a fundamental principle that underpins equipoise, that is, the physician's therapeutic obligation to provide the best care for their patient.[76]

Another challenge to the applicability of the uncertainty principle and clinical equipoise in Africa is posed by the prevalence and practice of traditional medicine. Simply put, the question is whether evidence affecting a physician's judgement or certainty in relation to equipoise should include their belief in the efficacy of traditional medicine. Or, where a physician is in equipoise, should the patient's preference or request for traditional medicinal therapy take the physician out of equipoise? While these questions also pertain to the ethics and integration of conventional and complementary and alternative medical practices,[77] they are important here for two reasons. First, the analysis above indicates that individual-theoretical equipoise is susceptible to disturbance by a wide range of evidence, including the physician's hunches, gut feelings and beliefs. In Africa, some physicians, despite their conventional training in university medical schools, still believe in traditional medicinal therapy and its efficacy for certain types of medical procedures. In that context, should a physician be out of equipoise when, although uncertain as to the relative therapeutic merits of a set of interventions (involved in the trial), they nevertheless believe that traditional medicinal therapy provides a better cure for the condition under investigation? Should it matter that the physician in that situation is even precluded by his professional ethics from prescribing traditional therapy? Second, the use of traditional medicine is widespread in Africa, and there is an increasing demand for traditional medicinal therapies by a significant number of African patients. The World Health Organisation estimates that 80 per cent of people in developing countries rely on traditional medicine for their various health needs.[78] In this connection, it might be asked whether a patient's preference for traditional medicinal treatment should be able to disturb equipoise. While there are no easy answers to these questions, they suggest that the concept of equipoise is not straightforwardly applicable in Africa.

75 Ibid., at 323–331.

76 Winston Chiong, 'The Real Problem with Equipoise' (2006), 6 American Journal of Bioethics 37 at 40.

77 For detailed analysis of the ethics, law, regulation and integration of conventional and complementary and alternative medicine: Michael H. Cohen, *Future Medicine* (Ann Arbor, Michigan: The University of Michigan Press, 2003); R. Fan and I. Holliday, 'Which Medicine? Whose Standard? Critical Reflections on Medical Integration in China' (2007), 33 J. Med. Ethics 454–461.

78 World Health Organisation, Press Release: WHO Launches the First Global Strategy on Traditional and Alternative Medicine, WHO/38/16 May 2002.

## Equipoise and the Duty to Provide the Best Treatment

Equipoise involves the idea that a known inferior treatment should not be given to participants in clinical research; nor should an inferior treatment be compared to the standard and accepted treatment for the disease under study. In such cases, equipoise does not exist. Put more positively, equipoise imposes a therapeutic obligation on physician-investigators to provide the best treatment for individual patients enrolled in clinical research. In this way, equipoise reconciles clinical research with physicians' clinical (therapeutic) obligation to their patients. To perform this role effectively, Alex London suggested that equipoise should be understood in the theoretical or individual sense highlighted above.[79] In essence, therefore, equipoise is consistent with a patient-centred approach to medical ethics.[80] As Marcia Angell correctly observed, an 'essential ethical condition for a randomized clinical trial comparing two treatments for a disease is that there be no good reason for thinking one is better than the other', otherwise 'the investigators would be guilty of knowingly giving inferior treatment to some participants in the trial'.[81] In other words, underpinning the requirement of equipoise is the duty on investigators to provide the best available treatment to all patients enrolled in a clinical trial.[82] Certainly, this should be a pivotal requirement for clinical trials conducted in Africa and, particularly, it challenges the ethics of placebo-controlled trials conducted in developing countries when proven and established treatments for the condition under study were available in developed countries.

Long before the eruption of the controversy (examined in chapter one) relating to the standard of care adopted for the clinical trial of a short-course zidovudine in the management of vertical transmission of HIV/AIDS in Africa and other developing

79 Alex J. London, 'Two Dogmas of Research Ethics and the Integrative Approach to Human-Subjects Research' (2007), 32 Journal of Law and Philosophy 99 at 105: 'if the normative force for the equipoise requirement is grounded in the physician's therapeutic obligation, then that requirement must locate the relevant uncertainty in the mind of the individual researcher and focus on the interests of the particular patient'.

80 Robert J. Levine, 'Uncertainty in Clinical Research' (1988), 16 Law, Medicine & Health Care 174 at 175, reproduced in George Tomossy and David N. Weisstub, *Human Experimentation and Research* (Aldershot: Ashgate Publishing, 2003) at 418.

81 Marcia Angell, 'The Ethics of Clinical Research in the Third World' (1997), 337 New Eng. J. Med. 847.

82 As observed by Winston Chiong, 'The Real Problem with Equipoise' (2006), 6 American Journal of Bioethics 37 at 38: 'This underlying rationale for the equipoise requirement (that is, duty on physicians to offer treatments that are in the best interests of the individual patient, without regard for the welfare of third parties) has seemingly gone unnoticed by many, who might wish to reject this uncompromising, traditional account of the therapeutic obligation while accepting the equipoise requirement as a constraint on clinical research. In fact, the two are inextricably linked'.

countries (conducted in the mid-1990s),[83] Freedman had already recognized that the 'principle underlying the requirement for equipoise' was that a 'patient be offered the best treatment known'.[84] While this requirement (that is, the duty to provide the best known treatment) has, in its various reformulations, become the common mantra of widely recognized research guidelines, its interpretation and application to clinical research in Africa proved very problematical, as shown by the controversy that trailed the short-course zidovudine trial in Africa and other developing countries. In reality, the particular trial was a product of economic necessity meant to fill the gap in developing countries' health care systems exposed by the availability of the antiretroviral drug, zidovudine (AIDS Clinical Trials Group Study 076), which, though the gold standard drug for the prevention of perinatal transmission of HIV/AIDS in developed countries, was too expensive and unaffordable in Africa and other developing countries. It was thought that a cheaper and shorter course of the drug might prove equally effective, useful and affordable in developing countries, but the problem lay in fashioning the appropriate research design for testing the less expensive regimen. In sum, the question boiled down to what should be the appropriate standard of care for the pregnant women in the control arm of the trial. In other words, should the HIV/AIDS pregnant women in the control arm of the trial receive a placebo (inactive substance) or the standard zidovidine therapy which, though available, was too expensive and unaffordable in developing countries?

At the time of the clinical trial, the applicable Helsinki Declaration was the 1989 version.[85] Guideline 11(2) recommended that the 'potential benefits, hazards and discomforts of a new method should be weighed against the advantages of the best current diagnostic and therapeutic methods'. Similarly, Guideline 11(3) required that in 'any medical study, every patient – including those of a control group, if any – should be assured of the best proven diagnostic and therapeutic method'. But the question raised by the short-course zidovudine trial was whether the 'best current' treatment, recommended by Guidelines 11(2) and (3) above, referred to the treatment available within the locality of the research (local standard) or to the best treatment available anywhere in the world (universal standard)? Of course, at the time of the research, there was no treatment in Africa for the prevention of vertical transmission of HIV/AIDS and the real question, therefore, was whether the pregnant women in the control arm should be given a placebo. Were this question to be answered by Torbjörn Tännsjö, his view (prescient but pessimistic) was that Guideline 11(3) not only prohibits placebo-controls where effective treatments exist, but also it

83 Peter Lurie and Sidney M. Wolfe, 'Unethical Trials of Intervention to Reduce Perinatal Transmission of the Human Immunodeficiency Virus in Developing Countries' (1997), 337 New Eng. J. Med. 853–856.

84 Freedman in Kuhse and Singer, supra, note 2, at 515.

85 World Medical Association, *Declaration of Helsinki – Recommendations Guiding Physicians in Biomedical Research Involving Human Subjects* (41st World Medical Assembly, Hong Kong, September 1989).

'was a ban on all controlled studies of new drugs'.[86] Torbjörn Tännsjö's approach would, therefore, endorse two conclusions for the short course zidovudine trial in developing countries. First is that all the HIV/AIDS infected pregnant women in the placebo-controlled arm of the trial were not 'assured of the best proven diagnostic and therapeutic method' (Guideline 11(3)) which at that time was zidovudine. Second is that even those in the experimental arm of the trial that received a short-course zidovudine also failed to receive the best proven therapeutic method which is a full-course zidovudine. But as chapter one shows, the controversy has, however, been analysed on the basis of the standard of care accorded to the control group rather than the experimental arm. In the wake of the controversy this trial generated, the Helsinki Declaration was amended in 1996 by re-wording the provision relating to standard of care in clinical research, though the 1996 version still retained the fundamental requirement of the 'best current' treatment.[87] The 2008 version of the Helsinki Declaration maintains this approach, stipulating in Guideline 32:

- The benefits, risks, burdens and effectiveness of a new intervention must be tested against those of the best current proven intervention, except in the following circumstances:
- The use of placebo, or no treatment, is acceptable in studies where no current proven intervention exists; or
- Where for compelling and scientifically sound methodological reasons the use of placebo is necessary to determine the efficacy or safety of an intervention and the patients who receive placebo or no treatment will not be subject to any risk of serious or irreversible harm. Extreme care must be taken to avoid abuse of this option.

The duty to provide the best therapy to clinical research subjects also appears in the guidelines prepared by the Council for International Organisations of Medical Sciences (CIOMS).[88] Guideline 11 of CIOMS:

- As a general rule, research subjects in the control group of a trial of a diagnostic, therapeutic, or preventive intervention should receive an

86 Torbjörn Tännsjö, 'The Morality of Clinical Research: A Case Study' (1994), 19 Journal of Medicine and Philosophy 7–21 (reprinted in Helga Kuhse and Peter Singer, *Bioethics: An Anthology* (Oxford: Blackwell Publishing, 2006) 525 at 527).

87 World Medical Association, *Declaration of Helsinki – Ethical Principles for Medical Research Involving Human Subjects* (48th World Medical Assembly, Somerset West, Republic of South Africa, 1996), Guideline 29: 'The benefits, risks, burdens and effectiveness of a new method should be tested against those of the best current prophylactic, diagnostic, and therapeutic methods. This dos not exclude the use of placebo, or no treatment, in studies where no proven prophylactic, diagnostic or therapeutic method exists'.

88 Council for International Organisations of Medical Sciences, International Ethical Guidelines for Biomedical Research Involving Human Subjects (Geneva: CIOMS, 2002).

established effective intervention. In some circumstances it may be ethically acceptable to use an alternative comparator, such as placebo or 'no treatment'. Placebo may be used:

- when there is no established effective intervention;
- when withholding an established effective intervention would expose subjects to, at most, temporary discomfort or delay in relief of symptoms;
- when use of an established effective intervention as comparator would not yield scientifically reliable results and use of placebo would not add any risk of serious or irreversible harm to the subjects.

Certainly, the duty to provide an 'established effective intervention' under Guideline 11 of CIOMS raises interpretive difficulties akin to those encountered in the analysis of similar provisions in the Helsinki Declaration. In other words, does an 'established effective intervention' refer to the standard of care obtainable locally or universally?

Arguably, equipoise answers this question by requiring a universal standard of care. This follows from its implicit duty on investigators to provide patients in clinical research with the best available treatment. In that sense, the HIV/AIDS-infected pregnant women assigned to the placebo-controlled arm ought to have received zidovudine, the standard but expensive therapy for the prevention of perinatal transmission of HIV/AIDS. The 2002 CIOMS Guidelines were prepared after the controversial short-course zidovudine trial and the commentary on Guideline 11 is extended in a way that shows the drafters' engagement with the issues raised by the controversy relating to the short-course zidovudine trial. For instance, the commentary on Guideline 11 recognized an exception to the use of a comparator other than an established effective intervention:

> An exception to the general rule is applicable in some studies designed to develop a therapeutic, preventive or diagnostic intervention for use in a country or community in which an established effective intervention is not available and unlikely in the foreseeable future to become available, usually for economic or logistic reasons. The purpose of such a study is to make available to the population of the country or community an effective alternative to an established effective intervention that is locally unavailable.[89]

Despite this clear exception, which derogates from the duty to provide the best treatment as ordained by equipoise, the commentary itself exhibits a cleavage of opinion among the drafters of Guideline 11 of CIOMS through the clear acknowledgement that 'some people strongly object to the exceptional use of a comparator other than an established effective intervention because it could result in exploitation of poor and disadvantaged populations'.[90] The commentary on

89 Ibid., commentary to Guideline 11, at 56.

90 Ibid., commentary to Guideline 11, at 57.

Guideline 11 also restated the three grounds underpinning the objection above; these are that a placebo-controlled trial might expose subjects to a risk of serious or irreversible harm that an established effective intervention would avoid; that scientific experts are not unanimous that in certain circumstances an active control (based on the established effective intervention) would not produce scientifically reliable results; and that an economic reason for the unavailability of an established effective intervention in a poor country cannot justify a placebo-controlled trial in that country if it would be unethical to conduct a similar trial in a rich country.[91] Thus, while the Helsinki Declaration holds on to the universal standard of care (arguably) underpinning the principle of equipoise, the CIOMS Guideline, with some trepidation, has relaxed the principle in order to cater for cases where, for economic reasons, the established effective intervention is not available in the area or country where the clinical research is being conducted.

In sum, the analysis above shows that a faithful adherence to the underpinning rationale of equipoise (that is, the investigator's therapeutic obligation to research subjects) means that clinical research in Africa should generally be based on active controls, and that participants in such trials should receive the best proven therapy even if that therapy is not available locally. This conclusion is unexceptionally recognized by Guidance Point 11 of UNAIDS Guidance Document: 'As long as there is no known effective HIV preventive vaccine, a placebo control arm should be considered ethically acceptable in a phase 111 preventive vaccine trial'.[92] While acknowledging that a vaccine with proven efficacy in preventing infection or disease from HIV does not currently exist,[93] the commentary to Guidance Point 11 of the UNAIDS Guidance Document observed that 'participants in the control arm of a future phase 111 HIV preventive vaccine trial should receive an HIV vaccine known to be safe and effective when such is available'.[94] These considerations are restated in Guidance Point 15 of the current 2007 UNAIDS Guidance Document: 'Participants in both the control arm and the intervention arm should receive all established effective HIV risk reduction measures'.[95] Thus, equipoise provides a theoretical prism for looking at the short-course zidovudine trial discussed in the previous chapter; the duty on investigators (imposed by equipoise) to provide clinical research subjects with the best proven therapy is probably the reason why the applicable standard of care in the short-course zidovudine trial proved to be the most critical consideration.

---

91 Ibid., commentary to Guideline 11, at 57.

92 UNAIDS, *Ethical Considerations in HIV Preventive Vaccine Research – UNAIDS Guidance Document* (Geneva: UNAIDS, 2000).

93 Ibid., commentary to Guidance Point 11, at 31.

94 Ibid., commentary to Guidance Point 11, at 31.

95 UNAIDS, *Ethical Considerations in Biomedical HIV Prevention Trials: UNAIDS/WHO Guidance Document* (Geneva: UNAIDS, 2007).

## Equipoise and Placebo-Controlled Randomized Trials

As the analysis above indicates, the controversy triggered by the short-course zidovudine trial in developing countries in the mid-1990s centred on the question of what the standard of care should be in international collaborative research sponsored in resource-poor countries by multinational pharmaceutical companies, Western governments or their agencies. However, the term 'standard of care' is conceptually ambiguous.[96] For instance, the US National Bioethics Commission (NBAC) identified three different applications or meanings of that term;[97] it might refer to treatment that is routinely available. That is the sense in which the NBAC employed the term; however, it might well mean the standard practice or what is normally done in a particular situation. Finally, it could refer to a level of conduct that must be attained. In terms of provenance, 'standard of care' is a medico-legal concept which captures the normative standard or level of conduct against which a doctor's treatment of their patient would be judged and, as such, it is a term peculiarly unsuited for application to the research context where it cannot, as opposed to patients, determine the treatment that should be provided to research subjects.[98] Despite its conceptual ambiguity, however, standard of care generally refers to the treatment that should be given to research subjects in the control arm of a drug trial; that is, whether the research subjects should receive a placebo (inactive substance or no treatment) or the best proven or established treatment for the condition under study. Ruth Macklin explored this issue from a philosophical perspective, and considered how the principle that justice is equality could impact on the determination of the appropriate standard of care in international collaborative research. She observed that while the principle that equality is justice ('treat like cases alike, and different cases differently') is potentially interpretable in both ways, that is, capable of both defending and disavowing research designs based on placebo-controls, there were, however, two factors that could tip the balance of interpretation in relation to the principle of justice as equality. These are the different harm-benefit ratios between industrialized and developing countries, and the different economic conditions existing between industrialized and developing countries; even then, these factors are open to contentious interpretation.[99] To a large extent, however, equipoise avoids this debate (on whether placebos should be used as the standard of care in international collaborative research) by requiring that no inferior treatment be given to research subjects in randomized

96 For an excellent exploration of this ambiguity: Ruth Macklin, *Double Standards in Medical Research in Developing Countries* (Cambridge: Cambridge University Press, 2004) at 38–44.

97 National Bioethics Commission, *Ethical and Policy Issues in International Research: Clinical Trials in Developing Countries, vol. 1* (Bethesda, Maryland: NBAC, 2001), at 9.

98 Ibid., at 9.

99 Macklin, supra, note 96, at 44–47.

and controlled clinical trials. Thus, equipoise abhors placebo-controlled trials when there is a known and effective therapeutic intervention for the condition under study.[100] Accordingly, where a known and effective treatment for a disease under study exists, an investigational drug should be tested against the established therapy. Furthermore, since an established treatment for the condition already exists, it would be absurd to claim that a state of clinical uncertainty exists relating to the comparative merits of an investigational treatment and a placebo.[101] Thus, equipoise would prohibit the placebo-controlled trial of a short-course zidovudine therapy conducted in Africa and other developing countries for the prevention of vertical transmission of HIV/AIDS. The expensive but gold standard full-course zidovudine treatment, rather than placebo, should have been given to the HIV/AIDS pregnant women in the control arm. In contrast, equipoise would support the community-based, placebo-controlled and randomized trials in Ghana, Tanzania and Bangladesh to test the efficacy of rectal artesunate as a pre-referral treatment for severe malaria in remote areas where standard malaria treatment is not available;[102] this is simply because of the absence of an established or standard alternative pre-referral treatment for severe cases of malaria in remote settings.[103]

The use of placebos in such critical and important international collaborative research, however, attests to its methodological orthodoxy in the design and conduct of clinical trials and justifies its description as the 'gold standard of clinical research'.[104] This status is attributable to the belief among some scientists that placebo-controlled trials provide the best method of testing whether an investigational treatment has a specific biological effect on a disease under study. A placebo-controlled trial also carries the advantage that it facilitates the running of smaller trials, lessens the incentives for sloppiness, and is conducive to the making of fewer assumptions of an implicitly historical nature.[105] Mormont has, however, suggested a human right dimension to the problem raised by placebo-designed

100 As Mormont observed: 'It remains the case that in circumstances where clearly effective medication exists, it is hardly defensible or practical (because superfluous) to administer a placebo. In general, a new molecule will be tested in comparison with an active drug'. Christian Mormont, 'Ethical Questions Pertaining to the Use of Placebos', in David N. Weisstub (ed.), *Research on Human Subjects: Ethics, Law and Social Policy* (Oxford: Elsevier Science Ltd., 1998) at 545.

101 B. Freedman, 'Placebo Controlled Trials and the Logic of Clinical Purpose' (1990), 1 IRB: A Review of Human Subjects Research 1–6.

102 Andrew Kitua, et al., 'The use of placebo in a trial of rectal artesunate as initial treatment for severe malaria patients en route to referral clinics: ethical issues' (2010), 36 J. Med. Ethics 116–120.

103 Ibid., at 118.

104 B. Freedman, C. Weijer and C. Glass, 'Placebo Orthodoxy in Clinical Research 1: Empirical and Methodological Myths' (1996), 42 J.L. Med. & Ethics 243.

105 Baruch A. Brody, 'When are Placebo-Controlled Trials No Longer Appropriate?' (1997), 18 Control Clinical Trials 602 at 603.

studies.[106] Starting from the premise that the ethical and methodological validity of a placebo-controlled trial depends on the subject's ignorance of the placebo design, Mormont argues that placebo-controls involve the practice of deception in a way that conflicts with the subject's human right to self-determination, particularly the subject's right to know all aspects of the protocol, including its methodological design and reliance on placebos.[107] Accordingly, the use of placebos is ethically unacceptable as it strikes at the subject's right to self-determination.[108] But this need not be the case in a randomized clinical trial where the subjects are informed that the protocol is methodologically designed to include the use of placebos and that the subjects would be assigned randomly to the different arms of the trial (including the placebo arm) in a blinded manner. This preserves the subjects' right to self-determination while maintaining the methodological integrity of the trial. Mormont seems to have captured this possibility in his observation that the 'individual right to self-determination can be exercised in deciding to renounce the right; in other words, the subject who has freely accepted to participate in an experiment can decide not to be party to subsequent decisions'[109] and that having 'a right does not mean one has the duty to exercise it'.[110]

In an interesting article, Freedman, Weijer and Glass recounted the popularity and scientific orthodoxy of placebo trials, characterizing the 'belief that placebos provide uniquely important insight into the biological effects of a treatment, the *placebo orthodoxy*, and the policy that belief has generated on the part of regulators, *placebo practice*'.[111] (Italics in the original) The authors then set out to articulate, and refute, five myths that underpin the placebo orthodoxy and practice: (a) Placebo-controlled trials provide an accurate baseline measure of a treatment's biological effectiveness. The authors argued that this myth was flawed since it was based on the assumption that investigators were able to maintain the blind of their study when, on the contrary, practical experience often showed that trials could be un-blinded by several factors; (b) Placebo controls are simpler than active controls in testing the effectiveness of new drugs. In other words, the use of placebos provides the quickest and most efficient way of determining the efficacy of a new treatment. Freedman and his colleagues, however, argued that placebo trials could be equally cumbersome if properly designed. For example, multiple studies of placebos of different colours and given at different dosages could be as cumbersome as studies with active controls; (c) Placebo-controlled trials are necessary to prevent medical science from halting. Freedman and his

106 Christian Mormont, 'Ethical Questions Pertaining to the Use of Placebos', in David N. Weisstub (ed.), *Research on Human Subjects: Ethics, Law and Social Policy* (Oxford: Elsevier Science Ltd., 1998) at 531–546.

107 Ibid., at 532.

108 Ibid., at 532.

109 Ibid., at 533.

110 Ibid., at 533.

111 Freedman, et al., supra, note 104.

colleagues impugned the validity of this myth and argued that medical research must be both scientifically and ethically valid. Furthermore, they observed that this myth ((c) above) was justifiable only in the case of a first generation treatment for a previously untreatable condition; (d) Concern for patient welfare requires the use of placebo rather than active controls, to allow for licensure of those drugs that are advantageous for some patient populations. Freedman and his colleagues, however, argued that the assumption of this myth ((d) above) was fallacious since active controls are not required for refractory populations. In other words, the case of refractory population is identical to situations where there is no established and effective treatment for the condition under study, thus making the use of placebo-control ethically justifiable; and (e) Insuperable statistical difficulties in using active controls mean that placebo controls remain the only feasible clinical trial approach. In response, Freedman and his colleagues argued that the difficulties alluded to by this myth could be avoided by employing an alternative trial design, such as the active control equivalence study (ACES) design. Consequently, Freedman and his colleagues suggested that while 'first-generation treatments designed for previously untreatable conditions, should be tested against placebo before receiving regulatory approval',[112] the '[s]econd-generation treatments, however, should be tested against accepted therapy, rather than, as at present, against placebo'.[113] Similarly, Marcia Angell observed that only 'when there is no known effective treatment is it ethical to compare a potential new treatment with a placebo. When a treatment exists, a placebo may not be used'.[114]

Interestingly, some of the myths on placebo orthodoxy and practice impugned by Freedman and his colleagues have been embraced by the CIOMS guidelines.[115] For instance, the commentary on Guideline 11 observed that when 'the objective is to establish the effectiveness and safety of an investigational intervention, the use of a placebo control is often more likely than that of an active control to produce a scientifically reliable result'.[116] Recall that this was the second myth on placebo orthodoxy and practice identified by Freedman and his colleagues above. Accordingly, the CIOMS guidelines endorse the use of placebo controls not only when there is no established and effective treatment for the condition under study, but also in cases where: (a) the use of placebo-controlled trials entail only minor risks; (b) the use of active controls would not yield reliable results; and

112 Ibid., at 243.

113 Ibid., at 244.

114 Marcia Angell, 'The Ethics of Clinical Research in the Third World' (1997), 337 New Eng. J. Med. 847.

115 For a good analysis of the provisions of international guidelines relating to the use of placebos, see H.-G. Ehni and U. Wiesing, 'International ethical regulations on placebo-use in clinical trials: a comparative analysis' (2008), 22 Bioethics 64–74.

116 Council for International Organisations of Medical Sciences, *International Ethical Guidelines for Biomedical Research Involving Human Subjects* (Geneva: CIOMS, 2002), commentary to Guideline 11 at 54–55.

(c) an established effective intervention is not available in the host country.[117] In contrast to CIOMS, the Helsinki Declaration sticks to its original view that 'a new intervention must be tested against those of the best current proven intervention'.[118] Freedman, Glass and Weijer noted that although this prescription, in the Helsinki Declaration, was poorly worded, it resonated with a widely accepted principle of research ethics; they further observed that the underlying principle of that prescription has withstood subsequent amendments of the Helsinki Declaration.[119]

In sum, therefore, the use of placebo-controlled trials in Africa, when a current and effective treatment for the disease under study exists, is not ethically justifiable. In light of the analysis above, equipoise would disapprove the placebo-controlled short-course zidovudine trial conducted in Africa and other developing countries in the mid-1990s to prevent the vertical transmission of HIV/AIDS.

## Equipoise and the Consent of Research Subjects

Should consent alone justify clinical research in the absence of equipoise? Put differently, if at the start of clinical research an honest null hypothesis does not exist (that is, a state of uncertainty regarding the relative merits of therapeutic regimens), could the investigator nonetheless proceed with the clinical trial on the basis of the trial participants' full and informed consent? Proceeding from the premise that clinical research is different from clinical practice, some commentators have answered this question in the affirmative, arguing that equipoise is flawed for conflating the two activities, and that it is sufficient for the moral defensibility of clinical research if the subjects were not exploited and gave full and informed consent.[120] Similarly, Veatch suggested that the informed consent of research subjects was a sufficient ethical condition for the randomization of patients in clinical trials; equipoise was therefore irrelevant.[121] Addressing a similar question, Victor Tunkel suggested that 'such randomized tests are acceptable in law and

117 Ibid., commentary to Guideline 11 at 55–59.

118 World Medical Association, Declaration of Helsinki: Ethical Principles for Medical Research Involving Human Subjects (59th WMA General Assembly, Seoul, October 2008), Guideline 32.

119 B. Freedman, K. Glass and C. Weijer, 'Placebo Orthodoxy in Clinical Research 11: Ethical, Legal, and Regulatory Myths' (1996), 24 J.L. Med. & Ethics 252 at 253.

120 Ezekiel J. Emmanuel and Franklin G. Miller, 'The Ethics of Placebo Controlled Trials – A Middle Ground' (2001), 345 New Eng. J. Med. 915–919; Franklin G. Miller and Howard Brody, 'What Makes Placebo Controlled Trials Unethical?' (2002), 2 American Journal of Bioethics 3–9; Franklin G. Miller and Howard Brody, 'Clinical Equipoise and the Incoherence of Research Ethics' (2007), 32 Journal of Medicine and Philosophy 151–165.

121 Robert Veatch, 'The Irrelevance of Equipoise' (2007), 32 Journal of Medicine and Philosophy 167–183.

ethics provided the patient knows he may be randomized, and what this means'.[122] Yet, consent is only a necessary but not sufficient condition for the ethics of clinical research. This applies to other normative frameworks that underpin the ethical appraisal of clinical protocols, such as beneficence, non-maleficence and justice; none by itself is a sufficient condition for the ethics of clinical trials. The need to comply with these principles (autonomy or consent, beneficence, non-maleficience and justice) in biomedical research is increasingly known in the bioethical community as principlism.[123]

Meslin and his colleagues' powerful critique of principlism observed that while it provides useful cognitive prompts for the ethical consideration of protocols, it lacks sufficient specificity and exhaustiveness for the evaluation of clinical trials.[124] Thus, the authors argued that principlism should be supplemented with a concept they identified as 'sensitivity to context'; that is, the context of a case should provide the specification and content for the relevant element of principlism sought to be applied.[125] This suggests that valid consent by itself (as an element of principlism) is not sufficient for the moral justification of clinical trials, hence Miller and Weijer warned against the 'conflation of [equipoise with the] analytically distinct questions concerning consent and the duty of care'.[126] For instance, a research subject's consent to undergo an experimental and life-threatening non-therapeutic surgery will hardly protect an investigator against any civil or criminal action brought against them to redress the injuries (or death) suffered by the subject.[127] In such cases, as the hypothetical above, the investigator is still ethically bound to ensure that the risks of clinical research are not disproportionate to its benefits.[128] While this ethical obligation is coterminous with consent, it exists independently of consent. Absent a favourable risk-benefit ratio, therefore, consent alone cannot justify a trial.[129] Analogous to the dangerous surgery example above, a patient's willingness to forgo the gold standard treatment

122 Victor Tunkel, 'Legal Aspects of Clinical Trials in the United Kingdom', in C.J. Williams (ed.), *Introducing New Treatments for Cancer: Practical, Ethical and Legal Problems* (Chichester, England: John Wiley & Sons, 1992) at13.

123 For a detailed examination of these principles, see Tom L. Beauchamp and James F. Childress, *Principles of Biomedical Ethics, 6th edn* (Oxford: Oxford University Press, 2009).

124 Eric M. Meslin, et al., 'Principlism and the Ethical Appraisal of Clinical Trials' (1995) 9 Bioethics 399–418.

125 Ibid., at 413–416.

126 Paul B. Miller and Charles Weijer, 'Equipoise and the Duty of Care in Clinical Research: A Philosophical Response to Our Critics' (2007), 32 Journal of Medicine and Philosophy 117 at 118.

127 Compare *R v Brown* [1994] 1 A.C. 212 (HL).

128 Generally: C. Weijer and P.B. Miller, 'When are research risks reasonable in relation to anticipated benefits?' (2004), 10 Nature Medicine 570–573.

129 Baruch A. Brody, 'When are Placebo-Controlled Trials No Longer Appropriate?' (1997), 18 Control Clinical Trials 602 at 606.

for a disease, in favour of a placebo, does not relieve the investigator from their ethical and legal obligation to treat the patient competently and in accordance with the prevailing and professionally determined standard of care. Ian Kennedy has even argued that (in the circumstances above) it is unethical to ask for a patient's consent to an inferior treatment, and that any consent given in that regard would be considered involuntary and invalid. Thus, he observed that a 'patient who is asked to consent to treatment which may, or will, involve something which he would prefer was not done, or involves waiving the doctor's obligation to put his interests first, may as a consequence be being subjected to improper pressure merely by being asked',[130] and that 'any consent given under such circumstances may be invalid, on the ground that it is not truly voluntary'.[131]

In the same vein, Freedman and his colleagues observed that a 'physician cannot escape the professional duty to practice competent medicine by eliciting patient consent'.[132] Interestingly, Torbjörn Tännsjö examined a case study in which a subject in the investigational arm of a trial died (a probable risk of the study) and the investigators were not in agreement as to whether it was morally defensible to continue the trial. Specifically, one of the issues that arose was whether it was ethically justifiable to continue the trial based on the full and informed consent given by the participants? Taken the competence of the subjects and the validity of their consents as a given, Torbjörn Tännsjö observed that it was not a decision the doctors could leave to their patients; in other words, the problem was not resolvable on the basis of consent alone.[133] This resonates with Freedman and his colleagues' rhetorical question: 'Should … an inept surgeon be free to continue to butcher patients because he has disclosed his deficiencies to patients?'[134]

The problems of consent highlighted above are exacerbated by the peculiar situation of Africa characterized, as it were, by high rates of illiteracy, profound trust of medical institutions, substitute decision-making, power-dependency relationships and general lack of familiarity with scientific and clinical research concepts.[135] Worse still, a recent survey of surgeons' opinions in Nigeria, regarding the practice of informed consent in their clinical practice, shows that most surgeons in western Nigeria failed to provide relevant and sufficient information

---

130 Kennedy, supra, note 14, at 221.

131 Ibid.

132 B. Freedman, K. Glass and C. Weijer, 'Placebo Orthodoxy in Clinical Research 11: Ethical, Legal, and Regulatory Myths' (1996), 24 J.L. Med. & Ethics 252 at 254.

133 Torbjörn Tännsjö, 'The Morality of Clinical Research: A Case Study' (1994), 19 Journal of Medicine and Philosophy 7–21 (reprinted in Helga Kuhse and Peter Singer, *Bioethics: An Anthology* (Oxford: Blackwell Publishing, 2006) 525 at 527).

134 B. Freedman, K. Glass and C. Weijer, 'Placebo Orthodoxy in Clinical Research 11: Ethical, Legal, and Regulatory Myths' (1996), 24 J.L. Med. & Ethics 252 at 254.

135 Similar factors inhibiting informed consent were noted for the Palestinian refugee community in Lebanon: R. Nkkash, J. Makhoul and R. Afifi, 'Obtaining informed consent: observations from community research with refugee and impoverished youth' (2009) 35 J. Med. Ethics 638–643.

to their patients before obtaining the patients' consent[136]. Similar challenges are noticeable in the clinical research setting in Nigeria.[137] The controversy that trailed the consent procedure employed by Pfizer in its trovan trial in Nigeria in the mid-1990s (examined in the previous chapter) should erase any doubt regarding the insufficiency of consent as an ethical justification of clinical trials in Africa and other developing countries. In the trovan trial, parents of children that participated in the trial were largely illiterate and clearly misunderstood the consent process; they thought they were consenting to treatment on behalf of their children rather than consenting to clinical research; it is doubtful if those parents even understood the concept of clinical research. Even in industrialized countries where rates of literacy are high, obtaining an informed consent can pose significant challenges. For instance, a qualitative study on informed consent in the UK by Stead and colleagues observed that the majority of trial participants poorly understood the science of clinical trials and the concepts explained in the information sheets, such as randomization and placebo; thus, the subjects' consent was uninformed and invalid.[138] If this problem exists in developed countries with a long history of medical research, then it is bound to be exacerbated in developing African countries where, in addition to high rates of illiteracy and rudimentary research culture, some biomedical research concepts have no equivalents in local African languages.[139] For instance, a study of the consent process in an influenza vaccine trial in South Africa found that the majority of the trial participants (poor Black South Africans) struggled with the comprehension of scientific concepts described in the trial information leaflets, such as placebo and randomization.[140] Similarly, Hill and colleagues carried out a study to examine the comprehension of consent process by research participants in Ghana who were subjects in a placebo-controlled vitamin A supplementation trial (investigating the impact of vitamin A supplementation on maternal mortality in Ghana). The authors found that as

---

136 T.O. Ogundiran and C.A. Adebamowo, 'Surgeons' opinions and practice of informed consent in Nigeria' (2010), 36 J. Med. Ethics 741–745. A study of informed consent in Pakistan recorded a similar result for Pakistani surgeons: A.M. Jafarey and A. Farooqui, 'Informed consent in the Pakistani milieu: the physician's perspective' (2005), 31 J. Med. Ethics 93 at 95.

137 P. Marshall, et al., 'Voluntary Participation and Informed Consent to International Genetic Research' (2006), 96 American Journal of public Health1989–1995 (examined genetic epidemiological studies of hypertension in Nigeria and the USA in order to identify factors associated with voluntary participation and comprehension of the purpose of studies among the research subjects).

138 M. Stead, et al., 'Hello, hello – it's English I speak!: a qualitative exploration of patients' understanding of the science of clinical trials' (2005), 31 J. Med. Ethics 664–669.

139 A. Bhan, M. Majd and A. Adejumo, 'Informed Consent in International Research: Perspectives from India, Iran and Nigeria' (2006), 3 McMaster University Medical Journal 36 at 40.

140 K. Moodley, et al., 'Informed consent and participant perceptions of influenza vaccine trials in South Africa' (2005), 31 J. Med. Ethics 727–732.

much as 93 per cent of the study participants failed to understand the concept of placebo because they thought that all the vitamin A capsules were the same; that is, none contained an inactive substance.[141] In contrast, where the research design does not involve the use of technical concepts, such as placebo and randomization, African research subjects are more likely to comprehend the consent process and information contained in the consent forms. Thus, in a research bronchoscopy study conducted in Malawi, which did not involve the use of placebo or randomization, it was reported that most of the research subjects were satisfied with the consent process and the amount of information they received.[142]

In sum, therefore, consent is not a sufficient framework for the ethical justification of clinical research in Africa. Furthermore, the analysis concerning the interplay of equipoise with consent provides a good framework for examining scandalous clinical research in Africa (such as Pfizer's trovan trial), particularly those in which the consent of African research subjects was projected as the ethical justification for the clinical research.

## Conclusion

Clinical research must not only be scientifically valid; it must also be ethically justifiable. In the 1970s, Fried suggested that the concept of equipoise was a potential normative framework for evaluating the ethics of clinical research. Freedman took up Fried's suggestion and fleshed it out in the 1980s, although he embedded equipoise in a different epistemic ground, by reconceptualizing it as clinical equipoise. Freedman's conceptualization has attracted much criticism, including calls for its total abandonment in favour of other normative criteria for the moral defensibility of clinical research, for instance, the principle of exploitation. In contrast, some commentators have argued for the retention of equipoise as the foundational ethical prop for clinical trials, albeit with some alterations or philosophical rehabilitation, in order to make it a much more robust criterion for clinical research. Consequently, equipoise has remained a relevant principle of clinical research, and has continued to dominate the bioethical imagination of scholars and practitioners alike.

Understandably, the application of equipoise in Africa is undermined by a notorious absence of direly needed health infrastructure, health services and effective therapy for common diseases. In Africa, this makes it extremely difficult or challenging to meet the requirements implied by equipoise, such as the duty to refrain from giving a participant a known inferior treatment, and the disavowal of a placebo-controlled trial where an effective treatment for the condition being

141 Z. Hill, et al., 'Informed consent in Ghana: what do participants really understand?' (2008), 34 J. Med. Ethics 48–53.

142 N. Mtunthama, et al., 'Malawians permit research bronchoscopy due to perceived need for healthcare' (2008), 34 J. Med. Ethics 303–307.

studied exists. While it is not easy to state the version of equipoise applicable to clinical research in Africa, it is argued that equipoise provides a valuable normative framework for evaluating the ethics of biomedical research conducted in developing countries of Africa. Furthermore, equipoise could be used to enforce the physician's therapeutic obligation within the context of international collaborative research conducted in Africa. Thus, equipoise demands that physicians conducting clinical trial in developing African countries have a duty to provide their subjects with the best proven or established treatments. As such, where established treatments exist for the conditions being studied, equipoise prohibits the implementation of placebo-controlled clinical trial designs in developing African countries. Similarly, the consent of African research subjects is not sufficient to justify clinical research that lacks equipoise. Accordingly, this chapter suggests that in addition to the deployment of equipoise as the moral criterion for evaluating clinical research in Africa, it is also a useful analytical prism for interrogating the biomedical research that went awry in Africa. The previous chapter considered some of these scandals in further depth.

# Chapter 3
# Case Studies of Research Governance in Africa

## Introduction

Research governance is used here to denote the structures and process (as well as their interactions) that govern the conduct of biomedical research in Africa.[1] Through analysis of the historical underpinnings of current research guidelines in Uganda, Tanzania and Nigeria, and the political, social and cultural influences that conditioned their development, this chapter provides an account of the regulatory and oversight mechanisms established for the protection of research subjects in African countries.

Although the debate on the regulation of international collaborative research in developing countries has raged for many years, yet there is hardly any comparable analytical focus on the existence, substance and operation of domestic research guidelines in individual African countries. Interestingly, the US Office of Inspector General identified this gap in its 2001 Report, observing that the 'FDA's informational void concerning the performance of foreign institutional review boards is of particular concern for emerging sites with little experience in conducting clinical research'.[2] Usually, research involving human subjects in developing countries is analysed on the basis of major international research guidelines. These include the Declaration of Helsinki and CIOMS guidelines,[3] and two well-known specialist guidelines, the UNAIDS/WHO Guidance Document which regulates HIV/AIDS vaccine research,[4] and the ICH Harmonised Tripartite Guideline: Guideline for Good Clinical Practice which regulates the conduct

---

1 For a theoretical and detailed analysis of 'governance' in the context of health research involving human subjects: Michael McDonald, *The Governance of Health Research Involving Human Subjects* (Ottawa: Law Commission of Canada, 2000).

2 Department of Health and Human Services, Office of the Inspector General, *The Globalization of Clinical Trials: A Growing Challenge in Protecting Human Subjects* (DHHS, 2001), at 18.

3 World Medical Association *Declaration of Helsinki, Ethical Principles for Medical Research Involving Human Subjects* (59th WMA General Assembly, Seoul, 2008); Council for International Organisations of Medical Sciences (CIOMS), *International Ethical Guidelines for Biomedical Research Involving Human Subjects* (Geneva: CIOMS, 2002.

4 Joint United Nations Programme on HIV/AIDS and World Health Organisation, *Ethical Considerations in Biomedical HIV Prevention Trials: UNAIDS/WHO Guidance Document* (Geneva: UNAIDS/WHO, 2007).

of clinical trials,[5] and was promulgated for adoption by regulatory bodies of the European Union, Japan and USA. Although these international guidelines provide an excellent model for regulatory emulation, the need for local or national domestic guidelines in African countries has never been greater. The reasons have been discussed in the introductory chapter of this book; for instance, international guidelines have not taken the peculiar local circumstances of Africa into consideration; only a local guideline can achieve that end. Also, the provisions of international guidelines often conflict, thereby confusing African countries and their researchers as to which guideline should provide the rule of action. More importantly, and following from the divergent provisions of international guidelines, sponsors and investigators from developed countries involved in externally-sponsored research in Africa often make strategic use of international guidelines. In other words, they only adhere to an international guideline that supports their objectives or national interests; accordingly, international guidelines that are thought to be inconvenient, or whose provisions are thought to impose burdensome duties on investigators and sponsors, are often ignored.[6] Furthermore, the strategic and tendentious use of international research guidelines in developing countries by sponsors and investigators from developed countries is often facilitated by the ambiguity of the guidelines, which create a need for their interpretation. This means that an international guideline whose requirements are perceived to be burdensome could be interpreted into irrelevance. What all this means is that not only do African countries need to promulgate national or domestic guidelines that take their local circumstances into consideration; also, the analytical emphasis on international guidelines, with respect to research involving human beings in developing countries, wrongly assumed that research guidelines in Africa were either non-existent or poorly developed, and that ethical review procedures in Africa were rudimentary at best. While some of these assumptions remain valid, especially with regard to the independence, competence and performance of ethics committees in some African countries, on the whole, however, these assumptions are inconsistent with the reality of research governance in most African countries. For instance, in an empirical study conducted by Nancy Kass and colleagues, they observed that 'research ethics review is increasingly routine in Africa'.[7] Similarly, based on a survey of the experiences of developing countries' researchers, Hyder and colleagues opined that 'ethical guidelines in developing countries exist and are able to offer some protection to research subjects, which is different from the

---

5 International Conference on Harmonisation of Technical Requirements for Registration of Pharmaceuticals for Human Use, *ICH Harmonised Tripartite Guideline: Guideline for Good Clinical Practice* (1996).

6 P. Laurie and D.B. Greco, 'US exceptionalism comes to research ethics' (2005), 365 Lancet 1111; Sylvester C. Chima, 'Regulation of biomedical research in Africa' (2006), 332 BMJ 848 at 848.

7 Nancy Kass, et al., 'The Structure and Function of Research Ethics Committees in Africa: A Case Study' (2007), 4 PLoS Medicine 26 at 29.

hypothesis that such local guidelines are either non-existent or entirely worthless'.[8] By focusing on research guidelines in selected African countries, therefore, this chapter proposes to correct the misconstruction of research regulation in Africa, and to highlight the increasing sophistication of research governance in some African countries.

The case studies in this chapter serve at least four purposes. First: to provide a guide for investigators, especially foreign investigators, intending to conduct biomedical research involving human subjects in the referenced countries. Second: to show that regulatory frameworks governing research in some developing African countries have reached a level of sophistication comparable to the systems in most industrialized countries. Third, the case studies provide a more specific and detailed analysis of the response of some African countries to the scandals examined in the earlier chapters (especially chapter one). Lastly, the case studies provide a context for the analyses in chapters 5, 6 and 7 relating to legal liability issues that arise from the conduct of biomedical research involving human subjects in Africa and other developing countries. To achieve these objectives, this chapter provides a normative account of research governance in the referenced countries, and offers a criticism of some the regulations (for example, the Ugandan research guideline) that require foreign investigators to be affiliated with local institutions. In addition, this chapter explores the factors that influenced the development of research guidelines in Uganda, Tanzania and Nigeria; the contents of these guidelines; their conformity with the political, social and cultural circumstances of the countries involved; and some of the difficult issues that arise from the referenced countries' guidelines. Accordingly, while the first section of this chapter considers research governance in Uganda, the subsequent sections examine research governance in Tanzania and Nigeria respectively. The author was not successful in his attempts to access research protocols that were rejected or approved under the guidelines examined in this chapter; the regulatory authorities and ethics review committees in the referenced countries refused to permit such access because of the confidentiality of the data. Nonetheless, it can be surmised that most research undertaken in Africa, including some of those mentioned in chapter one and other chapters, which were published after the promulgation of the relevant guidelines, were actually reviewed on the authority of those guidelines.

## Uganda

Although biomedical research institutions in Uganda have always been active in health research, it was the HIV/AIDS pandemic in that country, however (as well as in some other African countries), that catalysed Uganda's currently huge

---

8 A.A. Hyder, 'Ethical Review of Health Research: A Perspective from Developing Country Researchers' (2004) 30 J. Med. Ethics 68 at 71.

biomedical research activities.[9] The 1990s witnessed an influx of research funds and foreign research collaborators into Uganda. This resulted in significant local capacity building and improvement in health care delivery. Above all, the concerted biomedical research efforts helped to stem the tide of HIV/AIDS transmission and infection in Uganda. For instance, the prevalence rate dropped from over 18 per cent in the 1990s to 6.4 per cent in 2005.[10] But the laudable and expansive research efforts in Uganda to combat the scourge of HIV/AIDS and other serious diseases brought in their wake a correlative increase in the use of Ugandans as research subjects. Thus, concerns began to be expressed regarding the rights, safety and welfare of Ugandans used as research subjects in biomedical research endeavours. There arose an obvious need to protect them against exploitation. Frameworks developed to confer the needed protection included the promulgation of national research guidelines and institution of oversight mechanisms; these frameworks of protection are examined later in this chapter.

*Background to Research Subject Protection in Uganda*

Concerns about the participation of Ugandans as research subjects in various biomedical studies since the 1990s are better understood in their historical, economic, and socio-cultural contexts. Historically, Ugandans experienced politically oppressive and exploitative regimes under Milton Obote and Idi Amin between 1962 and 1985 (the combined periods of their regimes).[11] This adverse political experience has exacerbated the sensitivity of Ugandans to relationships of power dependency or imbalance. Quite naturally, Ugandans are acutely aware of their susceptibility to exploitation and abuse of power and they tend to judge research relationships in that light. For the above reasons, Ugandans are cautious (if not suspicious) in their dealings with investigators because international research collaborations in Africa have the characteristic features of power or relational imbalance. But that does not necessarily mean that research collaborations in Uganda and other African countries are actually exploitative. Foreign researchers bring in research money. Consequently, they dictate the research agenda, albeit with some local input. Many difficulties arise when the research agenda is not within the control of a developing country. It might, for instance, lead to the execution of research projects that fail to address the needs or priority needs of a developing country. Take the case of malaria, a priority health problem in many developing countries in comparison to cardiovascular diseases that are prevalent

9 Generally: K. Cook, D. Mbori-Ngacha and E. Marum, 'Shadow on the Continent: Public Health and HIV/AIDS in Africa' (2002), 360 Lancet 67–72; Editorial (Lancet), 'The Economics of HIV in Africa' (2002) 360 Lancet 1.

10 Uganda AIDS Commission, *Uganda Guidelines for AIDS Vaccine Research* (UAC, 2006) at 3.

11 Generally: G.W. Kanyeihamba, *Constitutional and Political History of Uganda: From 1894 to the Present* (Kampala, Uganda: Centenary Publishing House Ltd., 2002).

in industrialized countries. It might be that unless the research agenda is controlled by local researchers, cardiovascular diseases rather than malaria would be the focus of a protocol (involving foreign collaborators) intended to be carried out in a developing country.

Similarly, Yohana Mashalla lamented that researchers in developing countries neither control biomedical studies involving international collaboration, nor is the result of such studies usually relevant to the needs of developing countries. More pertinently, he observed that international collaborations have 'triggered concern on the potential for research to cause harm either in the physical sense or psychological harm'.[12] Thus, while capacity for biomedical research has been on the increase across many parts of Africa,[13] it will be extremely naive (regardless of what appears on paper) to regard international research collaborations in most parts of Africa as being forged on the basis of equality.[14] As the saying goes, whoever pays the piper dictates the tune. Those that bring in research money from abroad generally have a dominant hold on the research agenda. Costello and Zumla have even given a colonial slant to this undesirable outcome by observing that the current model of most international research collaboration is semi-colonial in nature.[15] The authors alleged that western foreign researchers dominate the setting of research priorities and project management in developing countries through the establishment of independent research sites that are staffed and controlled by expatriate researchers (what the authors called 'Annexed Sites'). The authors warned that this model of research investment has serious opportunity costs and negative consequences that outweigh the potential benefits of the research.[16] Furthermore, relational and power imbalance can exist even outside the spheres of international biomedical research collaboration, such as the lopsided power relationship between developing countries' physician-researchers and their subjects. The physician-researcher in Africa is seen by the ordinary research subject as possessing superior knowledge and wielding enormous power and resources. In other words, the physician-researcher is seen as an authority figure. Consequently, the average African research subject not only trusts the physician-researcher but also finds his or her authority practically irresistible. This type of relationship could potentially lead to exploitation. The point, therefore, is that

---

12 Yohana J. Mashalla, 'Preface', in TANHER Forum, *Guidelines for Health Research in Tanzania* (TANHER Forum, 2001) at ix.

13 European Commission, *Ethics, Research and Globalisation: Europe and its Partners Building Capacity in Research Ethics* (European Commission: Directorate-General for Research, 2007).

14 B. Maina-Ahlberg, et al., 'North-South health research collaboration: Challenges in institutional interaction' (1997) 44 Soc. Sci. Med. 1229–1238.

15 Anthony Costello and Alimuddin Zumla, 'Moving to research partnerships in developing countries' (2000), 321 BMJ 827–829.

16 Ibid., at 827. Also, Tessa Tan-Torres Edejer, 'North-South research partnership: the ethics of carrying out research in developing countries' (1999), 319 BMJ 438–441.

relational and structural power imbalance exists in the execution of biomedical research in Uganda and other Africa countries, irrespective of whether or not such research involves international collaboration. Because such research relationships of dependency or power imbalance are potentially exploitative, Uganda is justified in its concern that lax oversight of research in its territories might lead to the exploitation of Ugandan research subjects.

There is another dimension to the Ugandan historical and political experiences that impact on biomedical research in that country. It is the rumour of biomedical research exploitation which, in turn, is rooted in power imbalance. Rumours on the purpose, goal and impact of biomedical research in Uganda are usually strong; they are disseminated widely and prevail for a long time. Most importantly, research rumours have a tellingly negative effect on the scientific enterprise, especially in developing countries. While lacking in substance, research rumours in Uganda have become such a troubling phenomenon that commentators cannot easily ignore it. For instance, Sana Loue and colleagues recalled a rumour to the effect that the existence of HIV/AIDS in Uganda was a hoax used by foreigners as a pretext to experiment on Ugandans in order to devalue them.[17] There was also a strong rumour in Uganda that people from industrialized countries introduced HIV/AIDS into Uganda but that they later turned round to accuse East Africans of being the originators of the disease.[18] Some Ugandans regard this type of accusation as an extension of the colonial oppression suffered by many African countries (colonized by industrialized countries). Ugandans also think that the accusation that East Africans were the originators of HIV/AIDS is consistent with stereotypes of Africa as a continent prone to disease and lacking in dignity. Naturally, these rumours have generated ill-feelings among Ugandans towards international collaborative research. However, the actual impact of these rumours on the conduct of biomedical research in Uganda is yet to be empirically ascertained. Nevertheless, there are indications that rumours in the research setting have produced some adverse consequences. As highlighted in chapter one, for example, the clinical trial of HIV-1 vaccine in Uganda was nearly marred by rumours that volunteers would be deliberately exposed to HIV infection through the administration of contaminated polio vaccines (that is, contaminated with HIV).[19] The immediate outcome of this rumour was a disruption of the polio vaccination exercise coordinated by the Ugandan Ministry of Health. It is an outcome that resonates with a similar experience in Nigeria (concerning polio vaccination) in 2004. In that year, some Muslims in many states of northern Nigerian rumoured that polio vaccines contained toxic substances that were deliberately designed to

17 Sana Loue, et al., 'Research Bioethics in the Ugandan Context: A Program Summary' (1996), J.L. Med. & Ethics 47 at 49.

18 For a similar discussion: E. Tabor, et al., 'Did HIV and HTLV Originate in Africa?' (1990), 264 JAMA 691–692.

19 Roy D. Mugerwa, et al., 'First Trial of the HIV-1 Vaccine in Africa: Ugandan Experience' (2002), 324 BMJ 226–229.

render children infertile and expose them to HIV infection. As part of the rumour, it was said that the US planned the alleged contamination of polio vaccines in Nigeria in order to further its policy to depopulate Africa.[20] As in Uganda, the ensuing controversy led to the temporary suspension of the polio campaign in Nigeria.[21]

In addition to the factors above, there are other economic and social circumstances that condition Ugandans' heightened concern about participation in scientific studies as research subjects. While health care infrastructure and delivery in Uganda flourished in the period after independence, things quickly turned for the worse in the past few decades.[22] With a per capital annual health expenditure of about US$6, access to health care services in Uganda is severely limited. For a deadly and expensive disease like HIV/AIDS, it means that (absent the supply of low-cost generic antiretroviral drugs) the Ugandan government cannot afford patented and cost-prohibitive antiretroviral drugs required for the treatment of HIV/AIDS.[23] Consequently, some Ugandans can only access antiretroviral therapies through participation in research projects as volunteers. Thus, participation in research projects has become a beneficial, rather than a risky, activity.[24] It should be expected that in this type of economic and social setting, there would be stiff competition among poor African HIV/AIDS patients for enrolment in HIV/AIDS research protocols. Not infrequently, therefore, successfully recruited subjects for HIV/AIDS protocols consider themselves to be extremely lucky.[25] It has become a sort of therapeutic lottery. This means that the pressure to get crucial treatment for a deadly disease, in a health care setting characterized by poor resources and inadequate infrastructure, is capable of giving rise to issues of voluntariness (of participation). Consequently, Ugandans are understandably anxious to ensure that biomedical research conducted in their

---

20 Fiona Fleck, 'Nigerian president holds key to global polio eradication' (2004), 328 BMJ 544; Abiodun Raufu, 'Traditional rulers in northern Nigeria call for halt to polio vaccination' (2004), 328 BMJ 306.

21 Abiodun Raufu, 'Nigeria postpones programme of polio immunisation' (2004), 328 BMJ 1278.

22 C.P. Dodge and P.D. Wiebe (eds), *Crisis in Uganda: The Breakdown of Health Services* (Oxford: Oxford University Press, 1985).

23 For the impact of cost and patents on access to antiretroviral drugs in Africa: M.A. Santoro and T.M. Gorrie (eds), *Ethics and Pharmaceutical Industry* (Cambridge: Cambridge University Press, 2005); R.N. Nwabueze, 'What Can Genomics and Health Biotechnology Do for Developing Countries' (2005), 15 Albany Law Journal of Science & Technology 369–432.

24 Bernard Dickens, et al., 'Research on Human Populations: National and Internal Ethical Guidelines' (1991), 19 Law, Medicine & Health Care 157; Larry Gostin, 'Ethical Principles for the Conduct of Human Subject Research: Population-Based Research and Ethics' (1991), 19 Law, Medicine & Health Care 191 at 196.

25 A. Zarembo, 'Guatemala: life-or-death lottery – the medicine is scarce; it must be allotted somehow', Newsweek, 5 July 1999, 25–27.

country would not exploit the vulnerability of their citizens due to poverty and disease. Note that this concern also raises the issue of justice and post-trial access to medication (more fully explored in chapter four).

Equally important is the significant level of illiteracy (especially in the rural areas of Uganda) which affects the comprehension and operation of the consent process. A consent process that is not attuned to the special needs of an illiterate community would lead to exploitation. Illiteracy in some segments of Uganda is likely to exacerbate other factors that engender ethical difficulties, such as therapeutic misconception, non-familiarity with biomedical research concepts, and cultural norms that give male heads of families or communities authority to approve (or disapprove) a family or community member's participation in research; much of this was examined in chapter two in relation to the interface of equipoise with consent. In sum, therefore, it is not surprising that in response to the problems above, Uganda has developed various regulatory structures to guide the conduct of biomedical research involving human participants in Uganda.

### *Ugandan Research Guideline*

One of the moves towards tighter regulatory oversight of biomedical research in Uganda was the development of a clearly articulated research guideline that governs the conduct of research involving human participants. The Ugandan guideline[26] is a model of excellence in Africa, not only for its acculturation of the popular bioethical principles that govern research on human beings.[27] It also exemplifies the debate, public education and academic engagement that should generally precede the promulgation of research guidelines. In terms of provenance, the Ugandan guideline is traceable to a 5-day symposium held in Jinja (Uganda) in 1994. The symposium was intended to examine the relevance of bioethical principles (such as autonomy, beneficence, non-maleficence and justice) to Uganda and their compatibility with the Ugandan culture and local circumstances.[28] It was attended by various stakeholders, including representatives of governmental agencies and commissions, professional organizations, biomedical researchers and ethicists. While participants at the symposium generally supported the adoption of the bioethical principles above, they recommended, however, a contextual adaptation of these principles to suit the peculiar circumstances of Uganda.

In 1996, a follow-up conference was organized to further the objectives of the 1994 Jinja symposium. But this conference could not reach a consensus on any

---

26 Uganda National Council for Science and Technology, *National Guidelines for Research Involving Humans as Research Participants* (Kampala: UNCTS, 2007) (Hereafter, National guidelines).

27 These include autonomy, nonmalficence, beneficence and justice. For elucidation of these principles: T.L. Beauchamp and J.F. Childress, *Principles of Biomedical Ethics, 5th edn* (New York: Oxford University Press, 2001).

28 Sana Loue, supra, note 17.

of the matters the participants discussed because the number of attendees was small and the issues raised in the conference were complex. Nevertheless, the attendees were able to delegate the responsibility of producing a draft research guideline to David Okello, Medi Kawuma, and Sana Loue; the trio were also the major organizers of the conference. The objective of the 1996 conference was that the proposed draft guideline would be reviewed in a subsequent conference. Okello, Kawuma and Loue took their assignment seriously and proceeded with dispatch. They consulted with various stakeholders and produced a new draft research guideline. In 1997, the draft guideline was presented for review at the National Consensus Conference (NCC) held in Kampala, Uganda (July, 1997). To ensure adequate attendance, the NCC was widely advertised. Participants at the conference covered a range of stakeholders, including representatives of governmental organizations and departments, churches, non-governmental organizations, professional bodies and students. The NCC debated extensively on most of the provisions of the draft guideline before its voting members unanimously accepted its adoption.[29] The guideline contains comprehensive provisions on various aspects of research involving human participants, including sections on prior ethical review of research, registration and accreditation of institutional review committees, consent procedures (that take account of local circumstances) and special protection for vulnerable groups, such as pregnant women, foetuses, children, prisoners, soldiers, mentally ill and behaviourally disordered and refugees. Thus, through a democratic process that spanned three years, Uganda was able to develop a research guideline that suits its local circumstances.[30]

A decade later, the guideline was reviewed by the Uganda National Council for Science and Technology.[31] As a result of the review, modifications were made to the guideline in order to incorporate recent and contemporary developments. For instance, new provisions were added to cover research with stored human biological samples.[32] Furthermore, the title of the guideline was amended to indicate its broader scope and coverage of all types of research involving human subjects. Previously, the guideline applied only to 'health research'.[33] The new guideline, however, applies to all aspects of research involving human intervention, whether

29 Sana Loue and David Okello, 'Research Bioethics in the Ugandan Context 11: Procedural and Substantive Reform' (2000), 28 J.L. Med. & Ethics 165–173.

30 Uganda National Health Research Organisation, *Guidelines for the Conduct of Health Research Involving Human Subjects in Uganda* (Entebbe, Uganda: Ministry of Health, 2000).

31 UNCST, National Guidelines, supra, note 26.

32 For some of the ethical issues that might arise in connection with stored biological samples: Simon K. Langat, 'Reuse of Samples; Ethical Issues Encountered by Two Institutional Ethics Review Committees in Kenya' (2005), 19 Bioethics 537–549.

33 But the definition of health research is extensive enough to cover activities that are not traditionally recognized as 'health research': Global Forum for Health Research, *Monitoring Financial Flows for Health Research* (Geneva: Global Forum for Health Research, 2001) at 3.

social or behavioural, and includes research on traditional medicine. Similarly, the amended guideline extends to all research conducted by public and private institutions, governmental and non-governmental organizations, as well as private individuals.[34]

### *Ethics Review of Research in Uganda*

Uganda operates a layered approach to research ethics review; it starts at the institutional level and culminates at the national level instantiated by the National Council for Science and Technology.

#### *Institutional Review Committees*

Every institution engaged in research involving human participants in Uganda must set up an institutional review committee (IRC) or rely on a similar committee established by another institution and recognized by the Uganda National Council for Science and Technology (UNCST).[35] An IRC must be registered and accredited by the UNCST.[36] In Uganda, there are a number of established institutions that conduct health research. These institutions have set up IRCs that are accredited and recognized by the UNCST. They include the Uganda AIDS Commission; the Uganda Virus Research Institute; the Uganda Youth Development Link; the Mulago Hospital; the Medical Research Council; the Medical Biotechnology Laboratories; the Centre for Disease Control; the Makerere Institute for Social Research; and the Makerere Medical School. In addition, many of them have secured the US Federal Wide Assurance (FWA).[37] An IRC must be composed of at least five members and must be multi-disciplinary in nature. The composition of an IRC must also reflect the different nationalities of the country and must be gender-sensitive.[38] Furthermore, an IRC must be composed in a manner that facilitates a complete and adequate review of research commonly undertaken by its affiliated or parent institution.[39] Interestingly, the Ugandan guideline requires compulsory ethics training for every member of an IRC, and this must be done within one year of appointment. Additional or continuing ethics training is required to be undertaken, at least once every two years.[40] On whether illiteracy should impair membership of an IRC, the guideline provides that the 'lack of formal education

34 National Guidelines, supra, note 26, art. 1.5.

35 Ibid., art. 4.1.

36 Ibid., articles 3.4 and 4.2.

37 Fogarty, AIDS International Training Program, *A Survival Guide for Conducting International Collaborative Research in Uganda* (San Francisco: Fogarty AITRP, University of California, 2004) at 9.

38 National Guidelines, supra, note 26, art. 4.3.

39 Ibid., art. 4.3.a.

40 Ibid., art. 4.3.f.

shall not be a reason for excluding an individual from IRC membership'.[41] There are, however, practical problems to the training of such (illiterate) members. It is difficult to imagine that bioethical training would be readily and easily absorbed by illiterates. Consequently, it appears that the bioethical training requirements in the Ugandan guideline are not likely to be satisfied by potential 'illiterate' members of an IRC. For illiterates, this would be a practical and effective bar to membership despite the permissive provisions of the guideline. But as regards other members, the bioethical training requirements are laudable. It will go a long way to meeting the criticism that most members of research ethics committees in Africa lack the requisite skills for conducting a proper and efficient ethics review.[42] Chapter four provides further analysis of the training needs and other capacity problems that confront research ethics committees in Africa.

The major responsibility of an IRC is to protect the rights, safety and wellbeing of research participants.[43] Consequently, the Ugandan guideline incorporated the ethical principles of autonomy, beneficence, non-maleficence and justice as the standards for proper evaluation of research protocols.[44] In addition, the Ugandan guideline contains detailed provisions on the procedures for operating an IRC,[45] including conditions for an expedited review,[46] and requirements for exemption from the ethical review process.[47]

*Review of International Collaborative Research*

International collaborative research is implicated in the Ugandan requirement, entailing a compulsory IRC review of research protocols. This arises from two premises. First, every research protocol in Uganda must originate at the institutional level. Second, Ugandan institutions generally review only protocols from their own researchers. It follows, therefore, that foreign researchers are excluded from the ethics review process, unless they obtain an affiliation status with one or more of the relevant local institutions. In the alternative, they could appoint a local colleague as a co-principal investigator. For this reason, article 4.5.4. b provides that 'an international collaborative research project should have a co-principal investigator in Uganda which must be employed and/or affiliated to a recognized local institution that is relevant to the area of the proposed research'. Accordingly,

41 Ibid., art. 4.3.b.

42 Nancy E. Kass, et al., 'The Structure and Function of Research Ethics Committees in Africa: A Case Study' (2007), 4 PLoS Medicine 26–31. Also, Nuffield Council on Bioethics, *The Ethics of Research Related to Healthcare in Developing Countries* (NCB, 2002); National Bioethics Advisory Commission, *Ethical Issues in International Research: Clinical Trials in Developing Countries: Report and Recommendations of the National Bioethics Advisory Commission* (Bethesda, NBAC: 2001).

43 National Guidelines, supra, note 26, art. 4.4.

44 National Guidelines, supra, note 26, arts. 2.3, 4.7 and 5.

45 For instance, ibid., art.4.5.

46 Ibid., art. 5.2

47 Ibid., art. 4.5.3.

one of the application forms for research permission (UNCST/RC 1) requires an applicant to state the particulars of their local institution (or to which they are affiliated), such as the institution's address, fax, telephone number and email.

Based on personal experience from field research in Uganda, it can be said that considerable delays are frequently encountered in an application for institutional affiliation. Depending on the circumstances, it can take between one to three years, though this may be avoided by making an early application. While applications for institutional affiliation are usually fast-tracked for foreign researchers who appoint local investigators and bring in much-needed research funds, it is much worse for a lone foreign researcher with funds too insufficient to appoint local investigators or invest (financially) in the local institution. In the latter case, the applicant might have to experience the full length of the bureaucratic delays. Such delays are likely to frustrate some important but small-scale studies planned for Uganda by foreign researchers. Take, for instance, a research project which seeks to interview volunteers under strict conditions of anonymity and confidentiality. The size of the project is small and the budget is insufficient to appoint a local co-investigator. Anticipated risks to subjects are minimal provided their privacy and confidentiality are secured. It might also be assumed that there are no insurmountable language difficulties or other challenges peculiar to the locality. Yet, it may take a foreign researcher more than one year to process successfully an application for institutional affiliation. Usually, the local institution would require the (foreign) researcher to apply for a formal position, such as Visiting Scholar or Visiting Professor. Success of the visiting professorial application might, however, turn on other imponderable factors, including the availability of office space (even if not strictly needed by the researcher), availability and willingness of a local colleague to serve as a host, and the interest of the department or faculty in the research topic. It might be that in the end, the application for affiliation would still be turned down even though little or no institutional support was needed for a successful execution of the project. It is suggested, therefore, that this type of research should be reviewed directly by the UNCST and thus dispense with the requirement for an institutional affiliation. Interestingly, Malawi has a similar institutional affiliation requirement.[48] The National Research Council of Malawi justified that procedure on the need 'to promote (international) collaboration, improve on capacity building and exchange of expertise'.[49] While these objectives are laudable, their inflexible application would (for reasons already stated) be counter-productive. Affiliation status should only be a desirable, and not mandatory, requirement for collaborative studies.

---

48 NRCM, *Procedures and Guidelines for the Conduct of Research in Malawi* (NRCM, Office of the President and Cabinet, 2002).

49 Ibid., at 4.

*Mid-Level Institutional Review*

IRCs conduct only an initial review of a protocol. A protocol might be rejected, approved or sent back with recommendations for some modifications after the initial review. While an IRC's review of a protocol is not final it nevertheless has the authority to halt, suspend or terminate an approved research that turned out to be harmful or deviated from the approved protocol.[50] Once a protocol passes successfully through the initial review stage, a sort of mid-level institutional review might be engaged. A mid-level review is only relevant for certain protocols. For instance, a proposed study on HIV/AIDS is likely to be sent to the Uganda AIDS Commission (UAC) for comments. The Uganda AIDS Commission is an apex policy institution on HIV/AIDS in Uganda. The UAC acts in an advisory capacity with respect to protocols referred to it and, thus, its services could be engaged by a researcher, an IRC or both. In practice, investigators usually obtain a letter of support from the UAC which is included in their application package for a national review.[51] But the UAC's advisory services should not be confused with its own mandatory ethical review structures. For instance, the UAC has its own IRC through which it conducts the initial review of projects undertaken by its staff. The UAC's IRC is a specialist review body. The UAC was established by statute in 1992 to promote and coordinate HIV/AIDS research and related activities in the country.[52] It is responsible for policy formulation in the area of HIV/AIDS. The UAC is also statutorily empowered to establish programme priorities, take the lead in national planning and monitoring, spearhead advocacy for HIV/AIDS activities, identify obstacles to the national response, mobilize and monitor resource allocation and utilisation, foster linkages among partners, organize information documentation and exchange, and promote HIV/AIDS research in Uganda.[53] There are also other HIV/AIDS specialist institutional review committees in Uganda, such as the Science and Ethics Committee of the Uganda Virus Research Institute (Entebbe); the Institutional Review Committee of the Joint Clinical Research Centre (Kampala); and the AIDS Research Committee of the UNCST.

A mid-level review might be relevant even for non-HIV/AIDS protocols. For instance, studies relating to the experimental use of hazardous substances would require a mid-level review. Accordingly, the Ugandan guideline mandates the establishment of an Institutional Bio-Safety Committee (IBC) by institutions that undertake research on potentially hazardous substances of a physical, chemical, biological and similar nature. An IBC must be certified by the UNCST. It must also be composed of at least a bio-safety officer and three other persons with relevant qualification.[54] An IBC's function is to 'minimize potential human and

50 National Guidelines, supra, note 26, art. 4.5.5.

51 UAC, supra, note 10, at 24.

52 Uganda AIDS Commission, Cap. 208, 1992.

53 UAC, supra, note 10, at 31.

54 National Guidelines, supra, note 26, art. 3.5.4.1.

environmental harm that may be associated with research on or with potentially hazardous substances such as pathogens, radioactive material and applications of biotechnology, especially recombinant DNA techniques and processes'.[55] An IBC discharges this function through a bio-safety review of research proposals relating to the use of potentially hazardous substances. An IBC is obliged to notify an IRC or the UNCST of any research involving the use of potentially hazardous substances in its institution. It must also ensure that there are adequate provisions and facilities for the proper storage and disposal of hazardous materials. Furthermore, an IBC must ensure the provision of appropriate bio-safety training for technical staff and must develop a health monitoring plan for all high-risk personnel engaged in work involving the use of hazardous substances.[56] It is, however, the responsibility of an investigator to ensure that protocols involving the use of hazardous substances underwent a bio-safety review.[57]

*Review at the National Level*

After a successful initial review by an IRC (and a mid-level review if relevant) the protocol must be forwarded to the Uganda National Council for Science and Technology (UNCST) for final approval. The UNCST is a national review body. It is empowered to review all research protocols in Uganda involving human subjects.[58] The existence of a framework for national review, as in Uganda, has some advantages. For instance, a national review ensures the availability of a critical mass of expertise competent to review every type of research, especially those complex studies that might be beyond the skill and competence of local institutions. Moreover, a national review body is better positioned to assess the relevance of a study for the needs and health priorities of the country.[59] Furthermore, by reviewing every relevant research in the country, a national review body serves as a clearing house for research information. Consequently, it is in a better position to avoid the potential waste resulting from the duplication of research efforts. The drawback, however, is that a national review process might entail additional delays and costs.

The UNCST was established by statute in 1990 as a semi-autonomous governmental agency. It is empowered to advise on, develop and coordinate national policy on all matters relating to science and technology.[60] Its specific research agenda includes undertaking scientific and technological research and development (R&D), establishing research and experimental development institutions, providing scientific and technological documentation and information services, acting as a clearing house for information on research and experimental

55 Ibid., art. 3.5.4.2.
56 Ibid., art. 3.5.4.2. a-e.
57 Ibid., art. 3.5.4.1.
58 Ibid., arts. 3.1 and 3.2.
59 Loue and Okello, supra, note 29, at 167.
60 Uganda National Council for Science and Technology Act 1990, c. 209.

development taking place in Ugandan institutions and research enterprises, and disseminating research results, findings and developments.[61] To discharge these functions, the UNCST is given enormous powers (direct and incidental), including the power to establish specialized committees, research councils and organizations.[62] The UNCST exercised this power to establish a specialized committee that reviews protocols provisionally approved by institutional review committees. Certainly, the UNCST does not rubber-stamp protocols that were provisionally reviewed by an IRC. In contrast, the UNCST may wish to reject a provisionally approved protocol or may require some modifications to be made to the protocol. Instead of conducting a review through its specialized committee, the UNCST may wish to adopt a peer review mechanism.[63] This means that a protocol would be sent to one or more experts for review on behalf of the UNCST. The external reviewer's comments usually inform the decision of the UNCST to approve or reject a protocol. In principle, the UNCST's approval is evidence of a protocol's sufficient compliance with ethical requirements. In Uganda, however, an approved study cannot be undertaken unless research permit and security clearance are secured from the Office of the President.

*Research Secretariat in the Office of the President*

There is a Research Secretariat in the Office of the Ugandan President. It is involved in the chain of processes relating to research involving human participants. The Research Secretariat of the President's Office intervenes in the research process mainly on grounds of national security.[64] Consequently, a presidential clearance must be obtained before the commencement of any study. The application process for a presidential permit is, however, partly administered by the UNCST. Thus, investigators usually submit Form RS 6 (research clearance form from the Research Secretariat, Office of the President) to the UNCST as part of their application package for final ethical approval. If the UNCST decides to approval a protocol, it then liaises with the Research Secretariat of the Office of the President for the issuance of a research permit. This means that investigators are not personally involved in the process for securing presidential clearance.[65] A research permit from the Office of the President would ordinarily mark the end of the governance process, at least at the approval stage. However, where a protocol relates to clinical trial an investigator must obtain a further permit from the National Drug Authority.[66]

61 Ibid., s. 4.
62 Ibid., s. 5.
63 UAC, supra, note 10, at 23.
64 National Guidelines, supra, note 26, arts. 3.1 and 5.
65 http://www.uncst.go.ug
66 National Guidelines, supra, note 26, art. 3.3.

*National Drug Authority*

The National Drug Authority (NDA) was established by statute to regulate the safety, quality, efficacy, handling and use of drugs or drug-related products in research.[67] NDA's intervention in the research process relates mainly to clinical trials. Where a clinical trial involves the use and importation of experimental products, the investigator must obtain a certificate from the NDA authorizing the importation. The certificate is usually part of the application package submitted to the UNCST for ethical approval. However, the NDA issues a certificate of importation only after satisfying itself as to the safe handling, use, safety, quality and efficacy of the product based on data submitted by the investigator. For unlicensed experimental products manufactured in Uganda, the NDA conducts rigorous tests and analysis of their safety before authorizing their use. In addition to a certificate of importation, an investigator must obtain (from the NDA) a certificate permitting the conduct of clinical trial in Uganda in relation to products referenced in the certificate. In Uganda, it is an offence to undertake a clinical trial without permission from the NDA.[68]

In conclusion, the oversight mechanisms above characterize the governance of research involving human participants in Uganda (especially, governance at the research approval stage). Uganda's layered approach to research governance might be criticized for its dilatory effect on the processing of research applications. It is, thus, arguable that the multiple review structures in Uganda could discourage potentially useful research. In contrast, it is arguable that structural delays in the governance of research involving human subjects in Uganda are justified by the protective goals intended to be achieved by the Ugandan guideline. Delays in the research process occasioned by procedural safeguards may not be a disproportionate price to pay for protection of the rights, dignity and welfare of research subjects. In the light of recent and historical research scandals examined in chapter one, it is unlikely that any country would sacrifice research subjects' protection just for the sake of getting quick and speedy scientific research results. This is consistent with the principle that the protection of research subjects must take priority over the benefits of research to science and humanity.[69] Thus, the utilitarian principle of the greatest good for the greatest number may not hold well in the context research involving human subjects.[70]

67 National Drug Policy and Authority Act, c. 206.

68 Section 40, National Drug Policy and Authority Act.

69 For a trenchant criticism of this principle: J. Harris, 'Scientific Research is a Moral Duty' (2005), 31 J. Med. Ethics 242–248; and the reply by S. Shapshay and K.D. Pimple, 'Participation in Biomedical Research is an Imperfect Moral Duty: A Response to John Harris' (2007), 33 J. Med. Ethics 414–417.

70 Generally, John S. Mill, *Utilitarianism* (Indianapolis: Hackett Publishing Co., 1979. Edited by G. Sher and originally published in 1861).

**Tanzania**[71]

Tanzania's history of research subjects' protection is significantly different from that of Uganda; while the research subject protection measures in Uganda were triggered substantially by the HIV/AIDS pandemic and influx of huge foreign research funds, Tanzania's oversight mechanisms responded to more internal factors, such as the development of national health priorities, and the resultant increase in biomedical research activities. In common with other developing countries, however, Tanzania presents the usual factors that attract international collaborative research. These include high (prevalence) rate of HIV/AIDS; heavy burden of communicable (and even non-communicable) diseases; and availability of abundant research subjects, due to diseases, illiteracy, poverty, lack of access to health care, inadequate health care infrastructure, low per capita health expenditure and other socio-cultural factors. These factors are partly responsible for the (relatively) huge international research investment that has taken place in most parts of Africa since the 1990s. Increased research activities, in turn, highlight the need for a more proactive and systematic approach to subject protection.

In Tanzania, the impetus for development of oversight mechanisms is traceable to the concerted efforts of a few biomedical research institutions led by the National Institute of Medical Research (NIMR). The NIMR is a semi-autonomous governmental agency. Its mandate is to promote and coordinate health research in Tanzania. In 1998, the NIMR became completely dissatisfied with the lack of cooperation and sharing of knowledge among Tanzania's health research institutions. This resulted in the duplication of research efforts, unproductive institutional rivalry and waste of resources. Part of the problem was that each institution feared domination by the others.[72] Consequently, the results of research from Tanzania's health institutions were not effectively communicated to the public, policy makers and the industry. This made the development of evidence-based health policies utterly difficult. In 1998, however, the NIMR responded to these problems by initiating talks, and dialoguing, with other research institutions in Tanzania. Discussions focused on the best way to achieve co-operation among Tanzanian health research institutions and how to coordinate their efforts in order to accelerate health research in Tanzania. The NIMR's organizational efforts were largely successful and culminated in a proposal to set up an independent research body to be known as the Tanzania National Health Research Forum. This proposal was regionally approved by the Fifth African Essential National Health Research

71 G. Ndossi, 'Research in Tanzania', in T. Lemmens and T. Archibald (eds.), *The Regulation and Organization of Research Ethics Review* (Toronto: Brown Book Co., 2006) 13–14; Stephen E.D. Nsimba, 'The United Republic of Tanzania, East Africa', in T. Mduluza (ed.), *A Gateway to Biomedical Research in Africa* (New York: Nova Science Publishers, Inc., 2007) 81–89.

72 Andrew Y. Kitua, 'Coordinating health research to promote action: the Tanzania experience' (2000), 321 BMJ 821–823.

Meeting for Africa held in Ghana in 1998. It was also nationally approved at a workshop held in Bagamoyo (Tanzania) in 1998. The approval was confirmed at a subsequent national workshop in 1999. The new body was formally launched by the Tanzanian Minister of Health in February 1999.[73]

*Tanzania National Health Research Forum*

As mentioned above, the Tanzanian National Health Research Forum (TANHER Forum) was formed in 1998 and formally launched in 1999. It is a non-religious, non-governmental and non-political organization. The TANHER Forum's goals are the facilitation of scientific corporation and the promotion (and implementation) of health research in Tanzania. The TANHER Forum also serves as an advisory and consultative body on health research to the government of Tanzania and other interested parties. The TANHER Forum is poised to promote and support health research in Tanzania, develop and periodically revise essential national health priorities, approve the work of the national health research coordinating committee and the national health research ethics committee, develop and update guidelines for the conduct of scientifically and ethically sound research in Tanzania, promote the establishment of networking and coordination of funds for health research, provide guidelines for partnership in health research and, finally, promote and enhance the use of health research results for planning, policy, and decision making.[74] Soon after its formation, the TANHER Forum developed a set of national health research priorities based on comprehensive and widely circulated questionnaires covering all aspects of the health system in Tanzania.[75] To facilitate easy dissemination of research results, the TANHER Forum established a journal that publishes twice a year: the Tanzania HEALTH Research Bulletin. As regards research regulation, the TANHER Forum initiated the promulgation of a national guideline for research involving human participants. The guideline was drafted by the National Health Research Ethics Committee, a subsidiary of the TANHER Forum.

*The National Health Research Ethics Committee (NHREC)*

The National Health Research Ethics Committee (NHREC) is a branch of the TANHER Forum. It is responsible for developing strategies for the protection of the rights, safety and welfare of research subjects in Tanzania.[76] The NHREC is

73 Ibid., at 822.

74 Ibid., at 822; Sirkku K. Hellsten, 'Bioethics in Tanzania: Legal and Ethical Concerns in Medical Care and Research in Relation to the HIV/AIDS Epidemic' (2005), 14 Cambridge Quarterly of Healthcare Ethics 256 at 260.

75 NIMR, *Tanzania Essential National Health Research, & Priority Setting* (Dar es Salaam, Tanzania: NIMR, 1999).

76 TANHER Forum, *Guidelines on Ethics for Health Research in Tanzania* (TANHER Forum, 2001), at 13 (afterwards, Tanzanian Guidelines).

particularly entrusted with the duty of drafting and implementing ethical guidelines on health research in Tanzania. In addition, the NHREC must periodically revise the applicable guidelines in the light of contemporary circumstances. The NHREC also advises the government of Tanzania on ethical issues relating to health research in Tanzania; it equally helps to disseminate information relating to the rights of communities and subjects involved in health research.[77] Furthermore, the NHREC is the accrediting body for institutional research ethics committees in Tanzania. As part of its oversight functions, the NHREC monitors and coordinates the activities of accredited institutional research ethics committees in Tanzania. The NHREC is also empowered to participate in national and international discussions relating to the ethics of health research. Overall, the NHREC aims to enhance the ethics and standards of health research, as well as the quality of discussions relating to health research in Tanzania.[78] In furtherance of its functions, the NHREC developed a national health research guideline which was published in 2001.[79]

*Tanzanian Research Guideline*

*Guidelines on Ethics of Health Research in Tanzania* incorporates the cultural values and local circumstances of Tanzania into the popular, but by no means consensus, principles (autonomy, beneficence, nonmalficence and justice) that guide research involving human subjects.[80] The guidelines, however, apply to health-related research only, defined as 'activities involving subjects undertaken with the prime objectives of testing a hypothesis and permitting conclusions to be drawn for the purpose of contributing to medical knowledge'.[81] Practically, this restriction may not mean much since 'health research' connotes a much more expansive and flexible concept. For instance, it was defined to include 'the study of health determinants, population health issues, and many non-medical factors related to health (economic, social, cultural, legal, etc.)'.[82] This means that health research may extend to the pursuit of knowledge that is not strictly medical, provided it is capable of application in the health field. Interestingly, the Tanzanian guidelines also regulate research on animals.[83]

In line with other national and international guidelines, the Tanzanian guideline considers prior ethics review of research as an indispensable process for the safety

77 Hellsten, supra, note 74, at 260–261.

78 Tanzanian Guidelines, supra, note 76, at 13–14.

79 Ibid.

80 Chapter four offers a criticism of principlism (autonomy, beneficence, nonmalficence and justice) and highlights alternative theories that could underpin research involving human subjects.

81 Tanzanian Guidelines, supra, note 76, at xiii.

82 McDonald, supra, note 1, at 32.

83 Tanzanian Guidelines, supra, note 76, at 67.

and protection of research subjects.[84] To make up for the scant provisions on the operating procedures for ethics committees, the Tanzanian guideline expressly incorporates the World Health Organisation's operational guidelines for ethics committees.[85] The deliberations of ethics committees in Tanzania must be guided by the ethical principles of autonomy, beneficence, nonmalficence and justice. To that end, the guideline stipulates that the Helsinki Declaration shall be the basis for elaborating the applicable ethical principles in Tanzania.[86] Furthermore, the guideline contains detailed provisions for the protection of research subjects, and special protection for vulnerable groups including minors, the mentally disordered, the mentally ill, demented and unconscious persons, people with learning disabilities, the elderly, pregnant women, prisoners and, interestingly, students.[87] Finally, the guideline contains directions to help potential investigators regarding the making of applications for the ethics review of research in Tanzania.

### *Ethics Review of Research in Tanzania*

The ethics review system in Tanzania is national in character, at least in theory. In practice, however, the process is significantly decentralized. The National Institute of Medical Research (NIMR) is the national review body. It was established by statute in 1979 to conduct, promote and coordinate health research in Tanzania.[88] The Tanzanian research guideline provides that every biomedical research involving human subjects must receive ethical clearance from the NIMR and 'under no circumstances can any research involving human beings be conducted or initiated in Tanzania without the permission of NIMR'.[89] The NIMR receives, reviews, and considers protocols for approval through its committee known as the Medical Research Coordinating Committee (MRCC).[90] The MRCC is responsible for the supervision of health research in Tanzania. It is empowered to review the scientific, medical and ethical aspects of research proposals with a view to granting ethical clearance.[91] The MRCC discharges its ethics review functions through a sub-committee known as the National Health Research Ethics Review Committee (NHRERC).

While the NIMR has authority to review every biomedical research involving human subjects in Tanzania, it has nevertheless encouraged health research institutions in Tanzania to set up an institutional ethics review committee (IREC).

84 Ibid., at 8–12 and 70–75.

85 Ibid., at 74; also: WHO, *Operational Guidelines for Ethics Committees that Review Biomedical Research* (Geneva: WHO, 2000).

86 Tanzanian Guidelines, supra, note 76, at 16–19.

87 Ibid., at 24–31.

88 National Institute of Medical Research, Act of Parliament No. 23, 1979.

89 Tanzanian Guidelines, supra, note 76, at 70.

90 Ibid., at 71.

91 http://www.nimr.or.tz.

IRECs review and, where appropriate, issue ethical clearance for research proposals submitted by the employees of their institutions. Similarly, they can review studies proposed to be undertaken in their institutions by non-employees.[92] IRECs' jurisdiction is however significantly limited. They can only review studies proposed to be undertaken exclusively by Tanzanian nationals. Thus, IRECs cannot review proposals involving international collaborative research.[93] Foreign investigators must, therefore, submit their proposals directly to the NIMR. Despite this limitation, IREC has helped to reduce the workload of the NIMR. Similarly, IREC has improved the efficiency of the NIMR by reducing the delays involved in granting ethical clearance certificates. Where an ethical clearance certificate is issued by an IREC, it must be lodged with the NIMR for documentation, scrutiny and monitoring purposes. In addition to its status as a national review body, the MRCC's National Health Research Ethics Review Committee (NHRERC) operates as the institutional ethics review committee (IREC) for research undertaken by the NIMR. The NIMR's research is done through its centres at Muhimbili, Mwanza, Amani, Tabora, and Tukuyu; but its headquarters is in Dar es Salaam. Recently, however, the NIMR has encouraged the formation of separate and full-fledged IRECs for its research centres. While IRECs currently exist for the NIMR's research centres, they are only allowed to conduct the initial reviews of protocols. This means that their decision is provisional and must be forwarded to the NHRERC for final approval.[94] But there seems to be increasing efforts to empower IRECs at the NIMR's centres.[95] The ultimate goal is to give them power to grant final ethical clearance certificates.

For international collaborative research, the NIMR has the exclusive power to issue ethical clearances. Although an IREC might receive and review international collaborative research protocols, it can only comment on and forward the protocol to the NIMR for final review and ethical clearance.[96] Unlike the situation in Uganda, neither the NIMR nor the Tanzanian research guideline insists on institutional affiliation before foreign investigators can undertake their studies in Tanzania. This liberal approach is likely to facilitate an expedited review of small-scale and interview-based studies proposed by foreign investigators. In practice, however, foreign investigators might discover that it is extremely difficult to conduct an elaborate study of any significance without the help of local co-investigators or institutional affiliation. While the grant of an ethical clearance certificate marks the end of ethics review process for research intended to be undertaken exclusively by Tanzanians, foreign investigators would need to proceed to the Tanzanian Commission for Science and Technology in order to obtain a research permit.

92 Tanzanian Guidelines, supra, note 76, at 71–72.

93 Ibid., at 72–73.

94 Joyce K. Ikingura, 'Health Research Ethics Review and Needs of Institutional Ethics Committees in Tanzania' (2007), 9 Tanzania Health Research Bulletin 154 at 155.

95 Ibid., at 155.

96 Tanzanian Guidelines, supra, note 76, at 74.

*Tanzanian Commission for Science and Technology (COSTECH)*

COSTECH is the only institution empowered to issue research permits to foreigners undertaking research in Tanzania.[97] It was established by statute in 1986 to promote, monitor and coordinate all research and development (R&D) activities in Tanzania.[98] COSTECH's specific research remit includes advising the government on all matters relating to scientific research, formulating policy on the development of science and technology and advising on its implementation and monitoring. COSTECH also coordinates activities relating to scientific research conducted by all persons and organizations in Tanzania; it acquires, stores, and disseminates scientific and technological information, in addition to initiating, formulating and implementing research policies and programmes in Tanzania.[99] COSTECH issues research permits to foreigners whose research proposals were ethically cleared by the NIMR. For this reason, the NIMR works harmoniously with COSTECH and forwards to it copies of all relevant ethical clearance certificates.

*Tanzania Food and Drugs Authority*

Finally, where a proposal involves the conduct of clinical trials, the investigators must obtain a clinical trial certificate under the Tanzania Food, Drugs and Cosmetics Act (TFDA).[100] TFDA is the regulatory body for clinical trial of drugs and medical devices in Tanzania. It issues a clinical trial certificate only for studies that comply with the provisions of the Act and are supported by ethical clearance certificates issued by research ethics committee in Tanzania.

In conclusion, Tanzania has developed sophisticated research guidelines and oversight mechanisms in response to internal factors that are markedly different from those underpinning the guidelines in Uganda. In further contrast to Uganda, Tanzania's research governance structure is more monolithic than layered, though the NIMR is increasingly pursuing a policy of decentralization. The current system of a single ethics review in Tanzania, through a national body, is likely to avoid the delays inherent in layered systems. It is a feature that is likely to be attractive to foreign investigators for whom time is of the essence.

97 In Uganda, a similar function is performed by the Research Secretariat of the Office of the President.

98 The Tanzanian Commission for Science and Technology Act, No. 7 of 1986. For a good history of the commission: Benedict C. Mukama and Charles S. Yongolo, *Development of S & T System and Experience of Tanzania on S & T Data Collection* (Presentation at the Regional Workshop on Science and Technology Statistics at Entebbe, Uganda, 17–22 September 2005).

99 COSTECH Act, supra, note 98, s. 3.

100 Tanzania Food, Drugs and Cosmetics Act, 2003.

**Nigeria**

Although Nigeria gained political independence from the United Kingdom in 1960, biomedical research activities in the country date back to the colonial era. In 1920, the Rockefeller Foundation initiated a colonial research enterprise in the West Coast of Africa known as the 'Rockefeller Foundation Yellow Fever Commission to the West Coast of Africa'.[101] In 1925, the Yellow Fever Commission, as it was generally called, built a Research Unit in Yaba, Lagos. Few details are known about any clinical trial or other activities by the Yellow Fever Commission, but, considering that ethics review was developed in the 1960s,[102] yellow fever research would probably raise only issues of informed consent.

In 1954, the British colonial government established the West African Council for Medical Research for its West African territories of Nigeria, Ghana, Gambia, and Sierra Leone.[103] The main function of the Council was to arrange for the conduct of medical research in those West African territories and to provide medical research information concerning West Africa to the British government. Legislation establishing the Council was not specific on the type of medical research to be conducted or sponsored by the Council, nor did it contain any provision relating to the ethics review of research protocols conducted under the auspices of the Council. In 1952, the Nigerian colonial government established the University College Hospital, Ibadan (UCH).[104] UCH was established as a teaching hospital of the University of Ibadan (then University College, Ibadan). Part of the mandate of the UCH was to carry out clinical research or other medical experimentation, though no research guideline was specifically mentioned. At that period, however, the main medical research guideline was the Nuremberg Code. Following the UCH research mandate, subsequent teaching hospitals established in Nigeria were given the same clinical research jurisdiction. These include the University of Nigeria Nsukka Teaching Hospital, University of Lagos Teaching Hospital, University of Benin Teaching Hospital, and Obafemi Awolowo University Teaching Hospital (formerly, University of Ife).

In 1972, the then Nigerian Military government established the Medical Research Council of Nigeria (MRC).[105] The federal agency was responsible for the promotion, coordination and conduct of medical research in Nigeria. In 1977,

---

101 National Institute of Medical Research, Yaba, Lagos, Nigeria: http://www.nimr-ng.org.

102 P. Ferguson, 'Do Researchers Feel an LREC Hinders Research?' (2001), 165 Bull. of Med. Ethics 17 at 19.

103 West African Council for Medical Research Ordinance, Laws of the Federation of Nigeria and Lagos, Cap. 215, 1958.

104 University College Hospital Act, Laws of the Federation of Nigeria and Lagos, Cap. 205, 1958.

105 Decree No. 1, Medical Research Council of Nigeria, 1972.

however, the National Science and Technology Development Agency (NSTDA)[106] was established by statute to advise the federal government on matters relating to scientific research and development. The NSTDA Decree repealed the Medical Research Council of Nigeria Decree 1972. Pursuant to the NSTDA Decree, the Research Institute's Order of 1977[107] established the National Institute of Medical Research in Yaba, Lagos (NIMR). The assets and rights of the MRC were transferred to the NIMR. The NIMR is authorized to conduct medical research related to health problems in Nigeria and to cooperate with Nigerian medical schools and universities in the provision of necessary facilities for the training of medical researchers in Nigeria. Though the NIMR is a major institute concerned with human medicine and research in Nigeria, it was not, until recently, governed by any formal national guideline for the conduct of research involving human subjects. In 1980, the NSTDA was dissolved and merged with the Ministry of Science and Technology by the National Science and Technology Act.[108] The new Act, however, retained the NIMR established under the repealed NSTDA Decree.[109] It also authorized the Minister for Science and Technology, with the approval of the President, to establish further research institutes in the country. In the exercise of this power, the Minister established the Nigerian Institute for Pharmaceutical Research and Development (NIPRD) in 1987 to conduct and promote indigenous pharmaceutical research and development. The NIPRD aims to develop and commercialize drugs, biological products and pharmaceutical raw materials from indigenous resources. Consequently, clinical trials of drugs and products developed by the NIPRD must receive prior ethics clearance.

*Background to Research Subject Protection in Nigeria*

Nigeria can relate with the peculiar situations in Africa that create potential opportunities for the exploitation of research subjects. These include poverty, disease, and illiteracy among a substantial portion of the population. In Nigeria, as in many other African countries, poverty and disease have combined to produce abundant research subjects. Cheap and readily available research subjects facilitate the conduct of clinical trials. In contrast to Africa, many people in industrialized countries are reluctant to take part in clinical trials. For instance, it was estimated that only one in three hundred and fifty Americans would agree to take part in a drug trial.[110] Naturally, the drug industry is happy to conduct trials in countries

---

106 Decree No. 5, National Science and Technology Development Agency Decree, 1977.

107 Research Institutes (Establishment, etc.) Order 1977, Annual Volume of the Laws of the Federal Republic of Nigeria, 1977.

108 National Science and Technology Act 1980.

109 Ibid., s. 2.

110 Sonia Shaw, 'Globalising Clinical Research: Big Pharma Tries Out First World Drugs on Unsuspecting Third World Patients', The Nation, 1 July 2002 (page unknown).

where it is easy to recruit subjects and produce a quick and decisive result for drug registration. Most African countries offer this opportunity, by not only having an abundant store of potential research subjects; also, these subjects are the most appropriate for clinical trials since many of them are not likely to have been previously treated for the disease proposed to be studied, nor are they likely to have received any medications at all for other conditions.[111] Poverty, prevalence of disease and general lack of access to health care in Nigeria would mean that many Nigerian research subjects will easily satisfy the descriptions above. Furthermore, a drug company might want to use Nigeria as a trial site just for market purposes; for example, to develop a market for an investigational drug if eventually approved by the regulatory authorities.[112] Other factors have also contributed to the attraction of international collaborative research in Nigeria, including the expansion of contract research organizations (CROs) into developing countries like Nigeria,[113] willingness of the US Food and Drug Administration (FDA) to accept data for drug registration generated from clinical trials in Nigeria, low visibility of biomedical research regulations (until recently), relatively cheaper cost of clinical trials, poor health care infrastructure, low per capita health expenditure, and inadequate access to health care services in Nigeria. In common with Uganda and Tanzania (and, indeed, other African countries), the factors above contextualize concerns in Nigeria that research subjects might be needlessly exposed to exploitation.

However, the greatest impetus for the protection of research subjects in Nigeria is the controversial (Pfizer's) trovan trial in 1996. This has already been examined extensively in chapter one, and its legal aspects are analysed further in chapter seven. Due to the scandal, there was a huge loss of public confidence in health researchers in Nigeria. The scandal also damaged the peculiarly strong trust that characterized the physician-patient relationship in Nigeria. Consequently, many Nigerians (especially in northern Nigeria) have become suspicious of western medicine and drug trials. The trovan scandal equally had adverse consequences for the Nigerian government. Since the government was implicated in the trovan trial (partly through the grant of import permit for the investigational drug), most Nigerians have lost faith in the ability of their government to protect them against unjustifiable research risks. More than a decade after the scandal, many Nigerians are still suspicious of any health programme administered by the government. As noted in the section on Uganda, for instance, there were allegations (basically rumours) in 2004 that polio vaccines in Nigeria were deliberately contaminated. These rumours were strengthened by wide publication of the trovan trial that took place only a few years previously. Consequently, the polio immunization campaign conducted by the Nigerian government in 2004 was adversely affected.

---

111 Office of Inspector General, *The Globalisation of Clinical Trials: A Growing Challenge in Protecting Human Subjects* (US Department of Health and Human Services, 2001), at 8.

112 Ibid., at 8.

113 Ibid., at 9.

A prominent spokesperson from northern Nigeria (where the controversial Pfizer trial took place) attributed the failure of the polio campaign in 2004 to lack of public support :[114] 'The Council (Supreme Council of Sharia) harbours strong reservations on the safety of our population not least because of our recent experience in the Pfizer scandal, when our people were used as guinea pigs with the approval of the federal ministry of health and the approval of all the relevant UN agencies'.[115]

Nigerian government adopted a two-pronged action to redeem its battered image and restore public confidence in biomedical activities. First, it filed a criminal action against Pfizer in the Federal High Court at Abuja, Nigeria.[116] Kano state (where the trial took place) also filed a criminal charge in 2007 (through the Attorney-General of that state) against Pfizer and other persons.[117] The criminal charges alleged that Pfizer conducted the trovan trial without informed consent of the subjects and in a criminally negligent manner, leading to the death of some of the participating children and other side-effects, including deafness, muteness, paralysis, brain damage, loss of sight, and flawed speech.[118] Second, the federal government took active steps to pass legislation on research governance in the country.[119] The National Health Act 2011 authorized the promulgation of an enforceable code containing principles that govern biomedical research involving human subjects; it also provides mechanisms for the setting up of institutional and national research ethics committees.[120]

*Nigerian Research Guideline*

The *National Code of Health Research Ethics*[121] is a formal and official document that governs the conduct of health research involving human participants in Nigeria.[122] It was promulgated pursuant to the powers given to the National Health

---

114 Dr Ibrahim Datti Ahmed, the secretary general of the Supreme Council of Sharia in Nigeria.

115 Abiodun Raufu, 'Nigeria postpones programme of polio immunisation' (2004), 328 BMJ 1278.

116 *Attorney-General of the Federation v Pfizer Inc. & Ors.*, FHC/ABJ/CR/27/07 (dated 3 May 2007. On file with author).

117 *State v Pfizer Inc. & Ors., Charge No. K/21c/07* (on file with author).

118 *A-G v Pfizer*, supra, note 116, *State v Pfizer*, supra, note 117. Also: Mike Oboh, 'Nigerian state files criminal suit against Pfizer', Reuters, 30 May 2007 (http://www.uk.reuters.com).

119 National Health Act 2011.

120 Ibid., sections 33 and 34.

121 Federal Ministry of Health (Nigeria), *National Code of Health Research Ethics* (Abuja, Nigeria: Federal Ministry of Health, 2007). (Afterwards, National Code).

122 For a good historical account of the development of the Nigerian research guideline: Clement A. Adebamowo, et al., 'Developing Ethical Oversight of Research in Developing Countries: Case Study of Nigeria', in Olayiwola Erinosho, *Ethics for Public*

Research Ethics Committee by the National Health Act 2011.[123] As in Tanzania, the Code's jurisdiction is limited to all 'health research involving human participants, conducted, supported or otherwise subject to regulation by any institution in Nigeria'.[124] But as noted above, health research is viewed very broadly and encompasses studies on the determinants of health and other social, economic, cultural and legal (non-medical) factors that are related to health.[125] The Nigerian research Code considers prior ethics review as an indispensable framework for the protection of research subjects.[126] The Code contains provisions for the expedited review of protocols,[127] and for the exemption of certain protocols from the review process.[128] In line with some popular principles governing the conduct of biomedical research, otherwise known as principlism,[129] the Nigerian Code incorporates the ethical principles that govern research involving human subjects, such as autonomy, beneficence, justice, fair selection of participants, presence of social or scientific value and clinical equipoise.[130] As regards clinical trials, the Code expressly refers to the ICH-GCP guidelines[131] for further guidance.[132] There are also provisions relating to the transfer of animal, plant and herbal samples and other biological materials out of Nigeria.[133] Although the Nigerian research Code enjoys some statutory backing,[134] it does not contain any specific penal sanction for the breach of its provisions beyond the power of research ethics committees to suspend or terminate an approved research,[135] instigate professional disciplinary action, or report to the appropriate civil or criminal authorities.[136]

---

*Health Research in Africa* (Ago-Iwoye, Ogun State, Nigeria: Olabisi Onabanjo University Press, 2008) at 13–31.

123 National Health Act 2011, section 33(6).

124 National Code, supra, note 121, at 3.

125 McDonald, supra, note 1; Global Forum for Health Research, supra, note 33.

126 National Code, supra, note 121, at 7–12 and 27–31.

127 Ibid., at 4–5 and 17–18.

128 Ibid., at 6 and 19–20.

129 In the context of research, principlism refers to the four principles that govern research: autonomy, beneficence, nonmalficence and justice. Generally: Richard B. Davies, 'The Principlism Debate: A Critical Overview' (1995), 20 Journal of Medicine and Philosophy 85–105; Beauchamp and Childress, supra, note 27, at 1–23. Chapter four offers a criticism of principlism and highlights other alternative theories.

130 National Code, supra, note 121, at 35–42.

131 International Conference on Harmonisation of Technical Requirements for Registration of Pharmaceuticals for Human Use, *ICH Harmonised Tripartite Guideline: Guideline for Good Clinical Practice – E6* (1996).

132 National Code, supra, note 121, at 26 and 42.

133 Ibid., at 24–25.

134 National Health Act 2011, section 33(6).

135 National Code, supra, note 121, at 20–22.

136 Ibid., at 57.

*Ethics Review of Research in Nigeria*

Although Nigeria operates a national system of ethics review, considerable power is given to institutional ethics review committees. National Health Research Ethics Committee (NHREC) is the national review body, established by section 33 of the National Health Act 2011. The NHREC, however, dates back further in history. In the early 1980s it was informally developed as a national ethics review framework but could not make any significant impact on the research process in Nigeria. Eventually, and partly due to insufficient funding and support, it became moribund.[137] In 2011, however, the National Health Act revived and freshly empowered the NHREC.

*National Review by the NHREC*

The NHREC is empowered to develop, issue, implement, and revise guidelines to govern biomedical research in the country,[138] and to register, accredit and monitor institutional health research ethics committees.[139] Specific functions of NHREC include:[140]

- to determine the guidelines for the functioning of health research ethics committees;
- to register and audit health research ethics committees;
- to set norms and standards for conducting research on humans and animals, including norms and standards for conducting clinical trials;
- to adjudicate complaints about the functioning of health research ethics committees and hear any complaint by a researcher who believes that he has been discriminated against by a health research ethics committees;
- to refer to the relevant statutory health professional council matters involving the violation or potential violation of an ethical or professional rule by a health care provider;
- to institute such disciplinary action as may be prescribed against any person found to be in violation of any norms and standards, or guidelines, set for the conduct of research under the Health Act; and
- to advise the Federal Ministry of Health and State Ministries on any ethical issues concerning research.

Apart from the adjudicatory, consultative, advisory and regulatory functions above, the NHREC is authorized to undertake particular ethics review functions.

137 Address of Prof. Eyitayo Lambo, Nigerian Minister of Health, at the inaugural ceremony of the National Health Research Ethics Committee held at the Conference Hall of the Federal Ministry of Health, Abuja, on 5 October 2006 (on file with the author).

138 National Health Act 2011, section 33 (6)(a); Code, at 1.

139 Ibid., section 33 (6)(c); Code, at 7–12.

140 Ibid., section 33 (6)(a–f); National Code, supra, note 114, at 1–2.

For instance, the Institutional Health Research Ethics Committees (HREC) are obliged to forward complex protocols to the NHREC, especially those protocols that the HREC members lack the competence and technical ability to review.[141] Similarly, ethics review application may be made directly to the NHREC where a protocol involves a multi-site study (three or more Nigerian sites).[142] The NHREC may also review research protocols that have a nationwide coverage. Where there is no HREC in any institution, and that institution does not have an ethics cooperative agreement with a registered HREC,[143] an investigator (from that institution) may make a direct application to the NHREC.[144] Above all, the NHREC may at its discretion review any health research involving human subjects in Nigeria.[145] This omnibus provision makes it a truly national review body. In practice, however, the HRECs review the bulk of research protocols in Nigeria. The NHREC may review a protocol in one of three ways. First, it may authorize any HREC in Nigeria to review a protocol on behalf of the NHREC. In that case, the HREC would be acting as the institutional review committee for that protocol (HREC of record). Second, the NHREC may constitute itself into a review committee. As such, it is authorised to exercise all the powers of an HREC under the Nigerian research Code. Lastly, the NHREC may wish to establish an ad hoc HREC to review a particular protocol.[146]

*Institutional Review by HREC*

Unlike the NHREC, a Health Research Ethics Committee (HREC) is institutional in nature and operation. The National Health Act 2011 requires every institution, health agency and health establishment at which health research is conducted to establish or have access to an HREC.[147] HRECs must be registered and accredited by the NHREC.[148] Among other things, HRECs are designed to protect the rights, safety and welfare of research participants, as well as those of researchers and communities participating in research.[149] HRECs must be constituted in such a way as to ensure a complete and adequate review of a health protocol; consequently, regard must be had to the members' experience, expertise, gender, qualifications, diversity, religion and socio-cultural backgrounds.[150] The Nigerian research Code requires that all members of an HREC must complete a training

141 National Code, supra, note 121, at 16 and 27.
142 Ibid., at 23.
143 For the conditions and dynamics of such agreements: ibid., at 10–11.
144 Ibid., at 27.
145 Ibid., at 27.
146 Ibid., at 27–28.
147 National Health Research Act 2011, section 34 (1).
148 Ibid., section 34 (1).
149 National Code, supra, note 121, at 27–31.
150 Ibid., at 13.

programme approved by the NHREC.[151] Unlike Uganda, however, compulsory bioethical training in Nigeria is facilitated by the absence of provisions permitting illiterates to be members of HRECs. The jurisdiction of HRECs is limited to protocols proposed to be undertaken within the premises of a parent institution or to protocols originating from permanent employees of a parent institution.[152] Where ethics review cooperative agreement exists, a HREC's jurisdiction would be extended accordingly.

HRECs in Nigeria, unlike Uganda, are authorized to issue final ethical clearance for research proposals.[153] The Nigerian research Code provides that an HREC 'shall review prescribed application materials and have authority to approve, require modifications in (to secure approval) or disapprove all health research activities covered by this Code'.[154] While the Code clearly gives an investigator a right to appeal the HREC's decision to terminate an approved research that became unexpectedly harmful or terminated for failing to comply with the Code, existing law and HREC requirements,[155] it is not clear whether an investigator can appeal an HREC's decision to reject a protocol in the first place. In other words, beyond the opportunities to make further representations to the HREC, can an investigator appeal against an HREC's decision to reject a protocol?[156] This is obviously an interpretational and practical difficulty. It makes sense to think that if a right of appeal exists against a decision to terminate an approved protocol, then a similar right should exist against a decision not to approve the protocol in the first place. Ideally, appellate jurisdiction over rejected protocols should be within the remit of a national review body. The Nigerian research Code contains an interesting provision pertaining to the right of appeal, an issue that is not clearly dealt with in the Ugandan and Tanzanian guidelines. It provides: 'Any dispute arising from any quarters, including research participants, researchers, sponsors, institutional officials or any other source, about the appropriate interpretations or intentions of any section of this code, other than matters of legality, shall be referred to NHREC for clarification and elaboration'. This may provide a basis for arguing that a right of appeal exists against a decision to reject a protocol. Much, however, turns on the meaning of 'dispute', 'clarification' and 'elaboration' in the quotation above. Where an investigator complains that the rejection of their protocol by an HREC was unfair and unjustifiable, a dispute requiring elaboration and clarification by the NHREC would presumably arise. Furthermore, the NHREC's assumption of appellate jurisdiction over rejected protocols may be consistent with the avoidance of forum shopping. Having regard to the jurisdiction of HRECs, however, there is not much room for forum

151 Ibid., at 8.
152 Ibid., at 10.
153 National Health Act 2011, section 33 (2)(b).
154 National Code, supra, note 121, at 15.
155 Ibid., at 20–21.
156 Ibid., at 15–16.

shopping. This means that absent an appellate jurisdiction, an investigator whose protocol was rejected by the HREC can only mount pressure on the NHREC to exercise its discretion by reviewing the protocol directly.

*International Collaborative Research in Nigeria*

As in Uganda, international collaborative research in Nigeria must go through ethical clearance at the institutional level. Accordingly, the Code requires principal investigators to be based in the local institution where the research is proposed to be undertaken.[157] This means that foreign investigators proposing biomedical studies in Nigeria must appoint local co-investigators or, alternatively, get affiliated to a local institution in Nigeria where the research is intended to take place. The criticisms made with respect to similar provisions in Uganda are equally applicable here.

*Institutional Bio-Safety Review*

Where an institution conducts research involving hazardous substances of a physical or biological nature such as pathogens, radioactive material, recombinant DNA techniques and processes (and other biotechnological applications), then it has to establish an institutional bio-safety committee (IBC).[158] An IBC shall consist of a bio-safety officer and three other appropriately qualified persons. An IBC must also be registered with the NHREC. It is the investigator's responsibility to notify an IBC of any research protocol involving classified hazardous substances. As a framework, an IBC is developed to minimize any potential human or environmental harm in research involving classified hazardous substances. Accordingly, an IBC is authorized to conduct bio-safety review of protocols involving the use of such substances; it must also ensure the provision of suitable storage and disposal facilities for all materials involved in work with hazardous substances. The Nigerian research Code is, however, not clear on whether protocols reviewed by an IBC must also be reviewed by the institution's HREC, at least where research subjects are involved. It seems that such a double review should be the norm. After all, the Code provides that all health research involving human subjects must be reviewed by HREC. Exclusive review by an IBC would not satisfy that requirement.

*National Agency for Food and Drug Administration and Control*

The National Agency for Food and Drug Administration and Control (NAFDAC) was established by statute as a semi-autonomous governmental agency under

157 Ibid., at 23.
158 Ibid., at 53–54.

the Ministry of Health.[159] The NAFDAC is empowered to regulate and control the importation, exportation, manufacture, advertisement, distribution, sale and use of food, drugs, cosmetics, medical devices, bottled water and chemicals. The NAFDAC also has the power to conduct appropriate and relevant tests to ensure compliance with standard specifications designated and approved for the effective control of the quality of the items mentioned above. In addition, the NAFDAC is the appropriate federal agency to determine the suitability or otherwise of medicine, drugs, food products, cosmetics, medical devices or chemicals for human and animal use.[160] Although the statute establishing the NAFDAC did not expressly mention clinical trials, the NAFDAC's functions make it obvious that its permission is a necessary condition for clinical trials, at least those involving the use and importation of drugs and medical devices.[161] Moreover, the Nigerian research Code expressly makes NAFDAC's permission a condition precedent for the conduct of clinical trials in Nigeria to test the efficacy and safety of products.[162]

In conclusion, it can be said that the development of research guidelines in Nigeria was largely a response to the scandalous trovan trial conducted by Pfizer (in Nigeria) in the mid-1990s. The Nigerian guideline, as well as those of Uganda and Tanzania, underscores how peculiar local circumstances condition the promulgation and contents of research guidelines in Africa. More interestingly, Nigeria's research guideline is backed by legislation and, therefore, legally enforceable, unlike the guidelines in Uganda and Tanzania. The policy decision to adopt a legally enforceable guideline in Nigeria may not be unconnected with the trovan tragedy. Generally, the regulatory system in Nigeria combines the approaches in Uganda and Tanzania. While Nigeria has a national review body, like Tanzania, it also operates institutional review committees, like Uganda. Unlike Tanzania, however, the national review body in Nigeria does not exercise exclusive jurisdiction over ethics review. Similarly, while institutional ethics review committees in Nigeria are empowered to give final ethics clearance or approval for research protocols, their counterparts in Uganda can only conduct initial reviews (without the power to give final approval to protocols).

## Conclusion

Although this chapter focused on a few African countries, yet it provides evidence of completed and ongoing international collaborative biomedical research in

159 National Agency for Food and Drug Administration and Control Act, Cap. N1 (Laws of the Federation of Nigeria, 2000).

160 Ibid., section 5.

161 NAFDAC's authority over clinical trials would seem to derive from NAFDAC Act, section 5. See also, NAFDAC (Regulatory and Registration Directorate), Documentation Guidelines for Clinical Trial in Nigeria.

162 National Code, supra, note 121, at 51.

Africa and the responses of African countries to the issue of research subject protection. Interestingly, the chapter showed that Uganda, Tanzania, Malawi and Nigeria (as well as some other African countries) have developed sophisticated frameworks for biomedical research oversight, comparable to the systems found in industrialized countries. This challenges popular belief, especially in the Western world, that developing African countries mark a zone of regulatory low visibility in relation to the oversight of biomedical research.

In the past ten years or so, Uganda, Tanzania, Malawi, Nigeria and some other African countries have developed sophisticated regulatory systems to protect human subjects of biomedical research and promote scientifically and ethically sound research. The regulatory system in place includes the review of research protocols by properly constituted, functional and multi-disciplinary ethics review committees. Some African countries like Uganda and Ethiopia even have hierarchically ordered ethics review systems, ranging from institutional (through regional, in case of Ethiopia) to national review bodies.[163] Some countries, like Malawi, have even integrated bioethics into the curricula for the training of physicians and other scientific researchers. Chapter three also suggested that sensitivity to the protection of research subjects is currently high in many African countries. It seems unlikely that the types of unethical (and controversial) research that took place in Africa in the past fifteen years will be repeated easily in that region. Countries like Uganda, Malawi, Cameroon, Ethiopia, Tanzania, Nigeria, Botswana, Zimbabwe and Kenya have well-developed research ethics guidelines.[164] Others that do not currently have research ethics guidelines are in the process of developing one. In the interim, such countries rely mainly on international research guidelines, including the Helsinki Declaration, the CIOMS, and the ICH-GCP. Research guidelines in Africa seek to adapt popular principles (principlism) governing research involving human participants to the peculiar context of Africa. While these efforts are laudable, they should not give rise to complacency. As chapter four will show, there still remains some significant practical problems in the oversight of research in Africa.

---

163 Ethiopian Science and Technology Commission, *National Health Research Ethics Review Guideline* (Addis Ababa, 2005).

164 Some of these guidelines were discussed in chapters two and three. However, for Cameroon, Kenya, Botswana and Zimbabwe, the guidelines are: Ministry of Public Health (Cameroon), *Ministerial Decree No. 079 on the Creation and Organisation of an Ethics Committee Regulating all Research Involving Human Beings* (22 October 1987); National Council for Science and Technology (Kenya), *Guidelines for Ethical Conduct of Biomedical Research Involving Human Subjects in Kenya* (NCST, 2004); Ministry of Health (Kenya), *National Guidelines for Research and Development of HIV/AIDS Vaccines* (MoH, 2005); Health Research and Development Committee (Bostwana), *Guidelines for the Review of Research Proposals* (Ministry of Health, Bostwana, 2005). Medical Research Council (Zimbabwe), *Guidelines for Researchers and Ethics Review Committees in Zimbabwe* (MRC, 2004).

# Chapter 4
# The Machinery of Ethics Review: Nature, Functions and Scope

## Introduction

As mentioned in chapter one, many current research guidelines embody an important procedural ethics requirement developed as part of the national and international responses to research scandals explored in chapter one. In furtherance of that analysis, chapter three explored the regulatory frameworks in selected African countries and highlighted the provisions relating to ethics review. In essence, prior ethics review has become a pre-eminent requirement in bioethics and a cornerstone of the regulation of research involving human participants.[1] This means that a research protocol must receive the prior approval of an ethics committee before its execution. The system of ethics review is widely accepted as an indispensable framework for the protection of the rights and welfare of research subjects. It also helps to build public confidence in the integrity of the research process. Increasingly, prior ethics review has become an important condition for the funding of research involving human subjects, especially international collaborative research; as suggested in chapter one, ethics review requirements in the guidance documents of international organizations and sponsors in industrialized countries were partly responsible for the establishment and proliferation of ethics committees in many African countries. Accordingly, this chapter examines the constitution, mechanism and dynamics of ethics review committees. Following this introduction, the next section examines the ethical and scientific review functions of ethics committees in order to emphasize the sub-optimal performance of most ethics committees in Africa. The section examines other functions of ethics committees, including legal review and responsibilities of research ethics committees; fostering of public trust and confidence in the research enterprise; and the monitoring of approved research. The next section examines the review of international collaborative research, followed by analysis of bioethical capacity building and training of members of research ethics committees in Africa; funding of ethics committees and the charging of fees for review; and, lastly, the problems raised by the existence and operation of commercial or for-profit ethics review boards.

---

1 For a good analysis of the role of ethics committees as regulatory authorities: S. McGuinness, 'Research ethics committees: the role of ethics in a regulatory authority' (2008), 34 J. Med. Ethics 695–700.

## Functions of Research Ethics Committees

Ethics committees perform important ethical, scientific, legal and social functions. While their role is arguably indispensable for any country concerned about the ethical conduct of research involving human subjects, the need for ethics committees is much more pronounced in developing countries, especially African countries, where regulations might be weak and the vulnerabilities of research subjects more systemic, due to disease, poverty and lack of access to health care. Thus, ethics committees in developing countries have the potential to offer the much-needed protection through a rigorous evaluation of research protocols. It is, therefore, disheartening that a study conducted by the World Health Organisation (WHO) Regional Committee for Africa found that only 60 per cent of the (surveyed) member states had functional ethical review committees.[2] While ethics committees have proliferated in Africa in the last few years, their operations are still bedevilled by budgetary constraints, inadequate infrastructure, poor staffing levels and insufficient training for their members. For instance, a recent study of thirty-one ethics review committees across various parts of Africa found that a total of 38 per cent of their members had not received any form of training in health research ethics.[3] The analysis that follows, regarding the functions of ethics committees, puts this tragedy in context.

### *Ethical Review*

A fundamental task of ethics review committees is to ensure that proposed studies are ethically sound. With respect to clinical drug trials, part of this duty could be discharged by applying the normative framework of equipoise already examined in chapter two. More generally, a protocol's ethical validity depends on its compliance with certain popular (four) principles that guide the conduct of research involving human subjects.[4] Research guidelines in many developing countries (for instance, Nigeria, Tanzania, and Uganda) have expressly incorporated these principles, including autonomy, beneficence and justice. Thus, an ethics committee must ensure that a research protocol respects the autonomy of

2 Joses M. Kiriga and Charles Wambebe, 'Status of National Health Research Systems in Ten Countries of the WHO African Region' (2006), 6 BMC Health Services Research 135.

3 A. Nyika, et al., 'Composition, training needs and independence of ethics review committees across Africa: are the gate-keepers rising to the emerging challenges?' (2009), 35 J. Med. Ethics 18–193.

4 Harris observed that the 'four principles constitutes (sic) a useful "checklist" approach to bioethics for those new to the field, and possibly for ethics committees without substantial ethical expertise (of which local research ethics committee is this not true?) approaching new problems': J. Harris, 'In praise of unprincipled ethics' (2003), 29 J. Med. Ethics 303 at 303.

research participants, has a favourable risk-benefit ratio, and must fairly distribute the burdens and benefits of research. Beauchamp and Childress deployed principlism to characterize adherence to these principles (autonomy, beneficence, non-maleficence and justice), as well as projecting them as the criteria for ethical validity in bioethics.[5] Principlism is not a general moral theory; rather, it provides 'a framework for identifying and reflecting on moral problems';[6] it also expresses the 'general values underlying rules in the common morality'.[7] Lee observed that 'principlism has been celebrated as one of the most important methodological inventions of modern practical ethics, particularly in Anglophone scholarship'.[8] While principlism has become a popular analytical framework in bioethics, there is, however, no consensus regarding its utility, sufficiency and universality.[9] For instance, Meslin and colleagues argued that the contents of principlism were too amorphous and lacked the specificity necessary to provide useful guidance on practical moral problems.[10] The authors of principlism appear to have conceded this point and, in the subsequent editions of their book, proceeded to show how the four principles could be specified and balanced.[11] Tom Walker, however, argues that while principlism is a necessary framework in bioethics, it is by no means sufficient.[12] For instance, principlism does not capture other norms by which moral judgements are made by most people who think seriously about morality. Walker illustrates this with recent works in anthropology and psychology which show

5 T.L. Beauchamp and J.F. Childress, *Principles of Biomedical Ethics, 5th edn.* (Oxford: Oxford University Press, 2001), at 12. In the UK, the leading exponent of principlism is Raanan Gillon, see R. Gillon, 'Four Scenarios' (2003), 29 J. Med. Ethics 267–268.

6 Beauchamp and Childress, supra, note 5, at 15.

7 Ibid., at 12.

8 Marvin J.H. Lee, 'The problem of "thick in status, thin in content" in Beauchamp and Childress' principlism' (2010), 36 J. Med. Ethics 525 at 525.

9 Even some proponents of principlism agree that its claims are sometimes either overstated (for instance, Ruth Macklin) or fail to give due weight to the relevance of other complimentary ethical theories, such as virtue ethics (for instance, A.V. Campbell): R. Macklin, 'Applying the four principles' (2003), 29 J. Med. Ethics 275–280; A.V. Campbell, 'The virtues (and vices) of the four principles' (2003), 29 J. Med. Ethics 292–296.

10 E. Meslin, et al., 'Principlism and the ethical appraisal of clinical trials' (1995), 9 Bioethics 399–418. For similar criticisms: S. Holm, 'Not just autonomy – the principles of American biomedical ethics' (1995), 21 J. Med. Ethics 332–338, observing at 337: 'we are presented with a structure for moral reasoning which cannot give any definite answers to moral problems'; J. Harris, 'In praise of unprincipled ethics' (2003), 29 J. Med. Ethics 303 at 303: 'the [four] principles allow massive scope in interpretation and are, frankly, not wonderful as a means of detecting errors and inconsistencies in argument'.

11 Beauchamp and Childress, supra, note 5, at 15–23. Also, T.L. Beauchamp and J.F. Childress, *Principles of Biomedical Ethics, 6th edn* (New York: Oxford University Press, 2009); T.L. Beauchamp, 'Methods and principles in biomedical ethics' (2003), 29 J. Med. Ethics 269–274.

12 Tom Walker, 'What principlism misses' (2009), 35 J. Med. Ethics 229–231.

that some people reflect on moral problems from the ethics of autonomy (respect – not identical with autonomy in principlism), community (interdependency) and divinity (purity), which lie outside the epistemic boundaries of principlism.[13] Thus, principlism does not capture all the norms by which most people identify moral problems and work through moral dilemmas.[14] Principlism also undermines and obfuscates the significant contribution of dignity to the analysis of moral dilemmas.[15] Some of the criticisms above inspired a search for alternative ethical frameworks to be used in the evaluation of research involving human subjects, especially in developing countries. For instance, Benatar and Singer argued that the ethics of international collaborative research should move away from the narrow discourse of research subject protection to a broader view of the standard of care (treatment for participants in the control arm of a trial), involving issues of human rights (social and economic rights) and the linking of research with development in poor countries.[16]

In a more recent work, Benatar and Singer argued that the ethics of research in developing countries should be linked with improvements in health and capacity building;[17] thus, they identified 'two overarching principles that encapsulate the ethical requirements for research associated with moral progress and enhanced social justice in developing countries'.[18] The first principle is that research conducted in developing countries should contribute to improved health care in the host community; this principle, the authors argued, is best realized through the development of collaborative partnerships and effective strategic alliance.[19] The second principle complements the first and entails that research undertaken in developing countries should contribute to sustainable capacity building in research, by enabling 'host country researchers to solve their own research problems in the future'.[20] The authors suggested that the two principles above, underpinned by the value of (global) solidarity, should 'replace a narrow research ethics framework, focused on protection of vulnerable participants, with a broader framework that

13 Ibid., at 229–230.

14 But Sokol argues that the four principles are so indeterminate that it would not be easy to find cases or moral rules that lie outside their confines: D. Sokol, 'Sweetening the scent: commentary on "What principlism misses"' (2009), 35 J. Med. Ethics 232–233.

15 Charles Foster, *Human Dignity in Bioethics and Law* (Oxford: Hart Publishing, 2011). 113–114.

16 S.R. Benatar and P.A. Singer, 'A New Look at International Research Ethics' (2000), 321 BMJ 824–826.

17 S.A. Benatar and P.A. Singer, 'Responsibilities in International Research: A New Look Revisited' (2010), 36 J. Med. Ethics 194–197.

18 Ibid., at 195.

19 A similar proposal was developed by D.W. Dowdy, 'Partnership as an ethical model for medical research in developing countries: the example of the "implementation trial"' (2006), 32 J. Med. Ethics 357–360.

20 S.A. Benatar and P.A. Singer, 'Responsibilities in International Research: A New Look Revisited' (2010), 36 J. Med. Ethics 194 at 195.

could emancipate them and their communities, improve inadequate healthcare systems, promote social justice and foster development'.[21] Similarly, Ezekiel J. Emanuel and his colleagues, drawing from their previous work,[22] articulated a sort of non-exploitation framework as the ethical criterion of clinical research in developing countries;[23] this involves eight principles (collaborative partnership; social value; scientific validity; fair selection of study population; favourable risk-benefit ratio; independent review; informed consent; and respect for recruited participants and study communities) and thirty-one benchmarks that specify practical measures to determine the extent to which clinical research in developing countries satisfies the enumerated principles. Thus, the authors observed that 'these principles and benchmarks constitute a systematic framework that specifies core practical considerations necessary to ethically justify research in developing countries'.[24] In sum, therefore, although principlism is not universally accepted as the criterion of ethical validity in biomedical research, the analysis below draws on its framework to highlight the ethical review of research involving human subjects in Africa. However, non-maleficence is not given a separate treatment because it is collapsed with the analysis of beneficence. This is consistent with the approach in the *Belmont Report*,[25] although Beauchamp and Childress analysed non-maleficence as a separate ethical principle.[26]

*Autonomy*

Autonomy is the freedom of action; it is the right of a human being to make a choice based on the factors of agency and liberty.[27] Being autonomous individuals, research participants must not be involved in a study without their informed consent. Similarly, they should be able to withdraw from a study at any time without being subjected to any direct or indirect punishment, nor required to provide a reason for doing so.[28] Protection of the right to withdraw from a research procedure is crucial in most African countries because physicians

---

21 Ibid., at 196.

22 E.J. Emanuel, et al., 'What makes clinical research ethical?' (2000), 283 JAMA 2701–2711.

23 E.J. Emanuel, et al., 'What Makes Clinical Research in Developing Countries Ethical? The Benchmarks of Ethical Research' (2004), 189 Journal of Infectious Diseases 930–937.

24 Ibid., at 935.

25 National Commission, *Belmont Report: Ethical Principles and Guidelines for the Protection of Human Subjects of Research* (National Commission, 1979).

26 Beauchamp and Childress, supra, note 5, at 113–164.

27 Ibid., at 57–58.

28 But consider the proposal that a subject's mindless and whimsical withdrawal from research, which imperils the validity of the result of the research, should be compensated through a legally enforceable contract: Sarah J.L. Edwards, 'Assessing the Remedy: The Case for Contracts in Clinical Trials' (2011), 11 The American Journal of Bioethics 3–12; for a criticism of this proposal: John A Lynch, '"Through a Glass Darkly": Researcher

and researchers are seen as authority figures. To discharge this function, ethics committees in Africa demand that research proposals should be accompanied by consent forms and an information sheet that give details of relevant information to potential volunteers. Such information must include the pertinent and mandatory statement that volunteers are free to withdraw from the research with impunity. Considering the lack of local (African) linguistic equivalence for many biologic and scientific concepts, ethics committees encourage investigators to develop strategic and practical means of enhancing subjects' understanding of the terms of the protocol.[29] For instance, Phoenix suggested the 'use of literacy tests on consent documents'.[30] Also relevant is the concept of a battery-operated 'speaking' book, which deploys a user-friendly and simple English (with local translations) to educate communities with low levels of literacy on what it means to be part of a clinical trial; such a device is expected to complement the informed consent process.[31] Furthermore, the guideline in Nigeria provides that the consent form and information sheet must be capable of being understood by a person with at least nine years of formal education in Nigeria, and that an ethics committee 'may require researchers to provide translations of consent process appropriate to the socio-cultural characteristics of the population to be studied'.[32] Guidelines also make special provisions for obtaining the consent of incompetent persons, such as minors and incompetent adults.[33] Due to the oral culture prevailing in most parts of Africa, ethics committees do not insist on written signed consent forms, though the giving of oral consent must be documented by the investigator.[34] Another feature of the consent process in Africa, that takes its peculiar culture and tradition into consideration, is the power conferred on ethics committees to observe the consent process in order to ensure compliance with ethical guidelines.[35]

---

Ethnocentrism and the Demonization of Research Participants' (2011), 11 The American Journal of Bioethics 22–23.

29 Consider the use of the concept of surgery or 'an operation', familiar in local Malawian language, to explain research autopsy on paediatric cadavers: J.M. Mfutso-Bengu and T.E. Taylor, 'Ethical Jurisdictions in Biomedical Research' (2002), 18 Trends in Parasitology 231.

30 Janet A. Phoenix, 'Ethical considerations of research involving minorities, the poorly educated and/or low-income populations' (2002), 24 Neurotoxicology and Teratology 475 at 476.

31 Ames Dhai, et al., 'A pilot study evaluating an intervention designed to raise awareness of clinical trials among potential participants in the developing world' (2010), 36 J. Med. Ethics 238–242.

32 Nigerian Federal Ministry of Health, *National Code of Health Research Ethics* (FMoH, 2007) at 37 and 40.

33 For instance, Uganda National Council for Science and Technology, *National Guidelines for Research Involving Humans as Research Participants* (UNCST, 2007) at 33 and 35–36.

34 Ibid., at 26; Nigerian Code, supra, note 32, at 39.

35 Nigerian Code, supra, note 32, at 17; UNCST, supra, note 33, at 16.

Furthermore, ethics committees recognize (and ought to recognize) the hierarchical social and communal tradition in Africa which might require the investigator to obtain a supplemental consent, that is, consent of a third party in addition to the individual consent of the research participant.[36] The third party might be the community leader or elder(s), chief, father or husband. There is a serious debate on whether this second consent is necessary, but most of the issues in the debate border on ethical relativism. While this is not the place to resolve the controversy, it must be said that there is an increasing recognition that consent procedures should be responsive to the peculiarities of the social and political traditions in Africa.[37] Some African scholars, for instance, accept that the consent of a relevant third party (chief, elders, husband, or father) is desirable provided it is given as an addition to the voluntary and individual consent of the research subject. Rather than undermine the autonomy of the African research subject, such additional consent can be a catalyst for the process of individual informed consent. Thus, Diallo and his colleagues argued that the involvement (and consent) of a community chief, or community leaders, would help to disseminate information relevant to the proposed study and thereby assist in the recruitment of subjects based on informed consent.[38] Similarly, Ndebele observed that once the context allows for the making of a free decision on participation, and the volunteers are not (directly or indirectly) pressurized to enrol as subjects in research approved by their community leaders, it does not hurt to get the permission of the community: 'The community leaders … need to be taken as gatekeepers and, as such, as another layer of protection besides the ethics committee as they assist in ensuring that their people are protected'.[39] Ndebele also observed that 'acknowledging the existence of gatekeepers is to acknowledge the existence of other political systems and structures besides the Western democratic model of governance which hinges on individual freedoms'.[40] The opinions above seem to be consistent with most research guidelines in Africa. While these guidelines clearly emphasize the necessity and sufficiency of voluntary and individual informed consent, they still encourage investigators to obtain the consent of a relevant third party. For instance,

36 For a good analysis of this cultural aspect of informed consent: Patricia A. Marshall, 'Human Rights, Cultural Pluralism, and International Health Research' (2005), 25 Theoretical Medicine and Bioethics 529–557.

37 For insightful analysis of the consent provisions in the Nigerian guidelines, see Joseph O. Fadare, 'Informed Consent in Human Subject Research: A Comparison of Current International and Nigerian Guidelines' (2010), 5(1) Journal of Empirical Research on Human Research Ethics 67–74.

38 D.A. Diallo, et al., 'Community Permission for medical Research in Developing Countries' (2005), 41 Clinical Infectious Diseases 255–260.

39 Paul Ndebele, 'African thoughts and perspectives on research ethics: Identifying some central problem areas', in The ENRECA Health Research Network, *Ethics and Health Research in Low Income Societies: Ethical Capacity Building – Obstacles and Challenges* (Copenhagen: ENRECA, 2003), at 17.

40 Ibid., at 18.

the Ugandan guideline provides that 'a community leader may not consent to the participation of community members in research without the individual research participant's informed consent'.[41] In other words, a community leader's consent is not sufficient for an individual's participation in research unless it is supported by the informed consent of that individual. In stronger terms, the Nigerian guidelines even require the submission of 'an agreement between sponsor, institution, researchers and the community indicating adequate community consultation and agreement with the proposed research'.[42]

*Beneficence*

In addition to ensuring the autonomy of research participants, ethics committees in Africa must also ensure that a protocol evinces a favourable risk-benefit ratio. In general, the principle of beneficence requires that potential harm to research participants must be reasonable in relation to the anticipated benefits of the study.[43] In other words, the risks must not outweigh the benefits of the research. Chapter one examined research scandals in Africa in which volunteers were exposed to unnecessary and avoidable harm, arguably in breach of the principle of beneficence. To avoid similar tragedies in the future, ethics committees in Africa must take their beneficent role very seriously. However, the calculation of risks and benefits of research are not open to exact mathematical quantification because they depend on a variable set of factors and circumstances. These include the type of research being conducted, the product or process being tested, the phase of the research (in case of drug trials), the circumstances of the research subjects and the locality of the research. In any event, ethics committees must ensure that research participants are not exposed to foreseeable harm and that a framework exists for the compensation of research-related injuries. Similarly, the disease and poverty that characterize the African landscape impose a special obligation on ethics committees in relation to the assessment of harm. For instance, participation in an HIV/AIDS study in Africa might (in the case of unjustifiable disclosure) entail risks beyond those foreseeable in a developed country. People living with HIV/AIDS (PLWA) in Africa are prone to social stigmatization and discrimination that go beyond those suffered by PLWA in most Western countries. In addition, PLWA in Africa stand the risk of being denied employment and, thus, their economic means of livelihood.[44] Consequently, ethics committees reviewing an HIV/AIDS protocol (or other diseases with a social stigma) must ensure not only the adequacy of arrangements for the protection of the privacy of research participants and the confidentiality of data obtained from them; such committees must also adopt creative approaches to risk assessment that encompass all types of harms, whether physical, psychological, social or economic.

41 UNCST, supra, note 33, at 23.

42 Nigerian Code, supra, note 32, at 30. Also: TANHER Forum, *Guidelines on Ethics for Health Research in Tanzania* (2001) at 49–50.

43 Beauchamp and Childress, supra, note 5, at 165–214

44 A South African case in point is *Hoffman v South African Airways* (2000) 1 SA 1.

For this reason, Monnye criticized the South African research guideline[45] for clearly (or expressly) recognizing physical and psychological harms, but failing to refer explicitly to social and economic harms.[46]

The economic and socio-cultural risks latent in an HIV/AIDS protocol in Africa, which might be unanticipated by an ethics committee, are not dissimilar to those involved in an HIV/AIDS study in China. As in Africa, a positive diagnosis for HIV/AIDS in China is widely perceived to lead to the discrimination and stigmatization of the victim. Worse still, a person diagnosed with HIV/AIDS in China might be exposed to involuntary detention.[47] In an interesting analysis relating to the standards that should guide a US Institutional Review Board (IRB) in the evaluation of cross-cultural protocols, White deployed an AIDS research in China to demonstrate the peculiar research risks arising from socio-political and cultural systems that do not share Western concepts of human rights. The AIDS research involved a proposal by some American scientists to provide training for Chinese epidemiologists in risk-behaviour assessment for sexually transmitted diseases (including HIV/AIDS). Pursuant to the protocol, the Chinese trainees would return to China in order to test a questionnaire developed in the course of their training, and would also conduct a face-to-face interview with patients attending a clinic for sexually transmitted diseases.[48] Although the research protocol was approved by the relevant institutional ethics committees in the USA and China, White argued that the approval given by the US IRB carried a false assumption that the IRB members were familiar with the social and political contexts of HIV/AIDS research in China.[49] She further argued that since the US IRB members were geographically, politically, and culturally distanced from China, they were not in a position to identify, nor deal with, important (but unanticipated) socio-political risks associated with the study, such as involuntary detention for a positive diagnosis of HIV/AIDS.[50] While White's observations were made in the context of a foreign review of a collaborative study, they are also relevant to the local review of a collaborative protocol in Africa and highlight the need for sensitivity

45 MRC (South Africa), *Guidelines on Ethics for Medical Research* (MRC, 2001–2002), paragraph 10.6.1.

46 Segoane L. Monnye, 'Protection of Human Participants from Risks in Biomedical Research: An Analysis of the Law of South Africa and International Ethical Guidelines' (2003), 22 Med. Law 73–94.

47 Mary T. White, 'Guidelines for IRB Review of International Collaborative Medical Research: A Proposal' (1999), 27 Law, Medicine & Ethics 87–94; Y.G. Wang, 'AIDS Policy and Bioethics: Ethical Dilemmas Facing China in HIV Prevention' (1997), 11 Bioethics 323–27; B.R. Liu, 'Legal Regulations of AIDS Detection and Administration in P.R. China' (1992), 3 International Journal of Bioethics 25–7; M.L. McCall, 'AIDS Quarantine Law in the International Community: Health and Safety Measures or Human Rights Violations?' (1993), 15 Loyola of Los Angeles International and Comparative Law Annual 1001–28.

48 White, supra, note 47, at 88.

49 Ibid., at 88–89.

50 Ibid., at 88–89.

to culture-specific risks. Unlike US IRB members, however, ethics committee members in Africa cannot be said to be ignorant of the socio-political and cultural contexts of biomedical research in their territories. Nevertheless, there is a need for vigilance in order to protect subjects from risks that do not appear on protocols but arise from systemic cultural, social and political inequities.

*Justice*

As part of its mandate, an ethics committee must ensure that a research protocol satisfies the requirements of justice. There are different conceptions of justice, including procedural justice, formal justice, corrective justice, restorative justice, and distributive justice.[51] In the research setting, however, justice mainly refers to distributive justice.[52] Until recently, many collaborative research studies undertaken in Africa failed to satisfy this requirement. For instance, there were cases where the research was not responsive to diseases common in the community or was merely undertaken to obtain data for drug approval in a developed country.[53] The Pfizer trovan study examined in chapter one is illustrative. Thus, ethics committees in Africa need to be vigilant in assessing the distribution of the benefits and risks of research. Accordingly, they must ensure that a proposed study addresses a health condition prevalent in the community (or country) from where the subjects are recruited (even if the health condition is also present in other countries), and that a particular community is not habitually used as research subjects for a particular disease, unless this can be justified by the investigator. As well, ethics committees should ensure that there are arrangements in place for making the product of the study (in the case of drug or vaccine trials) available to the participants and members of their community (and, possibly, to the country as a whole). A qualitative study in Kenya, testing the views of potential HIV/AIDS research participants, clinician researchers and administrators on the fairness of discontinuing (beneficial) therapy after a trial, found that all the stakeholders regarded the discontinuance of (post-trial) therapy as unfair.[54] At the international level, however, there is a debate on whether post-trial benefits should be obligatory or directory.[55] While various international guidelines word the requirement differently, most of them fail to impose a clear ethical or legal obligation. For

51 Peter Westen, 'The Empty Idea of Equality' (1982), 95 Harv. L. Rev. 537.

52 Mary Simmerling, et al., 'Introducing A New Paradigm For Ethical Research In The Social Sciences: Part 1' (2007), 101 Northwestern University Law Review 837 at 856–857.

53 A. Costello and A. Zumla, 'Moving to research partnerships in developing countries' (2000), 321 BMJ 827–829; T.T. Edejer, 'North-South research partnerships: the ethics of carrying out research in developing countries' (1999), 319 BMJ 438–441.

54 D.N. Schaffer, et al., 'Equitable treatment for HIV/AIDS clinical trial participants: a focus group study of patients, clinician researchers, and administrators in western Kenya' (2006), 32 J. Med. Ethics 55–60.

55 R. Macklin, *Double Standards in Medical Research in Developing Countries* (Cambridge: Cambridge University Press, 2004), 77–82.

instance, CIOMS guidelines only require sponsors and researchers to make products resulting from research 'reasonably available' for the benefit of the population or community involved in the research.[56] As the commentary to CIOMS guidelines acknowledged, the concept of 'reasonable availability' is 'complex and will need to be determined on a case-by-case basis'.[57] The Declaration of Helsinki, while using a sort of obligatory tone, however restricts access to post-trial benefits to the trial participants: 'At the conclusion of the study, patients entered into the study are entitled to ... share any benefits that result from it, for example access to interventions identified as beneficial in the study or to other appropriate care or benefits'.[58] In a directory fashion, similar to CIOMS above, the US National Bioethics Advisory Commission recommended that '[R]esearchers and sponsors in clinical trials should make reasonable, good faith efforts before the initiation of a trial to secure, at its conclusion, continued access for all participants to needed experimental interventions that have been proven effective for the participants'.[59] More emphatically, the Nuffield Council on Bioethics, while accepting that the availability of post-trial treatment should be discussed at the planning stage of research, imposes the main responsibility for its provision on the host country's government.[60] Notice that while most of the guidelines above fail to impose any clear legal and ethical duty on the provision of post-trial benefits, they also vary in the stipulation of the class of people entitled to such benefits. For instance, although the Declaration of Helsinki limits the class of beneficiaries to research participants, CIOMS extends the class to the community at large.[61]

Arguably, the provision of post-trial benefits are better couched in non-obligatory terms, such as those embodied in most of the guidelines above.[62] An absolute requirement to make post-trial benefits (such as the proven intervention in a drug trial) available to the participants or their community might be counter-

---

56 Council for International Organisations of Medical Sciences/WHO, *International Guidelines for Biomedical Research Involving Human Subjects* (Geneva; CIOMS, 2002) Guidelines 10 and 21.

57 Ibid., at 53.

58 World Medical Association, *Declaration of Helsinki: Ethical Principles for Medical Research Involving Human Subjects* (59th WMA General Assembly, Seoul, 2008) Art. 33.

59 National Bioethics Advisory Commission (NBAC), *Ethical and Policy Issues in International Research: Clinical Trials in Developing Countries* (Bethesda, MD: NBAC, 2001) at 74.

60 Nuffield Council on Bioethics, *The Ethics of Research Related to Healthcare in Developing Countries* (London: NCB, 2002) at 122–125.

61 For analysis of these differences and their implications, see Macklin, supra, note 55, at 82–88.

62 In contrast, it was argued from the perspectives of justice and beneficence that the provision of post-trial benefits should be obligatory: Zhiyong Zong, 'Should post-trial provision of beneficial experimental interventions be mandatory in developing countries' (2008), 34 J. Med. Ethics 188–192.

productive. For instance, such a mandatory prescription ignores that the distribution and administration of drugs are matters subject to the requirements of a particular country, and therefore beyond the control of an investigator or sponsor. In other words, even if a sponsor makes a successful investigational drug available to the relevant authorities of a country, there is no guarantee that it will reach the research subjects or the community involved in the study. Furthermore, an absolute post-trial obligation might defeat the conduct of a potentially beneficial research in Africa, especially where the sponsor and investigator are unable to commit to the financial expenses involved. Moreover, insistence on post-trial benefits ignores other significant benefits that accrue from the conduct of international collaborative research, such as the training of healthcare or research personnel, construction of healthcare facilities and other physical infrastructure, provision of public health measures and health services, additional diagnostic tests, distribution of medications and vaccinations, provision of emergency evacuation services, and collateral benefits such as employment and enhanced economic activities, determining disease prevalence in the studied population and drug resistance patterns, providing antibiotics for respiratory infections and the digging of bore holes for the supply of clean water.[63] Consequently, it has been suggested that the imposition of post-trial obligation does not necessarily avoid exploitation (since it is concerned with the type rather than the quantum of benefits) and should be replaced with a 'Fair Benefits' framework which, in addition to supplementing other ethical principles, would ensure that the research is relevant to the health needs of a developing country population, does not exploit the vulnerabilities of the studied population, and must pose few risks to the participants.[64]

The concept of 'fair benefits', which emphasizes both collateral benefits and interventional products of research, resonates with the 'development-oriented approach' to justice formulated by Alex London[65] and endorsed by Angela Wasunna.[66] London criticized the current approach to ethics in international research which defines justice in terms of compliance with the ethical principles of non-maleficence, autonomy, and beneficence. This 'minimalist view', as he

63 M. El Setouhy, et al., 'Fair Benefits for Research in Developing Countries' (2002), 298 Science 2133–2134. It was even argued that the obligation to provide collateral benefits should be standardized as an 'infrastructure charge' policed by ethics review committees in developing countries: Angela Ballantyne, 'Benefits to Research Subjects in International Trials: Do They Reduce Exploitation or Increase Undue Inducement?' (2008), 8 Developing World Bioethics 178–191.

64 El Setouhy, supra, note 63. The 'Fair Benefits' framework was strongly criticized by Udo Schuklenk, who argued that communities in most developing countries lack the education and expertise necessary to extract fair benefits from the developed world's for-profit trial sponsors: U. Schuklenk, 'For-Profit Clinical Trials in Developing Countries – Those Troublesome Patient Benefits' (2010), 10 The American Journal of Bioethics 52–54.

65 Alex J. London, 'Justice and the Human Development Approach to International Research' (2005), 35 Hastings Centre Report 24–37.

66 Angela Wasuna, 'Researchers Abroad' (2005), Hastings Centre Report 3.

calls it, militates against critical and significant considerations of much larger and broader social justice issues that constitute the background of international collaborative research. Although London criticized the 'Fair Benefits' framework for being significantly minimalist in orientation,[67] his support of microbicide research in developing countries, as a high priority health activity that illustrates his vision of justice, is consistent with the principles espoused by the 'Fair Benefits' framework. Wasunna's contribution to this debate, however, explored the claim that political corruption, which obviates a fair distribution of research benefits in developing countries, could be overcome by allowing researchers and sponsors to deal directly with the relevant subjects or concerned community. In other words, the question is whether researchers/sponsors should give direct assistance to the relevant population without involving their politically elected representatives.[68] Wasunna, however, argued that such direct assistance might be inconsistent with the law of the developing country involved; it also has the potential to undermine the developing country's sovereignty.[69] Thus, in agreement with London, Wasunna suggested a 'strategic, development-oriented approach that strengthens the local institutions that can evolve into vital bedrocks for democracy and reform'.[70] Consistent with the views above, some African research guidelines have adopted a liberal and flexible approach to the provision of research benefits. For instance, the Nigerian research guideline provides that international collaborative studies should be 'integrated with comprehensive capacity building, technology transfer and health care delivery strategies that address significant local health problems and add value to local participants of research, including researchers, institutions, communities and the country.'[71] As regards post-trial benefits, the Nigerian guideline requires investigators to provide 'assurances that reasonable efforts shall be made to ensure that the benefits of research are made available to the community where the research was conducted'.[72] Similarly, the Ugandan guideline directs that if 'the investigational product is found to be beneficial, the investigator should assist to secure its provision, without charge, to participants in the research project following the conclusion of the research'.[73] Arguably, the non-absolute rendition of post-trial obligation embodied in African guidelines above is an indirect acknowledgement that other benefits accrue from the conduct of research; it might be that both quantitatively and qualitatively, these other benefits are enough to satisfy the requirements of justice.

67 London, supra, note 65, at 26.

68 Although Alex London would not agree that such guidelines have gone beyond the minimalist approach to research benefits or ethics. London, supra, note 65.

69 Ibid.

70 Ibid.

71 Nigerian Code, supra, note 32, at 35.

72 Ibid., at 32.

73 UNCST, supra, note 33, at 30.

*Scientific Review*

In addition to ethical validity, an ethics committee should ensure that a research protocol is scientifically sound. There is a debate however as to whether the scientific and ethical reviews of protocols should be conducted as separate activities, and by different review bodies. In other words, are research ethics committees bound to accept the science of a protocol as presented? Put differently, can research ethics committees, mainly concerned with the ethics of research and protection of research subjects, review the science of a protocol and, if found scientifically unsound, reject same for that reason? Dawson and Yentis strongly argued that the distinction between science and ethics in relation to research ethics review is not only incoherent; ethics committees should be also obligated to review research protocols for their scientific validity; thus ethics committees should have the power to reject any protocol that is based on poor science.[74] The Nigerian guideline adopts this approach, and stipulates that for 'research to be ethical, it must have scientific validity'.[75] In the same vein, Emanuel and colleagues observed that '[S]cience and ethics do not conflict; valid science is an ethical requirement'.[76] Thus, research that is scientifically unsound is bound to be ethically indefensible.[77] This correlation (between science and ethics) was clearly adumbrated by McDonald, who argued that it is morally blameworthy to execute a protocol that is scientifically impaired and unlikely to produce any useful result, and thus, expose participants to unnecessary and avoidable harm:

> Such risks may be substantial, e.g., death or major trauma due to the bad design of clinical trials of a new drug or exposure to violence by the breach of confidence of a victim of sexual abuse. Or the risk may be low, in which case there is a misuse and abuse of the research subject's time, effort and good will. The second reason focuses on veracity and promise keeping. Through the informed consent process, a researcher implicitly assures potential subjects that the research is likely to contribute to the advancement of knowledge.[78]

---

74 A.J. Dawson and S.M. Yentis, 'Contesting the science/ethics distinction in the review of clinical research' (2007), 33 J. Med. Ethics 165–167.

75 Nigerian Code, supra, note 32, at 35.

76 E.J. Emanuel, et al., 'What Makes Clinical Research in Developing Countries Ethical? The Benchmarks of Ethical Research' (2004), 189 Journal of Infectious Diseases 930 at 933.

77 For similar reason, the Warner Report was criticized for divorcing scientific review from ethical review: M. Epstein and D.L. Wingate, 'Is the NHS Research Ethics Committees System to be Outsourced to a Low-Cost Offshore Call Centre? Reflections on Human Research Ethics After the Warner Report' (2007), 33 J. Med. Ethics 45–47.

78 M. McDonald, The Governance of Health Research Involving Human Subjects (Ottawa: Law Commission of Canada, 2000), at 31–32.

Consequently, an ethics committee must ensure that a protocol's design and methodology are consistent with sound scientific principles.[79] Further guidance is provided by the Nigerian Code:

> Research lacking clear scientific objectives; using invalid methodology; that is underpowered; lacking equipoise (for clinical studies); whose operationalising plans are inadequate within the context of the environment where research would be conducted; lacks plausible data analysis plan (including a specific role for a Data and Safety Monitoring Board [DSMB] in clinical trials) and research with biased measurements of outcome is unethical.

Sound scientific review of research protocols is so important that some African research guidelines provide for a separate institutional committee (Scientific Committee) which reviews only the scientific aspects of a protocol.[80] A scientific review is usually done before the submission of a protocol to an institutional ethics committee.[81] The World Health Organisation (WHO) African Regional Office found that 50 per cent of its member states have scientific review committees.[82] The conduct of separate scientific review (by a Scientific Committee) does not, however, preclude an ethics committee from assessing (or re-assessing) the scientific validity of a protocol. For instance, the Ugandan guideline stipulates that it is 'important for IRCs (institutional review committees) to review the scientific soundness of the research proposals'.[83] Similarly, the Malawian research guideline provides that ethics committees must review 'proposals for scientific, professional and ethical merits'.[84] To this end, research guidelines in Africa usually require the composition of an ethics review committee to include a scientific member.[85] In meeting this requirement, some ethics committees in Africa have gone too far in the appointment of scientists as members and have been accused of lopsided compositions in favour of scientific members.[86]

---

79 Nigerian Code, supra, note 32, at 35.

80 UNCST, supra, note 33, at 7–8.

81 Ibid., at 7.

82 Joses M. Kiriga and Charles Wambebe, 'Status of National Health Research Systems in Ten Countries of the WHO African Region' (2006), 6 BMC Health Services Research 135.

83 UNCST, supra, note 33, at 15.

84 NRCM, *Procedures and Guidelines for the Conduct of Research in Malawi* (2002), 3.0, and 10.0.

85 For instance, Ethiopian Science and Technology Commission, *National Health Research Ethics* (2005), at 45; UNCST, supra, note 33, at 14; Nigerian Code, supra, note 32, at 13.

86 D.E. Elsayed and N.E. Kass, 'Assessment of Ethical Review Process in Sudan' (2007), 7 Developing World Bioethics 143–148; N.E. Kass, et al., 'The Structure and Function of Research Ethics Committees in Africa: A Case Study' (2007), 4 PLoS Medicine 26–31.

### *Legal Review and Responsibilities*

In addition to ethical and scientific reviews, should protocols be assessed for their legality by research ethics committees? Obviously, this is a debatable question.[87] It has been observed that while researchers are prone to 'court proceedings and to criminal and civil sanctions', as chapters five, six and seven make clear, there is, however, 'no external procedures for assessing the legality of a research project before it takes place'.[88] This follows from the fact that while most international and national guidance documents emphasize the ethical review function of ethics committees, only a few of them refer to issues concerning the legal review of protocols by ethics committees.[89] Interestingly, it might be argued that the functions of ethics committees are essentially legal in nature, although the performance of legal functions sits oddly with the description of a body as an ethics committee. While the literature addressing the legal responsibilities of ethics committees is few and far between, and the topic is generally glossed over by commentators and research guidelines,[90] it is certainly the case that ethics committees must strive to protect the welfare, dignity and rights of human research subjects.[91] This protective public function implies that ethics committees are obliged to undertake the legal assessment of research protocols. For instance, it is arguable that the 'rights' of research subjects, entrusted to the care of ethics committees, should be understood both in their legal (Hohfeldian) and non-legal (moral) senses.[92] The Ugandan guideline illustrates this approach by listing the legal and non-legal rights to which research subjects are entitled.[93] Despite the Ugandan example, giving a

87 Charles Warlow, 'Should research ethics committees be observing the law or working by ethical principles?' (2005), 1 Research Ethics Review 23–26.

88 T.M. Douglas, 'Ethics committees and the legality of research' (2007), 33 J. Med. Ethics 732 at 732.

89 For instance, National Health and Medical Research Council, Australian Research Council, Australian Vice-Chancellors' Committee, National Health and Medical Research Council, *National Statement on Ethical Conduct in Human Research* (Canberra; Commonwealth of Australia, 2007).

90 For a discussion of the ambiguity surrounding the legal function of RECs in England: D. Beyleveld, 'Law, Ethics, and Research Ethics Committees' (2002), 21 Medicine and Law 57–75; and generally: Douglas, supra, note 88.

91 For instance, Department of Health, *Governance Arrangements for NHS Research Ethics Committees* (2001) – GAFREC, provides in paragraph 2.2 that the role of research ethics committee 'is to protect the dignity, rights, safety and wellbeing of all actual and potential research participants'.

92 For Hohfeldian analysis of legal rights in terms of jural relations, see W.N. Hohfeld, 'Some Fundamental Legal Conceptions as Applied in Judicial Reasoning' (1911), 23 Yale Law Journal 16; W.N. Hohfeld, 'Fundamental Legal Conceptions as Applied in Judicial Reasoning' (1917), 26 Yale Law Journal 710.

93 UNCST, supra, note 33, at 3.

clear legal review mandate to ethic committees, ethics committees are generally not considered to have an obligation to review protocols for their legality.

Research guidelines contribute to this ambivalence. For instance, the Department of Health's Research Governance Framework (RGF) provides that '[I]t is not the role or responsibility of NHS research ethics committees to give legal advice, nor are they liable for any of their decision in this respect'.[94] In contrast, GAFREC requires ethics committees 'to have due regard to the requirements of relevant regulatory agencies and of applicable law'.[95] The two provisions above appear to be conflicting. In line with the RGF, John Saunders observed that although the 'work of ethical review is not primarily about the law,' yet 'the REC member ... should have some background understanding of legal issues – the basic ones arising from the European Clinical Trials Directive ..., the Mental Health Act, the Human Tissue Act and the legal background to issues of consent, confidentiality, data protection and indemnity'.[96] Roy-Toole roundly condemned the RGF and GAFREC provisions, arguing that ethics committees have a clear duty to consider and give an opinion on the legality or illegality of a protocol. He therefore opined that the 'law must be applied in an ethical review and in the formal opinion of the ethics committee. The committee must deal with illegality and the method of their dealing is to be reflected in their final opinion'.[97] In support of the legal review functions of ethics committees, Stephen Baker and colleagues argued that since ethics committees are analogous to public authorities, they have an obligation to protect the legal rights of research participants by ensuring compliance with the UK Human Rights Act 1998, the Data Protection Act 1998 and the Human Tissue Act 2004.[98] Furthermore, ethics committees, being emanations of the State 'must obey EC law over any contradictory domestic law'.[99] Similar arguments in support of legal review by ethics committees were made by Lehtonen and Halila in the context of research regulation in Finland. Thus, the authors argued that since ethics committees in Finland are creatures of regional authorities, they must be considered as public bodies bound by the norms

---

94 Department of Health, Research *Governance Framework for Health and Social Care* (2005).

95 GAFREC, supra, note 91, at paragraph 2.6.

96 John Saunders, 'More Guidelines on Research Ethics?' (2007), 33 J. Med. Ethics 683.

97 Christopher Roy-Toole, 'Illegality in the research protocol: the duty of research ethics committees under the 2001 Clinical Trials Directive' (2008), 4 Research Ethics Review 111 at 115. For a similar line of argument, see Desmond R. Laurence, 'Research ethics committees and the law: indemnity and independence' (2006), 2 Research Ethics Review 140–143.

98 Stephen Baker, et al., 'Research Ethics Committees and the Law in the UK', in D. Beyleveld, et al., *Research Ethics Committees, Data Protection and Medical Research in European Countries* (Aldershot, Ashgate Publishing, 2005) at 271–289.

99 Ibid., at 281. Also: *Foster v British Gas Plc* [1990] ECR 1–3313.

of administrative law.[100] Consequently, the 'RECs in Finland can only approve studies that are considered lawful'.[101] The Finnish position is further clarified by section 17 of the Medical Research Act, which mandates ethics committees to 'examine whether the research plan has taken account of the provisions of this Act, the provisions on data protection, the international obligations concerning the status of research subjects and the regulations and guidelines that govern medical research'.[102] In France, however, the uncertainty surrounding the legal review function of ethics committees is minimized through the making of a regulatory distinction between 'ethics committees' and 'legal committees'.

However, French ethics committees do not undertake the actual review of research proposals. Rather, French ethics committees concentrate on leading discussions and reflections on ethical issues relating to a particular area of biomedicine. Reports of such committees have the potential to influence future legislation relating to the subject matter of the report. Consequently, concerns have been raised as to the legitimacy and impact of such committees on the democratic process.[103] In Canada, however, Verdun-Jones and Weisstub observed that the habitual conduct of general reflection on ethical issues is certainly not one of the functions of research ethics boards (REB) in Canada as traditionally understood both in Canada and the USA: 'One major problem with the localized nature of the IRB system is that the boards themselves do not engage in general reflection about the nature of the broad ethical principles that should guide research in the United States'.[104] For this reason, Katz recommended that a separate entity should be established in the USA to develop, reflect and debate on important ethical policies with a view to providing advice to institutional review boards:

> The policy questions underlying the tensions between the inviolability of subjects of research and advancing the frontiers of knowledge require more careful articulation and resolution than can be gleaned from the federal regulations so far enacted. The concerns I have raised and the recommendations I have made need to be examined, debated and decided by a national regulatory body to which the IRBs can also turn for advice and guidance on difficult problems that require resolution.[105]

---

100 Lasse A. Lehtonen and Ritva Halila, 'The General Legal Responsibility of Research Ethics Committees in Finland', in Beyleveld, et al. (eds), supra, note 98, at 46.

101 Ibid., at 46.

102 Medical Research Act, No. 488/1999, as amended by 295/2004 (Finland).

103 Minou B. Friele, 'Do Committees Ru(i)n the Bio-Political Culture? On the Democratic Legitimacy of Bioethical Committees' (2003), 17 Bioethics 301–318.

104 Simon Verdun-Jones and David N. Weisstub, 'The Regulation of Biomedical Research Experimentation in Canada: Developing an Effective Apparatus for the Implementation of Ethical Principles in a Scientific Milieu' (1997), 28 Ottawa L. Rev. 297 at 310.

105 J. Katz, 'Human Experimentation and Human Rights' (1993), 38 Saint Louis University L.J. 7 at 39.

Although the US National Bioethics Advisory Commission (NBAC) and the UK Nuffield Council on Bioethics currently perform, to a large extent, the ethical and policy roles articulated by Katz, yet both bodies, in contrast to France, cannot rightly be described as ethics committees whether in the US or the UK.

While only one ethics committee is statutorily established in France, that is, the National Consultative Ethics Committee (CCNE), there are, however, a few research organizations that developed their own (non-statutory) ethics committees, such as the National Centre for Scientific Research (CNRS). The protection of research subjects in France is the responsibility of bodies known as the Consultative Committees for the Protection of Persons Participating in Biomedical Research (CCPPRBs). Judging from their remits, these are basically legal committees because they are clearly given the powers to conduct a legal assessment of research proposals. CCPPRBs were established under a 1988 French legislation that makes their consultation, opinion and approval mandatory for the conduct of biomedical research involving human subjects. This law was amended in 2004 to implement the European Directive 2001/20/EC of 4 April 2001 on Good Clinical Practice; consequent upon the amendment, the CCPPRBs are currently known as the 'Committees for the Protection of Persons'.[106] Although the French Code of Public Health requires CCPPRBs to be composed in a manner that 'guarantee(s) their independence and diversity of knowledge in the field of biomedicine and in relation to ethical, social, psychological and legal issues',[107] yet Brigitte Feuillet argued that 'these authorities (CCPPRBs) cannot be considered as ethics committees. Rather, they are groups with a multidisciplinary composition responsible for verifying that the legal rules relating to the protection of the person involved in a research project are respected'.[108] As Feuillet further argued, the opinion of a CCPPRB is not ethical but legal in nature because it verifies the conformity of a protocol with the rules for the protection of research subjects. While Feuillet's analysis of the legal review functions of ethics committees was clearly made in the context of the French regulatory system, it is arguable that her observations are transposable to other jurisdictions. Feuillet even hinted at this possibility in her observation that the European Directive of 4 April 2001 (mentioned above) required the intervention of an ethics committee (in biomedical research) for the protection of the rights and welfare of research participants; according to Feuillet, this means that 'the committee concerned is actually an authority responsible for ensuring the protection of the person and of his or her fundamental rights rather than an ethics committee *stricto sensu*'.[109] Thus, Feuillet's arguments suggest that what is

---

106 Law Relating to the Policies of Public Health, Official Journal no. 185 of 11 August 2004, 14277.

107 Article L.1123–2 of the Code of Public Health.

108 Brigitte Feuillet, 'The Role of Ethics Committees in Relation to French Biomedical Research: Protection of the Person and Personal Data' in D. Beyleveld, et al. (eds.), supra, note 98, at 59.

109 Feuillet in Beyleveld et al., supra, note 98, at 56.

traditionally understood as research 'ethics committees' in countries like England, the USA, Canada, Uganda and Nigeria perform legal, rather than solely ethical, roles since 'the role of an ethics committee should rather be to lead a discussion on ethical issues relating to a particular situation. However, the protection of the person, which includes obtaining his or her consent, is more a matter of defence of fundamental rights than an ethical issue'.[110] Therefore, Feuillet doubts that ethics committees in other jurisdictions should have a function beyond the protection of the legal interests of research subjects. Interestingly, Feuillet's arguments resonate with Riis' observation that the ethical review system is deeply rooted in human rights.[111] Nigeria, however, avoids the controversy (above) relating to the legal review function of ethics committees.

The Nigerian research Code contains express provisions relating to the legal task of ethics committees. For instance, it provides that in addition to possessing the relevant ethical, scientific and professional competence, an ethics committee must be 'able to ascertain the acceptability of proposed research in terms of institutional regulations, applicable laws, and standards of professional conduct and practice'; and to that end, an ethics committee must 'include persons knowledgeable in these areas and whenever feasible, a lawyer'.[112] As chapter five will show, a provision of this type could have significant impacts on the standard adopted for measuring the legal liability of an ethics committee. However, the potential risk of legal liability in relation to ethical and legal reviews of research protocols might dissuade qualified persons from serving as members of ethics committees. For those who are already members, the potential legal liability arising from the duty to conduct a legal assessment of protocols is likely to undermine their enthusiastic and calm review of research protocols. To avoid such consequences, the Nigerian research Code provides that the parent institutions of ethics committees must 'take full responsibility for all actions of each member of HREC in the course of performance of duties related to membership'.[113] Consequently, the parent institution must provide an insurance 'coverage for any liability of any member arising from service on HREC'.[114] In sum, therefore, while uncertainty remains in most jurisdictions in relation to the legal review function of ethics committees, the Nigerian research guideline has taken the happy route of making legal assessment of protocols a clear task of ethics committees in Nigeria; also, by making provisions for compulsory insurance coverage, the Nigerian guideline has ensured

110 Ibid., at 56.

111 Povl Riis, 'The Globalisation of ethical codes for biomedical research', in The ENRECA Health Research Network, Ethics and Health Research in Low Income Societies: Ethical Capacity Building – Obstacles and Challenges (Copenhagen, ENRECA Health Network, 2003) at 23–28.

112 Nigerian Code, supra, note 32, at 13.

113 Ibid., at 8.

114 Ibid.

the protection of members of ethics committees against potential legal liability arising from the discharge of their ethical and legal duties.

### *Fostering of Public Trust and Confidence in Research*

Public trust is essential for any meaningful progress in biomedical research and innovation. Lemmens rightly observed that '[P]ublic trust, ethical conduct in research and scientific progress are mutually dependent'.[115] As chapter one illustrated, research scandals engender loss of confidence in the research enterprise, especially research involving human subjects. The regulatory initiatives examined in chapter three were, in part, intended to restore public confidence in research, which was bruised by the scandals discussed in chapter one. However, more recent research scandals continue to create a climate of distrust. A good example is the paediatric organ and tissue retention scandal in England in 2000 which led to the erosion of confidence in the biomedical research process, as highlighted in the Report of the House of Commons Inquiry set up to investigate the matter.[116] One of the consequences of the paediatric organ and tissue retention scandal in England was the significant drop in the donation rates of transplantable organs and tissues in the period following the scandal.[117] The impact of the scandal was so serious that the (UK) government had to respond legislatively by enacting the Human Tissue Act 2004. In addition to meeting the sting of the scandal, the Human Tissue Act 2004 symbolizes the government's respect for the opinion and trust of British people. Recall that the trovan scandal in Nigeria (examined in chapter one) also had the effect of tarnishing the image or reputation of the Nigerian government. Nigerian people felt betrayed by the questionable roles of their government in the trovan scandal, and accused their government of complicity in that controversial and ethically questionable trial. Due to the trovan scandal, many Nigerians lost their trust in biomedical researchers. The prevailing climate of mistrust engendered by the trovan scandal was so intense that it disrupted the polio immunization programme run by the government in 2004. When this sort of mistrust becomes pervasive, it tends to be construed or misconstrued as an attack on science, or that 'scientists are objects of suspicion and are on the defensive'.[118]

---

115 Trudo Lemmens, 'In the Name of National Security: Lessons from the Final Report on the Human Radiation Experiments' (1999), 6 European Journal of Health Law 7 at 23.

116 The House of Commons, *The Royal Liverpool Children's Inquiry* (London: House of Commons, 2001). Also, Margaret Brazier, 'Retained organs: ethics and humanity' (2002), 22 Legal Stud. 550 at 556.

117 Generally, Brazier, supra, note 116.

118 John Harris, 'Scientific Research is a Moral Duty' (2005), 31 J. Med. Ethics 242. For a refutation of Harris' thesis: Sandra Shapshay and Kenneth D. Dimple, 'Participation in Biomedical Research is an Imperfect Moral Duty: A Response to John Harris' (2007), 33 J. Med. Ethics 414–417.

In sum, therefore, there is a need to foster trust in the biomedical research process.[119] Caulfield and colleagues observed that trust is necessary for the public acceptance of research and the conduct of clinical trials; without 'trust patients may hesitate to participate in research protocols'.[120] Therefore, one of the important functions of research ethics committees is to forge or deepen trust in the biomedical enterprise.[121] Interestingly, the establishment of trust in the research process helps to generate more funds for research. For instance, it was suggested that the emergence of institutional review boards in the USA was partly responsible for the progressive increase in biomedical research budgets and funding in that country.[122]

### *Monitoring of Approved Research*

The monitoring of approved research is an important function of ethics committees. As chapter three highlighted, ethics committees in most African countries are required to monitor the execution of any study which they reviewed and approved. Monitoring is, however, an onerous and resource-intensive responsibility. Considering that most ethics committees in Africa are inadequately funded, and lack sufficient manpower and relevant infrastructures, it is unlikely that their monitoring role would be effectively discharged. For similar reasons, it might not be even sensible to expect ethics committees in Africa to embark upon the monitoring of approved research. However, ethics committees in Africa might reduce the cost of monitoring approved research by engaging an expert monitor. The cost of hiring such an expert monitor might well be beyond the budget of most ethics committees in Africa. Unsurprisingly, most ethics committees in Africa adopt a practical approach to their monitoring duty, by asking investigators to submit periodic reports that provide detailed information concerning the research they have already done.[123]

---

119 D. Shalala, 'Protecting Research Subjects – What Must be Done' (2000), 343 New Eng. J. Med. 808–810; F. Miller, 'Trusting Doctors: Tricky Business When It Comes to Clinical Research' (2001), 81 Boston University Law Review 423–456.

120 Timothy Caulfield, et al., 'Research Ethics and the Role of the Professional Bodies: A View From Canada' (2004), 32 J.L. Med. & Ethics 365 at 367.

121 Robert A. Perlman, 'Introduction to the Practice of Bioethics', in Nancy S. Jecker et al. (eds.), *Bioethics: An Introduction to the History, Methods, and Practice* (Boston: Jones and Bartlett, 1997) at 260–261.

122 Nathan Hershey and Robert D. Miller, *Human Experimentation and the Law* (Aspen Systems Corporation, 1976) at 1–2.

123 Jean-Paul Rwabihama, et al., 'Ethics committees for biomedical research in some African emerging countries: which establishment for which independence? A Comparison with the USA and Canada' (2010), 36 J. Med. Ethics 243 at 244.

## Review of International Collaborative Research

As the analysis above shows, ethical review of research involving human participants is one of the most important functions of ethics committees. In international collaborative research, the effective discharge of this function requires special skill and adherence to certain procedures. Thus, this subsection proposes to revisit the ethical review function of ethics committees in order to highlight the particular problems involved in externally-sponsored studies.

### *Ethical Review of Externally-Sponsored Research in Developing Countries*

Externally sponsored research requires special ethics procedure; much of that is already evident from the country-specific studies undertaken in chapter three. For instance, some African countries (like Tanzania) require research protocols involving foreign collaboration to be reviewed exclusively by a national review body. Other countries, like Nigeria, Uganda and Malawi, insist on some affiliation (by foreign collaborators) with a local institution, as well as requiring an institutional review of externally-sponsored research protocols. Internationally, however, Guideline 3 of CIOMS (2002) makes special provisions for the ethical review of externally-sponsored research:

An external sponsoring organization and individual investigators should submit the research protocol for ethical and scientific review in the country of the sponsoring organization, and the ethical standards applied should be no less stringent than they would be for research carried out in that country. The health authorities of the host country, as well as a national or local ethical review committee, should ensure that the proposed research is responsive to the health needs and priorities of the host country and meets the requisite ethical standards.[124]

To qualify as an externally-sponsored research, the research (or part of a multi-part trial) should be undertaken in a host country 'but sponsored, financed, and sometimes wholly or partly carried out by an external international or national organization or pharmaceutical company with the collaboration or agreement of the appropriate authorities, institutions and personnel of the host country'.[125] Guideline 3 aims to ensure that biomedical research undertaken in a resource-poor country, such as many African and developing countries, is given proper ethical consideration that recognizes the rights, dignity, and welfare of the research subjects.[126] This provision is evidently crucial because of the low regulatory visibility under which biomedical research takes place in some African host countries, and the temptation for researchers from developed and wealthy sponsoring countries to think that the abundance of impoverished research

124 CIOMS, supra, note 56, Guideline 3.

125 Ibid., Guideline 3.

126 Robert J. Levine, 'International Codes of Research Ethics: Current Controversies and the Future' (2002), 35 Ind. L. Rev. 557 at 563.

subjects in a region of near regulatory void is a warrant for ethical impropriety.[127] Globalization not only of goods and services but also of clinical trials has brought the aforementioned temptation within the realm of reality.[128] Because of a number of factors present in developing countries – for instance low income, widespread unemployment, illiteracy, poverty and disease – citizens of developing countries are much more vulnerable and available to be research subjects.[129] These factors, in addition to a favourable regulatory climate in many developing countries, comparative reluctance by citizens of developed countries to enrol as research subjects, bureaucratic control of research in many wealthy nations, and low cost of conducting clinical trials in developing countries, make it more advantageous for some biomedical researchers and industries in the North to conduct their clinical trials in developing countries.

Regrettably, the globalization of biomedical research has left in its wake evidence of the unsavoury consequences of the economic inequality between the North and South.[130] For instance, Chang described how the human-subject experimentation relating to H. Pylori bacterium conducted by the United States National Cancer Institute in a rural province of China in 1998 led to an increase of about forty per cent in the disease infection.[131] Without any form of legally enforceable post-trial obligation on visiting researchers, research injuries of this kind will be rampant in developing countries. The willingness of drug agencies in some developed countries to accept data generated from a clinical trial in a developing country would only intensify the current rush for human research subjects abroad.[132] Though globalization of clinical trials is theoretically unproblematic, it is necessary that rapid internationalization of ethical guidelines and standards should accompany this globalization and hinder the potential opportunities for abuse of clinical trials in poor, developing countries. Thus, to reduce the risk of ethical misconduct during biomedical research in a host country, Guideline 3, above, stipulates a two-fold process of ethical review.

---

127 Ileana Dominguez-Urban, 'Harmonization in the Regulation of Pharmaceutical Research and Human Rights: The Need to Think Globally' (1997), 30 Cornell Int'l L.J. 245 at 270–271.

128 Mary Pat Flaherty and Joe Stephens, 'Pa. Firm Asks FDA To Back Experiment Forbidden in U.S.', Wash. Post, 23 February 2001, A3.

129 Sonia Shaw, 'Globalizing Clinical Research: Big Pharma Tries Out First World Drugs on Unsuspecting Third World Patients', The Nation, 1 July 2002, at 1–6; Dawn Joyce Miller, 'Research and Accountability: The Need for Uniform Regulation of International Pharmaceutical Drug Testing' (2001), 13 Pace Int'l L. Rev. 197 at 219–20.

130 Esther Chang, 'Fitting a Square Peg into a Round Hole?: Imposing Informed Consent and Post-Trial Obligations on United States Sponsored Clinical Trials in Developing Countries' (2002), 11 S. Cal. INTERDISC. L.J. 339.

131 Ibid.

132 US Food and Drug Administration, Guidance for Industry: Acceptance of Foreign Clinical Studies (2001) – available at http://www.fda.gov/cber/gdlns/clinical031301.htm.

First, the relevant ethical review board in the sponsoring country would scrutinize the proposed research for both its scientific and ethical validity. Even at this stage, the sponsoring country's review board is required to take into consideration the customs and traditions of the host country that may influence the ethics of the proposed research. Since members of the review board are geographically distanced and likely to be unfamiliar with the cultures of a foreign country, adequate cultural sensitivity, and an understanding of how the culture affects the review process, may be difficult to achieve. What ethical standards, therefore, should guide a foreign review board in the evaluation of a cross-cultural protocol? The problem is further exacerbated by a foreign review board's ignorance of unanticipated risks that are not usually stated in protocols but arise from systemic socio-political and cultural inequities.[133] A famous debate identified two approaches to this problem. The first is based on what Baker calls 'moral fundamentalism'.[134] It posits that ethical principles are universal in operation, cutting across cultures and territories, and applying to all people without discrimination. On this view, undiluted Western ethical standards should guide the evaluation of cross-cultural protocols in order to ensure adequate protection for research subjects.[135] The second approach is based on ethical relativism, which gives strength to the ethos of multiculturalism and the reality of our diversity.[136] It is based on the understanding that appropriate and sufficient protections for research subjects are conditioned by the prevailing social, cultural and political circumstances.[137] Thus, a research protocol involving an HIV/AIDS study in a territory which exposes people suffering from the disease to a risk of involuntary detention might be considered ethically indefensible in that territory, although the same research might be ethically justifiable in another territory. However, White has argued that both moral fundamentalism and ethical relativism are by themselves insufficient to guide members of an ethics committee.[138] Moral fundamentalism suffers from several limitations, including the tendency to generate a review that is ethically sound on paper but divorced from practical realities and unanticipated risks that might be present in a territory due to its oppressive socio-political system.[139] A rigid application of the universal approach might also warrant the conclusion that the circumstances in a particular developing country are such that it is impossible or extremely difficult to apply

133 White, supra, note 47.

134 R. Baker, 'A Theory of International Bioethics: Multi-Culturalism, Postmodernism, and the Bankruptcy of Fundamentalism' (1998), 8 Kennedy Institute of Ethics Journal 2001–31.

135 M. Angell, 'Ethical Imperialism? Ethics in International Collaborative Clinical Research' (1988) 319 New Eng. J. Med. 1081–83.

136 Baker, supra, note 134; L. Newton, 'Ethical Imperialism and Informed Consent' (1990), 12 IRB: A Review of Human Subjects Research 10–11.

137 R. Baker, 'A Theory of International Bioethics: The Negotiable and the Non-Negotiable' (1998), 8 Kennedy Institute of Ethics Journal 233–273.

138 White, supra, note 47.

139 Ibid., at 89.

Western ethical standards, thereby imperiling potentially beneficial research in a developing country.[140] Ethical relativism, on the other hand, involves the difficulties of obtaining the necessary contextual information and identification of the significant and relevant socio-political factors.[141]

In recognition of the problem above, the commentary on Guideline 2 recommends that a sponsor country's ethical review committee should include someone conversant with the customs and traditions of the host country.[142] But if we accept Benatar and Singer's call for a pro-active approach to international research ethics,[143] then a sponsor's ethics committee is even required to make socioeconomic and political determinations that might be external to strict ethical review. For instance, Benatar and Singer observed that a sponsor's ethics committee should have knowledge of:

(a) the sociology of pharmaceutical research; (b) the political relation between the sponsoring and host countries – for example, how the host country fits into the sponsoring country's policy, what economic aid is provided, the nature of any debt relations, and the extent of arms trading between the two countries; and (c) the human rights achievements of the sponsoring and host countries.[144]

Furthermore, Benatar and Singer argued that gross inequality in global health requires that foreign investigators should demonstrate a sufficient knowledge of the social, economic, and political circumstances of the host country in which their research is proposed to take place. Such cognitive requirement operates to the advantages of a host country because foreign investigators 'might influence political leaders in their countries to promote more equitable relations with the host country in which the research was conducted'.[145] As an ideal, Benatar and Singer's proposals are unobjectionable; but it might be unrealistic to expect a sponsor's ethics committee to reject a proposal simply because the investigator is not sufficiently knowledgeable about the socio-economic and political history of the host country.

The second stage of the two-fold review process of externally sponsored research is the submission of the protocol to the relevant ethics board in the host country, which must ensure that the proposed research is scientifically and ethically sound having regard to the overall circumstances of the host country. In particular, the US National Bioethics Advisory Commission recommended that 'clinical trials conducted in developing countries should be limited to those studies that are

---

140 Ibid.

141 Ibid., at 90.

142 CIOMS, supra, note 56, commentary on Guideline 2.

143 Solomon R. Benatar and Peter A. Singer, 'A New Look at International Research Ethics' (2000), 321 BMJ 824.

144 Ibid., at 826.

145 Ibid.

responsive to the health needs of the host country'.[146] It is important for the host country's ethics committee to review not only the ethical merit of the protocol, but also its relevance to the host country's priorities, which could be medical or socio-economic.[147] For instance, in a resource-poor host country with a small pool of doctors, which are desperately needed for more pressing medical emergencies, their diversion to externally-sponsored research on a less prevalent disease, such as cancer, may be in dissonance with the priorities of the host country.[148] Dickens noted the ability of sponsored studies in host countries to distort the priorities of the host and reflect those of the sponsors.[149] He observed that the 'diversion of assets from host countries' priorities to those of developed study-sponsoring countries, even when what is accomplished in a host country is of value, is a form of imperialism'.[150] Though a host country's ethical review could obviate this sort of ethical imperialism, considerable problems arise for host countries without any form of a regular and functional ethical review board. In a bid to attract potentially beneficial biomedical research, a poor host country may quickly raise an ethics committee with little or no idea of its mandate. Such a review committee will simply rubber-stamp the protocol at the expense of the rights, welfare, and dignity of research subjects. The Nuffield Council on Bioethics highlighted this concern:

> In some instances, researchers may submit research for approval in developing countries, only to have it 'approved' within a few days, with no amendments or changes proposed. Under these circumstances concerns have been expressed that officials in developing countries do not recognise the need for effective ethical review and consider it to be simply a formality.[151]

What should be done in these circumstances? Should a sponsoring country abandon the research due to the incapacity of ethical review in the host country? Should it conduct such research even when it compromises international ethical guidelines or domestic legislation of the sponsor? In other words, is under-regulation or zero regulation an excuse for conducting ethically problematic research in a host country? Though different answers to these questions are possible, a strict adherence to the provisions of the CIOMS guideline would

146 National Bioethics Advisory Commission, *Ethical Issues in International Research: Clinical Trials in Developing Countries: Report and Recommendations of the National Bioethics Advisory Commission* (NBAC, 2001) at 8.

147 Bernard M. Dickens, 'Research Ethics and HIV/AIDS' (1997), 16 Med. Law 187 at 195.

148 Similar impact was attributed to 'annexed research sites' in host countries: Anthony Costello and Alimuddin Zumla, 'Moving to Research Partnerships in Developing Countries' (2000), 321 BMJ 827.

149 Dickens, supra, note 148, at 195.

150 Ibid.

151 The Nuffield Council on Bioethics, supra, note 60.

mean that a sham ethical review is equivalent to no review at all. This means that, absent a competent and functional ethics committee in the host country, executing an externally-sponsored research protocol may amount to an infraction of international ethical guidelines. Moreover, the loose regulatory situation in the host country does not exempt the sponsor from any domestic legislation (in the sponsoring country) that compulsorily requires ethical review in a host country. Even without such a requirement, it is morally wrong for a foreign investigator or agency to conduct in a host country research that would be ethically problematic and impermissible in the sponsor's country.

Furthermore, the provisions of CIOMS relating to the constitution[152] and composition[153] of an ethics review board does not differentiate between a host and a sponsoring country, or a developing and a developed country. Thus, a sponsoring country should, despite the willingness of a host country to forgo strict compliance with ethical review requirements, insist on a proper review conducted by a competent ethics board. The sponsor should exhibit a stand on ethical review that countervails the desperation of a host country. Dickens suggests that a sponsor could assist in developing the ethical review capacity for the host country.[154] Another commentator suggests that funding ethical review in the host country should be reflected in the protocol and be part of the ethical review in the sponsoring country.[155] These suggestions are legitimate and acceptable provided the sponsor does not, in the guise of providing institutional capacity, supplant the ethical review in the host country. Thus, help should relate to such matters as training, education, and supply of equipment. Where, however, the sponsor is a private, multinational corporation with considerable commercial interest in the research, it may find the unsatisfactory regulatory situation in the host country very convenient, and probably unwilling to assist on real ethical review.

### *Conflict of Ethical Expectations*

Even with the availability of competent and efficient ethical review in both the sponsoring and host countries, cultural relativism potentially ensures contradictory review by both committees. For instance, a seroprevalance study in Tanzania entailed sampling the blood of an infant upon birth, as well as their mother's blood.[156] A US Institutional Review Board approved the study on the condition that the research participants should be informed of the test results. However, the Tanzanian authorities were not prepared to inform the research subjects about the

152 CIOMS, supra, note 56, Guideline 2.

153 Ibid.

154 Dickens, supra, note 148, at 828.

155 Robert Mittendorf 11, 'Primum Non Nocere: Implications for the Globalisation of Biomedical Research Trials' (2001) 25 Fletcher F. World Aff. 239 at 247.

156 Michele Barry, 'Ethical Considerations of Human Investigation in Developing Countries: The AIDS Dilemma' (1988), 319 New Eng. J. Med. 1083; White, supra, note 47.

blood draws and the test results. The Tanzanian authorities were just being sensitive to trauma that usually accompanies the disclosure of HIV status in Tanzania, coupled with the lack of effective intervention for the disease in Tanzania. Since the US and Tanzanian authorities were not able to resolve this ethical conflict the study was abandoned.[157] Thus, conflict in ethical expectations is a significant problem; it demands urgent attention and critical analysis.

As the Tanzanian study above shows, while a host country's ethical committee might find a proposed research ethical and consistent with the host's cultural norms and traditional lifestyle, an ethics committee of the sponsor, with a different cultural background, might however conclude that the same protocol is unethical. In that case, the protocol would fail to meet the requirements of concurrent review and concurrent approval. Thus, cultural and ethical differences might lead to the termination of potentially beneficial research. The Nuffield Council on Bioethics observed:

> Where there are irreconcilable differences between research ethics committees, a committee may choose not to approve the research. If a committee from a sponsoring country does not approve the research, the sponsor cannot fund it. If a research ethics committee from a developing country does not approve the research, then the research cannot be conducted within that country.[158]

There may be ways to negotiate out of this problem.[159] First, a protocol that satisfies the ethical requirement of the host country may easily find favour with the ethics committee in the sponsor-country, even when it does not strictly comply with the sponsor's ethical guidelines.[160] This may easily be the case where the sponsor country has cultural affinity with the host country. For instance, a US Institutional Review Board may be willing to accept the review of a Canadian Research Ethics Board due to significant cultural and legal affinities that exist between the two countries. Second, the host country's ethical review committee might be given a presumptive claim to ethical guidance. As Christakis and Panner elaborated:

> The host country for the research, or, more specifically, the representatives of research subjects, should have a presumptive claim to ethical guidance. In the event of a conflict, the host country's ethical standards, if they are more restrictive, should always prevail. In other words, if there are two interpretations

157 Ibid.

158 Nuffield Council on Bioethics, supra, note, 60, at 108.

159 Ibid, at 107–108, suggesting negotiation that mediates the differences between the two committees. Also, A.A. Christakis and J. Panner, 'Existing International Ethical Guidelines for Human Subjects Research: Some Open Questions' (1991), 19 Law, Medicine, & Health Care 214 at 219.

160 Dickens, supra, note 148, at 196.

> of what would be ethical – one favouring the research and the other barring the research – if the interpretation barring the research is favoured by the host community, the research must be viewed as unethical.[161]

Third, the host and sponsor country's ethical review committees may cooperate and agree that each reviews specific and different aspects of the protocol in a non-contradictory manner. This type of cooperation is encouraged by CIOMS.[162] The bioethical negotiation and mediation suggested above might, however, be difficult to achieve in some African countries. In Nigeria, for example, Marshall gathered empirical data suggesting that investigators in Nigeria perceived US institutions to be inflexible, and unwilling to modify protocols for cultural reasons highlighted by Nigerian investigators:

Nigerian investigators discussed administrative issues regarding the process of obtaining approval from ethical review committees. Several investigators commented on the difficulties of responding to the requirements of funding agencies in the United States and at local Nigerian institutions. They said it was particularly frustrating to try to respond to what they perceived as inconsistent requirements for ethical review. A physician in Lagos reported difficulties at many levels; dealing with the informed consent document itself, having to 'fight with Washington' to change the consent form, and then going through the process of making the form useful and appropriate for his patients in Nigeria.[163]

Despite the difficulties above, some African guidelines encourage negotiation and cooperation between ethics committees as a means of resolving ethical conflicts. The Ugandan guideline provides that, with the approval of the Uganda National Council for Science and Technology, 'an institution participating in a collaborative research project may enter into joint review arrangements for that particular research project in order to streamline the review process'.[164] Similarly, the Nigerian research Code provides that in international collaborative research 'ethics committees shall, as much as possible, consult with each other in order to resolve discordant reviews and generate consistent single response to multi-site research'.[165]

---

161 Christakis and Panner, supra, note 159, at 219.

162 CIOMS, supra, note 56, Guideline 3, commentary.

163 Patricia A. Marshall, 'The Relevance of Culture for Informed Consent in U.S.-Funded International Health Research', in National Bioethics Advisory Commission, *Ethical and Policy Issues in International Research, vol. 11, Clinical Trials in Developing Countries, Commissioned Papers and Staff Analysis* (NBAC, 2001), at C-25.

164 UNCST, supra, note 33, at 17.

165 National Code of Health Research Ethics, supra, note 32, at 23.

## Bioethical Capacity Building and Training of Members of Ethics Committees in Africa

To discharge its functions effectively, an ethics committee must be composed of competent and well-trained members, and this is particularly important in Africa where research subject protection is suboptimal. No doubt, review of research protocols by competent and independent ethics committee is a fundamental safeguard for the protection of research participants; it also promotes public confidence and trust in the ethics of biomedical research as argued in the sections above. In the last two decades, ethics review capacity has been boosted in most African countries by various bioethical training programmes organized for the training of African bioethicists. However, some African countries still lack expertise in ethics review. In Sudan, for instance, Elsayed and Kass observed that 93 per cent of ethics review members had not received any sort of training in ethics review, nor had the committees conducted any training courses for their members.[166] In a study of twelve ethics committees in nine African countries, it was reported that two of the committees had members with no ethical training.[167] Partly for this reason, some foreign researchers are sceptical about the competence of local ethics review boards in Africa; such scepticism might lead to attempts to circumvent local review procedures.[168] Therefore, recent guidelines in Africa emphasize the training and competence of ethics committee members. The Nigerian guideline insists that at the time of their appointment members of ethics committees must have completed a research ethics programme approved by the national review and accreditation body (NHREC).[169] A training programme of this sort would certainly entail some financial outlay for prospective members of ethics committees in Nigeria; as such, training-related expenses might be a disincentive to serving as a member of ethics committees in Nigeria. To address this problem, the Nigerian guideline stipulates that the 'institution setting up the HREC must provide resources for such training'.[170] Similarly, the Ugandan guideline requires each member of an institutional review committee to 'undergo at least one basic training in research ethics within one year of appointment, and thereafter, should undergo continued ethics education at least once every two years'.[171] Recall that on the basis of this provision, chapter three criticized the inclusion of people without

166 D.E.M. Elsayed and N.E. Kass, 'Assessment of the Ethical Review Process in Sudan' (2007), 7 Developing World Bioethics 143 at 145.

167 N.E. Kass, et al., 'The Structure and Function of Research Ethics Committees in Africa: A Case Study' (2007), 4 PLoS Medicine 26 at 27.

168 George Ulrich, 'Setting an Agenda for Strengthening Ethical Awareness and Accountability in Donor-Sponsored Research', in The ENRECA Health Research Network, supra, note 39, at 4.

169 Nigerian Code, supra, note 32, at 8.

170 Ibid.

171 UNCST, supra, note 33, at 14.

formal education in the Ugandan institutional review committees because of their potential inability to absorb formal training in Western-related concepts. While the bioethical training requirements in African guidelines are laudable, ethics review capacity in Africa would be further enhanced by the inclusion of bioethics in the curricula of medical schools in Africa.[172] This is already the approach of the College of Medicine, University of Malawi.[173]

Furthermore, many developing countries need international assistance to develop and strengthen their ethics review capacity. Benatar and Singer argued for the creation of a global alliance between international donors, with the aim of promoting bioethical capacity in developing countries. The proposed global alliance should be able to establish thirty bioethics training centres in developing countries, and each training centre should be able to produce twelve trainees annually.[174] Benatar and Singer estimated that the training project would cost about US$100,000,000.[175] Some international organizations and agencies are already responding to the training needs of developing countries in the area of ethics review capacity. At the US National Institutes of Health, for instance, the Forgarty International Centre (FIC) supports and promotes international collaborative research in priority global health areas, with the goal of reducing inequities in global health.[176] Part of FIC's objective is to 'develop human capital and build research capacity in the poorest nations of the world where the need is the greatest'.[177] Since 2001, FIC has provided annual grants and awards to support the ethics training of faculty members from institutions in developing countries. The Rockefeller Foundation provided a similar support in 1980 through the International Clinical Epidemiology Network (INCLEN); INCLEN identified and supported medical schools in a number of developing countries and trained their faculty members in clinical epidemiology. Recently, the US Office of Inspector General (OIG) recommended that the staff of the Food and Drug Administration (FDA) should continue to use the opportunity of their conference and other travels outside of the US to reach out and provide technical assistance to ethics committees in developing countries.[178] Furthermore, the OIG encouraged sponsors of research in developing countries to 'take steps to educate the non-US boards that they use,

172 Temidayo O. Ogundiran, 'Enhancing the African Bioethics Initiative' (2004), 4 BMC Medical Education 21.

173 Based on personal communication with Mr Paul Ndebele in July 2008, then of College of Medicine, University of Malawi.

174 S.R. Benatar and P.A. Singer, 'A New Look at International Research Ethics' (2000), 321 BMJ 824–826.

175 Ibid.

176 Gerald T Keusch, 'Welcome to Forgarty International Centre', available at http://www.fic.nih.gov/about/welcome.html.

177 Ibid.

178 Department of Health and Human Services, Office of the Inspector General, *The Globalisation of Clinical Trials: A Growing Challenge in Protecting Human Subjects* (2001), at 18.

particularly those that lack experience reviewing FDA-regulated research. One way that they could do this is by contracting with experienced US boards to help train the foreign boards'. [179]

Regionally, the Pan African Bioethics Initiative (PABIN) is an important forum for the promotion and systematic development of ethics review capacity in Africa. PABIN has organized several regional conferences since its inception. Similarly, the African Malaria Vaccine Testing Network (AMVTN), re-styled African Malaria Network Trust (AMANET), was established in 1995 to facilitate 'the planning, coordination and execution of malaria vaccine trials in Africa'.[180] AMANET's objectives include the development of research and ethics capacity in African countries in connection with its malaria vaccine project.[181] Furthermore, the South African Research Ethics Training Initiative (SARETI) provides Masters-level training in research ethics and non-degree training for members of research ethics committees in Africa, researchers and other stakeholders.[182] The SARETI programme is jointly run by the University of KwaZulu-Natal and the University of Pretoria, both in South Africa. In West Africa, the West African Bioethics Training Initiative provides similar bioethical programmes in the sub-region.[183] The proliferation of bioethical training programmes is also noticeable in other parts of the developing world. These include the Forum for Ethical Review Committees in Asia and the Western Pacific (FERCAP), the Latin American Forum of Ethics Committees in Health Research (FLACEIS), and the (Russian) Forum for Ethics Committees in the Confederation of Independent States (FECCIS). At the international level, the World Health Organisation has contributed to ethical capacity building in developing countries by developing the Operational Guidelines for Ethics Committees.[184] The WHO guideline facilitates ethical review around the world, and serves as a model for countries that plan to develop a written procedure for their ethics committees. The WHO's efforts were enriched by the Strategic Initiative in Developing Capacity in Ethical Review (SIDCER). SIDCER focuses on developing and disseminating the best practices in ethical review. Thus, SIDCER has established networks with various national and regional bioethical forums; the aim is to exchange information and develop capacity in ethical review around the world.[185] In sum, therefore, although much

179 Ibid., at 19.

180 The African Malaria Vaccine Testing Network, at http://www.amvtn.org.

181 Trust Rules, *The Constitution of the African Malaria Vaccine Testing Network*, Art. 7 (2002).

182 South African Research Ethics Training Initiative, at http://shsph.up.ac.za/sareti.htm.

183 See, http://www.westafricanbioethics.net.

184 WHO, *Operational Guidelines for Ethics Committees that Review Biomedical Research* (WHO: Geneva, 2000).

185 Juntra Karbwang, et al., 'Ethical Review and the Globalisation of Clinical Trials' (2002), Applied Clinical Trials 90–94.

progress has been made in developing ethical review capacity in most parts of Africa, there is no room for complacency. African countries should ensure that members of ethics committees operating in their territories receive sufficient training in research ethics review, and should make bioethics part of the curricula of their medical schools.

## Funding of Ethics Committees and the Charging of Fees for Ethics Review

Funding is a major problem for the operation of ethics committees in many developing countries, and the problem is exacerbated in African countries. For instance, an empirical study conducted in Nigeria indicated that some researchers had to pay for the administrative costs involved in the ethics review of their protocols by ethics committees in Nigeria despite the researchers' limited resources.[186] Furthermore, in a study of twelve ethics committees in nine African countries, Kass and colleagues reported that three of the committees had no operating funds at all.[187] Thus, it makes sense that research guidelines in Africa should embody provisions relating to the funding of ethics review committees. Without sufficient funding, and training programmes for ethics committees, members of ethics committees would be unable to discharge their important protective function. The Nuffield Council on Bioethics estimated that the operating costs of a research ethics committee in the UK was about £36,000 per annum and up to US$500,000 per annum in the United States.[188] Though the cost of operating a research ethics committee in Africa is likely to be lower, it still represents a significant amount that may unduly burden the parent institution of an ethics committee. Some research guidelines in Africa have addressed the funding problem in various ways. For instance, the Nigerian guideline demands that the parent institution of an ethics committee should provide to the national regulatory authority (NHREC) a statement of its commitment to fund (sufficiently) an institutional review.[189] Similarly, the Ugandan guideline requires an 'assurance' of resources to support an institutional review.[190] But these are just promises to fund an institutional review. It does not envisage, nor amount to, a legal obligation. Many research institutions and universities in Africa already complain that their various programmes and activities are inadequately funded by governments in their territories. Thus, the materialization of an institution's promise to fund its ethics committee depends on the institution's overall funding profile, which, at the moment, is generally bleak in Africa.

186 Marshall in NBAC, supra, note 163, at C-25.
187 Kass, supra, note 86, at 27.
188 The Nuffield Council on Bioethics, supra, note 60, at 106.
189 Nigerian Code, supra, note 32, at 8.
190 UNCST, supra, note 33, at 12.

The practice of charging fees for protocol evaluation might, therefore, be a more realistic solution to the problem of funding of ethics committees in Africa. This strategy has found favour with some African research guidelines. For instance, the Ethiopian research guideline outlines fees for protocol evaluation at the national level,[191] and this includes international collaborative research.[192] Foreign students conducting research in Ethiopia pay 2 per cent of the protocol budget; foreign researchers pay 3 per cent of the budget.[193] However, a lower scale of fees is prescribed for the evaluation of protocols that do not involve international financial sponsorship.[194] As shown by the Ethiopian scale of fees above, the practice of charging fees for protocol evaluation is likely to increase the overall cost of research. Thus, it might be a disincentive to the conducting of potentially beneficial research in Ethiopia if the researcher is not sufficiently funded. Malawi seems to have recognized this problem by opting out of the percentage approach to fees for protocol evaluation. Malawi operates a fee system that is fixed and reasonable in amount. Thus, the Malawian approach requires the Sectoral Research Co-ordinating Committees, or institutions that conduct research, to determine the 'fees in form of pegging fixed actual amounts as opposed to pegging a percentage of the total budget of the research study as the latter may circumstantially be too costly on the part of the researcher'.[195] In Nigeria, there are no compulsory fees for the evaluation of research protocols; fees are, however, at the discretion of ethics committees in Nigeria (HRECS). Thus, the Nigerian approach introduced some flexibility in the practice of charging fees for ethics review, and this ensures that beneficial but insufficiently funded studies are exempted from the payment of fees for ethics review. In exercising its discretion, regarding whether or not fees are payable and the amount of such fees, an HREC in Nigeria is influenced by several factors, including the estimated administrative costs of a protocol's review; the size, complexity, and duration of the study; and the status of the researcher and sponsor of the study.[196]

While the charging of fees for ethics review might offer a practical solution to the problem of funding ethics committees in Africa, the practice, however, presents some serious difficulties. Fee-charging may undermine the independence of ethics committees and raise a potential conflict of interest which is likely to be exacerbated by the operation of commercial or for-profit ethics committees. Responding to this problem, the Nuffield Council on Bioethics suggested that the relevant fees should be paid into a central fund or to a local or national government

191 Ethiopian Science and Technology Commission, *National Health Research Ethics* (2005), at 45.

192 Ibid., at 23.

193 Ibid., at 45.

194 Ibid.

195 NRCM, supra, note 84, at 5.

196 Nigerian Code, supra, note 32, at 28.

and devoted to financial support of ethics committees.[197] In sum, therefore, absent any visible form of governmental support for ethics committees in Africa and other developing countries, the option of charging fees for protocol evaluation is both prudent and pragmatic. However, there is a pressing need to develop ways to mitigate the negative impact of fees on the independence of ethics committees.

## Commercial Ethics Review Committees

Should commercial ethics review committees be developed and promoted in African countries? The review of research protocols by for-profit ethics review committees or boards marks a new trend in the history and development of the ethics review system. The number and scope of such commercial boards have continued to expand in the USA, Canada, and Europe.[198] An exhaustive analysis of the phenomenon of commercial review boards, their dynamics, and the problems they present to the protection of human research subjects is beyond the scope of this (already extended) chapter. Happily, an interesting and detailed exploration of the subject, in the context of conflict of interest, was undertaken by Lemmens and Freedman; they identified two types of commercial ethics review boards.[199] The first type is the free-standing boards. They are not part of or owned by contract research organizations (CROs); nor are they part of the structures of academic institutions and research centres. Such free-standing commercial review boards are known as independent review boards or non-institutional review boards (NIRB). NIRBs usually review protocols (for a fee) from CROs, private researchers and other clients. The second type is the commercial review boards. They are owned by CROs and review in-house research protocols (although, in theory, they may wish to review protocols from other organizations). Such review boards are also known as proprietary boards. Commercial review boards owe their existence to various factors. For instance, research conducted by, or within, pharmaceutical companies, such as phase 1 drug trials, are not usually reviewed by ethics boards of academic institutions. Since (by applicable regulations) such studies must also receive prior ethical approval, industry scientists are just left with the option of commercial review boards. For the same reason, medical research conducted by private physicians, not attached to academic institutions, are reviewed by for-profit ethics review boards. Commercial review boards are beginning to play a crucial

197 The Nuffield Council on Bioethics, supra, note 60, at 106.

198 Office of Inspector General, *Institutional Review Boards: The Emergence of Independent Boards* (Washington, DC: US Department of Health and Human Services, 1998); Trudo Lemmens and Benjamin Freedman, 'Ethics Review for Sale? Conflict of Interest and Commercial Review Boards' (2000), 78 Milbank Quarterly 547–584; Trudo Lemmens and Alison Thompson, 'Noninstitutional Commercial Review Boards in North America' (2001), 23 IRB: Ethics & Human Research 1–12.

199 Lemmens and Freedman, supra, note 198, at 549.

role in the regulation and conduct of research involving human participants.[200] Their increasing popularity, especially within the pharmaceutical industry, is attributable to certain advantages. These include fast or expedited review of research protocols, composition by competent and experienced members, quality review services, and ability to review multi-centre studies.[201]

The existence and operation of commercial ethics boards have raised some concerns. These concerns focus mainly on conflict of interest issues. Although problems relating to conflict of interest also arise with respect to institutional review boards, they are more acutely expressed by commercial review boards. For instance, the potential for financial conflict of interest is higher in commercial boards (due to their constitution and operation) than in institutional boards. Furthermore, in proprietary review boards, the members (or, at least, some of them) are likely to be recruited from the employees of a CRO; in turn, the CRO's economic existence depends on its ability to attract research contracts. Thus, the wages of the members of a proprietary board depend on the economic fortunes of the CRO. Also, obedience to superior authority, which is an inherent part of a corporate structure, might put additional pressure on members of proprietary boards. Moreover, where the employee benefit package of a CRO includes shares in the company, its proprietary board members would certainly appear to have a financial interest in the review process; more so because the outcome of a review process (arguably) has a correlative effect on the profit margins and value of shares of the company. Even when members of a proprietary board are recruited from outside, their objectivity is countervailed by the potential for negative reviews to lead to the termination of their appointments. For instance, a CRO might lose lucrative research contracts with pharmaceutical companies if its proprietary board is in the habit of rejecting protocols or recommending burdensome modifications. In that case, it might consider the option of terminating the appointments of members of its proprietary board. Although less intense, the challenges above are equally faced by NIRBs. For instance, Leslie Francis observed that consistent unfriendly reviews by an NIRB might lead to loss of lucrative contracts from CROs.[202] Thus, while rigorous and critical reviews by NIRBs are good for the protection of research subjects, they might eventuate to loss of valuable clients for NIRBs, especially if the outcome of the review is frequently negative. This possibility was highlighted in the empirical study undertaken by Lemmens and Thompson; they reported a case in which an NIRB's client refused to pay for the

---

200 Susan Gilbert, 'Trials and Tribulations' (2008), 38 Hastings Centre Report 14–18.

201 P.T. Kefalides, 'Research on Humans Faces Scrutiny: New Policies Adopted' (2000), 132 Annals of Internal Medicine 513–16; Lemmens and Freedman, supra, note 198, at 550–551.

202 L. Francis, 'IRBs and Conflicts of Interest', in R.G. Spece et al. (eds.), *Conflicts of Interest in Clinical Practice and Research* (New York: Oxford University Press, 1996) 418–36.

evaluation of a rejected protocol and threatened to do future business elsewhere.[203] This underscores the point that since members of commercial boards are paid for their services, the loss of service contracts by their employers (for example, CROs and NIRBs) would likely affect the remuneration or retention of their services, and in relevant cases, the value of their shares in the company. In essence, the considerations above imply the existence of a potential financial bias that might affect the professional judgement of commercial review boards. Even when actual bias is not present, the existence of a likelihood of bias is sufficient to warrant some concerns. Thus, actual or potential conflict of interest, especially on the part of commercial review boards, poses enormous problems for the protection of research subjects, and the maintenance of public trust in the research enterprise which, as argued above, is essential for any meaningful progress in biomedical research. Conflict of interest also undermines the credibility of both commercial review boards and institutional review boards. Thus, Lemmens and Freedman suggested the development of detailed and specific conflict of interest rules to countervail the risks inherent in the structure and operation of for-profit review boards.[204]

The concerns about the existence, structure and operation of commercial review boards have increased with the proliferation of CROs in many developing countries.[205] The 2001 report of the Office of Inspector General noted the presence of CROs in developing countries like Chile, (former) Czech Republic, Greece, the Philippines, Romania, Thailand, Asia and the Pacific Rim.[206] The Introduction to this book also noted the proliferation of CROs in India. Although the operational level of CROs in Africa is not clear,[207] it is likely that the globalization of clinical trials will ensure the presence of CROs in Africa sooner or later. In that eventuality, the current challenges to the protection of research subjects in Africa (due to the prevalence of disease, poverty, illiteracy, and lack of access to adequate health care) would be compounded by the problems of conflict of interest inherent in the structure and operation of commercial review boards. In the meantime, it is possible to illustrate the manner that the operations of commercial review boards might play out in Africa by reference to a recent scandal involving a CRO in Switzerland; the Swiss CRO was accused of 'importing' research subjects from

---

203 Lemmens and Thompson, supra, note 198, at 7.

204 Lemmens and Freedman, supra, note 198.

205 M. Huijstee and I. Schipper (eds), *Putting Contract Research Organisations on the Radar* (Amsterdam: SOMO, 2011) at 12, noting the significant presence of CROs in developing countries, including India, Brazil, Peru, China, Eastern Europe and Russia

206 OIG, supra, note 178, at 9.

207 It is interesting to note that a recent study on the operation of CROs in developing countries does not contain any significant country-specific information on the activities of CROs in Africa, in contrast to other regions of the developing world, such as Asia, Latin America, Eastern Europe and Russia: Huijstee and Schipper, supra, note 205.

poor eastern European countries.[208] For this reason, a prominent Indian physician-researcher suggested that CROs and commercial review boards should not be allowed to play a role in the conduct of research involving human subjects in developing countries.[209] Similarly, a recent work on the operation of CROs in developing countries observed that the 'CRO sector was characterized by an extreme lack of transparency'.[210]

Although the operation of commercial review boards raises some serious issues and concerns, yet there is no specific or express treatment of the subject in most research guidelines in Africa. The matter is thus generally left to interpretation. For instance, it is a matter of interpretation whether or not the Nigerian research guideline permits the operation of commercial review boards. A good starting point is the provision that health 'research that is conducted anywhere in Nigeria must comply with all sections of this code'.[211] This certainly includes every health research protocol that might be reviewed by a commercial board. Part of the requirements of the Nigerian Code, which must be adhered to, relates to provisions dealing with the registration and accreditation of ethics review committees by the national regulatory agency, the National Health Research Ethics Committee NHREC).[212] But can the NHREC register and accredit a commercial review board or ethics committee? The Code provides no specific or clear answer to this question. However, in stating the requirements for the registration of an ethics committee, the Code provides that in 'order for an institution to be able to conduct health research, the institution must have a registered health research ethics committee'. Notwithstanding that the meaning of 'institution' is crucial for the interpretation of the provision above, the Code fails to provide a definition of that term. Presumably, it excludes independent or non-institutional review boards (NIRBs) since, by definition, NIRBs do not conduct research; they only review research protocols. But what of proprietary review boards that form part of the structures of CROs? CROs not only conduct health research, it is usually their main, if not sole, business. Arguably, a CRO qualifies as an 'institution' capable of conducting health research as contemplated by the Nigerian research Code. If that is the case, then a CRO's proprietary board should be entitled to registration in Nigeria. On the other hand, it is arguable that the Nigerian Code contemplates only an 'institution' in the traditional sense of the term. The fact that proprietary (or commercial ethics review) boards of CROs are not usually described as 'institutional' boards lends credence to this argument. Even then, it is not easy to

---

208 For a good account of this scandal, see Trudo Lemmens, 'Federal Regulation of REB Review of Clinical Trials: A Modest But Easy Step Towards An Accountable REB Review Structure in Canada' (2005), 13 Health Law Review 39–50

209 M.S. Valiathan, 'Clinical Trials Should Promote Health Care', The Hindu (vol. 18), 18–31, August 2001 (page unknown): http://www.hinduonnet.com.

210 Huijstee and Schipper, supra, note 205, at 21.

211 Nigerian Code, supra, note 32, at 3.

212 Ibid., at 1.

frustrate or prohibit the operation of CROs in Nigeria. For instance, if we accept the latter interpretation above, it would only mean that a CRO cannot establish its own ethics board in Nigeria; but a CRO can obtain the review of its protocols by other lawful means. Such lawful means are, however, limited in Nigeria. Recall (from chapter three) that institutional ethics committees in Nigeria (HREC) can only review protocols originating from the permanent staff of their parent institutions, or protocols that were intended to be executed within the boundaries of the parent institution;[213] although this requirement generally excludes protocols from CROs, a CRO might nonetheless make a direct (ethics review) application to the Nigerian national review body, the NHREC. As suggested in chapter three, the discretionary jurisdiction of the NHREC is expansive enough to accommodate protocols from CROs.

The Ethiopian guidelines are also ambivalent regarding the status and operation of commercial review boards. For instance, after providing that 'all health researches involving human participants must be subjected to independent ethics review and this should be conducted by a health research ethics review committee', the Ethiopian guideline went on to establish the National, Regional and Institutional ethics committees.[214] Since a commercial review board cannot (logically) be said to be the national or regional ethics committee in Ethiopia, it can only claim recognition (or accreditation) in Ethiopia under the category of 'institutional' review committee. However, the Ethiopian guideline, like its Nigerian counterpart, does not define 'institution' in relation to the institutional ethics review committees (IERCs) established under the guideline. It only provides that the national review and regulatory body, the National Ethics Review Committee (NERC), should register and accredit ethics committees, including IERCs. In the absence of a working definition for 'institution' in the Ethiopian guideline, both the non-institutional review boards (NIRBs) and proprietary boards of CROs could claim to be 'institutions' and thus entitled to registration and accreditation in Ethiopia. Although the arguments made for and against the registration of commercial boards in Nigeria are equally applicable to Ethiopia, there is, however, a noticeable difference in the two countries that revolves around the NIRBs. In Nigeria, NIRBs, rather than proprietary boards of CROs, are clearly excluded from registration and accreditation. This is because Nigeria defined registration and accreditation requirements in terms of institutions that conduct health research. Since, generally, an NIRB does not conduct research, and only reviews research protocols, it is logically excluded from registration and accreditation in Nigeria. In contrast, Ethiopia defines (similar) registration and accreditation requirements in terms of ethics committees (see the quote above); therefore, the Ethiopian guideline potentially allows the registration and accreditation of NIRBs. The point, therefore, is that while uncertainty remains with respect to the registration and accreditation of commercial review boards in

213 Ibid., at 10.

214 ESTC, supra, note 85, at 20.

Nigeria and Ethiopia, there is a chance that both proprietary and non-institutional boards can gain recognition in Ethiopia; only proprietary boards of CROs might be recognized in Nigeria. This means that if commercial boards were considered undesirable in African countries like Nigerian and Ethiopia, then the gaps highlighted above need to be plugged.

Compared to Nigeria and Ethiopia, however, the Ugandan guideline contains the clearest provision on the status of commercial review boards. It provides that research involving human subjects must be reviewed initially by institutional review committees (IRC) accredited by the Uganda National Council for Science and Technology (UNCST).[215] The guideline defines 'institution' as meaning 'any entity or agency, whether public or private. The institution should have adequate capacity to conduct the proposed research project'.[216] This clearly includes a CRO (and its proprietary board) because it is a 'private' entity, and capable of conducting biomedical research within the terms of the definition above. On the other hand, the Ugandan provision excludes non-institutional boards which, though private entities, do not usually engage in biomedical research; they only review research protocols. This view finds support in similar provisions of the Ugandan guideline, for instance the requirement that 'Institutional Review Committees (IRCs) are established by institutions whose mandate includes carrying out research';[217] and that '[A]ll institutions in Uganda that conduct research involving humans as research participants should set up IRCs in accordance with these guidelines'.[218] The emphasis in the Ugandan guideline regarding the need for an institution to be able to conduct research before its IRC could be registered and accredited means that non-institutional review boards are logically excluded. Thus, only review boards of CROs are entitled to registration in Uganda; to that extent, Uganda and Nigeria approach the issue in a similar fashion. In sum, therefore, research guidelines in Africa and other developing countries should make clear and specific provisions relating to the registration and operation of commercial boards in their territories.

## Conclusion

The regulation of research based on prior ethics review is widely accepted as an important safeguard for the protection of research subjects. Through analysis of the functions, mechanisms and dynamics of ethics review, this chapter suggests that the framework of ethics review in Africa is too important to be left in the hands of the inexperienced and the untrained; nor should governments in Africa

215 UNCST, supra, note 33, at 7.
216 Ibid., at 46.
217 Ibid., at 7.
218 Ibid., at 12.

deny ethics committees the necessary operative funds.[219] Although much progress has been made in the last two decades in establishing bioethical capacity in many parts of Africa, some African countries still lack competent, independent and well-funded ethics committees; this is a potential source of harm to research subjects, as shown by Pfizer's clinical trial of trovan examined in chapter one. While an ethics committee's power to assess a protocol for its ethical acceptability is not in doubt, there is some uncertainty regarding an ethics committee's power, and indeed duty, to assess the legality of a research protocol, and to verify a protocol's scientific validity. In line with the approach of some research guidelines in Africa, this chapter suggested that ethics committees should have the power to reject a protocol that is scientifically invalid; research based on poor science is likely to produce harm to research subjects, and, therefore, should be considered unethical. Similarly, although legal assessment of research protocols is likely to be a potential source of delay in the ethics approval process, this chapter favours the assessment of research protocols for their lawfulness by ethics committees, and such protocols should be rejected if they violate the human rights or other legal rights of research subjects. Thus, it is necessary to ensure that the composition of ethics committees includes members with expertise in law. It has already been suggested that ethics committees in Africa must be sufficiently funded and trained so that they could discharge their onerous duties effectively. However, the assurance of funding for ethics committees is particularly problematic in Africa due to a general lack of needed resources. As a possible and practical solution to this problem, this chapter recommended the practice of charging fees for ethics review. While ethics committees in Africa should be allowed to charge reasonable fees for their services, they should, however, be mindful of the potential conflict of interest entailed by the practice of charging fees for ethics review. Furthermore, the operation of commercial ethics review boards in Africa raises serious problems and concerns, and exacerbates the problem of conflict of interest. Thus, this chapter suggested that research guidelines in Africa should make clear provisions relating to the acceptability, and conditions for the operation, of commercial review boards. Having examined issues relating to the functions and operations of ethics committees in this chapter, the next chapter (five) moves on to examine the legal liability of ethics committees and their members in connection with a review of research protocol.

---

219 Other commentators have also emphasized the need for more funding and better training of ethics committee members in Africa: Rwabihama, supra, note 123, at 247; Nyika, et al., supra, note 3.

# Chapter 5
# Legal Liability of Research Ethics Committees in Actions by Research Subjects

## Introduction

Apart from the possibility of judicial review of research ethics committees' decisions, judicial control may be exercised through a series of private law actions. Applications for judicial review of research ethics committees' decisions are most likely to be brought by aggrieved investigators whose protocols were rejected by ethics committees. This issue is considered in detail in the next chapter (chapter 6). Since any research-related injury suffered by a research subject must logically arise from the execution of an approved protocol, it would be absurd for an injured subject to seek judicial review of an already executed protocol. Nor does it make sense for a research subject to seek judicial review of a protocol even before he or she is recruited as a subject. In that case, the applicant will lack sufficient interest or standing to bring the application.[1] Even if standing is granted to a potential research subject on discretionary grounds, there is still the problem that he or she is 'exceedingly unlikely to be aware of the presence of such irregularities (that is, procedural irregularities that tainted the research approval process)'.[2] Therefore, the appropriate remedy for research subjects would lie in private law actions. While this chapter explores some of the private law actions that might be brought by an injured research *subject* against an ethics committee or its members, the next chapter will examine the *investigator's* legal remedies against research ethics committees and their members. By far, a claim in negligence appears to be the most suitable legal action that research subjects could bring against ethics committees and their members. In practice, however, research subjects would need to consider the practical wisdom of suing ethics committees and their members, having regard to their ability to satisfy any compensation awarded by the court against them. Pragmatism might dictate that the host or parent institution of an ethics committee should be sued rather than the ethics committee or its members.[3]

---

1 For instance, *R. v Inland Revenue Commissioners, Ex p. National Federation of Self Employed and Small Business Ltd.* [1982] A.C. 617 (HL).

2 Michael Hadskis and Peter Carver, 'The Long Arm of Administrative Law: Applying Administrative Law Principles to Research Ethics Boards' (2005), 13 Health Law Review 19 at 28.

3 That was the approach adopted by the Canadian case of *Weiss v Solomon* [1989] R.J.Q. 731 (C.S. civ.), and the American case of *Gregg v Kane*, 1997 WL 570909 (E.D. Pa.).

But, in theory, nothing prevents an aggrieved research subject from suing research ethics committees and their members either alone or in conjunction with other defendants. Furthermore, while it is clear that members of an ethics committee may be named individually as defendants in a civil suit (individual responsibility), it is far from clear whether an ethics committee could be sued as a body with its own separate legal personality. In other words, do research ethics committees have a right to sue and be sued in their 'corporate' names? This chapter attempts to answer these questions, in addition to exploring the potential liability of ethics committees and their members in negligence actions brought by aggrieved research subjects. Finally, this chapter examines the liability of members of ethics committees to professional disciplinary procedures instigated by aggrieved research subjects.

As in the subsequent chapters, this chapter's substantial reliance on cases and materials from the UK, US, Canada and Australia needs some explanation since this book is on research regulation in African countries. The law on medical negligence in most common law African countries, especially those referenced in chapter three, is relatively in a state of underdevelopment. For this reason, commentators who have written generally on the law of negligence in a common law African country, or specifically on medical negligence, have relied heavily on foreign cases as well.[4] Even where a few cases are available on medical negligence, those cases generally focus on the more or less straightforward issues of consent to treatment[5] or medical malpractice.[6] Some of these cases are examined in detail in chapters six and seven. Moreover, most of the available cases on negligence in common law African countries tend to simply apply the relevant English common law precedents on the issue for adjudication, without any significant assessment or discussion of the underlying principles involved.[7] Thus, Cottrell's observation in 1973 that on 'the whole, however, it cannot, unfortunately, be said that the decisions (on negligence) discussed earlier have contributed significantly to the jurisprudence of this subject' rings true even today.[8] Furthermore, in the specific context of biomedical research, there is a dearth of reported cases in the African

4 For a general analysis of the law of negligence in Nigeria, for instance: G. Kodilinye, *The Nigerian Law of Torts* (London: Sweet & Maxwell, 1982), 38–89. Although there has been an increase in the volume of Nigerian tort cases in recent years, most of them relate to conversion and detinue: R. Nwabueze and P. Okorie, 'Flexibility of Damages for Conversion and Detinue' (2009), 17 Afri. Jour. of Int'l & Comp. L. 102. In the case of specific work on medical negligence: C.O. Okonkwo, 'Medical Negligence and the Legal Implications', in B.C. Umerah (ed.), *Medical Practice and the Law in Nigeria* (Ibadan, Nigeria: Longman Nig. Ltd., 1989) 119–136.

5 For instance: *Baby Kasozi v Pope John's Hospital* [1974] EA 221 (Uganda).

6 *Medical and Dental Practitioners Disciplinary Tribunal v Okonkwo* [2001] 7 NWLR 206 (SCN); *Njereketa v Director of Medical Services* [1950] 17 EACA 60 (C.A. for E. Afri.).

7 Jill Cottrell, 'The Tort of Negligence in Nigeria' (1973), 17 J. Afr. L. 30 at 31.

8 Ibid., at 38.

countries (as explored in chapter three) and other common law African countries.[9] The dearth of cases on research ethics committees is, however, not limited to Africa. For instance, Biggs observed that 'there is at present no UK case law associated specifically with the work of RECs';[10] although she hastened to add that the situation was 'undoubtedly in part due to the difficulty in so doing (that is, bringing actions against RECs), but most overwhelmingly is the result of the good practice adopted by the NHS RECs both before and after the introduction of the Clinical Trials Regulation'.[11] For these reasons, this chapter relies heavily on cases from comparable and well-developed common law jurisdictions in the West in order to illustrate the arguments canvassed in the chapter. Wherever possible, however, available local or African cases are used to develop some of the issues raised in this chapter.

## Legal Personality of Research Ethics Committees

A research ethics committee can sue and be sued as an artificial entity only if it has a legal personality separate from those of its members. But questions relating to the legal personality of an ethics committee are not likely to arise where the claimant seeks only a judicial review of its decision. This is because, at common law, unincorporated tribunals are subject to prerogative remedies or judicial review.[12] In contrast, the legal personality of an ethics committee is most likely to be in contention where a claimant seeks private law remedies against an ethics committee on the basis or assumption that it is a corporate or quasi-corporate body. While the courts are yet to grapple with this issue, some (academic) commentators have expressed a largely negative opinion. For instance, Savulescu and colleagues speculate that research 'ethics committees probably lack the necessary personality to be a defendant in a civil action. Participants who have been harmed by research could sue either the health authority or individual members of the committee'.[13] Similarly, Brazier opined that the 'ethics committee itself lacks the necessary legal

9 Mpanga S. Ssemigavu, Protection of Human Subjects of Biomedical Research and Medical Interventions: The Legal and Ethical Concerns (Dissertation submitted in 1997 to the Faculty of Law, Makerere University, Uganda, in partial fulfilment of the requirement for the grant of Bachelors of Law) – on file with the author.

10 Hazel Biggs, *Healthcare Research Ethics and Law: Regulation, Review and Responsibility* (London: Routledge-Cavendish, 2010) at 54.

11 Ibid., at 59.

12 John A. Kavanagh, *A Guide to Judicial Review* (Toronto: Carswell Co. Ltd., 1978), at 167. See also, *R. v Ethical Committee of St Mary's Hospital* (Manchester), ex parte H. [1988] 1 FLR 512, where an action of ethics committee went through judicial review.

13 J. Savulescu, et al., 'Does setting good practice standards for research ethics committees increase their legal liability?' (1997), 314 BMJ 1833 at 1833.

personality to be a defendant in a civil action'.[14] Equally, McHale opined that 'an individual committee does not have any legal personality which is separate from that of their members' so that any action against 'an NHS REC ... would need to be brought against the body establishing the REC and individual members would be joined in the action'.[15] The issue is, however, much more complex than it appears from the opinions above.

Apart from legal personality acquired through registration and incorporation of an artificial entity or association, the easiest way an entity can establish a separate legal personality is to show that it is a creature of a statute under which it is given powers to sue and defend an action in its own name. In other cases, the court would have to determine whether a separate legal personality can be implied having regard to the prevailing facts and circumstances of a case. In *Fawehinmi v NBA (No. 2)*, the Supreme Court of Nigeria deployed a long line of English cases[16] to develop the criteria for the acquisition of a separate legal personality.[17] One of the issues in that case was whether the Nigerian Bar Association (NBA) (one of the defendants) was liable to be sued (or defend the action) in its name, having not been registered as a corporate body, nor created by a statute. The NBA was, however, recognized or mentioned in some statutes and subsidiary legislation in Nigeria. It was argued for the claimant that having regard to the several statutory and constitutional rights, privilege and powers conferred and duties imposed on the NBA, it was capable of being sued in its own name as a legal entity. In other words, that the NBA had in the circumstances been impliedly authorized by statute to sue or defend an action in its own name. The Supreme Court of Nigeria started by drawing a distinction between the recognition of an entity's separate existence (juridical personality), which is short of giving it a right to sue and defend actions in its own name, and the acquisition of a separate legal personality (juristic personality), which gives an entity the right to sue and defend an action in its own name.[18] It held that the NBA belonged to the former category: 'it is too late in the day to say now that the 1st respondent (NBA) has no existence at all known to the law apart from its members. But in my judgement that is not the same thing as saying that it is a legal persona which can sue and be sued *eo nomine* by virtue of the fact alone that it has an entity or existence known

14 Margaret Brazier, 'Liability of ethics committees and their members' (1990), Professional negligence 186 at 187.

15 J.V. McHale, 'Liability in the law of tort of research ethics committees and their members' (2005), 1 Research Ethics Review 53 at 54.

16 For instance: *Bonsor v Musicians Union* [1956] A.C. 104; *Knight and Searle v Dove* [1964] 2 All ER 307; *Taff Vale Railway Co. v Amalgamated Society of Railway Servants* [1901] A.C. 426; *Willis v Association of Universities of the British Commonwealth* [1964] 2 All ER 39; Vine v National Dock Labour Board [1957] A.C. 488.

17 *Fawehinmi v NBA* (No. 2) [1989] 2 NWLR 558 (SCN).

18 Ibid., at 608 (Agbaje, JSC), and at 648 (Oputa, JSC)

to the law and nothing else'. [19] The apex court confirmed its earlier decision in *Thomas v Local Government Service Board*[20] to the effect that creation by a statute alone does not give a statutory body a separate legal personality unless the statute expressly or impliedly gives it a right to sue or defend an action in its own name.[21] Such rights would be implied, however, where the exercise of powers under the statute would result in injustice to the claimant, and the injustice would be irreparable unless the statutory body's power to defend the claimant's action is implied in the circumstances.[22] This will be the case where a statutory body is not given express powers to sue or defend an action but it, nevertheless, exercises its statutory powers in a way that harms or infringes the rights of a claimant. Thus, legal personality is usually implied in order to obviate potential injustice. In the end, the Nigerian Supreme Court unanimously held in *Fawehinmi v NBA (No. 2)* that the statutory recognition given to NBA, through a right to appoint, nominate or elect some of its members to serve as members of various statutory bodies, did not justify a conclusion that the legislature thereby impliedly endowed the NBA with capacity to sue and defend actions in its own name. In addition, the Supreme Court held that a separate legal personality could not be implied for the NBA since it (NBA) cannot own land (except through trustees) or act through agents. Nor was injustice occasioned by depriving the NBA of a separate legal personality since it could always sue and defend actions in a representative capacity.

Based on the analysis above, it is difficult to say with certainty whether or not an ethics committee would be recognized as having a legal personality separate from those of its members. Much will depend on the facts and circumstances of each case. A few observations might, however, be in order. Generally, research ethics committees in universities are neither registered as corporate bodies nor created by statutes. They operate as one of the various administrative, non-statutory, structures or committees in the universities. Legal actions for wrongs committed by most university ethics committees are usually brought against the university rather than the committee in question. Consequently, a wrong committed by the research ethics committee of a university will not be left without a remedy. This avoids the need to imply a separate legal personality in order to obviate potential injustice;[23] the university would be answerable for the wrongs of its ethics committee.[24] Moreover, it is inconceivable that a statute (or charter) that established a university would contemplate that the university's ethics committee

19 Ibid., at 601 (Agbaje, JSC).

20 *Thomas v Local Government Service Board* [1965] 1 All N.L.R. 168 (SCN). Also, *Kpebimoh v The Board of Governors Western Ijaw Teachers Training College* [1966] N.M.L.R. 130 (HC); *The Solicitor-General Western Nigeria v Adedoyin* [1973] 3 U.I.L.R. 143 (CAW).

21 Fawehinmi, [1989] 2 NWLR 588 at 608.

22 Ibid., at 611; *Thomas v LGSB* [1965] 1 All N.L.R. 168.

23 *Thomas v Local Government Service Board* [1965] 1 All N.L.R. 168 (SCN).

24 Brazier thought that liability will not be vicarious but based on the institution's breach of a primary or secondary duty: Brazier, supra, note 14, at188.

could sue, or defend, an action in its own name. Accordingly, it will be extremely difficult to establish that a university research ethics committee has acquired a juristic status or legal personality. Even for ethics committees created by statutes, the cases above show that mere statutory evolution is not sufficient to create a separate legal personality. In addition, it must be proved that the statute expressly or impliedly conferred on the ethics committee a right to sue or defend actions in court. A claimant-investigator or research subject might, however, be able to establish a separate legal personality of an ethics committee by demonstrating that injustice or legal injury would arise if legal personality was denied. As a practical step, therefore, a claimant is better advised to sue not only the ethics committee, but also its individual members and the parent institution.

## Liability of Individual Members of Research Ethics Committees

For sure, each member of an ethics committee is separately (and individually) responsible for any harm suffered by a research subject as a result of the negligent review of a protocol. In a recent US case, for instance, members of an institutional review board (IRB – name of research ethics committees in the US) were individually named in a Complaint by a claimant. The case is discussed below.[25] The concept of individual liability, however, calls for the development of an appropriate standard of care. This task is compounded by the multidisciplinary composition of most research ethics committees. As such, it is desirable that different standards of care should be applied to determine the liability of members of an ethics committee. Thus, the standard of care applicable to the scientific or professional members should not apply to lay or community representatives. In the context of hospital ethics committees, which give advice on ethically charged medical problems, Merritt observed that each 'member may be held to a standard of reasonable competence and care for a member of that individual's profession' and that though 'standards of professional competence may be more sharply defined for some members of the committee (physicians, psychiatrists, lawyers) than for others (lay persons, clergy, academically trained ethical philosophers), this does not eliminate the possibility of formulating a standard of care.'[26] Discriminating standards of care are further justified by the actual practice of ethics committees; proceedings of most ethics committees are characterized by the domination of

25 *Robertson v McGee*, 202 WL 535045 (N.D. Okla). Generally: Randi Z. Shaul, et al., 'Legal liabilities in research: early lessons from North America' (2005), 6 BMC Medical Ethics 4; Mary M. Thomson, 'Bringing Research into Therapy; Liability Anyone?', in Trudo Lemmens and Duff Warring (eds), *Law and Ethics in Biomedical Research: Regulation, Conflict of Interests, and Liability* (Toronto: University of Toronto Press, 2006) at 183–205.

26 Andrew L. Merritt, 'The Tort Liability of Hospital Ethics Committees' (1987), 60 Southern Cal. L. Rev. 1239 at 1295.

scientific and professional members.[27] While the suggestion above implies a lower standard of care for lay members of an ethics committee, Bordas warned that a 'lay member or one who possesses no special expertise in the field being reviewed still has the responsibility of being conscious of his own ignorance', and that in such a case the standard of care would require him 'to know at least enough to conduct an intelligent inquiry as to what he does not know'.[28] Individual liability would also mean that habitual and unreasonable approval of protocols or their amendments by only the chairperson of an ethics committee (chair's action) would lead to the legal liability of that chairperson alone. In *Robertson v McGee*, for instance, the IRB chair (Dr Daniel C. Plunket) was accused, among other things, of a unilateral retroactive approval of deviations from the criteria originally approved by IRB for the enrolment of subjects.[29] If the case had gone to full trial, Dr Plunket alone would have been responsible for that wrong.

Similarly, where an ethics committee delegates the initial review of a protocol to one of its members (lead reviewer), then that member would be liable for any negligence or misrepresentation that led to the approval of a dangerous protocol by other committee members. It has even been hypothesized that if a lead reviewer 'wilfully provided incorrect or incomplete information to the other committee members in the process of that review, perhaps to mislead them into believing the trial is safer than it is, then that member might be held to be guilty of an offence'.[30] Individual liability, on the other hand, has its own defensive utility. For instance, members who voted against the approval of a protocol that turned out to be unsafe might be free from legal liability for the harm suffered by a research subject in connection with that protocol.[31] For this reason, it is crucial to have a record of how the members voted for each protocol. The availability of this much-needed evidence, however, depends on the procedures of an ethics committee, its record-keeping profile and the comprehensiveness of the minutes of its meetings. Where minutes of proceedings are deficient in details or the committee does not keep a record of how the members voted for each protocol, it might be difficult to prove a member's negative vote against an unacceptably risky protocol. Lapse of time

---

27 J.A. Goldner, 'An Overview of Legal Controls on Human Experimentation and the Regulatory Implications of Taking Professor Katz Seriously' (1993), 38 St Louis U. L.J. 63 at 106; A. Verdun-Jones and D.N. Weisstub, 'The Regulation of Biomedical Research Experimentation in Canada; Developing an Effective Apparatus for the Implementation of Ethical Principles in a Scientific Milieu' (1997), 28 Ottawa L. Rev. 297 at 311.

28 Linda M. Bordas, 'Tort Liability of Institutional Review Boards' (1984–85), 87 W. Va. L. Rev. 137 at 149.

29 Mary R. Anderlik and Nanette Elster, 'Lawsuits Against IRBs; Accountability or Incongruity? (2001), 29 J.L. Med. & Ethics 220 at 221.

30 Stephen Baker et al., 'Research Ethics Committees and the Law in the UK', in Deryck Beyleveld et al. (eds), Research Committees, Data Protection and Medical Research in European Countries (Aldershot: Ashgate, 2005) at 278.

31 John A. Robertson, 'The Law of Institutional Review Boards' (1979), 26 UCLA L. Rev. 484 at 532.

will likely compound the problems of poor record-keeping. Absent any recorded evidence, for instance, it might be difficult to recall how members voted on a particular protocol approved, say, ten or more years ago. Accordingly, it is prudent for members, especially those who voted against a high-risk research protocol, to insist that their negative votes are recorded even if the recording of votes is not part of the customary practice of their ethics committee. While many ethics committees have developed effective standard operating procedures (SOP), some still operate in a procedurally perfunctory manner despite international efforts in that regard.[32] Inadequate record-keeping and deficient review proceedings not only make it difficult to prove a member's vote; it also exposes ethics committees to negligent liability. In *Robertson v McGee*, for instance, it was alleged that: the Tulsa IRB minutes of meeting repeatedly lacked detail to document discussion of issues or adequate basis for requiring changes to protocols or informed consent documents; that there was no documentation reflecting that the Tulsa IRB reviewed or considered investigator brochures, case report forms or subject recruitment information related to studies under consideration; that in the case of expedited approval by the IRB chair, which was subsequently forwarded to the full board, the minutes only documented the unanimous approval of the board and lacked documentation of discussion of the administrative action; and that the Tulsa IRB did not keep a membership list older than two years.[33] Unfortunately, the case was dismissed for want of jurisdiction, and thus the legal implications of these allegations were not examined.

Secrecy of the proceedings of ethics committees adds another layer of complication to the evidential burden confronting a research subject who alleges negligence against members of ethics committees. Similar procedural difficulties are faced by a committee member who wants to prove a negative vote against a controversial protocol. Minou Friele remarked that the secrecy characterizing the proceedings of most ethics committees is antithetical to the culture of transparency

32 For instance: *World Health Organisation, Operational Guidelines for Ethics Committees that Review Biomedical Research* (Geneva: WHO, 2000).

33 *Robertson v McGee*, Case No. 01CV0060H (US District Court for the Northern District of Oklahoma) at13–14 (on file with author). Similarly, in the hexamathonium asthma study at Johns Hopkins University, which led to the death of 24-year-old Ellen Roche (a healthy volunteer), the Johns Hopkins IRB was accused of failing to uncover published literature about the toxic effects of inhaling hexamathonium, failing to ensure that volunteers were adequately warned of potential risks, conducting review of the study at an improperly convened meeting, and failing to keep proper minutes of meeting and documentation to show attendance at meeting and that research was reviewed according to correct procedures: J. Savulescu, 'Two Deaths and Two Lessons: Is it Time to Review the Structure and Function of Research Ethics Committees?' [2002] 28 J. Med. Ethics 1–2; J. Savulescu and M. Spriggs, 'The Hexamethonium Asthma Study and the Death of a Normal Volunteer in Research' [2002] 28 J. Med. Ethics 3–4.

which underlies the democratic process.[34] In the context of proposals for regulating research on the terminally ill, Annas also argued that since ethics committees are commonly dominated by expert members (in terms of composition), '[A] ll meetings of such review committees should be open to the public, because openness helps to dilute the power and democratically enfranchise the public'.[35] But there may be good reasons for excluding the public from the meetings of ethics committees. It is arguable that review of a protocol requires free, full and frank discussion, an objective that is not promoted by public access to the proceedings of ethics committees. Some research ethics committee members might feel very uneasy to condemn or reject a protocol in the presence of an investigator who is likely to be a colleague in the same institution. Frank discussion is even more likely to be stifled where the investigator is a highly established scholar and powerful figure in the institution. Fear of retaliation from such individuals is real. Apart from the investigator, access to other members of the public might inhibit efficacious review because of the propensity for a defensive review. In the public glare, for instance, some members would be more sensitive and overly conscious of wrongdoing, an attitude that might come with huge distraction and deviation from effective review. Arguably, therefore, members of ethics committees need not be put in a position where they have to constantly look over their shoulders in the course of a review.

Ashcroft and Pfeffer have explored other potential justifications for the secrecy of research ethics committees' meetings.[36] These include the need to maintain independence of review, protection of medical confidentiality, commercial and academic confidentiality, privacy of researchers and privacy of committees. In the end, the authors cautioned that secrecy could be used to 'hide inadequacies in the reviewing process or in the reviewers themselves'.[37] They further observed that there is no clear justification for the confidentiality of review meetings, nor are the grounds normally cited in justification sufficient to the purpose. The authors concluded that given 'that the culture of the NHS is shifting towards one of openness and accountability, and that researchers increasingly argue for public registration and reporting of clinical trials, the confidentiality position of committees is anomalous'.[38] But the legal impact of the secrecy rule on a claimant should not be exaggerated. For instance, a claimant could obtain a court order for the discovery, inspection and production of ethics committees' documents. Oral evidence could be admitted to prove a negative vote or the manner various

---

34 Minou B. Friele, 'Do Committees Ru(i)n the Bio-Political Culture? On the Democratic Legitimacy of Bioethics Committees' (2003), 17 Bioethics 301 at 311–312.

35 George J. Annas, 'The Changing Landscape of Human Experimentation: Nuremberg, Helsinki and beyond' (1992), 2 Health Matrix 119 at 137.

36 R. Ashcroft and N. Pfeffer, 'Ethics behind closed doors: do research ethics committees need secrecy?' (2001), 322 BMJ 1294–1296.

37 Ibid., at 1296

38 Ibid., at 1296.

members voted on a particular protocol. In desirable cases, a claimant might get the court to subpoena one or more members of an ethics committee to testify in court. The point, however, is that despite some potential evidential difficulties, each member of an ethics committee is individually liable for a review that caused injury to a research subject.

## Negligent Acts and Omissions of Research Ethics Committees

Whether sued individually or as a 'corporate' body, ethics committees are potentially liable in negligence for the poor execution of their duties. Each function of an ethics committee carries a potential risk of negligent liability. Take, for instance, the notion of equipoise (in clinical drug trials) examined in chapter two. An ethics committee which approved a research protocol or clinical drug trial that lacked equipoise would expose itself to legal liability in negligence. Legal liability would also arise where any of the conditions implied by equipoise were not met. For instance, where an ethics committee approves a clinical drug trial that is designed to give the participants a known inferior treatment; or plans to use a placebo-control arm for the investigation of a serious medical condition despite the availability of an effective treatment for that condition. Risk assessment is another example. This is one of the most important tasks of ethics committees; yet research guidelines do not provide any guidance beyond the general requirement that risks should be minimized and should be adjudged reasonable in relation to anticipated benefits.[39] There is no standard for assigning value to the risks in order to measure their reasonableness against the expected benefits of the research.[40] While this ambiguity gives much power and discretion to ethics committees, it nevertheless exposes ethics committees to potential tort liability at the suit of aggrieved subjects. An investigator's overzealous quest for knowledge might motivate their overestimation of the benefits of a research protocol or gross underestimation of its risks. This, ordinarily, should be easily spotted by an ethics committee. Sadly, an ethics committee might approve such protocols either out of its ignorance or deliberate attempt to facilitate the research of members of the host institution. Either way, legal liability would result if an ethics committee's inaccurate risk assessment caused injury to a research subject. It is highly unlikely, however, that an ethics committee would be ignorant of the terms or subject-matter of a protocol because its multidisciplinary composition ensures that one or more of its

39 For instance, Federal Ministry of Health (Nigeria), *National Code of Health Research Ethics* (FMoH, Nigeria, 2007), at 36–37. In the USA, 45 C.F.R. § 46.111(a) (2) (2002) provides that the 'IRB shall determine that … risks to subjects are reasonable in relation to anticipated benefits, if any, to subjects…'.

40 For risk assessment generally: L. Kopelman, 'Estimating Risk in Human Research' (1981), 29 Clinical Research 1–8; W. Ezekiel, et al., 'What Makes Clinical Research Ethical?' (2000), 283 JAMA 2701–2711.

members should be competent in a field of study under review. Even if this were not possible, an ethics committee should be able to engage an outside expert or external reviewer to provide an opinion on the recondite protocol. As chapter three highlighted, most guidelines permit the engagement of an expert or consultant and some ethics committees do so in practice, for instance, the Tanzanian National Institute of Medical Research. Thus, ignorance will hardly be an excuse for the negligent assessment of research risks.

Deliberate overestimation of the benefits (or underestimation of the risks) of a study could be condoned or overtly supported by an ethics committee. Motives for such support include the desire to help a colleague secure a career-enhancing research fund or the need to position the university/host institution for a favourable research ranking.[41] Since most ethics committee members are also members of the faculties of the host institution, they are naturally sensitive to the collegial context of the review and realize, as Katz observed, 'when sitting in judgement of a research protocol, that their proposals may soon be subjected to similar scrutiny'.[42] Katz further observed that 'it is unlikely that members of IRBs will hold investigators to a standard of disclosure and consent that would protect the subjects of research if doing so would place impediments on the conduct of research and, in turn, affect the well-being of their colleagues in decisive ways'.[43] Furthermore, Judge Cathell of the Maryland Court of Appeals observed that since ethics committees are 'primarily in-house organs' they are 'not designed, generally, to be sufficiently objective in the sense that they are as sufficiently concerned with the ethicality of the experiments they review as they are with the success of the experiments'.[44]Moreover, an ethics committee may feel intimidated to approve an unmeritorious protocol from a lead researcher in the university out of fear of possible retaliatory measures.[45]

Condoning inaccurate risk assessments would most likely occur where a member of an ethics committee competent in a protocol's field of study decides to be silent on technical issues during a review process. Other (non-expert) members would likely take the silence as a show of support for the protocol.[46] In such a case, the 'expert' member will be severally and jointly liable with the non-expert members. *Grimes v Kennedy Krieger Institute* possibly illustrates an ethics

41 Hazel G. Beh, 'The Role of Institutional Review Boards in Protecting Human Subjects: Are We Really Ready to Fix a Broken System?' (2002), 26 Law & Psychology 1 at 40; Adil E. Shamoo, 'Institutional Review Boards (IRBs) and Conflict of Interest' (1999), 7 Accountability In Research 201at 207.

42 J. Katz, 'Human Experimentation and Human Rights' (1993), 38 St Louis U. L.J. 7 at 41.

43 Ibid., at 41.

44 *Grimes v Kennedy Krieger Institute*, 782 A.2d 807 at 817 (Md. 2001).

45 Beh, supra, note 314, at 41.

46 Bordas, supra, note 28, 137 at 142.

committee's overt support for inadequate and inaccurate risk assessment.[47] The case involved a lead paint abatement study using children as research subjects, and conducted by researchers at the Kennedy Krieger Institute, an affiliate of Johns Hopkins University. The protocol design involved the exposure of children enrolled in the experimental arms of the study to lead poison; the control groups consisted of children living in lead paint abated buildings and new buildings that were free from paint dust. The institutional review board of the Johns Hopkins University queried the inclusion of a control group in the study since USA regulations preclude the use of children in research unless it was capable of providing direct benefits to the children, or involved no more than minimal risk.[48] Despite its observation on the ethically problematic use of children as controls in studies that held no direct benefits to them, the IRB went ahead to make suggestions to the investigators on how they could circumvent the applicable regulation:

> The next issue has to do with drawing blood from the control population, namely children growing up in modern urban housing. Federal guidelines are really quite specific regarding using children as controls in projects in which there is no potential benefit [to the particular children].
>
> To call a subject a normal control is to indicate that there is no real benefit to be received [by the particular children] … So we think it would be much more acceptable to indicate that the "control group" is being studied to determine what exposure outside the home may play in a total lead exposure; thereby, indicating that these control individuals are gaining some benefit, namely learning whether safe housing alone is sufficient to keep the blood-lead levels in acceptable bounds. We suggest that you … modify consent form[s] … accordingly.[49]

As would be expected, the Maryland Court of Appeals thoroughly castigated the approach taken by the IRB in that case. The court observed that the IRB not only abdicated its responsibility, it also suggested 'to the researchers a way to miscast the characteristics of the study in order to avoid the responsibility inherent in non-therapeutic research involving children'.[50] The court regretted that the IRB, whose 'primary function was to ensure safety and compliance with applicable regulations, encouraged the researchers to misrepresent the purpose of the research in order to bring the study under the label "therapeutic" and thus under a lower safety standard of regulation. The IRB's purpose was ethically wrong'.[51]

An ethics committee would also be liable to a research subject if it was negligent in the review of consent forms and processes or in monitoring a study. For instance, an injured research subject might allege that, with proper

47 *Grimes v Kennedy Krieger Institute*, 782 A.2d 807 (Md. 2001).

48 45 C.F.R. §46.405.

49 Grimes, 782 A.2d 807 at 814.

50 Ibid., at 813.

51 Ibid., at 817.

monitoring, an ethics committee would have timely discovered the potential danger that eventually caused harm to the subject. In other words, but for the negligence of the ethics committee, the research ought properly to have been stopped before the injury arose. Some of these issues arose in *Gregg v Kane*, where the claimant suffered injuries resulting from an experimental eye operation in the form of excimer laser surgery.[52] Against the defendants, the claimant alleged numerous and unauthorized deviations from the original protocol and the use of improper and insufficient consent forms. Regarding claimant's claim for lack of informed consent, Buckwalter J observed that 'the FDA regulations make IRBs … responsible for insuring that informed consent will be sought from all prospective subjects, in accordance with fairly detailed standards governing such consent'.[53] Thus, Buckwalter J concluded that given 'what occurred with respect to informed consent in Mrs Gregg's Case (claimant), Wills (the eye hospital defendant) could be found liable for not fulfilling its FDA-mandated responsibilities'.[54] Similarly, the claimant in *Kus v Sherman Hospital* suffered permanent damage in his eyes as a result of going through an investigational intraocular lens implantation.[55] The consent form approved by the defendant's IRB was, without the permission of the IRB, modified by the investigator to remove references to the investigational nature of the procedure. Thus, the claimant did not know that he was engaged in an experimental medical procedure. If the defendant's IRB had performed its continuing review function, the investigator's unauthorized conduct would have been detected and the injury to the claimant might have been averted. The court observed that the 'defence's expert witness … admitted that, if Sherman Hospital's IRB had audited any of Dr Vancil's (investigator) charts in the 1½ years before Kus' surgery, the IRB would have discovered Vancil's use of the modified consent form'.[56] Consequently, the court held that the defendant's failure, through its IRB, to perform a continuing review of the intraocular lens implantation study indicated negligence sufficient to deny the (defendant's) motion to dismiss the action.

## Recent Cases in Negligence against Research Ethics Committees

While the analysis above highlighted some of the circumstances in which ethics committees may incur liability in negligence, it does not provide an examination of the elements of negligence against which the actions (or omissions) of an ethics committee would be measured. This needs to be done. Recall that in *Grimes v Kennedy Krieger Institute*, the Maryland Court of Appeals severely castigated the action of Johns Hopkins University's institutional review board in helping

52 *Gregg v Kane*, 1997 WL 570909 (E.D. Pa.).
53 Ibid., at 4.
54 Ibid., at 4.
55 *Kus v Sherman Hospital*, 644 N.E.2d 1214 (App. Ct. Ill., 1995).
56 Ibid., at 1218.

the investigators through a mischaracterization of the study (as one capable of benefiting the children used as research subjects) in a way that avoids the onerous obligations imposed by applicable regulations on non-therapeutic research involving children. Yet, the *Grimes* court did not directly consider the question of whether a duty of care is owed by research ethics committees to research subjects and, if so, what are the bases for the imposition of such duty? The court's detailed analysis of duty of care owed by investigators to research subjects is not easily transposable to the ethics committee-research subject relationship, not least because of the obvious differences in the dynamics of the two sets of relationships. Nor is the author aware of any reported case where the duty of ethics committees to research subjects was directly in issue.[57] In the UK, such litigation was expected to result from the serious injuries (multiple organ failure) suffered by six men who participated in a phase one clinical trial of an investigational anti-inflammatory drug in 2006. The participants, however, accepted monetary compensation in return for their agreement not to sue.[58] Before considering recent cases in which ethics committees (or their members) were directly named as defendants in a suit, it may be relevant to consider in more detail two previously mentioned cases in which parent institutions were held liable for the negligence of their ethics committees. The first case is *Gregg v Kane*.[59] As earlier noted, the claimant in that case complained that the investigator/physician used consent forms unsuitable for the procedure involved in the protocol – excimer laser surgery. In addition, the consent forms were inadequate for failing to make sufficient disclosure of all possible risks involved in the procedure. Although the claimant in *Gregg* sued the investigator, hospital (Wills Ever Hospital), and sponsor of the (medical device) clinical trial (Visx Inc.), the IRB of Wills hospital was not sued. Nevertheless, Buckwalter J observed:

> Wills' Institutional Review Board (IRB), the body which approved the protocol in which Mrs Gregg was enrolled, was required by FDA regulations to make an independent risk assessment prior to its approval .... Yet neither the IRB statement granting unconditional approval nor the minutes of IRB meetings discussing the protocol contain any indication that such an assessment was done.

---

57 *Weiss v Solomon* [1989] R.J.Q. 731 (C.S. civ.), was decided mainly on the basis of vicarious liability, that is, the liability of a hospital for the negligence of its ethics committee. The court was not called upon to consider (and did not discuss) the question of ethics committees' (direct) liability to research subjects. Generally: Anderlik and Elster, supra, note 29.

58 For excellent discussion of the incident: Pamela R. Ferguson, 'Clinical Trials and Healthy Volunteers' (2008), 16 Med. L. R. 23–51; M. Brazier and E. Cave, *Medicine, Patients and the Law, 4th edn* (London: Penguin Books, 2007), 409–411. Author's enquiries with the Association of Research Ethics Committees show that there is no current litigation in the UK concerning the legal liability of research ethics committees. The author is grateful to David Anderson-Ford, Chair, Association of Research Ethics Committees, for this information.

59 *Gregg v Kane*, 1997 WL 570909 (E.D. Pa.).

> Nor is there any other evidence that the IRB performed the independent risk assessment.

For this failure on the part of Wills' IRB, the Wills Eye Hospital was held potentially liable in negligence to the claimant and, thus, the motion to dismiss claimant's action was refused. Similarly, in *Weiss v Solomon*,[60] the deceased claimant was recruited in a study that tested the efficacy of indomethacin (eye-drops) in the management of side-effects associated with cataract surgery. The procedure involved the administration of three fluorescein angiograms (injection of fluorescein dye) immediately after the application of the eye-drops. In the course of the above procedure, the claimant suffered cardiac arrest and died. Unbeknown to the investigators, the claimant suffered from a heart condition (hypertrophic cardiomyopathy), though the causal connection between the experimental procedure and the claimant's death was not clear. It was argued for the claimant that the defendant/hospital was liable for the negligence of its ethics committee (that reviewed the study) in approving the protocol without requiring that the recruitment criteria be altered to exclude persons like the claimant, and for not demanding a much more detailed disclosure of risks in the consent form (to include remote but serious risks of harm). After observing that the protection of research subjects was the responsibility of the investigator, the court further observed:

> It is the same for the defendant Hospital, which, by its Research Committee, approved the research protocol as well as the consent form to be obtained from each research subject. The Research Committee of the hospital must be aware of that which its participants and members know. Even if the consent form to be obtained from the research subject does not fall under any regulations, we should ask ourselves why the risk of the fluoroscein angiogram was minimized in the consent form, whereas it should have been explained in detail by the doctor in charge of implementing the research protocol.[61]

In contrast to the above, there are a few US cases in which ethics committees or their members were directly named as defendants in a claimant's action. For instance, in *Head v Colloton*,[62] Chairman of the Institutional Review Board (IRB) of the University of Iowa Hospitals was named as a defendant in the suit. In part, the case sought to compel the IRB to approve an amendment of an unrelated bone marrow transplant protocol in a way that risked breaching the confidentiality of a subject. This is probably the first case in which an IRB was sued; but its significance is diminished by the lack of judicial analysis or consideration of the

60 *Weiss v Solomon* [1989] R.J.Q. 731. For analysis of this case: B. Freedman and K.C. Glass, 'Weiss v Solomon: A Case Study in Institutional Responsibility for Clinical Research' (1990), 88 Law, Medicine & Health Care 395.

61 Weiss, supra, note 3, at 743–744.

62 *Head v Colloton*, 331 N.W.2d 870 (Sup. Ct. Iowa, 1983).

medico-ethical issues raised by the parties. The judges, instead, focused on the question of whether information in hospital records belonging to a potential bone marrow donor qualified as protectable patient information.[63] More recent cases involving ethics committees ended inconclusively. In *Gelsinger v University of Pennsylvania*,[64] Jesse Gelsinger participated in a gene therapy protocol conducted by researchers at the prestigious Institute of Human Gene Therapy in the University of Pennsylvania. The protocol was a phase one clinical trial of a gene transfer treatment for a rare metabolic disorder, ornithine transcarbamylase deficiency syndrome (OTC). Jesse suffered from a mild form of OTC (controlled by diet and medication) and, thus, did not stand to benefit (therapeutically) from the clinical trial. The protocol essentially involved the use of adenoviral vector (allegedly more dangerous than other viral vectors) to lodge a repair genetic material into the recipient's genome. As a result of the procedure, Jesse suffered multiple organ failure and died. The investigators were accused of using consent forms that did not sufficiently warn Jesse of the risks involved in the study, and of deliberately withholding the reports of previous adverse events in the use of the procedure on humans and animals. The institutional review board was blamed for conducting an insufficient ethical review of the protocol and for abdicating its monitoring functions. The case was quickly settled out of court within two months of its commencement.[65]

In *Robertson v McGee*,[66] members of the institutional review board (IRB) of the University of Oklahoma Health Sciences Centre – Tulsa were named in a suit brought by former research subjects in a cancer vaccine study conducted by the defendants. The Complaint alleged that the IRB was negligent in approving a protocol that was deficient in several respects. For instance, it 'failed to examine the design of the protocol … assure protection of the participants, review proposed amendments to the informed consent forms provided to the patient, approve advertisements for the Trial, ensure proper reporting, and make certain that the Trial comported with ethical standards'.[67] More particularly, the IRB was accused of approving instructions for self-administration of the experimental vaccine by the research participants without the supervision of the investigator, and of approving major amendments to the Trial protocol through an expedited review

63 An ethical background and context of the case was analysed by a member of the institutional review board that reviewed the protocol in that case: Dena S. Davis, 'Case Study "Dear Mrs. X …"' (1983), IRB November/December 6-9.

64 *Gelsinger v University of Pennsylvania* (Complaint filed on 18 September 2000, Philadelphia County Court of Common Pleas Trial Division. Posted on: http://www.sskrplaw.com/links/healthcare2.html – last visited on 16 December 2010).

65 Paul L. Gelsinger, 'Uninformed Consent: The Case of Jesse Gelsinger', in Lemmens and Warring (eds), supra, note 25, 12–32.

66 *Robertson v McGee*, Case No. 01CV0060H (US District Court for the Northern District of Oklahoma) (on file with author).

67 Robertson, supra, note 31, at 13.

process. Also, the IRB was blamed for not presenting Trial-related protocol waivers to the full Board for approval prior to the enrolment of research subjects; nor did it require approval of the Trial-related advertisements prior to use by the clinical investigator. There were also allegations of failure to report adverse events and enrolment of ineligible patients. However, the case could not proceed to trial due to the success of the defendants' motions to dismiss (the case) for want of federal subject matter jurisdiction.[68] Claimants unsuccessfully argued that a federal right of action (and therefore jurisdiction in a federal court) existed through the guarantees in the Nuremberg Code and the Declaration of Helsinki. Claimants further argued that the standards embodied in the above international documents were impliedly incorporated into the American Constitution. Finally, the claimants contended that a violation of federal regulations (45 C.F.R. Part 46), which were developed to protect the rights and dignity of research subjects, would give a right of action in the federal courts. In dismissing the case for want of jurisdiction, Senior Judge Cook observed that 'there is no private right of action for an alleged violation of international law for the protection of human research subjects under the Declaration of Helsinki and the Nuremberg Code', and further, that 'there is no private right of action under 21 C.F.R'.[69] The court held that a breach of federal regulations for the conduct of research would only attract the comprehensive enforcement mechanism structured around the US Food and Drug Administration (FDA). These judicial observations, in *Robertson v McGee*, mark a retreat from the enthusiasm shown by the Maryland Court of Appeal in *Grimes v Kennedy Krieger Institute* regarding the use of Nuremberg Code and US federal regulations to ground the (potential) tort liability of investigators and ethics committees. Thus, *Robertson v McGee* undermines efforts to hold ethics committees legally accountable through famous international research guidelines and the local regulations that incorporate them. As no case has yet determined the legal liability of ethics committees, the question of whether they owe a duty of care to research subjects would, therefore, be decided on first principles.

## Duty of Care

'Duty of care' is a relational concept. It aims to limit the tortious liability of a wrongdoer. Without such a concept, a wrongdoer would be liable for every harmful wrong even if no prior legal relationship existed with the claimant. Accordingly, the 'duty of care' is a legal control mechanism that requires the justification of negligent liability by reference to the existence of a legally recognizable relationship between the claimant and defendant.[70] In a sense, the existence or non-existence of

68 *Robertson v McGee*, 202 WL 535045 (N.D. Okla).

69 Ibid., at 3.

70 Generally: Winfield, P.H. 'The History of Negligence in the Law of Torts' (1926), 42 L.Q.R. 184.

a legal duty of care in negligence is a policy decision with full legal colouration. Much of this is evident in the authoritative proposition by Prosser and Keeton that the 'duty of care' is 'not sacrosanct in itself, but is only an expression of the sum total of those considerations of policy which lead the law to say that the plaintiff is entitled to protection'.[71] Commentators from other jurisdictions generally agree with that proposition. Writing before the Canadian Supreme Court decision in *Cooper v Hobart*,[72] Klar argued that 'if plaintiffs are always foreseeable, there is always a presumptive duty of care, and the only real issue in negligence actions in so far as the existence of a duty is concerned is policy'.[73] Rogers has also observed that the 'question duty or no duty ultimately depends in most (and perhaps all) cases on the court's assessment of what is fair, just and reasonable',[74] which in turn are constructed by 'matters which take in a much broader range of questions than technical issues of law'.[75] American cases have clearly accepted the dominance of policy in the analysis of negligence.[76] For instance, in *Vu v Singer Co.*, the court enumerated seven factors that must be balanced in determining whether a duty of care exists in a particular case: these are the foreseeability of harm to claimant, the degree of certainty that claimant suffered injury, the closeness of connection between defendant's conduct and injury suffered, the moral blame attached to defendant's conduct, the policy of preventing future harm, the extent of burden to defendant and the consequences to the community of imposing a duty to exercise care with resulting liability for breach, and, finally, the availability, cost, and prevalence of insurance for the risk involved.[77] Similar factors were identified by Prosser and Keeton; these include the 'convenience of administration, capacity of the parties to bear the loss, a policy of preventing future injuries, the moral blame attached to the wrongdoer, and many others'.[78]

The factors above were neatly packaged into a tripartite analytic framework by the Supreme Court of Canada in *Cooper v Hobart*,[79] following the House of Lords decision in *Anns v Merton London Borough*.[80] Thus, at the first level of analysis,

71 W. Page et al. (eds), *Prosser and Keeton on the Law of Torts*, 5th edn (St Paul, MN.: West Publishing Co., 1984), at 358.

72 *Cooper v Hobart* [2001] 206 D.L.R. (4th) 193 (S.C.C.).

73 L.N. Klar, 'Judicial Activism in Private Law' (2001), 80 Can. Bar. Rev. 215 at 221.

74 W.V.H. Rogers, *Winfield and Jolowicz on Tort*, 18th edn (London: Sweet and Maxwell, 2010), at 153.

75 W.V.H. Rogers, *Winfield and Jolowicz on Tort*, 16th edn (London: Sweet and Maxwell, 2002), at 128.

76 Generally, Guido Calabresi, *The Costs of Accidents: A Legal and Economic Analysis*, 2nd edn (New Haven: Yale University Press, 1970).

77 *Vu v Singer Co.*, 538 F.Supp. 26 at 29 (N.D. California, 1981).

78 Page, supra, note 64, at 359.

79 *Cooper v Hobart* [2001] 206 D.L.R. (4th) 193 (S.C.C.), per McLachlin, CJC and Major J.

80 *Anns v Merton London Borough* [1978] A.C. 728 (HL), per Lord Wilberforce. This case was overruled by *Murphy v Brentwood DC* [1991] 1 A.C. 398 (HL).

the claimant must establish that he or she was within the zone of defendant's foreseeability of harm.[81] At the second level of analysis, the claimant must establish the existence of a proximate relationship with the defendant. If these two hurdles were successfully scaled, then the claimant is said to have established a *prima facie* duty of care. It is only then that the third level of analysis is engaged, with the result that the burden of proof is shifted to the defendant to show any factor that ought to limit or negate that duty. The analysis at this last stage is laden with policy considerations; it focuses on policy factors outside the relationship between the claimant and the defendant. These include the effect of recognizing a duty of care on other legal obligations,[82] the legal system and society more generally. The Supreme Court of Canada calls this analysis a residual policy consideration since similar policy analysis takes place even at the second stage of proximity.[83] At that stage (proximity) though, the policy analysis is limited to factors arising from the relationship between the claimant and the defendant, rather than broader (and more general) policy factors involving the society and legal system. In the leading English case of *Caparo Industries plc v Dickman*,[84] the House of Lords adopted a tripartite formula that is essentially similar to the Canadian approach. Lord Bridge observed:

> What emerges is that, in addition to the foreseeability of damage, necessary ingredients in any situation giving rise to a duty of care are that there should exist between the party owing the duty and the party to whom it is owed a relationship characterized by the law as one of 'proximity' or 'neighbourhood' and that the situation should be one in which the court considers it fair, just and reasonable that the law should impose a duty of a given scope upon the one party for the benefit of the other.[85]

In the context of research ethics committees, therefore, any duty of care owed to a research subject would depend on the existence of foreseeability of harm, proximity of relationship and on the absence of any policy factor that undermines

---

81 An illustrative case of the problem of foreseeability of harm is the famous judgement of Cardozo CJ in the American case of *Palsgraf v Long Island Ry. Co.*, 248 N.Y. 339 (1928, C.A.).

82 For instance, consider *C.B.S. Songs Ltd. v Amstrad Consumer Electric plc* [1988] A.C. 1013 (HL), where the House of Lords refused to recognize a duty of care on the part of a manufacturer of tape-to-tape domestic audio system (which could facilitate copyright infringement) on the ground that to impose negligence liability would subvert the statutory regime on copyright.

83 Rogers also observes that proximity analysis is policy oriented: 'The necessary degree of proximity is the product of the court's conclusion on what is fair, just and reasonable': Rogers, supra, note 75, at 126. (16th edn).

84 *Caparo Industries plc v Dickman* [1990] 2 A.C. 605 (HL).

85 Ibid., at 617–618. Also: *Customs and Excise Commissioners v Barclays Bank Plc* [2007] 1 A.C. 181 (HL).

the imposition of liability in negligence. In an important article, Brazier was in no doubt that ethics committees owe a duty of care to research subjects;[86] but her analysis seems to focus on policy considerations (the last stage of duty analysis) without a clear or separate examination of proximity:

> When a claim does arise out of the nature of the trial itself, there can be little doubt that the ethics committee, and each of its members, owe a duty of care to the aggrieved patient or volunteer. The committee exists to safeguard patients' interests. Within the NHS, the Department of Health has laid down rules which provide that no clinical trial can proceed without the 'green light' from the local research ethics committee. In these circumstances it would be difficult to argue that it is not 'just and reasonable' to impose a duty to patients and volunteers on local research ethics committees and their members.[87]

In the same vein, but after discussing the elemental constituents of a duty of care, Biggs observed in her interesting book that 'it seems self-evident that an REC, whose primary role is to protect the dignity, rights, safety and welfare of actual and potential research participants, would owe a duty of care to somebody like Sam (research subject)'.[88] With some trepidation, however, it is difficult to share the confidence of both Brazier and Biggs. As shown below, the author's diffidence emanates from a discriminating analysis of the three components of the duty framework, which shows that the duty relationship between an ethics committee and a research subject is neither self-evident nor free from doubt.

Foreseeability of harm could be easily established. For instance, Klar observed that 'foreseeability of the plaintiff as a potential victim of harm from negligent conduct is easily established. There have been no Supreme Court of Canada cases, or in fact any reported recent cases from any court, where the plaintiff has failed on the foreseeability test'.[89] Where an ethics committee negligently reviewed a protocol that caused injury to a research subject, it is not difficult to imagine that

---

86 Similarly, De Ville observed that in 'a negligence-based suit involving IRB members, the existence of a duty is clear': K. De Ville, 'The Role of Litigation in Human Research Accountability' (2002), 9 Accountability in Research 17 at 26. Also, Susan V. Zimmerman, 'Translating Ethics into Law: Duties of Care in Health Research Involving Humans' (2005), 13 Health Law Review 13 at 15, observed, on the basis of *Weiss v Soloman* [1989] 48 C.C.L.T. 280 (Que. Sup. Ct), that it 'is therefore clear that in Canada, research ethics boards owe a direct legal duty to research participants and may be held liable for a breach of that duty'; but in Weiss case, although the court castigated the perfunctory manner in which the defendant-hospital's ethics committee reviewed the protocol in question, the ethics committee itself was not sued as a party and the court's statement in that regard would, therefore, be considered obiter.

87 Brazier, supra, note 14, at 187.

88 Biggs, supra, note 10, at 62.

89 Klar, supra, note 73, at 215.

a court would hold that injury to be reasonably foreseeable.[90] It is much more difficult to establish a proximate relationship between research ethics committees and injured research subjects. In the field of negligence, proximity is a common but inscrutable term.[91] Other than the assurance in *Donoghue v Stevenson*[92] that 'proximity' is not limited to physical proximity, there is no specific guide to the meaning of the term beyond its vague description as a direct and close relationship which would justify the imposition of liability in negligence. Proximity is therefore a conclusory term, a characteristic that gives the courts great leeway in deciding whether the defendant should be liable for the claimant's loss. Accordingly, in *Caparo v Dickman*, Lord Bridge warned that:

> [t]he concepts of proximity and fairness ... are not susceptible of any such precise definition as would be necessary to give them utility as practical tests, but amount in effect to little more than convenient labels to attach to the features of different specific situations which, on a detailed examination of all the circumstances, the law recognizes pragmatically as giving rise to a duty of care of a given scope.[93]

Rogers equally highlighted the conclusory nature of 'proximity' in his observation that the 'reality would seem to be that "proximity" amounts to a statement of a conclusion that there is a duty of care'.[94] This ambiguity could be exploited by both the claimant and the defendant in a case where it is alleged that an ethics committee owes a legal duty of care to a research subject.

On one hand, it is arguable that research ethics committees do not stand in a proximate relationship with research subjects. Many reasons account for this position. Ethics committees rarely have physical or direct contact with research subjects, save for exceptional instances where an ethics committee decides to supervise the administration or execution of the informed consent process. Moreover, most protocols are approved before the recruitment of subjects begins, so that ethics committees do not know in advance or at all who would be the subjects of a particular protocol. Any knowledge of research subjects is likely to be at the level of generalization, such as their characteristics, origin, race, citizenship, age and health status. This sort of detachment from specific research subjects speaks

90 Thus, while Gold was right to observe that it 'is therefore foreseeable that an REB would have research subjects within its reasonable contemplation', her conclusion, essentially on the basis of foreseeability alone, that 'it is plain that a duty of care towards research participants by REB exists in Canada', is not convincing: Jennifer L. Gold, 'Watching the Watchdogs: Negligence, Liability, and Research Ethics Boards' (2003), 11 Health L.J. 153 at 160.

91 Rogers, supra, note 75, at 115–117.

92 *Donoghue v Stevenson* [1932] A.C. 562 at 581 (HL), per Lord Atkin.

93 *Caparo v Dickman* [1990] 2 A.C. 605 at 618.

94 Rogers, supra, note 75, at 116.

to the protective public function of ethics committees, which is to protect the public from unethical and unacceptably risky research. In that light, it is arguable that ethics committees occupy a position that is analogous to the Commissioner of Deposit-taking Companies in *Yueun Kun Yeu v Attorney-General of Hong Kong*,[95] where the Privy Council held that the Commissioner did not owe a duty of care to depositors with various financial institutions in Hong Kong (regulated by the Commissioner) partly because its statutory function was for the benefit of the public generally, rather than for the benefit of particular members of the public who deposited money with Hong Kong financial institutions. In the same way, ethics committees could be likened to the Registrar of Mortgage Brokers in *Cooper v Hobart*, who also owed its statutory duty to the public rather than to particular investors with the brokers regulated by the Registrar. Similarly, in *Hill v Chief Constable of West Yorkshire*,[96] it was held that there was no proximity between the police and victims of crime generally since the protective function of the police is for the benefit of the public at large.

On the other hand, it is arguable that proximity exists between ethics committees and research subjects. To begin with, the cases above could easily be distinguished. Apart from not being concerned about the liability of ethics committees, it is arguable that while the major function of the statutory bodies in those cases was the protection of the public at large, ethics committees (in contrast) protect particular subjects of specific protocols; it is only through this (specific) protection that the public at large is indirectly protected. Furthermore, ethics committees do not just give a general opinion on the ethics of research.[97] Instead, they review particular protocols to determine (among other things) whether the risks posed to the (particular) subjects of that research were reasonable. Thus, although ethics committees do not generally come into contact with research subjects, and those subjects are generally recruited after the approval of a protocol, yet ethics committees are hardly in doubt that each protocol raises a question of protection for particular research subjects rather than the public at large. Ethics committees' realization of and knowledge of the specific need for protection (of research subjects) raised by particular protocols is a possible anchorage for finding the existence of proximity. Support might come from a few English cases where it was held that proximity arose from the wrongdoer's knowledge of the use to which a tort victim put information from the wrongdoer.[98] Furthermore, research subjects are conceivably willing to participate in research only after it

95 *Yueun Kun Yeu v Attorney-General of Hong Kong* [1988] A.C. 175 (PC).

96 *Hill v Chief Constable of West Yorkshire* [1989] A.C. 53 (HL). Also: *Goodwill v British Pregnancy Advisory Service* [1996] 1 W.L.R. 1397.

97 As chapter four shows, it is even doubtful whether it is a proper function of research ethics committees to give a general opinion on matters of ethics instead of assessing the ethical acceptability of a particular protocol.

98 *Cann v Wilson* [1888] 39 Ch. D 39; *Candler v Crane Christmas & Co. Ltd* [1951] 2 K.B. 164 (C.A.) per Denning LJ; *Hedley Byrne & Co. Ltd. v Heller & Partners Ltd* [1964]

has been approved by an ethics committee. In other words, successful recruitment is based on the anticipation and expectation of a research subject that the protocol went through a successful ethics review, as well as their reliance on the representations of an ethics committee (through the protocol's approval) that the protocol was safe. In *Sutherland Shire Council v Heyman*, Mason J of the High Court of Australia suggested, though in the context of public authorities, that these factors (expectation, representation, dependence and reliance) might give rise to proximity:

> [t]here will be cases in which the plaintiff's reasonable reliance will arise out of a general dependence on the authority's performance of its function with due care, without the need for contributing conduct on the part of a defendant or action to his detriment on the part of the plaintiff. Reliance or dependence in this sense is in general the product of the grant (and exercise) of powers designed to prevent or minimize the risk of personal injury or disability, recognized by the legislature as being of such magnitude or complexity that individuals cannot, or may not take adequate steps for their own protection. This situation generates on one side (the individual) a general expectation that the power will be exercised and on the other side (the authority) a realization that there is a general reliance or dependence on its exercise of the power.[99]

However, even if the relationship between ethics committees and research subjects was found to be proximate in nature, it might be easy to establish policy factors that militate against the imposition of liability. An essential consideration would be whether a legal system could cope with immunity from negligence actions which the non-imposition of liability would practically and automatically confer on ethics committees. Placing ethics committees above liability for negligence substantially amounts to keeping them beyond judicial control and the reach of law. It is doubtful that any legal system would tolerate judicial immunity (from negligence) for ethics committees when similar immunity is not available to other comparable institutions. Thus, Robertson was right to suggest that although 'insurance against personal liability should ease the board members' fears of suits, institutional immunity is neither necessary nor desirable'.[100] Moreover, it is arguable that the imposition of liability would lead to more responsible conduct on the part of ethics committees.[101] Savalescu, Chalmers and Blunt observed that 'it is a sorry reflection of the post-modern values of some researchers, clinicians,

---

A.C. 465 (HL); *Smith v Bush* [1990] 1 A.C. 831 (HL); *Caparo Plc v Dickman* [1990]2 A.C. 605 at 620–622 (HL).

99 *Sutherland Shire Council v Heyman* [1985] 60 ALR 1 at 30. Similar observations were made by Lord Hoffmann in *Stovin v Wise* [1996] A.C. 923 at 954 (HL).

100 Robertson, supra, note 31, 484 at 535.

101 For the deterrent effect of a law suit through prospective liability: De Ville, supra, note 86, at 17–43.

and even members of ethics committees that they accuse those seeking to improve practice of increasing their own legal liability'.[102] Lawsuits may also set the tone of agenda on relevant public policy debates which, eventually, could stimulate regulatory and legislative reforms that aim to foster stricter standards of ethical review. De Ville highlighted the educative value of lawsuits in the field of research involving human subjects.[103] He observed that just as discrimination and sexual harassment lawsuits played a central role in changing social behaviour, high-profile 'litigation can expedite a cultural shift regarding the target of the litigation and help identify the problems that regulatory bodies and institutional players need address', and consequently 'the legal action in the research arena may inspire a genuine consciousness change in which those engaged in research and research oversight have a greater appreciation for the rights and interests of research subjects'.[104] In addition to the advantages above, the subjection of ethics committees to legal liability for inadequate review of research protocols ensures that research subjects harmed by the execution of such protocols should be able to seek appropriate compensation.[105]

There are, however, weighty policy factors against the imposition of liability. Considering that ethics committees, especially in Africa, complain of lack of resources and unwillingness of people to serve as members, the imposition of liability would further deter potential members from serving. As Brazier observed, the prospect of liability would mean that more and 'more [individuals] will refuse to serve and those in post will be hesitant to express forthright opinions'.[106] Although this problem might be assuaged by the provision of liability insurance (by the host institution) there is still a risk that unrestrained exposure to liability would lead to the practice of defensive review, what Robertson defined as 'taking positions that would unnecessarily restrict research simply to avoid the risk of liability'.[107] In the end, it seems that the availability of liability insurance for ethics committees would be the decisive point. As the acquisition of liability insurance becomes routine for members of ethics committees, the courts will be less hesitant or reluctant to shield them from liability for negligence.[108]

---

102 J. Savalescu et al., supra, note 13.

103 De Ville, supra, note 86, at 17.

104 Ibid., at 38.

105 Robin F. Wilson, 'Rethinking the Shield of Immunity: Should Ethics Committees be Accountable for their Mistakes' (2002), 14 Health Care Ethics Committee Forum 172.

106 Brazier, supra, note 14, at 189.

107 Robertson, supra, note 31, at 535.

108 Generally, on the impact of insurance in the imposition of liability for negligence: *Nettleship v Weston* [1971] 2 Q.B. 691 (C.A.).

## Standard of Care and Breach of Duty

Even if research ethics committees were found to owe a duty of care to research subjects, a claimant would still need to prove that the defendant breached that duty by failing to observe the appropriate standard of care. The standard of care is generally that of a hypothetical reasonable person in the circumstances of the defendant.[109] In the context of research ethics committees, the question becomes: what is the standard of care for ethics committees and their members? If it is assumed that an ethics committee has a legal personality separate from those of its members then the standard of care would be that of a prudent and competent ethics committee. To delineate this standard, regard must be had to the relevant provisions of national and international research guidelines where the obligations, composition and functions of research ethics committees are set out.[110] The dynamics of these international instruments and the manner in which they can inform the standard of care were explored in chapter one and should not detain us here. It suffices to say, however, having regard to the analysis at the beginning of this chapter, that research ethics committees are unlikely to claim successfully the status of a separate legal personality. Consequently, the standard of care test would rather apply to members of ethics committees. In other words, what is the standard of care to which each member of an ethics committee must conform? This resonates with the thesis that legal responsibility of ethics committees operate at the individual (and not 'corporate') level. Ascertainment of the appropriate standard of care for members of ethics committees is complicated by the multidisciplinary composition of most ethics committees. Analysis of this problem, and its possible solutions, was undertaken in the section (above) concerning the legal liability of individual members of ethics committees. It merits re-emphasizing, however, that professional members will be judged according to their professional codes.[111] Thus, Duffus, P of the Ugandan Court of Appeal observed in *Pope John's Hospital v Kasozi* that what 'the court had to do was to decide on the facts before it whether the … appellant as a medical practitioner … exercised such a standard of care as a normally skilled member of his profession may reasonably have been expected to exercise in the particular circumstances of this case'.[112] In England and Wales, physician members of research ethics committee will be judged according to whether a particular review conformed to a responsible body of professional

109 *Blyth v Birmingham Waterworks Co.* [1856] 11 Ex 781 at 784, per Alderson B; also *Roe v Minister of Health* [1954] 2 Q.B. 66 (CA).

110 For instance, World Medical Association, Declaration of Helsinki: Ethical Principles for Medical Research Involving Human Subjects ($59^{th}$ WMA General Assembly, Seoul, October, 2008); *World Health Organisation, Operational Guidelines for Ethics Committees that Review Biomedical Research* (Geneva: WHO, 2000).

111 T. Lemmens and B. Freedman, 'Ethics Review for Sale? Conflict of Interest and Commercial Research Review Boards' (2000), 78 Millbank Quarterly 547 at 571–572.

112 Pope John's Hospital v Kasozi [1974] E.A. 221 at 226.

opinion.[113] Note, however, that the Bolam rule is just a general test. The court is quite free to disregard a body of professional opinion that it considers unreasonable or illegal. Moreover, in some cases there may not be any body of professional opinion. This might be the case with new or emerging fields of practice, such as ethics review. While non-professional members are not subject to professional codes, they are, however, under a duty to be conscious of their ignorance and to exercise the care required of a person called upon to review a subject which is partly beyond his or her skill. If a research subject successfully proved that an ethics committee and its members breached the duty of care by failing to exercise the stipulated standard of care, then liability would depend on the presence of causation.

## Causation[114]

Causation is likely to present the most difficult problem for research subjects who allege negligence against ethics committees and their members. At the most basic level, causation is a causal link between the defendant's breach of duty and damage suffered by a claimant.[115] Absent cases of multiple causation, where the analysis is further complicated,[116] the traditional test for causation is the 'but for' test. In other words, the question is whether but for the conduct of the defendant the damage would have occurred?[117] Research involving human subjects presents an interesting context for the application of the 'but for' test. Ethics committees and their members approve research protocols that are ethically valid and free from unacceptable risks to research subjects. Thus, their duty sounds in mere approval or rejection of protocols. However, the execution of approved protocols lies within the province of investigators. As Bassiouni and colleagues observed, there is a 'belief that a responsible, ethical and informed investigator is the one on whom the ultimate responsibility for the conduct of the experiment and welfare of the subjects lies'.[118] McHale also observed that the 'primary responsibility for

---

113 *Bolam v Friern HMC* [1957] 1 WLR 582; *Sidaway v Royal Bethlem Hospital* [1986] A.C. 871 (HL). Generally: J. Montgomery, 'Time for a Paradigm Shift? Medical Law in Transition' (2000), 53 Current Legal Problems 363.

114 For a detailed analysis of causation: Rogers, supra, note 75, 209–262.

115 In *African Continental Bank v A-G (Northern Nigeria)* [1967] 1 All N.L.R. 76 at 81, Brett, JSC observed that it 'has not been shown that the plaintiff's loss resulted from the opening of the account in the name of "P.N. Oku"'.

116 For instance: *Baker v Willoughby* [1970] A.C. 467 9HL); *Jobling v Associated Dairies Ltd* [1982] A.C. 794 (HL).

117 *Barnett v Chelsea & Kensington Hospital Management Committee* [1969] 1 Q.B. 428; *McWilliams v Sir William Arrol & Co. Ltd* [1962] 1 W.L. R. 295.

118 M.C. Bassiouni, et al., 'An Appraisal of Human Experimentation in International Law and Practice: The Need for International Regulation of Human Experimentation' (1981), 72 J. Crim. L. & Criminology 1597 at 1652.

the conduct of the trial is with the researcher';[119] this means that it is the primary responsibility of an investigator to ensure that research subjects are not exposed to unnecessary and unacceptable risks of harm. As this primary responsibility is arguably *dehors* the duty of ethics committees, any harm suffered by a subject is likely to be caused by an investigator's breach of their primary duty. Dickens observed that 'a lapse of due care by … the Research Ethics Board (REB) may not exonerate the investigator, but rather afford a research subject remedies against the REB (parent) institution'.[120] No one can argue that an investigator is justified to imperil the life and safety of research subjects simply because the relevant protocol was approved by a research ethics committee. This means that even when a protocol was negligently approved, any resulting harm would, in fact, have been caused by the act or negligence of the investigator. Therefore, it cannot be said that but for the negligence of the ethics committee the harm would not have occurred. It makes better sense to say that but for the negligence of the investigator the injury would not have occurred. In this sense, the investigator's fault is taken to have broken the chain of causation.[121] Even then, ethics committees would not escape liability if a claimant established that the investigator's wrongful conduct was reasonably foreseeable. In other words, it was something the ethics committee knew was likely to happen. In such cases the chain of causation is said to remain intact.

Several cases have proved the difficulty of showing that the conduct of a third party (investigator) was something so likely to happen that the chain of causation remains intact.[122] There is little prospect for a successful argument that an investigator's wrongdoing was so much within the contemplation of an ethics committee that the chain of causation is not broken. Such an argument would be inconsistent with the generally shared belief that research activities are undertaken by competent investigators.[123] It also assails the general public trust in the ability of investigators to conduct their investigations ethically and skilfully. Public reactions to research scandals were fuelled, in part, by a feeling that this trust was betrayed.[124] That in itself generally means that most people, as well as ethics committees, do not expect harmful and unethical conduct on the part of investigators. Simply put, a research subject alleging negligence against an ethics

---

119 J.V. McHale, 'Liability in the law of tort of research ethics committees and their members' (2005), 1 Research Ethics Review 53 at 54.

120 Bernard M. Dickens, 'Conflicts of Interests in Canadian Health Care Law' (1995), 21 Am. J.L. & Med. 259 at 274.

121 Presumably, the investigator might be able to recover from the ethics committee on the basis of joint liability or through 'contribution proceedings'.

122 *Lamb v Camden London Borough* [1981] Q.B. 625 (C.A.); *Ward v Cannock Chase District Council* [1986] Ch. 546.

123 It might be otherwise where an ethics committee approves research that it knows will be conducted by an incompetent researcher.

124 Explored in chapter one.

committee would be hard pressed to prove that an investigator's negligence did not break the chain of causation. For as McHale observed, 'establishing the link between the approval of the trial protocol and the ultimate injury suffered by the research subject would be problematic from the outset due to the interface with the role of the researcher themselves which may ultimately constitute a "novus actus interveniens" and thus break any chain of causation'.[125] But this conclusion assumes that the wrongdoing of the investigator, which successfully breaks the chain of causation, relates to deviations from the approved protocol. Presumably, ethics committees are entitled to assume that investigators would be faithful to approved protocols. Accordingly, unauthorized deviations cannot be said to be within the contemplation or foreseeability of ethics committees. Where, however, the wrongdoing of the investigator relates to scientific flaws that were overlooked by an ethics committee, different considerations might apply. In other words, it is arguable that where an investigator's tortious conduct resulted from faithful adherence to an approved protocol which embodies a scientific flaw overlooked by an ethics committee, then the chain of causation is presumably not broken (so that the ethics committee and its members would remain liable to the research subject). This aspect of the argument, in turn, raises the question of whether ethics committees are bound to conduct a scientific review in addition to ethics review, a matter that was thoroughly dealt with in chapter four.

## Liability to Professional Discipline

Whatever the outcome of a negligence suit, professional members of ethics committees might be liable to professional disciplinary procedures in connection with a review process that falls short of the standards required by a particular profession.[126] Threats of professional disciplinary action obviously have a deterrent effect on ethical misbehaviour. In 1996, for instance, the name of a medical investigator (Dr Jyoti Argawala) was struck off the medical register because he forged ethical approvals for his research projects.[127] Although Dr Argawala was professionally disciplined in his capacity as an investigator, similar consequences would probably have befallen him if he had committed the unethical acts as a member of an ethics committee. Similarly, in 2007, Dr Andrew Wakefield, Professor John Walker-Smith and Professor Simon Murch, authors of a controversial paper in *Lancet* linking MMR vaccine and autism, faced a Fitness to Practice Panel (FTP) set up by the General Medical Council (GMC).

125 J.V. McHale, 'Liability in the law of tort of research ethics committees and their members' (2005) 1 Research Ethics Review 53 at 57.

126 Generally: Timothy Caulfield, et al., 'Research Ethics and the Role of the Professional Bodies: A View From Canada' (2004), 32 J.L. Med. & Ethics 365–368.

127 Douglas Carnall, 'Doctor Struck Off for Scientific Fraud' (1996) 312 BMJ 399–400.

They were accused of undertaking research with twelve children without proper ethical approval and for failing to conduct their study along the lines for which ethical approval was sought. They were also accused of not treating their young research subjects in accordance with the ethical approval given for the study.[128] More interestingly, Lemmens and Freedman highlighted a case in which the New Zealand Medical Council found the chairman of an ethics committee guilty of professional misconduct for the perfunctory approval and monitoring of a study in which women with cervical cancer died.[129]

Considering the difficulty and complexity of negligence suits against ethics committees and their members, professional disciplinary procedures may be the only realistic way of bringing ethics committees and their members to justice. Most professional codes, however, require that the impugned conduct must be incompatible with a professional status or amounts to infamous conduct in a professional respect.[130] Some of the modern professional codes simply require that the action or omission amounts to serious professional misconduct. They all seem to mean the same thing, that is: infamous conduct in a professional respect, conduct incompatible with a person's professional status and serious professional misconduct.[131] But it is not always easy to discipline a professional person for misconduct in connection with ethical review process. Take, for instance, a solicitor who is a member of an ethics committee. As a professional solicitor, he or she is mostly interested in protecting the interests of a client. In that sense, the solicitor is generally disinterested in ethical review process unless a client's interest is involved. As a member of an ethics committee, however, the solicitor travels outside the client-solicitor relationship and faces a different relationship with a new responsibility, that is, to ensure that research subjects (not clients) are protected. In this capacity, should the Law Society be able to proceed against the solicitor for incompetent or negligent review of protocols? Has the solicitor acted in a professional respect? Some of the answers to these questions raise issues relating to the nature, scope, functions and jurisdictions of research ethics committees covered in the previous chapter (chapter four). That chapter raised the important question of whether a review process involves legal functions. Acceptance of that proposition would mean that the solicitor (in the example above) could generally be said to be acting in a professional respect. Interestingly, a few cases have given some guidance as to what it means to be acting in a professional respect or to be guilty of serious professional misconduct.

---

128 Denis Campbell, 'I told the truth all along, says doctor at the heart of autism row', the *Observer*, Sunday 8 July 2007 (page unknown).

129 Lemmens and Freedman, supra, note 111, 547 at 572.

130 Remigius N. Nwabueze, 'Breach of Trust as a Professional Misconduct' (2009), 7 Commonwealth Journal of Law & Legal Education 17; Alec Samuels, 'Serious Professional Misconduct' (2005), 73 Medico-Legal Journal 166.

131 Samuels, supra, note 130, at 166.

As a starting point, it is open to a professional disciplinary body to adopt a broad, but measured, approach to the question of what conduct amounts to serious professional misconduct.[132] Accordingly, it was held in *Baxendale-Walker v Law Society* that an extraordinarily reckless letter of reference written by a solicitor in his professional capacity amounted to a serious professional misconduct.[133] Furthermore, the Court of Appeal held in *Marten v Royal College of Veterinary Surgeon's Disciplinary Committee* (where a veterinary surgeon failed to provide nursing care for his own animals) that the concept of professional misconduct includes those which are not only personally disgraceful but also bring disgrace on the profession in which the professional practises.[134] But in *Skidmore v Dartford and Gravesham NHS Trust*, the House of Lords supported the view that a professional misconduct is properly so called when it arises in the course of a professional relationship.[135] Nevertheless, Sir Anthony Clarke, MR, observed in *Meadow v General Medical Council* that 'there is ample authority for the proposition that a professional may face FTP (fitness to practice) proceedings, not just for conduct strictly within his professional capacity, but also for conduct in his private capacity'.[136] The Master of Rolls, however, acknowledged that 'this is, of course, a case in which the allegations related to conduct within Professor Meadow's professional capacity'.[137] Going back to the example of a hypothetical solicitor who is also a member of an ethics committee, it would mean that although his or her ethical review misconduct was not strictly committed in a professional respect, yet it is likely to reflect negatively not only on his reputation as a person, but also on the profession (of solicitors) in which he or she practises. Therefore, following *Marten v Royal College of Veterinary Surgeon's Disciplinary Committee*, the Law Society should be able to proceed against the solicitor for serious professional misconduct. The point, however, is that in addition to bringing a suit in negligence, an injured research subject can instigate professional disciplinary proceedings against members of ethics committees. The drawback is that this line of action is not available against those members of ethics committees that do not belong to any organized profession.

---

132 This latitude of action was judicially conceded to the Ontario (Canada) College of Optometrists in *Cox v College of Optometrists of Ontario* [1988] 65 O.R. 2d 461 (Ont. Div. Ct.).

133 *Baxendale-Walker v Law Society* [2007] 3 All ER 330 (CA).

134 Marten v Royal College of Veterinary Surgeons' Disciplinary Committee [1966] 1 QB 1 (CA).

135 *Skidmore v Dartford and Gravesham NHS Trust* [2003] T.L.R. 1 at 4 (HL).

136 *Meadow v General Medical Council* [2007] 1 All ER 1 at 15 (CA).

137 Ibid., at 15.

## Conclusion

It is not clear whether research ethics committees qualify as legal persons. In practice, however, aggrieved research subjects are likely to sue every potential defendant, including ethics committees, individual members of ethics committees and parent institutions of ethics committees.[138] Negligence is the most likely private law action that research subjects could bring against ethics committees and their members. However, the viability of a suit in negligence suffers from uncertainty as to the existence of a proximate relationship between ethics committees and research subjects. There are also policy factors that militate against the imposition of liability in negligence against ethics committees and their members. Furthermore, causation is a difficult hurdle to scale in negligence actions brought by research subjects against ethics committees or their members. Therefore, professional disciplinary proceedings seem to be the most viable control mechanism against ethics committees and their members; but non-professional members of ethics committees are not within the reach of professional disciplinary sanctions.

138 Mary M. Thomson, 'Bringing Research into Therapy: Liability Anyone?', in Lemmens and Warring (eds), supra, note 25, at 183–205.

# Chapter 6
# Liability of Research Ethics Committees in Actions by Investigators

## Introduction

While the previous chapter explored the potential legal liability of research ethics committees in actions by research subjects, such as an action in negligence, this chapter examines the potential legal liability of research ethics committees and their members in actions brought against them by investigators. As chapters three and four highlighted, research ethics committees might for good or bad reasons reject a protocol or grant their approval subject to a substantial modification of the protocol. Such modifications may be difficult to implement or may not be finished in good time to secure anticipated research funding. Thus, an ethics committee's decision to reject, or recommend substantial modification to, a protocol might adversely affect the investigator's economic and social interests, or interests in their reputation. For instance, in the course of the proceedings of an ethics committee, a member of the committee might make imputations of incompetence against the investigator which lower the investigator in the estimation of right-thinking members of the society; also, such defamatory remarks might be contained in a letter refusing the grant of ethics approval, written by the committee to the investigator and copied to the sponsor. Furthermore, the denial of ethics approval might lead to the loss of an investigator's lucrative research contract with a sponsor. Most uncommonly, an ethics committee and its members might intentionally procure the breach of an investigator's research contract or, otherwise, inflict economic loss on the investigator by behaving unlawfully towards a third party. In the situations above, there are potential legal remedies available to an investigator aggrieved by unlawful actions of an ethics committee and its members. Unlike chapter five, where an action in negligence was the principal legal route for vindicating the complaints of research subjects against ethics committees and their members, an investigator's legal remedies against an ethics committee and its members sound in the administrative law action of judicial review; an action for injunction; the torts of procuring a breach of contract, and causing loss by unlawful means; an action for negligent economic loss; and action for defamation; and the claim of a legal and constitutional right to research. Thus, this chapter proposes to examine these familiar common law and constitutional forms of action in the unique and novel context of research ethics committees and their members.

## Judicial Control and Review of Decisions of Research Ethics Committees

An ethics committee may reject or disapprove a protocol after due consideration. Although such decisions are rare, they do occur.[1] For instance, in an empirical study exploring the experiences and attitudes of researchers from developing countries, Hyder and colleagues reported that seventeen per cent of respondents abandoned their research projects as a result of unfavourable decisions by ethics committees.[2] Similarly, Hamburger, while challenging the constitutionality of research regulation through the framework of ethics committees, argued that ethics committees constitute a system of licensing contrary to the First Amendment of the US Constitution, and that 'far from making a single outrageous assault on this Amendment, IRBs modify or censor well over 100,000 research proposals every year in the United States and stifle countless others that get abandoned or never get started'.[3] In the same vein, Caroline Bledsoe and colleagues observed: 'With IRB demands spiralling, however, projects such as faculty summer research or student research projects with sharp time constraints were hard hit. International trips had to be cancelled, undergraduate projects were abandoned, and at least one tenure clock had to be set back because of IRB delays'.[4] This suggests that the outcome of an ethics approval process might be extremely negative for an investigator, in the sense of being productive of severe social, economic or professional consequences. An investigator aggrieved by a decision of an ethics committee might accuse it of bias or allege errors that substantially affected its decision. Where internal appeal procedures exist, the investigator might resort to them. Hadskis and Carver, however, argued that the legal mechanism of judicial review 'cannot be successfully pursued until available internal appeal mechanisms have been exhausted'.[5] Similarly, Robertson suggested that although an investigator has 'no legal right to appeal an adverse IRB decision after notice and hearing' an appellate process should nevertheless be established in order to ensure fairness and

---

1 However, a survey of ethics committees in twenty African countries found that no committee had ever rejected a research protocol: Jean-Paul Rwabihama, et al., 'Ethics committees for biomedical research in some African emerging countries: which establishment for which independence? A comparison with the USA and Canada' (2010), 36 J. Med. Ethics 243 at 244–245.

2 A.A. Hyder, et al., 'Ethical Review of Health Research: A Perspective from Developing Country Researchers' (2004), 30 J. Med. Ethics 68 at 70–71.

3 Phillip Hamburger, 'Getting Permission' (2007), 101 Northwestern University Law Review 405 at 407.

4 Caroline H. Bledsoe, et al., 'Regulating Creativity: Research and Survival in the IRB Iron Cage' (2007), 101 Northwestern University Law Review 593 at 620.

5 Michael Hadskis and Peter Carver, 'The Long Arm of Administrative Law: Applying Administrative Law Principles to Research Ethics Boards' (2005), 13 Health Law Review 19 at 27.

promote confidence in the review process.[6] He observed that such an 'appellate process might include recourse at three levels: (1) reconsideration by the IRB, (2) institutional review of the IRB decision, and (3) review of the institutional decision by a regional or national body'.[7] Where an institutional or national appellate review process does not exist, an investigator might wish to apply to the courts for judicial review of the decision. While, theoretically, a research subject might also be able to seek judicial review of the decision of an ethics committee to approve a protocol,[8] it will be seldom pragmatic or advantageous to do so. A research subject aggrieved by an ethics committee's decision to approve a particular study should simply refuse to participate in the study or withdraw from further participation.

In any case, the reviewability of a decision of an ethics committee will depend on the status or qualification of an ethics committee as a public authority. The question, therefore, is whether ethics committees qualify as public authorities? If so, what standard of review should apply to their decisions? Commentators disagree on the right answers to these questions. For instance, while Lehtonen and Halila accepted that ethics committees in Finland are public bodies subject to administrative law norms, they however observed that the 'opinion of an ethics committee is not considered as an administrative decision that could be re-evaluated by the administrative courts'.[9] More hesitatingly, Lemmens and Freedman suggested that ethics committees were situated somewhere on the continuum between public curators and administrative licensing boards.[10] Consequently, they argued that the 'rules of administrative law ought to inspire us in refining the rules by which IRBs are organised'.[11] In much stronger terms, however, Stephen Baker and colleagues suggested that ethics committees are public authorities both under the UK statutory and common law, because they derive their power from statutory bodies, perform public functions, and are given responsibilities under statutory law.[12] Similarly, Kennedy observed that ethics committees are subject to legal duties and could be liable to judicial review for their non-performance.[13]

---

6 John A. Robertson, 'The Law of Institutional Review Boards' (1979), 26 UCLA L. Rev. 484 at 527.

7 Ibid., at 527.

8 J.V. McHale, 'Guidelines for Medical Research – Some Ethical and Legal Problems' (1993), 1 Med. L. Rev. 160 at 180.

9 Lasse A. Lehtonen and Ritva Halila, 'The General Legal Responsibility of Research Ethics Committees in Finland', in D. Beyleveld, et al. (eds), *Research Ethics Committees, Data Protection and Medical Research in European Countries* (Aldershot: Ashgate Publishing Ltd, 2005) at 48.

10 T. Lemmens and B. Freedman, 'Ethics Review for Sale? Conflict of Interest and Commercial Research Review Boards' (2000), 78 Milbank Quarterly 547 at 554.

11 Ibid., at 554.

12 Stephen Baker, et al., in Beyleveld, et al. (eds), supra, note 9, at 281.

13 I. Kennedy, 'Research Ethics Committees and the Law', in C. Gilbert Foster (ed.), *Manual for Research Ethics Committees* (Centre of Medical Law and Ethics, Kings College, London, 1991).

However, not all ethics committees, especially university ethics committees, could fit into the analysis of Stephen Baker and colleagues above. Certainly, for-profit ethics committees (examined in chapter four) are not within the contemplation of Stephen Baker and colleagues above.

It is proposed to approach the questions above by making a distinction between statutory and non-statutory ethics committees. Statutory ethics committees refer to those that are set up under a statute or whose authority comes directly from a statute. They qualify as statutory bodies and, as such, are historically subject to judicial review by the courts.[14] Paradigmatic examples of statutory ethics committees are the UK Ethics Committee Authority (UKECA), ethics committees established pursuant to the Medicines for Human Use Regulation 2006 (UK) and the Nigerian National Health Research Ethics committee established under the National Health Act 2011. These are probably the sort of ethics committees which Stephen Baker and colleagues above had in mind. In contrast, non-statutory ethics committees are private bodies established on a more or less informal basis by a university, research institution or similar bodies. As chapters one and three indicated, ethics committees in most parts of Africa are institutional in nature in the sense of being established by a university or an academic research institution; such committees are usually non-statutory in nature.[15] Because of their non-statutory underpinning, a different basis of reviewability has to be found for the decisions of institutional ethics committees. Thus, the question is whether the courts should be able to control the actions of such committees? If so, what is the basis for such judicial intervention? Note that the answers to these questions do not turn on the legal personality of institutional or non-statutory ethics committees because, traditionally, the decisions of unincorporated associations are open to judicial review.[16] This will become much clearer from analysis of the cases below.

14 Elizabeth Giussani, *Constitutional and Administrative Law* (London: Sweet & Maxwell, 2008), at 251.

15 This is so even when the parent institution (for instance, a university) is established by a statute. University ethics committees are usually not expressly established under the governing university statutes, and are usually the product of a sub-delegation of authority under such statutes. Thus, the relationship of university research ethics committees with the governing university statutes is too remote to make them statutory bodies; and at any rate, such ambiguous statutory flavour undermines the analogy of university ethics committees with the quintessential statutory ethics committees identified above. Hadskis and Carver, however, argue that university ethics committees (in Canada at least, but generalizable to other jurisdictions) are statutory in nature because they are either the emanations of an exercise of power granted under the relevant university statutes or sub-delegatees of powers delegated to certain committees or councils under university statutes. Thus, to 'the extent this describes the basis for REB activity at a university, it will be seen as acting pursuant to statutory power': Hadskis and Carver, supra, note 5, at 21.

16 For a similar opinion: John A. Kavanagh, *A Guide to Judicial Review* (Toronto: Carswell Co. Ltd., 1978), at 167.

Canadian courts approached the questions above from the perspective of functions discharged by a private, non-statutory, body. Thus, the question was whether the impugned decision was given by a body whose duties or responsibilities were public in nature. Accordingly, *In re Polten and Governing Council of the University of Toronto*,[17] the Ontario Divisional Court held that the decision of the Subcommittee on Academic Appeals,[18] which acted on behalf of the Governing Council of the University of Toronto (a statutory body), was a judicial act subject to review by the court. Although the Ontario Divisional Court eventually held that there was no breach of the rules of natural justice in that case, it reasoned that the university's responsibility for the education of the citizens of the Province of Ontario was a 'public responsibility that should be subject to some measure of judicial control'.[19] This clearly evinces an approach to judicial review based on the public nature of the responsibilities of the body whose decision is impugned or sought to be reviewed. In other words, the emphasis is on the nature of functions performed by a private body rather than the source of its powers. It is arguable, however, that *Re Polten,* based on its own facts, is not an authority for the proposition above; rather, *Re Polten* more clearly illustrates the review of decisions given by statutory (rather than non-statutory) bodies. For instance, the Subcommittee on Academic Appeals did not act in its own name as an authoritative or independent committee of the University of Toronto. Instead, the Subcommittee on Academic Appeals acted in the name (and on behalf) of the Governing Council of the University of Toronto, which is a statutory body. Therefore, to the extent that the impugned decision was attributed to the Governing Council, rather than the Subcommittee on Academic Appeals, *Re Polten* arguably illustrates the judicial review of decisions of statutory (and not non-statutory) bodies.[20] Consequently, *Re Polten* offers only a limited assistance in the search for answers to the questions above.

*Re Vanek and Governors of the University of Alberta* supports the analysis of *Re Polten* above.[21] In *Re Vanek*, two tenure committees of the University of Alberta, Canada, refused to recommend Professor Vanek for tenure (in the sense of permanency of employment). Prof. Vanek applied to the court for an order of *certiorari* to quash the adverse reports and recommendations of the tenure

---

17 *In re Polten and Governing Council of the University of Toronto*, [1975] 59 D.L.R. (3d) 197.

18 Which refused to accept the applicant's doctoral dissertation for not meeting the requirements for the award of a Ph.D degree of the University of Toronto.

19 Polten, supra, note 17, at 212.

20 For similar reasons, the Supreme Court of Canada agreed with the Court of Appeal of Saskatchewan that a section of the statute that established the University of Saskatchewan 'created a statutory duty to be performed by the faculty council subject to appeal to the senate and that compliance with the statutory duty may be controlled and enforced by the ordinary courts': *King v University of Saskatchewan* [1969] 6 D.L.R. (3d) 120 at 125 (SCC).

21 *Re Vanek and Governors of the University of Alberta* [1975] 57 D.L.R. (3d) 595 (Alberta Sup. Ct. App. Div.).

committees. Among other things, Cavanagh J of the Alberta Supreme Court held that *certiorari* was not available to the claimant because none of the tenure committees was a statutory body. On appeal to the Appellate Division of the Supreme Court of Alberta, Clement JA observed that the '(tenure) committees and their functions were established not as bodies prescribed by statute as a matter of public policy, but rather as a matter of choice in the exercise of a discretion granted by the statute relating to affairs internal to the university'.[22] Thus, this suggests a test of judicial review based on the source of a tribunal's powers; in other words, whether or not the source of a tribunal's power is statutory or prerogative. A faithful and consistent application of the 'source of power' test would certainly put the decisions of private bodies beyond the scope of judicial review. For instance, Clement JA observed that the tenure committees were 'institutions private to the university',[23] and also, were 'non-statutory tribunals to which are applicable the words of Judson J in *Port Arthur Shipbuilding Co. v Arthurs*[24] .... "It is clear that the prerogative writs of prohibition and certiorari will not lie against a non-statutory tribunal"'.[25] Thus, *Re Vanek* would underpin an argument that most research ethics committees in Africa are private and non-statutory bodies and that their decisions are beyond judicial review in (African) courts. Certainly, *Re Vanek*'s test of reviewability based on the source of a tribunal's power conflicts with the previously analysed test based on the public nature of a tribunal's function, as established in *Re Polten.*[26] It is possible to harmonize both tests. For instance, a proper application of the 'public function' test developed in *Re Polten* is likely to yield an outcome similar to the application of *Re Vanek*. For example, the tenure committees in *Re Vanek* were not only non-statutory and private bodies; also, their functions were not of a public nature and affected only a single individual (that is, Professor Vanek) as opposed to members of the public. Thus, applying the *ratio* of *Re Polten* to the facts of *Re Vanek*, it is certainly the case that *Re Vanek* did not engage any 'public responsibility' sufficient to trigger legal intervention through the mechanism of judicial review. This view accords with the recent observation of La Forest J of the Supreme Court of Canada, that 'universities are statutory bodies performing a public service. As such, they may be subjected to the judicial review of certain decisions .... In a word, the basis of the exercise of supervisory jurisdiction by the courts is not that the universities are government, but they are public decision-makers'.[27]

22 Ibid., at 600.

23 Ibid., at 606.

24 *Port Arthur Shipbuilding Co. v Arthurs* [1968] 70 D.L.R. (2d) 693 at 697 (Sup. Ct. Can.).

25 Vanek, supra, note 21, at 607.

26 A similar point was highlighted by John A. Kavanagh, *A Guide to Judicial Review* (Toronto: Carswell Com. Ltd., 1978), at 162.

27 *McKinney v University of Guelph* [1990] 76 D.L.R. (4th) 545 at 638.

In England, on the other hand, the courts have at least since the middle 1980s accepted the 'public function' test as one of the recognized ways of determining the reviewability of administrative decisions.[28] A good example is the decision of the Court of Appeal in *Regina v Panel on Take-Overs and Mergers, Ex Parte Datafin Plc.*[29] In that case, the applicant accused a bidding competitor of acting in concert with other parties to breach the City Code on Take-overs and Mergers. The applicant's complaint to the Panel on Take-overs and Mergers was dismissed for lack of merit. The Panel was an unincorporated association and had no legal personality; it also lacked statutory, prerogative and common law powers. The applicant applied to the High Court for judicial review of the Panel's decision, and sought orders of *certiorari* and *mandamus*. The High Court dismissed the applicant's application, holding that since the Panel was not a statutory body its decision was not open to judicial review. While the Court of Appeal dismissed the applicant's appeal on the merits, it held that the decision of the Panel was open to judicial control and review. As Sir John Donaldson MR observed:

> It [the Panel] is without doubt performing a public duty and an important one. This is clear from the expressed willingness of the Secretary of State for Trade and Industry to limit legislation in the field of take-overs and mergers and to use the panel as the centrepiece of his regulation of that market. The rights of citizens are indirectly affected by its decisions, some, but by no means all of whom, may in a technical sense be said to have assented to this situation, e.g., the members of the Stock Exchange. At least in its determination of whether there has been a breach of the code, it has a duty to act judicially and it asserts that its *raisin d'etre* is to do equity between one shareholder and another. Its source of power is only partly based upon moral persuasion and the assent of institutions and their members, the bottom line being the statutory powers exercised by the Department of Trade and Industry and the Bank of England. In this context I should be very disappointed if the courts could not recognize the realities of executive power and allowed their vision to be clouded by the subtlety and sometimes complexity of the way in which it can be exerted.[30]

More tersely, Lloyd LJ observed: 'I do not agree that the source of the power is the sole test whether a body is subject to judicial review .... Of course the source of the power will often, perhaps usually, be decisive'.[31] Thus, Lloyd LJ encouraged the courts to look not just at the source of the power, but also at the nature of the power; so that if the 'body in question is exercising public law functions, or if

---

28 But the test arguably goes as far back as the famous judgement of Lord Parker C.J. in *Reg. v Criminal Injuries Compensation Board, Ex parte Lain* [1967] 2 Q.B. 864 at 882.

29 *Regina v Panel on Take-Overs and Mergers, Ex Parte Datafin Plc* [1986] 1 Q.B. 815 (CA).

30 Ibid., at 838–839.

31 Ibid., at 847.

the exercise of its functions have public law consequences, then that may … be sufficient to bring the body within the reach of judicial review'.[32]

In the context of regulatory bodies, the *Datafin* analysis has been applied to hold that the decision of a prosecuting authority of the Bar Council (the Professional Conduct Committee – PCC) was a reviewable judicial act.[33] Some recent cases, especially in the fields of sports and religion, have, however, sought to interpret restrictively the meaning of public duty, public powers and public functions; these cases suggest that, to be reviewable, the powers of a non-statutory body must not only have some public consequences; the powers must also be governmental in nature.[34]For non-statutory ethics committees, however, a choice need not be made between a liberal and restrictive interpretation of the *Datafin* decision above. As underscored in chapter four, research ethics committees perform protective public functions which impact significantly on the rights and welfare of research participants, and by extension, the general public. Therefore, research ethics committees perform an important public duty, and this should be sufficient to make their decisions subject to judicial review. As already noted, provided that the duties of ethics committees are public in nature, it is irrelevant that ethics committees are non-statutory in nature (for purposes of judicial review). This is illustrated by *R v Ethical Committee of St Mary's Hospital (Manchester) Ex p. Harriot*[35] in which a local ethics committee was established to provide advice and guidance on fertility treatments. The committee was an informal and non-statutory body, basically providing a forum for discussion amongst professionals. The applicant sought to quash the advice of the committee, which approved a decision of the applicant's physician to remove the applicant from a list of patients awaiting fertility treatment. On behalf of the committee, however, it was argued that its advice was not open to judicial review. Although the court dismissed the applicant's application on the merits, it refused to accept the committee's contention that its advice was not judicially reviewable. Thus, Schiemann J observed that if 'the committee had advised, for instance, that the IVF unit should in principle

32 Ibid.

33 *Reg. v Bar Council, Ex p. Percival* [1991] 1 Q.B. 212 at 228–229 (DC). Also, *R. v Advertising Standards Ltd. Ex p. Direct Line Financial Services* [1998] C.O.D. 20.

34 For instance, *Law v National Greyhound Racing Club Ltd.* [1983] 1 W.L.R. 1302 (C.A.); *Reg. v Jockey Club, Ex p. Aga Khan* [1993] 1 W.L.R. 909 (C.A.); *Reg. v Chief Rabbi, Ex, p. Wachmann* [1992] 1 W.L.R. 1036 (Q.B.D.). In the last case, for instance, Simone Brown J observed: 'To say of decisions of a given body that they are public law decisions with public law consequences means something more than that they are decisions which may be of great interest or concern to the public or, indeed, which may have consequences for the public. To attract the court's supervisory jurisdiction there must be not merely a public but potentially a governmental interest in the decision-making power in question', at 1041.

35 *R v Ethical Committee of St Mary's Hospital (Manchester) Ex p. Harriot* [1988] 1 FLR 512 (QBD).

refuse all such treatment to anyone who was a Jew or coloured, then I think the courts might well grant a declaration that such a policy was illegal'.[36]

Moreover, as suggested in chapter three, institutional or non-statutory research ethics committees in some African countries are intricately woven into the fabric of statutory regulations; thus, such committees could be said to be exercising some governmental power. For instance, some protocols approved by institutional review committees in Uganda must be approved by the statutory national review body (UNCST), the Research Secretariat of the Office of the Ugandan President and other governmental executive agencies such as the National Drug Authority. Similar structures are applicable in Tanzania through the intervention of the NIMR, COSTECH and the TFDA in the research regulatory process. Consequently, institutional or non-statutory research ethics committees in Africa are underpinned by state power, and as such, reflect direct and indirect, or potential, governmental interest.[37] In other words, even on Hoffmann LJ's restrictive interpretation of the *Datafin case* in *Reg. v Jockey Club*, to the effect that a reviewable 'power needs to be identified as governmental in nature',[38] it is arguable that the decisions of non-statutory ethics committees in some African countries are judicially reviewable because their powers enjoy the blessing of governments in their territories; in other words, such committees are governmental in operation.

## Grounds of Review

Having argued above that the decisions of research ethics committees are open to judicial control or review, the next point is to determine the grounds upon which the review may be undertaken. However, only a cursory analysis of this important topic is given below; extended discussion is available in standard administrative law books.[39] In *Council of Civil Service Unions v Minister for Civil Service*,[40] Lord Diplock developed three categories that underpin the exercise of supervisory jurisdiction; these categories are illegality (or unlawfulness), irrationality (or unreasonableness) and procedural impropriety (or unfairness). While it is possible for the decision of an ethics committee to be challenged on any of these three grounds,[41] procedural impropriety is, however, likely to be the most recurrent ground of challenge. Allegations of procedural impropriety or unfairness engage

36 Ibid., at 518–519.

37 *Reg v Jockey Club*, supra, note 34, at 926 (Farquharson LJ).

38 Ibid., at 931.

39 For instance, Paul Craig, *Administrative Law 6th edn* (London: Sweet & Maxwell, 2008); Wade, H.W.R. and C. Forsyth, *Administrative Law, 9th edn* (Oxford; OUP, 2004).

40 *Council of Civil Service Unions v Minister for Civil Service* [1985] 1 A.C. 374 (GCHQ).

41 As in *R v Ethical Committee of St Mary's Hospital (Manchester) Ex p. Harriot* [1988] 1 FLR 512 (QBD).

the rule against bias, which, in turn, is one of the twin pillars of natural justice: *audi alteram partem* (let the other side be heard) and *nemo judex in causa sua* (no one should be a judge in his or her own cause). A decision-maker's bias may arise from financial interest, personal involvement in a case or the prejudgement of a case. In every situation, however, it is necessary to identify the nature of the impugned interest of the decision-maker because the outcome of a review depends on the type of interest involved in a particular case.

In English law, the approach is to distinguish between direct and non-direct interests. While a direct interest automatically disqualifies the decision-maker (and, thus, a ground for review), a non-direct interest requires proof of a real danger of bias (in order to attract the sanction of disqualification).[42] Financial interests exemplify cases of automatic disqualification. A decision-maker's direct financial interest would result to automatic disqualification even if the amount involved is small or insignificant. Thus, in *Dimes v Grand Junction Canal*,[43] Dimes lost an appeal before the Lord Chancellor, Lord Cottenham, and appealed to the House of Lords. He alleged that Lord Cottenham was a substantial shareholder in the Grand Junction Canal (one of the parties to the case) and was, therefore, automatically disqualified from hearing the appeal. On the facts of the *Dimes* case, Lord Cottenham's shareholding gave him a direct financial interest in the Grand Junction Canal company. Although the House of Lords observed that there was no proof of actual bias on the part of Lord Cottenham, nor was such an inference possible on the facts of that case, yet the House of Lords had to set aside the decision of the Lord Chancellor (Lord Cottenham) because of his direct financial interest in the case. The House of Lords reasoned that a contrary decision would make Lord Cottenham a judge of a case in which he had an interest. However, not every financial interest would lead to an automatic disqualification. For instance, a remote or non-direct financial interest will not suffice. *R v Rand*[44] is a case in point. In that case, two justices had taken part in a decision involving the Bradford Corporation. It turned out that the justices were trustees of an institution that held bonds in the Bradford Corporation. Since the justices were simply trustees, and therefore did not have any beneficial interest in the bonds, the alleged financial interest was too remote. Accordingly, the court held that the two justices were not (automatically) disqualified unless a real likelihood of bias was proved.[45]

Financial interests do not, however, exhaust the range of relevant and automatically disqualifying direct interests. Recent cases show that a direct personal, proprietary or other non-financial interest could engage the automatic

42 *R v Gough* [1993] A.C. 646 (HL); *Porter v Magill* [2001] UKHL 67 (HL); *Lawal v Northern Spirit* [2003] UKHL 35 (HL).

43 *Dimes v Grand Junction Canal* [1852] 10 E.R. 301.

44 *R v Rand* [1865-66] L.R. 1 Q.B. 230.

45 Also, *Locabail (UK) Ltd. v Bayfield Properties Ltd.* [2000] Q.B. 451.

disqualification rule.[46] A good example is the case of *R v Bow Street Metropolitan Stipendiary Magistrate Ex p. Pinochet Ugarte (No. 2)*,[47] where the House of Lords had to consider whether a judge was disqualified from hearing a case because he had a personal interest in promoting a cause espoused by one of the parties to the case before him. *Ex p. Pinochet Ugarte No. 2* was one of the series of cases concerning the efforts of the Spanish government to extradite (from the UK) a former Chilean dictator and Head of State, Senator Pinochet, to Spain to face charges of crimes against humanity. On the question of whether the former Head of State was entitled to immunity from prosecution, the House of Lords ruled three to two against Senator Pinochet; Lord Hoffmann agreed with the majority. On behalf of Senator Pinochet, it was alleged that Lord Hoffmann was a director and chairperson of Amnesty International Charity Limited, a subsidiary of one of the parties to the case, that is, Amnesty International. It was argued, therefore, that Lord Hoffmann's decision was tainted with bias and ought to be set aside. Lord Browne-Wilkinson observed that the rules on automatic disqualification for bias were not limited to financial cases and were equally applicable to cases of personal interest in the promotion of a cause. Lord Browne-Wilkinson further observed that it was immaterial that Amnesty International Charity Limited (of which Lord Hoffman was a director and chairperson) was just a subsidiary of Amnesty International because they are 'various parts of a movement working in different fields but towards the same goals'.[48] Therefore, Lord Browne-Wilkinson set aside the majority's decision, and concluded that if 'the absolute impartiality of the judiciary is to be maintained, there must be a rule which automatically disqualifies a judge who is involved, whether personally or as a director of a company, in promoting the same causes in the same organization as is a party to the suit'.[49]

In relation to research ethics committees, the analysis above suggests that a strict application of the rule against bias would have a detrimental effect on the decisions of research ethics committees, whether institutional or for-profit. For instance, institutional or university research ethics committees generally have substantial interests in approving protocols that attract much-needed research funds to their institutions, and also protocols that have the potential to heighten their institutions' research profile. Similarly, institutional ethics committees are generally interested in the approval of protocols that have the potential to enhance an investigator's (colleague) career progression. Furthermore, members of an institution's ethics committee may have a substantial personal or professional interest in the research questions identified by a protocol; thus, they might be anxious to grant an ethics approval in order to ensure that those questions are

---

46 *R v Altrincham Justices, Ex p. N. Pennington* [1975] Q.B. 549 at 552; *Webb v The Queen* [1994] 181 C.L.R. 41 at 74.

47 *R v Bow Street Metropolitan Stipendiary Magistrate Ex p. Pinochet Ugarte (No. 2)* [2000] 1 A.C. 119 (HL).

48 Ibid., at 135.

49 Ibid.

fully researched or investigated. This type of personal interest might be direct enough to warrant an automatic disqualification. But the problem here is more theoretical than practical since the decision of the 'biased' ethics committee (in the examples above) favours the investigator, who should have been the person to complain about bias. Furthermore, issues of bias are exacerbated by the nature and operation of for-profit ethics committees; much of this is evident in the analysis in chapter four. Members of commercial or proprietary ethics committees are hired and paid by the same organizations that submit protocols to them for ethics review. Similarly, the viability of organizations like CROs generally depends on the outcome of ethics review process undertaken by proprietary or for-profit ethics boards. Therefore, it is arguable that members of commercial ethics committees have a direct and significant financial or non-financial interest in the ethics review process and should be automatically disqualified from reviewing research protocols. Thus, members of ethics committees should give serious attention to issues of conflict of interest.

## Injunctions

Generally, actions for injunctions fall within the courts' equitable jurisdiction. An injunction might be sought either alone or in conjunction with other judicial remedies; it could also be claimed as a temporary or permanent relief or both. In practice, however, injunctive claims are usually coupled with a claim for the declaration of a right. Injunctions could be restrictive, in the sense of restraining a party from behaving in a particular manner; or mandatory, in the sense of compelling a party to behave in a certain way. Both mandatory and restraining orders of injunction are potentially available to an investigator (or research subject) against an ethics committee. Moreover, the availability of an injunction may be a necessary predicate to the success of an investigator's action against an ethics committee. For instance, where an investigator alleges that he or she suffered loss (economic or reputational – examined below) as a result of the negligent or intentional action of an ethics committee (or its members) in connection with the review of a protocol, it is obvious that the success of the suit would depend largely on the availability of evidence relating to the proceedings of the ethics committee. This evidence is likely to be documentary because most ethics committees are required by relevant regulations and guidelines to employ written procedures;[50] but it is a piece of evidence that would rarely be in the possession of an investigator (or research participant), partly because the proceedings of ethics committees

50 WHO, *Operational Guidelines for Ethics Committees That Review Biomedical Research* (Geneva; WHO, 2000). Also: Federal Ministry of Health (Nigeria), *National Code of Health Research Ethics Committee* (Abuja, Nigeria: FMH, 2007), Section K (47–49).

are (generally) not held in public.[51] Moreover, an ethics committee embroiled in litigation that questions the competence and standard of its review would have no incentive to disclose voluntarily the record of its proceedings, and would be happy to claim the protection of its records on privacy and confidentiality grounds.[52] In these circumstances, an investigator's suit would fail before its inception unless he or she secures a judicial order, in the nature of an injunction, compelling the disclosure and handing over of relevant documents to the investigator.[53] As Robertson observed, if 'IRBs are to be legally accountable for their torts, it is necessary to allow plaintiffs access to IRB records pertaining to the protocol in question'.[54] The predicament of an investigator in relation to documents needed to substantiate his or her legal rights is analogous to the difficulty faced by the claimant in *Head v Colloton*.[55] Head was a leukaemia patient and in dire need of a bone marrow transplant. The defendants were the administrators of a bone marrow transplant registry kept by the University of Iowa Hospital. The registry contained a list of donors whose blood had been tissue-typed for purposes of determining their suitability for a potential bone marrow donation to a donee. It transpired that Head became aware that there was a person on that list who could become a suitable donor to him, but the hospital and the defendants failed to reveal the identity of that person; nor did that person accept the hospital's general invitation to make a donation. Head, therefore, sought an injunction to compel the defendants to reveal the identity of that potential donor (through the court or his counsel) so that he could make a specific and personal appeal to that potential donor. The court held that the information on the bone marrow registry, containing the identity of the potential bone marrow donor, was a confidential hospital record of a patient, and thus, was exempt from public access under the Iowa public records statute. Similarly, in *Halikas v The University of Minnesota*,[56] the claimant-researcher needed an injunction to forestall the publication and dissemination of the report of an inquiry conducted by his university's Institutional Review Board. The claimant alleged that the report, which resulted in the suspension of his research activities, was detrimental to his reputation and career. However, the court refused to grant

---

51 McHale, supra, note 8, at 163. As to confidentiality and handling of ethics committees' documents in Nigeria: A.O. Adejumo, 'Health Records and Reports' (paper presented at a seminar on National Code of Health Research Ethics in Abuja, Nigeria, 14–15 December 2006 – on file with author).

52 In *Konrady v Oesterling*, 149 F.R.D. 592 (US Dist. Ct., 1993), it was held that Minnesota's statutory peer review privilege did not extend to the records and proceedings of an Institutional Review Board (that is, research ethics committee in the USA).

53 It is possible that procedural relief, in the form of discovery and inspection of documents, might offer some assistance; this strategy was adopted in *Doe v Illinois Medical Center*, 696 N.E. 2d 707 (App. Ct. Ill., 1998).

54 Robertson, supra, note 6, at 536.

55 *Head v Colloton*, 331 N.W.2d 870 (Sup. Ct. Iowa, 1983).

56 *Halikas v The University of Minnesota*, 856 F.Supp. 1331 (US Dist. Ct. 4th Div., 1994).

the injunction on the ground that the claimant failed to surmount the threshold requirements for the grant of an action.

While an investigator's claim for an injunction might be sought as a final remedy, the need is most felt at the beginning of an action when the viability of an investigator-claimant's case depends on access to crucial documents. Thus, most claims would be for a temporary relief in the nature of an interlocutory (or interim) injunction compelling an ethics committee to make disclosures of documents in its possession. Therefore, an investigator contemplating an action for such temporary remedies would want to know the requirements for the grant of an interlocutory or interim injunction. Interestingly, the House of Lords enunciated the threshold requirements for interim injunctions in the famous case of *American Cyanamid Co. v Ethicon*, where the claimant sought an interim order of injunction to restrain the defendant from infringing the claimant's patent on surgical sutures.[57] In order to avoid considering the merits of the case at the preliminary stage of an application for interim injunction, the House of Lords observed that a claimant only needs to establish that his or her suit raises a serious question to be tried. Otherwise, the court would have to conduct a mini-trial by going into the merits of a claimant's case to see whether the claim reveals a strong probability of success (or a strong *prima facie* case). The latter approach, according to the House Lords, was prone to injustice and should be avoided.[58] Furthermore, the House of Lords held that once a claimant has crossed the initial hurdle of establishing that the claim raised a serious question that ought to be tried, then the court should move on to consider the extent to which each party would be adequately compensated in damages if the court's decision on injunction was unfavourable to that party. Assuming each party's loss was not sufficiently remediable by the award of damages, the next step would be to consider the balance of convenience. Should the balance of convenience weigh evenly, and fail to preponderate in favour of any party, the court could tip the balance by considering the relative strength of the case made by each party. In other words, the merit or relative strength of each party's case is to be considered as a last resort; that is, only when the analysis on balance of convenience failed to yield a decisive result.

The framework of *American Cyanamid* was approved and adopted by the Nigerian Supreme Court in *Obeya M. S. Hosp. v A-G.*[59] However, some English cases have questioned the proposition that the *American Cyanamid* dispensed with the need for an applicant to establish a strong *prima facie* case.[60] Critics of the *American Cyanamid* rely on the House of Lords decision in *Hoffmann-La Roche v Sec. State, Trade and Industry*, which was delivered about the same time as the

57 *American Cyanamid Co. v Ethicon* [1975] AC 396 (HL).

58 Generally, J. Leubsdorf, 'The Standard for Preliminary Injunctions' (1978), 91 Harvard L. Rev. 525.

59 *Obeya M. S. Hosp. v A-G.* [1987] 7 SCNJ 42 (SCN).

60 For analysis of some of those cases: K. Gray, 'Interlocutory Injunctions Since American Cyanamid' (1981), 40 CLJ 307.

*American Cyanamid.* In *Hoffmann-La Roche,* Lord Diplock, who also delivered the House of Lords judgement in *American Cyanamid,* observed that 'to justify the grant of such a remedy the claimant must satisfy the court first that there is a strong prima-facie case'.[61] Because of the conflict in the two decisions of the House of Lords above, Laddie J, in *Series 5 Software Ltd. v Clarke*, held that the *American Cyanamid* had not made any sea- change to the requirements for the grant of an interim injunction.[62] Thus, Laddie J held that it was proper for a court to consider any clear view it might have regarding the relative strength of each party's case. Unlike Nigeria, the Supreme Court of Uganda favours the approach in *Series 5 Software Ltd. v Clarke.* Thus in *Kavuma v Hotel International Ltd.*,[63] the Supreme Court of Uganda held unanimously that an applicant for a temporary injunction must, among other things, satisfy a judge that their claim raises a *prima facie* case; the applicant must also show a probability of success – that they would be successful in the substantive suit. In sum, therefore, an investigator who is able to satisfy the requirements above can apply for an interim or interlocutory injunction, a potentially useful remedy in suits against research ethics committees and its members.

## Procuring the Breach of a Research Contract

In addition to a claim for judicial review of an ethics committee's decision and a claim for injunction to restrain or compel an ethics committee to behave or act in a particular manner, an investigator might also bring an action in tort against an ethics committee or its members for procuring a breach of the investigator's research contract. Thus, an investigator may allege that the rejection of their protocol by an ethics committee led to the breach of the investigator's research contract with a sponsor. While such allegations are rare, the potential for their occurrence is heightened by the increasing pace and scope of university-industry partnership. For instance, some research conducted by investigators in universities and university teaching hospitals are generously funded or sponsored by industrial partners under contracts that include clauses on confidentiality and intellectual property rights. Sometimes such contracts go awry due to irreconcilable conflict of interests, as dramatized by the Olivieri saga.[64] Dr Nancy Olivieri conducted a clinical trial of deferiprone to determine its safety and efficacy in the treatment of thalassemia and other conditions characterized by iron overload. The trial was sponsored by Apotex Inc. (a big Canadian pharmaceutical company) and

61 *Hoffmann-La Roche v Sec. State, Trade and Industry* [1975] AC 295 at 360.

62 *Series 5 Software Ltd. v Clarke* [1996] 1 All ER 853.

63 *Kavuma v Hotel International Ltd.* [1993]11 KALR 73 (SCU).

64 J. Thompson, P. Baird and J. Downie, *Report of the Committee of Inquiry on the Case Involving Dr Nancy Olivieri, the Hospital for Sick Children, the University of Toronto, and Apotex Inc.* (Toronto: Canadian Association of University Teachers, 2001).

was performed at the Hospital for Sick Children, an affiliate of the University of Toronto, where Olivieri was employed as a researcher. Although the initial results of the trial were encouraging, subsequent results showed that deferiprone not only performed poorly against the gold standard drug (deferoxamine); it also showed signs of toxicity (hepatic fibrosis).[65] Obviously concerned about the safety of patients enrolled in the trial, Olivieri proposed to inform the research participants of the adverse and unexpected result. In addition, Olivieri intended to present the results of the trial in a scientific meeting. The ethics committee that reviewed the study was quite supportive of the approach proposed by Olivieri. Apotex, however, relied on the confidentiality agreement between it and Olivieri to insist on non-disclosure of the results of the trial, and threatened Olivieri with a lawsuit. Subsequently, the Hospital for Sick Children set up a panel to review the matter; in its report, the panel strongly criticized the conduct of Olivieri. Consequently, the hospital's medical advisory committee referred Olivieri's case to the Ontario College of Physicians and Surgeons for investigation and, if possible, commencement of a professional disciplinary action against Olivieri based on research misconduct. Olivieri was not only vindicated by the decision of the Ontario College of Physicians and Surgeons; she was also cleared of any wrongdoing by the report of a panel set up by the Canadian Association of University Teachers.[66]

While Olivieri's case more aptly illustrates a researcher-sponsor conflict of interest, breach of academic freedom and the failure of universities and research institutions to support their researchers for fear of diminishing the prospect of generous grants from potential sponsors, it equally highlights the potential economic interests that could be affected adversely by the rejection of a protocol. For instance, assume for a moment that instead of the researcher-sponsor conflict involved in Olivieri's case, her complaint bordered on the rejection of her protocol by the hospital or university's research ethics committee; in that case, she would have suffered the loss of a lucrative research contract with Apotex. Of course, this does not imply that such contractual considerations, rather than issues of scientific and ethical validity, should underpin decisions of research ethics committees. It will be highly unusual for an ethics committee to reject a protocol with the intention of procuring a breach of an investigator's research contract with their sponsor. However, there are circumstances, such as academic rivalry, in which it might be reasonable to suppose that an ethics committee, composed of an investigator's colleagues, intended to procure a breach of the investigator's research contract by rejecting a protocol submitted to them by the investigator. The investigator might

65 D.G. Nathan and D.J. Weatherall, 'Academic Freedom in Clinical Research' (2002), 347 New England Journal of Medicine 1368–1371; E. Gibson, F. Baylis, S. Lewis, 'Dances with the Pharmaceutical Industry' (2002), 166 Canadian Medical Association Journal 448–450.

66 Nathan and Weatherall, supra, note 65; Gibson, et al., supra, note 65.

bring a tort action against the ethics committee and its members for procuring a breach of the investigator's contract.

The tort of procuring a breach of contract was developed in 1853 in the famous case of *Lumley v Gye*.[67] In that case, the parties were proprietors of rival opera houses. The claimant accused the defendant of inducing the famous operatic singer, Johanna Wagner, to breach her performance contract with the claimant so that she would be free to perform for the defendant's opera house. At that time, the only recognized and relevant cause of action was the action for enticement or procurement of a servant to leave their master's service. Extending the principle underlying the master and servant cases, Erle J observed:

> It is clear that the procurement of the violation of a right is a cause of action in all instances where the violation is an actionable wrong, as in violations of a right to property, whether real or personal, or to personal security: he who procures the wrong is a joint wrongdoer, and may be sued, either alone or jointly with the agent, in the appropriate action for the wrong complained of.[68]

The action for procuring a breach of contract is an accessory liability tort. This means that the defendant's liability is secondary to the primary liability of a third party. In the context of research ethics committees, it means that the liability of an ethics committee and its members for procuring a breach of research contract is dependent on, and secondary to, the primary liability of the sponsor of the investigator. This means that if, for any reason, the sponsor is not held to be (primarily) liable to an investigator for a breach of research contract, then the secondary liability of an ethics committee and its members would not arise, whether or not they acted maliciously in procuring a breach of the research contract. Lord Hoffmann observed in *Mainstream Properties Ltd* v *Young* that 'one cannot be liable for inducing a breach unless there has been a breach. No secondary liability without primary liability'.[69] This feature of *Lumley v Gye* implies that it is of little assistance to investigators who intend to sue ethics committees and their members for procuring a breach of research contract. For instance, research contracts and grants are usually made on the condition that the investigator secures ethics approval. Such conditions are usually imposed by the funder of research or forms part of an institution's requirement for the conduct of research; it might also be part of an investigator's contract of employment with their institution. Thus, where a funder withdraws research funding for failure to secure an ethics approval, they (funder) cannot be accused of unlawfully breaching the research contract with an investigator. It means that the primary liability of the funder which is necessary to trigger an accessory liability under *Lumley v Gye* does not

---

67 *Lumley v Gye* [1853] 2 E & B 216. Also: S. Waddams, 'Johanna Wagner and the Rival Opera Houses' (2001), 117 L.Q.R. 431.

68 Lumley, supra, note 67, at 232.

69 *Mainstream Properties Ltd. v Young* [2008] 1 AC 1 at 31 (HL).

exist. In such cases, ethics committees and their members are practically immune from liability for *Lumley v Gye* tort.

In addition to the problem of primary liability, other elements of *Lumley v Gye* present significant difficulties to an investigator contemplating an action against an ethics committee or its members for procuring a breach of contract. In *Mainstream Properties Ltd v Young*,[70] for instance, the House of Lords overhauled the principles established in *Lumley v Gye*, as well as clarifying the elements of the action. First, the claimant must prove that the defendant had knowledge of the contract which the defendant is alleged to have induced or procured its breach. Knowledge of the precise terms of the contract is not necessary, however. Thus, Lord Denning MR observed in *Emerald Construction Co. v Lowthian* that it was enough 'if they (defendants) did not know the actual terms of the contract, but had the means of knowledge – which they deliberately disregarded'.[71] Furthermore, knowledge of a particular field or trade that undergirds a contract qualifies as sufficient knowledge of the contract, at least, for purposes of the tort of inducing a breach of contract.[72] In relation to ethics committees, however, it is relatively easy to prove that an ethics committee had some knowledge of the investigator's contract with a sponsor. For instance, some ethics committees require investigators to indicate sponsorship information on the protocol. Some investigators, however, provide research sponsorship information voluntarily. Thus, although ethics committees might not know the precise terms of contract between an investigator and a sponsor, they know enough to bring them within the element of *Lumley v Gye* above.

Second, there must be an inducement or persuasion. In the context of research ethic committees, it means the investigator must establish some persuasion or inducement directed by an ethics committee at a sponsor. As Rogers observed, there 'must be persuasion directed at a party to the contract'.[73] This may take the form of a direct contact between an ethics committee and the investigator's sponsor regarding the quality of the proposal or outcome of the review process; or a letter sent directly by an ethics committee to the investigator's sponsor informing the latter of an adverse decision taken on the protocol by the ethics committee. Third, the claimant must prove that the defendant intended to procure a breach of contract. In relation to ethics committees, therefore, it must be shown that an ethics committee intended to procure a breach of an investigator's contract with a sponsor. This means that the tort of inducing a breach of contract is an intentional tort. Thus, it is not sufficient to prove that the action of an ethics committee and its members was reasonably foreseeable to induce a breach of the investigator's

70 *Mainstream Properties Ltd. v Young* [2008] 1 AC 1 (HL).

71 *Emerald Construction Co. v Lowthian* [1966] 1 WLR 691 at 700–701.

72 *Merkur Island Shipping Corporation v Laughton* [1983] 2 AC 570 at 591 (HL, per Lord Diplock).

73 W.V.H. Rogers, *Winfield & Jolowicz on Tort, 18th edn* (London: Sweet and Maxwell, 2010), at 868.

research contract.[74] In essence, therefore, an ethics committee that acted honestly in rejecting a protocol cannot be accused of intentionally inducing a breach of contract between a sponsor and an investigator, even if the decision turned out to be unreasonable.[75] Thus, the element of intention ensures that *Lumley v Gye* provides only a marginal remedy to investigators. In sum, it must be quite an exceptional or remarkable case in which an ethics committee would reject a protocol simply to procure the termination of an investigator's contract. While an internal and academic rivalry between an investigator and members of an ethics committee might increase the chances of such unlawful behaviour, there are, however, some countervailing factors, such as the multi-disciplinary composition of ethics committees, and the risk of damage to professional reputation inherent in the malicious and unreasonable rejection of a research protocol. Thus, an investigator's action against an ethics committee or its members for inducing a breach of research contract does not have much prospects of success.

## Causing Loss by Unlawful Means or Unlawful Interference with Economic Interests

An investigator aggrieved by the rejection of their protocol might bring another economic tort action for damages against an ethics committee and its members; this is the tort of unlawful interference with economic interests which causes loss through unlawful means.[76] However, this cause of action has less prospects of success than the action for inducing a breach of contract examined above. The tort of causing loss by unlawful means can be traced to the old cases of *Garret v Taylor*[77] and *Tarleton v M'Gawley*;[78] both cases involved an unlawful intimidation of a third party with the intention of causing economic loss to the claimant. In contrast to *Lumley v Gye* tort, the action for causing loss by unlawful means is not based on accessory liability; both torts are, however, based on intention. In *Mainstream Properties Ltd v Young*, Lord Hoffmann observed that the 'defendant's liability (in tort of causing loss by unlawful means) is primary, for intentionally causing the plaintiff loss by unlawfully interfering with the liberty of others'.[79] In essence, the tort has two important elements.

First, the defendant must have acted unlawfully towards a third party. Questions usually arise as to what counts as unlawful means. Delivering the lead majority judgement in *Mainstream Properties Ltd v Young*, Lord Hoffmann observed

74 *Millar v Bassey* [1994] EMLR 44 (CA), which favoured such approach, was rejected by the House of Lords in *Mainstream Properties v Young*, supra, note 69.

75 Compare *British Industrial Plastics Ltd v Ferguson* [1940] 1 All ER 479 (HL).

76 For judicial analysis of this tort: *Allen v Flood* [1898] AC 1 (HL).

77 *Garret v Taylor* [1620] Cro Jac 567.

78 *Tarleton v M'Gawley* [1794] Peake 270.

79 *Mainstream Properties Ltd v Young*, supra, note 69, at 19.

that unlawful means 'consists of acts intended to cause loss to the claimant by interfering with the freedom of a third party in a way which is unlawful as against that third party and which is intended to cause loss to the claimant. It does not ... include acts which may be unlawful against a third party but which do not affect his freedom to deal with the claimant'.[80] Lord Nichols of Birkenhead was, however, willing to extend unlawful means to 'embrace all acts a defendant is not permitted to do, whether by the civil law or the criminal law'.[81] Returning to ethics committees, this tort requires that for liability to ensue, an ethics committee must act unlawfully, in a way that interferes with the freedom of a sponsor to deal with an investigator, and with the intent of causing loss to the investigator. It is hard to imagine that an ethics committee would commit such outrageous conduct, which also exposes it to a suit by the sponsor. No decent ethics committee is capable of such illegal action. An ethics committee's interference with the liberty of a sponsor could give rise to both civil and criminal liability. It is a route that would not be trodden by any reasonable ethics committee. This cause of action might, however, be available for acts done outside the review process.

Second, there must be an intention to cause loss to the claimant. In other words, the interference with the liberty of a third party must have been intended to cause loss to the claimant. The intention to cause loss to the claimant must be an end in itself or a means to an end; nothing short of that would suffice. As Lord Nichols of Birkenhead explained, a 'high degree of blameworthiness is called for, because intention serves as the factor which justifies imposing liability on the defendant for loss caused by a wrong otherwise not actionable by the claimant against the defendant'.[82] Again, it is unlikely that an ethics committee and its members would satisfy this mental element. As chapter four highlighted, protocols are usually accepted or rejected on the basis of their scientific and ethical merits, not with the intention of inflicting economic loss on the investigator. Also, it is not conceivable that an ethics committee or its members would go out of their way to commit a civil or criminal wrong against a sponsor with the intention of causing economic or professional loss to an investigator. In sum, therefore, the tort of causing loss by unlawful means is of little assistance to an investigator contemplating an action against an ethics committee and its members. However, the investigator could bring a claim for negligent economic loss examined below.

## Negligent Economic Loss

Unlike the cases of intentional economic loss considered above, an investigator might bring a case of negligent economic loss against an ethics committee and its members. For instance, the investigator might allege that the ethics process

80 Ibid., at 32.
81 Ibid., at 57.
82 Ibid.

was conducted in a negligent manner, and that the rejection of the protocol inflicted foreseeable economic loss on the investigator through the loss of a research contract. Currently, no such claim has been made in practice. Indirectly, the absence of such claims provides evidence that ethics committees conduct their reviews prudently and competently. But the prudence and competence of ethics committees need not be exaggerated. For instance, chapters three and four suggested that some ethics committees in Africa lack the significant training and expertise necessary to review research protocols. This might result to a claim for negligent infliction of economic loss.

This is not the place for a detailed analysis of the complex tort of negligent economic loss. Interestingly, Bruce Feldthusen has developed some useful (five) categories for analysing questions of pure economic loss in negligence.[83] Feldthusen's categories of economic loss have been approved by the Supreme Court of Canada;[84] they are negligent misrepresentation, negligent performance of a service, defective products or building structures, relational economic loss, and public authority's failure to confer an economic benefit. Of these five categories, the second category is the most relevant to an investigator's complaint that a negligent ethics review caused them an economic loss. However, some cases of negligent statements (first category) might involve an underlying performance of a service.[85] *Ross v Caunters* illustrates cases of economic loss arising from negligent performance of a service.[86] In *Ross v Caunters*, a gift bequeathed to the claimant under a Will became void because the Will was witnessed by the claimant's husband contrary to section 15 of the Wills Act 1837. The defendant-solicitor who prepared the Will was negligent in failing to inform the testator about the requirements of section 15 of the Wills Act. Judgement was given for the claimant. Sir Robert Megarry V-C observed that the solicitor's duty to the testator 'included a duty to confer a benefit on the plaintiff. When a solicitor undertakes to a client to carry through a transaction which will confer a benefit on a third party, it seems to me that the duty to act with due care which binds the solicitor to his client is one which may readily be extended to the third party who is intended to benefit'.[87] *Ross v Caunters* was approved by the majority of the House of Lords in *White v Jones*,[88] although in the latter case, the House of Lords was concerned with extending the duty of care developed in *Hedley Byrne*

83 Bruce Feldthusen, *Economic Negligence, 4th edn* (Toronto: Carswell, 2000) at 1–2.

84 *Winnipeg Condominium Corp. No. 36 v Bird Construction Co.* [1995] 1 S.C.R. 85; *Bow Valley Husky (Bermuda) Ltd. v Saint John Shipbuilding Ltd.* [1997] 3 S.C.R. 1210.

85 For liability in respect of negligent statements: *Hedley Byrne & Co. Ltd. v Heller & Partners Ltd.* [1964] A.C. 465 (HL).

86 *Ross v Caunters* [1980] 1 Ch. 297.

87 Ibid., at 309.

88 *White v Jones* [1995] 2 A.C. 207 (HL).

*& Co. Ltd. v Heller & Partners Ltd.*[89] Feldthusen argued that, to succeed in an action for negligent performance of a service, a claimant must establish (a) that the defendant voluntarily undertook to perform a specific service for the benefit of the claimant; (b) that the claimant relied on the defendant to perform the undertaking; and (c) that the claimant was injured by negligent performance of the service.[90] As with other cases of negligence, the action for negligent economic loss requires the establishment of a relationship of duty between a claimant and defendant; this was explored in detail in chapter five. For negligent economic loss, however, a duty relationship is established on the basis of the defendant's voluntary undertaking to perform a service for the claimant. Where the undertaking is directed at a third party instead of the claimant, *Ross v Caunters* would extend the undertaking to the claimant provided it was made for the claimant's benefit.

How does the analysis above apply to ethics committees? The task of ethics committees involves the performance of service; much of this is highlighted in chapter four. Thus, the work of ethics committees engages the second category of pure economic loss in negligence outlined above. Therefore, a negligent review of protocol qualifies as a performance of service, with the potential to inflict economic loss on an investigator. Beyond identifying the relevant category of pure economic loss, a claimant-investigator needs to prove the elements of an action for pure economic loss outlined above. On the first element, an undertaking made for the benefit of a claimant, an investigator must prove that the ethics review process was undertaken for his or her benefit. This is a critical requirement in an action for negligent performance of service.[91] Feldthusen observed that 'in the ordinary case of this type, recovery by an incidental beneficiary is difficult to justify'.[92] But as chapter four implied, it would be difficult for an investigator to prove that an ethics review process was undertaken for their benefit. Ethics committees perform a protective public function. This means that ethics review is undertaken for the primary purpose of protecting research subjects from unjustifiable research risks and injury. Although ethics approval might be beneficial to an investigator, for instance, by helping the investigator secure a research grant, or to satisfy the condition of a grant, yet such benefits are not the primary purpose for conducting an ethics review; rather, the benefits are incidental to the task of ethics committees. In essence, it is difficult for an investigator to prove that they are the foreseeable beneficiary of an ethics review process. Furthermore, as some investigators would rather wish to operate without an ethics review system, it is difficult to say that the system is meant for their benefit. The trovan scandal examined in chapter one, as well as the analysis in chapter four, implies that some investigators would be happy to operate without the system of ethics review. Also, some empirical studies on the

89 *Hedley Byrne & Co. Ltd. v Heller & Partners Ltd.* [1964] A.C. 465 (HL).

90 Feldthusen, supra, note 83, at 120.

91 *Biakanja v Irving*, 320 P.2d 16 (Sup. Ct. Cal., 1958); *Whittingham v Crease & Co.* [1978] 5 W.W.R. 45 (B.C. Sup. Ct.).

92 Feldthusen, supra, note 83, at 146.

operation of ethics committees in many parts of Africa suggest that some research protocols were undertaken without the benefit of ethics review. All this challenges the view that ethics review is undertaken for the benefit of an investigator. Moreover, concerns about the inadequacy of an ethics review are usually expressed in relation to the safety of research subjects (the real beneficiaries of the review process), and not for the benefit or protection of an investigator. Thus, any benefit that accrues to the investigator from the ethics review process is incidental to the protection of research subjects. Incidental benefits are, however, insufficient to ground an action for negligent performance of service. In sum, therefore, an investigator's action for pure economic loss has little prospects of success.

## Defamation

Defamation is defined as the publication of a statement which reflects on a person's reputation and tends to lower him or her in the estimation of right-thinking members of society generally,[93] or tends to make them shun or avoid him.[94] As explained below, there are several circumstances in which an investigator might bring an action in defamation against a member or members of an ethics committee. To succeed in such an action, the investigator must establish three elements necessary for the constitution of a cause of action in defamation: (a) the alleged statement must be defamatory. This is usually a question of fact and is generally determined on the basis of a hypothetical reasonable person; (b) the defamatory statement must refer to the claimant-investigator; and (c) the statement must be published or communicated to a person other than the claimant-investigator. Derogatory statements and imputations of incompetence falsely made against an investigator, in the course of a protocol evaluation, by one or more members of an ethics committee might satisfy the three elements above.

It is arguable, however, that the effectiveness of research ethics committees would be severely undermined unless the members are able to speak freely and frankly on every aspect of a protocol, including the professional character, integrity and competence of an investigator. In addition to posing a risk of defamatory action against members of an ethics committee, such a full and frank discussion exacerbates the tension between informational freedom necessary for an efficient

93 *Sim v Stretch* [1936] 52 T.L.R. 669.

94 W.V.H. Rogers, *Winfield & Jolowicz on Tort, 18th edn* (London: Sweet and Maxwell, 2010) at 570; also, *Youssopoff v MGM* [1934] 50 T.L.R. 581; *Reynolds v Times Newspapers Ltd* [2001] 2 A.C. 127 (HL). Some Nigerian cases on the subject include: *African Press Ltd. v Ikejiani* [1953] 14 WACA 386; *Bakare v Oluwide* [1962] 2 All NLR 324; *African Newspapers Ltd. v Coker* [1973] 1 NMLR 386; *Ukpoma v Daily Times Nig. Ltd.* [1979] 2 LRN 357; *Lardner v The Sketch Publishing Co. Ltd.* [1979] 3 LRN 276; *Nthenda v Alade* [1974] 4 ESCLR 109; *Omo-Osagie v Okutubo* [1969] 2 All NLR 175; *Agoaka v Ejiofor* [1972] 2 ESCLR 109.

review of a protocol and the equally important need to protect the reputation of an investigator. While it would be unusual for members of an ethics committee to descend into scurrilous and unwarranted imputation against the character of an investigator, such defamatory attacks are not improbable. As suggested in chapter four, the evaluation of an investigator's competence to conduct a proposed study is a vital part of the ethics review process. No one can possibly argue that it is ethically justifiable to approve a research protocol submitted by an investigator who is reasonably judged by the members of an ethics committee to be professionally incompetent. It is imaginable, however, that legitimate discussions on the competence of an investigator could be exploited by one or more committee members for extraneous and personal purposes. For instance, professional rivalry and personal conflicts could motivate false and malicious statements against an investigator. Such malice might be more difficult to check if exhibited by the only committee member with expertise in the protocol's field of study. Ordinarily, the non-professional or lay members of an ethics committee should be able to provide the needed balance and show greater sensitivity to such ill-motivated statements. However, the practical domination of ethics review proceedings by professional members, as shown in chapters three and four, is likely to undermine such a counter-balancing role for lay members. Thus, where there is no love lost between an investigator and a member (or some members) of an ethics committee, the review process could be misconstrued as an opportunity for mischief. In essence, a malicious and false statement against an investigator may not only amount to actionable defamation; it could also skew the outcome of a review process.

Furthermore, a defamatory statement made by a member of an ethics committee against an investigator, and published to other members or non-members of an ethics committee, might be oral, for instance made during a speech in the course of the committee's proceedings, or embodied in writing, such as when the speech (above) is recorded in writing and forms part of the committee's record of proceedings. Similarly, defamatory statements against an investigator might be contained in a letter rejecting his or her application for ethics approval (but publication must be proved) or in a similar letter sent to the investigator's sponsor. The distinction above gives rise to two issues that are evidentiary on the one hand and classificatory on the other. For instance, how could an investigator establish or prove the publication of a defamatory statement made orally by a member or members of an ethics committee during the course of proceedings which were not open to the public? This evidentiary difficulty was considered in more detail in chapters three, four and five, and it suffices to say that an investigator might overcome this difficulty by engaging the procedural remedy of discovery. The cases below are paradigmatic of that approach. In a similar situation, Adkins J (dissenting) observed that a 'suit on defamation which occurs during the committee proceedings can be prosecuted only if discovery of the committee proceedings is permitted. To deny discovery under these circumstances is to deny access to the courts for redress of injury'.[95] The classificatory problem, on the other hand, resonates with the distinction between slander and libel (explored below). For instance, while the defamatory letters mentioned above, as well as the committee's record of proceedings embodying the defamatory statements, would constitute a libel, the oral defamatory statements would amount to a slander.

## Libel and Slander

The law of defamation used to revel in a fast-diminishing distinction between libel and slander.[96] As noted above, libel refers to defamatory statements in a written or permanent form. In contrast, slander generally refers to oral defamatory remarks. It is not always easy to draw a line between the two, more so in a technological world where the means of communication and data storage are numerous and highly developed. In relation to ethics committees, however, the simplest form of libel would be the recording of a defamatory statement on the written records of the committee. Provided such records are generally accessible, through discovery or other legitimate means, an investigator could relatively easily establish the existence of a libellous statement concerning him or her. This eventuality might, however, trigger a sort of defensive recording of committees' proceedings, meaning that defamatory remarks might be deliberately left out of the records of a committee. Accordingly, it seems likely that the defamation of an investigator would more commonly take the form of a slander. Because of its ephemeral character, coupled with the secrecy of most meetings of ethics committees, slanderous allegations would be much more difficult to prove by an investigator, although the civil processes of discovery and the subpoena of witnesses would come in handy. Worse still, slander is not generally actionable unless special (or actual) damages are proved; this contrasts with libel where damage or injury to the claimant's reputation is assumed and, thus, is actionable *per se*. In four categories of cases, however, slander is actionable *per se.* These are imputation of a criminal offence punishable with imprisonment; imputation of disease; imputation of unchastity to a female; and imputation of unfitness or incompetence. In the context of research ethics committees, the first and, more probably, the last categories are likely to be relevant. As mentioned above, the imputation of an investigator's unfitness or lack of competence to execute a protocol might be entirely false or actuated by malice. Unfortunately, there are as yet no reported cases (as far as the author is aware) in which an investigator sued a member or members of research ethics committee in defamation. But there are a few cases in the US where aggrieved physicians sued their colleagues for defamatory statements published to their hospital's staff privileges committees. These US cases might be of analogical

95 *Holly v Auld*, 450 So.2d 217 at 223 (S. Ct. Florida, 1984).

96 Rogers, supra, note 73, at 570–572.

relevance to a defamatory action brought by an investigator against a member or members of a research ethics committee.

In *Samuelson v Susen*,[97] the claimant alleged that he was denied certain medical privileges as a result of defamatory statements published by the defendants while testifying before a medical review committee or hospital staff privileges committee. By way of discovery, the claimant sought to depose eight members of the staff privileges committee (to whom the defamatory statements were allegedly published). The proposed deponents objected to the discovery on the basis of an Ohio statute (Ohio Revised Code § 2305.251) which protects the confidentiality of the proceedings and records of review committees, including hospital staff privileges committees. Seitz CJ upheld the proposed deponents' objection, holding that the Ohio Code above is 'an explicit bar to the discovery of the proceedings of an Ohio committee reviewing an application for hospital staff privileges'.[98] A more liberal approach was taken by an Illinois court in *Matviuw v Johnson*.[99] Before the executive committee of the Alexian Brothers Medical Centre in Illinois, the defendant allegedly made scathing and defamatory statements concerning the claimant which carried imputations of professional incompetence, dishonesty and unethical practices. As a result of these defamatory statements, the claimant was not reappointed as a staff of Alexian Brothers Medical Centre. The claimant brought a defamatory action against the defendant and also sought discovery of data and proceedings of the executive committee. The trial court upheld the defendant's objection that the claimant's action was not maintainable under the Illinois Medical Studies Act (Ill. Rev. Stat. 1977), which confers absolute privilege on proceedings of hospitals' executive committees. The Illinois Appellate Court, however, held that the Medical Studies Act, by virtue of the exception contained in it, only confers a qualified privilege. While emphasizing that confidentiality was necessary for the effective functioning of hospital review committees, McNamara, J, nevertheless observed that there is 'no useful purpose to be served by allowing one physician to defame another before a medical executive committee and prohibiting the defamed party from seeking a remedy'.[100] The court opined that the need for protection was sufficiently met by the grant of qualified privilege only. In the more recent case of *Doe v Illinois Masonic Medical Centre*, the Appellate Court of Illinois (First District) has held that the privilege under the Medical Studies Act applies to the proceedings and records of research ethics committees.[101] The US states' divergent approaches to this issue are

97 *Samuelson v Susen*, 576 F.2d 546 (US Ct. App. 3rd Cir., 1978).

98 Ibid., at 552.

99 *Matviuw v Johnson*, 70 Ill.App.3d 481 (App. Ct. Ill., 1979).

100 Ibid., at 487.

101 *Doe v Illinois Masonic Medical Centre*, 696 N.E.2d 707 (App. Ct. Ill., 1998). A contrary decision was reached by a Minnesota court in *Konrady v Oesterling*, 149 F.R.D. 592 (US Dist. Ct., 1993).

further illustrated by *Auld v Holly*.[102] Dr Auld's application for staff privileges was denied by the credentials committee of a Florida hospital as a result of defamatory statements allegedly made and published by the defendants to the committee. The defamatory statements included allegations that Dr Auld performed unnecessary surgery, abandoned his patients in the hospital, rendered inefficient post-operative care, was dismissed from his previous hospital employment and ran out of town (of previous employment) because of too many malpractice law suits against him. Consequently, Dr Auld brought an action in defamation and sought discovery of the records of the credentials committee. The trial court dismissed Dr Auld's action. The case was, however, remanded for a new trial by the District Court of Appeal, Florida (Fourth District), which held that the statutory immunity against discovery of a medical review committee's records did not apply in defamation suits brought by a doctor against members of a credential committee. The court also certified its decision to the Supreme Court of Florida. However, the majority of the Supreme Court of Florida observed that the 'discovery privilege ... includes defamation action arising out of the matters which are the subject of evaluation and review by hospital Credentials Committee'.[103]

In principle, therefore, the cases above suggest that members of an ethics committee are individually responsible for any unjustifiable defamatory remarks they make against the character and reputation of an investigator. Where, however, a statement by a committee member concerning an investigator is false and malicious, but not defamatory in the legal sense, the investigator might sue the concerned committee member for malicious falsehood. For instance, in *Kaye v Robertson*,[104] a newspaper was held liable in malicious falsehood for publishing what it falsely claimed to be an interview to which the claimant consented. To succeed in an action for malicious falsehood, however, the claimant must establish that a false statement was made by the defendant to a third party, that the defendant acted with malice, and that the claimant suffered actual or pecuniary damage.[105] While the last element could present a difficult hurdle for an investigator-claimant, it might be established by showing that the false statement led to the denial of an ethics approval and, consequently, the loss of a lucrative research grant. Finally, a committee member sued in defamation might rely on certain well-recognized defences examined in the section below.

## Defences to a Defamation Suit

To avoid the liability of its members in actions for defamation, an ethics committee might be well-advised to establish a practice whereby an investigator is required to

102 *Auld v Holly,* 418 So.2d 1020 (Dist. Ct. App. Florida, 1982).
103 *Holly v Auld,* 450 So.2d 217 at 221 (S. Ct. Florida, 1984).
104 *Kaye v Robertson* [1991] F.S.R. 52.
105 Rogers, supra, note 73, at 664–665.

sign, before the evaluation of a protocol, a bond releasing the committee members from civil liability in connection with statements made by them or information furnished to them concerning the protocol. It is not clear, however, whether public policy would countenance such a release, especially if the defamatory statement was made in absolute bad faith and with malice.

A much more common defence is the defence of qualified privilege. Privilege protects communication that is otherwise defamatory. While absolute privilege is a complete defence and, thus, bars a cause of action from arising, qualified privilege, in contrast, is defeated by the presence of malice, in the sense of improper purpose or lack of belief in the veracity of a statement. The defence of absolute privilege applies in a limited set of circumstances which do not contemplate the proceedings of an ethics committee. These are statements made in Parliament; reports, papers, votes and proceedings ordered to be published by Parliament; judicial proceedings; communication between certain officers of state; and fair and accurate contemporaneous reports of court proceedings.[106] Qualified privilege, in contrast, has a wider ambit. It reaches to all instances where a statement (allegedly defamatory) concerning a claimant was made by a defendant to a third party, provided the defendant was under a legal, moral or social duty to make the statement to the third party who, in turn, had an interest in receiving the statement.[107] Thus, most cases in which qualified privilege is in issue would turn on the analysis of this duty-interest correlation. However, the concept of duty relevant to qualified privilege is very broad and goes beyond legal duties. For instance, Lindley LJ observed in *Stuart v Bell*:

> I take moral or social duty to mean a duty recognized by English people of ordinary intelligence and moral principle, but at the same time not a duty enforceable by legal proceedings, whether civil or criminal.[108]

Interest, on the other hand, includes not only business or financial interest, but also any tangible interest. Accordingly, it was observed that '[S]o long as the interest is of so tangible a nature that for the common convenience and welfare of society it is expedient to protect it, it will come within the rule'.[109] It is arguable, therefore, that each member of an ethics committee has, at least, a moral and social duty to communicate to other members of the committee statements regarding the skill and competence of an investigator, although such statements might turn out to be defamatory. Correspondingly, committee members have an interest to receive such statements. Absent malice, therefore, the defence of qualified privilege should cover or protect communications made in the course of ethics review.

---

106 Ibid., at 619–626.

107 *Reynolds v Times Newspapers Ltd.* [2001] 2 A.C. 127 (HL); *Watt v Longsdon* [1930] 1 K.B. 130.

108 *Stuart v Bell* [1891] 2 Q.B. 341 at 350.

109 *Howe v Lees* [1910] 11 C.L.R. 361 at 377.

Justification and fair comment are other possible defences. Thus, a member of an ethics committee, sued as a defendant in a defamation law suit, might prove that what he or she said was true. In that case, the defence of justification is available to that member even if his or her statement was actuated by malice. Furthermore, the defence of justification does not need to relate to every bit of the defamatory matter or statement; it is sufficient if the defence is just as broad as the charge.[110] It is also possible for a member of an ethics committee sued in an action for defamation to allege that his or her statements amount to fair comment on a matter of public interest. As in qualified privilege, the defence of fair comment is not available for malicious defamatory statements made by a defendant.[111] A cardinal requirement of the defence of fair comment is that the impugned statement must be of public interest. Thus, it must cover 'matters in which the public is legitimately interested as well as matters in which it is legitimately concerned'.[112] For a defendant-member of an ethics committee, therefore, the requirement of public interest might pose problems for defamatory statements published beyond the confines or relevance of the committee's proceeding. For instance, while it is certainly the case that the public has an interest in the protection of research subjects through the process of ethics review, it is arguable that no such legitimate interests exist with respect to defamatory statements made by a member of an ethics committee against an investigator. Thus, it is doubtful that the defence of fair comment applies to actions in defamation brought against members of an ethics committee.

## Right to Research

An investigator might argue that the rejection of their protocol amounts to an interference with their right to research.[113] Furthermore, it might be argued that regulatory or policy restrictions on scientific inquiry inherent in the requirement for ethics review violate the scientist's right to research.[114] But is there a legally

110 Rogers, supra, note 73, at 602.

111 *Peter Walker Ltd. v Hodgson* [1909] 1 K.B. 239.

112 Rogers, Supra, note 73, at 610.

113 Note that a 'right to research' is a component, but much narrower than the claim, of 'academic freedom' which, as Eric Barendt observed, could be analysed at three levels: the rights of individual scholars; institutional autonomy; and the rights of academics to self-rule or to participate in academic government. See, Eric Barendt, *Academic Freedom and the Law: A Comparative Study* (Oxford: Hart Publishing, 2010) at 22–34.

114 For instance, Hamburger argued that an ethics review process constitutes a system of licensing or a prior restraint on speech in a manner that is incompatible with the First Amendment of the US Constitution: P. Hamburger, 'Getting Permission' (2007), 101 Northwestern University Law Review 405. Barendt also explored the legality and legitimacy of an ethics review process and its impact on academic freedom, observing that while 'there can be little objection in principle to the requirements to obtain the approval of an ethics committee before conducting a clinical trial, the extension of these requirements

or constitutionally recognized and protected right to research?[115] Hamburger has suggested that rather than seeking to establish or develop a special right to research, it is better to focus analytical efforts on getting a clear judicial acknowledgement that the freedom of speech and press under the First Amendment of the US Constitution includes, at its core, freedom form licensing.[116] In an interesting article, however, Robertson developed a framework for the comprehensive analysis of a right to research, and the amenability of such right to constitutional protection.[117] It should be noted at the outset that an argument for the constitutional protection of a right to conduct scientific inquiry does not necessarily involve a claim that such right enjoys absolute immunity from governmental interference.[118] Rather, the conferment of a constitutional status on the right to research only ensures that potentially infringing regulations pass a stricter test of constitutional validity than would have been the case were there no such constitutional protection.[119] Thus, in the similar context of academic freedom, Barendt suggested that the constitutionalization of academic freedom ensures that it is 'a fundamental constitutional value, which must shape the interpretation and application of other laws'.[120]

Robertson opined that confusion in the analysis of a right to research stems mostly from the conflation of two components which ought to be kept separate; these are the freedom to choose the end or topic of research, and the freedom to choose the means of research, that is, the manner for conducting the research, including experiments on human subjects. Barendt also agreed that the 'freedom of research', as broadly understood, engages two constituent elements, that is, 'the right of individual academics to choose the subject of their research and how they propose to study it – their research methodology'.[121] Obviously, the public is more likely to be affected directly by choices relating to the means or methods of research, for instance the use of human research subjects in biomedical research, than by choices relating to the end of research, such as the selection of cloning as a research topic. Generally, however, an assertion of a right to research involves a claim 'to be free from government direction or intervention in choosing topics

to research in the social sciences and humanities is much more controversial': Barendt, supra, note 113, at 208.

115 While there is no simple answer to this question, it also involves the issue of whether a Bill of Rights or Constitution applies horizontally as well as vertically.

116 Hamburger, supra, note 3, at 492.

117 John A. Robertson, 'The Scientist's Right To Research: A Constitutional Analysis' [1977] 51 Southern California L. Rev. 1203–1279.

118 This was also highlighted by Barendt, supra, note 113, at 202–204; Amedeo Santosuosso, et al., 'What constitutional protection for freedom of scientific research?' (2007), 33 J. Med. Ethics 342–344; P.B. McDonald, 'Government regulation or other "abridgements" of scientific research: the proper scope of judicial review under the First Amendment' (2005), 54 Emory L. Rev. 979–1091.

119 Robertson, supra, note 117, at 1209–1210

120 Barendt, supra, note 113, at 49.

121 Ibid., at 202.

of research and in selecting means to carry out the research … [it] does not, however, include a claim that the government must fund any particular activity designed to advance knowledge'.[122] An unrestrained freedom to select the means of research might engage some protectable interests that are undermined by the methods chosen to generate the desired knowledge. For instance, compelled or involuntary participation in a research project (as a subject) is sure to threaten the research subject's personal autonomy and bodily security. The occurrence of this risk is less likely where what is asserted is the mere right of a scientist to select a research topic. Thus, the two aspects of a right to research, that is, the end and the means of research, attract different levels of legal and constitutional protection. As Robertson observed:

> Although scientists want to be free of restraints on their choice of research ends, many scientists would not claim as part of the treasured freedom of scientific inquiry an unrestricted right to select any means they find scientifically valid or interesting. For example, few would claim a right to experiment on the property of another without permission, on humans who do not consent to the experiment, or even on their own property or consenting subjects if the experiment will directly cause great damage to others. Thus, the right to experiment – the right to select appropriate means of conducting research – is a weaker right than the right to select the end of research.[123]

Therefore, assuming that a constitutional right to research exists,[124] governmental interference with that right could occur at three levels of regulations or restrictions: (a) Prohibitive restrictions that target the end or topic of research; for instance, the government might prohibit any type of scientific activity in a particular area, such as the general ban on human cloning research in some jurisdictions. This type of restriction is likely to attract the presumption of constitutional invalidity and would require a heavy burden of justification to be valid.[125] (b) Restrictions on means or manner of research. This category would encompass the requirement in most jurisdictions that research involving human subjects must receive prior ethics approval in order to be ethically justifiable. Manner restrictions of this type seem to be constitutionally permissible since they 'limit the means and not the end of research, they usually do not prevent the development of the desired knowledge altogether … [although they] do increase the cost of doing research and thus may

---

122 Robertson, supra, note 117, at 1206.

123 Ibid.

124 Santosuosso and colleagues identified three levels at which such a right could be said to exist, and observed that the right is expressly protected in the Constitutions of Germany, Italy, Slovenia, Spain and Greece: Amedeo Santosuosso, et al., 'What constitutional protection for freedom of scientific research?' (2007), 33 J. Med. Ethics 342–344.

125 Robertson, supra, note 117, at 1207 and 1248–1253.

slow or reduce the development of knowledge and its benefits in a given area'.[126] (c) Finally, restrictions may be indirectly imposed on scientific inquiry through governmental policy on research-funding and resource allocation decisions.[127] In the US, for instance, governmental research bodies, such as the National Institute of Health, condition the grant of federal research funds to universities and research centres on the development of local ethics review frameworks, and a commitment to adhere to substantive ethical principles, such as those stated in the Belmont Report.[128] Hamburger, however, argued that, in practice, US universities are pressured to give assurances that they would follow the Common Rule,[129] not only for federally-funded research, but also for all research involving human subjects conducted by their institutions regardless of the source of funding;[130] for this reason, Hamburger has argued that such conditions on funding violate the First Amendment of the US Constitution. In contrast, Weinstein argued that restrictions on research, such as requirements for ethical review, imposed directly by force of law do not violate the First Amendment because of the distinction between speech and conduct, and to the extent that research involves some communicative elements, such elements do not speak to the core value protected by the First Amendment.[131] Since direct restrictions on research do not encounter constitutional problems, Weinstein argued, it should be much more obvious that similar restrictions on research imposed indirectly, merely as a condition for federal research funding, are entirely compatible with the protections of the First Amendment; or, conversely, to the extent that direct restrictions on research encounter problems with the First Amendment, the constitutional difficulties are eased away by making such restrictions conditional on the receipt of federal funding.[132]

But on the crucial question of whether a constitutional right to research actually exists, Robertson argued that such a constitutional right was derivable from the US Constitution, through its protection of the right to liberty and privacy (Fourteenth Amendment), the right of association and, more significantly, the

126 Ibid., at 1253.

127 Ibid., at 1208 and 1267–77.

128 National Commission, *Belmont Report: Ethical Principles and Guidelines for the Protection of Human Subjects of Research* (National Commission, 1979).

129 Health and Human Services (Common Rule), Title 45 Code of Federal Regulations, Part 46 (2005).

130 P. Hamburger, 'Getting Permission' (2007), 101 Northwestern University Law Review 405 at 441. Charrow, however, argued that the practical extension of the Common Rule to non-federally funded research, although voluntarily undertaken by USA universities, might not be legally enforceable by the US federal government: Robert Charrow, 'Protection of Human Subjects: Is Expansive Regulation Counter-Productive' (2007), 101 Northwestern University Law Review 707 at 716–718

131 James Weinstein, 'Institutional Review Boards and the Constitution' (2007), 101 Northwestern University Law Review 493–497–542.

132 Ibid., at 550–551.

right of free speech (First Amendment).[133] Arguably, the protection of the First Amendment encompasses all the essential preconditions of speech, including the creation, gathering, dissemination, and reception of information. A contrary argument presents a lot of difficulties; for instance, protecting the dissemination or publication of information without a corresponding protection for the initial act of creating that information leads to absurdities. Thus, Robertson argued that the right to receive information from a willing speaker and a journalist's right to gather information very closely resemble scientific activities that come under the rubric of research. As he observed, 'much acquisition or research involves activities traditionally protected by the first amendment, such as speaking, talking, writing, and publishing'.[134] This means that 'social science and other research that use interviews with willing respondents would be protected by the speech clause because the interviewer and interviewee would be exercising the traditional first amendment right to talk to each other, rather than because they are engaged in research'.[135] In contrast to Robertson, Irwin has argued that while a right to research exists, its source is not the freedom of speech protected by the First Amendment but, rather, the freedom of thought and inquiry embedded in the protection of the First Amendment.[136] Weinstein, however, disagreed with both Robertson and Irwin's attempts to locate a right to research within the core or interstices of the First Amendment, arguing instead, that to the extent that a right to research existed, it was more properly found within the liberty interests protected by the Due Process Clauses of the Fifth and Fourteenth Amendments; however, after noting the reluctance of the US Supreme Court to expand the substantive reach of the Due Process Clauses, Weinstein expressed a 'doubt that the Court would recognize a right to research as a liberty specially protected by the Due Process Clauses'.[137] Although the existence of a constitutional right to research has not been the subject of litigation in the US, especially in relation to research ethics committees, there are, however, a few US cases where the existence of a right to research was generally acknowledged.[138] In other jurisdictions, however, the question relating to the existence of a right to research has not received much judicial analysis.

---

133 Robertson, supra, note 117, at 1212–1240.

134 Ibid., at 1217.

135 Ibid.

136 Dana R. Irwin, 'Freedom of Thought: The First Amendment and the Scientific Method' (2005), Wis. L. Rev. 1479.

137 James Weinstein, 'Institutional Review Boards and the Constitution' (2007), 101 Northwestern University Law Review 493 at 545.

138 *Henley v Wise*, 303 F.Supp. 62 (N.D. Ind. 1969); *In re Popkin*, 460 F.2d 328 (1st Cir., 1972); *Richards of Rockford, Inc. v Pacific Gas & Electric Co.*, 71 F.R.D. 388 (N.D. Cal. 1976); *Trachtman v Anker*, 563 F.2d 512 (2nd Cir., 1977). Generally: Roy G.. Spece and Jennifer Weinzieri, "First Amendment Protection of Experimentation: A Critical Review and Tentative Synthesis/Reconstruction of the Literature" (1998), 8 S. Cal. Interdisc. L.J. 185.

Interestingly, the European case of *Kenedi v Hungary* provides a judicial analysis of the scientist's right to research under the European Convention for the Protection of Human Rights and Fundamental Freedoms.[139] In that case, Mr Kenedi, a Hungarian national and historian, was an expert on the functioning of the secret services of totalitarian and dictatorial regimes, and he had published several works in that area. In order to research and publish an academic work on the functioning of the Hungarian State Security Service in the 1960s, he applied to the Hungarian Ministry of Interior for access to certain documents in its possession; the Ministry denied Kenedi's request. Kenedi then applied to the domestic court and got an order which granted him unrestricted access to the relevant documents, but for the purposes of research only. The Hungarian authorities, however, delayed in complying with the order of the domestic court; even at the time of his application to the European Court of Human Rights, Kenedi had not been given unrestricted access to all relevant documents as ordered by the domestic courts. In the European Court of Human Rights, therefore, Kenedi argued that the government of Hungary had interfered with his rights under the European Convention, particularly the right to freedom of expression under Article 10 of the Convention. While the Hungarian government admitted an interference with Kenedi's right to freedom of expression under the Convention, it argued that the interference was justifiable under Article 10(2) of the Convention. In its judgement, the European Court of Human Rights (ECHR) observed that Article 10 of the Convention protects both the publication of the result of research and the precondition for that publication, that is, research. Thus, the ECHR 'notes that the intended publication (of the applicant's historical study) fell within the applicant's freedom of expression as guaranteed by Article 10 of the Convention';[140] the ECHR also emphasized that 'access to original documentary sources for legitimate historical research was an essential element of the exercise of the applicant's right to freedom of expression'.[141] On the basis of the arbitrariness exhibited by the government of Hungary, and the inordinate delay involved in the enforcement of Kenedi's right to research as an inherent part of his freedom of expression, the ECHR held that the Hungarian government's action was neither justifiable nor prescribed by law under Article 10(2) of the Convention.

In Nigeria, the right to research is grounded in the constitutional protection of private and family life; right to freedom of thought, conscience, and religion; right to freedom of expression and the press; and the right to peaceful assembly and association.[142] The Ugandan Constitution not only contains similar provisions,

139 *Kenedi v Hungary* (Application no. 31475/05), European Court of Human Rights (Second Section), 26 May 2009.

140 Ibid., at para. 33.

141 Ibid., at para. 43.

142 Respectively, sections 37, 38, 39 and 40 of the 1999 Nigerian Constitution (Lagos; Federal Government Printer, 1999).

as in the Nigerian Constitution above,[143] it also comes much closer to granting explicit protection on the right to research. For instance, while section 29(b) of the Ugandan Constitution protects the 'freedom of thought, conscience and belief which shall include academic freedom in institutions of learning', section 37 protects the right of a person 'to belong to, enjoy, practise, profess, maintain and promote any culture, cultural institution, language, tradition, creed or religion in community with others'. Certainly, 'academic freedom' in section 29(b) above includes the pursuit of scientific inquiry, knowledge or research. Similarly, it is arguable that the pursuit of knowledge through research is included in the meaning of 'culture' as provided by section 37 of the Ugandan Constitution above.

In sum, therefore, the analysis above suggests that an investigator's legal objection to the existence of an ethics review process, or the rejection of their protocol for non-compliance with the ethics requirements, might have a constitutional flavour or underpinning. However, in research involving human subjects, such objections fall into the category of restrictions bordering on the means and manner of research. In that category, an investigator's claim of a right to research is much weaker. Worse still, the claim of a right to research is extremely tenuous where the research was funded on the condition that ethics approval must be obtained. Thus, an investigator who is unable to satisfy the ethics requirement would be hard pressed to argue that the rejection of their protocol amounts to a violation of their constitutional right to research.

## Conclusion

As this chapter highlighted, an ethics review process might implicate significant professional, social and economic interests of an investigator. Particularly, the rejection of a research protocol for want of ethical justification might expose the investigator to substantial economic injury; for instance, the withholding of ethics approval might lead to the loss of funding from a potential sponsor. Also, an ethics committee or its members might intentionally procure the breach of a research contract, or cause the loss of research contract by acting unlawfully towards a third party. Similarly, the negligent performance of an ethics review might result in pure economic loss. Apart from these potential economic injuries, the proceedings of an ethics committee might involve the publication of statements injurious to the reputation of an investigator. Thus, this chapter examined the judicial remedies open to an investigator aggrieved by the rejection of their protocol; these remedies include the administrative law process of judicial review; the tort actions of procuring a breach of contract, causing loss by unlawful means, and negligent economic loss; an action for defamation; and a claim of legal and constitutional

143 For instance, sections 27 (privacy), 29 (conscience, expression, movement, religion, assembly and association), 30 (education) and 37 (culture) of the Constitution of the Republic of Uganda 1995.

right to research. Of these numerous common law and constitutional actions, however, this chapter suggested that the administrative law action for judicial review and the action for judicial injunction offer the best chance of success to an investigator who contemplates an action against an ethics committee and its members.

## Chapter 7

# Legal Liability of Investigators in Actions by Research Subjects

### Introduction

Research involving human participants, especially clinical trials of drugs and medical devices, may expose subjects to potential risks of harm. In some cases, the risks may not be avoidable, such as where there is no reliable evidence on the toxicity or side effects of a new drug. A phase 1 clinical trial, which assesses the toxicity and dosage of an investigational drug, is a case in point. Thus, apart from ensuring that research participants voluntarily consent to undergo such risks, one of the cardinal functions of research ethics committees is to evaluate the risks and benefits of a study, and to ensure that study-related risks are reasonable in relation to the anticipated benefits; the ethical principle for the effectuation of this analysis is generally known as beneficence, and this was explored in chapter four. In some cases, on the other hand, the risks of a study or injuries caused to research participants might not only have been avoided; they might have been actually caused by the deliberate or negligent action of an investigator. For instance, the design of a study may be so fraught with risks of harm that its subsequent execution can only be regarded as being intended or calculated to inflict injuries on the research subjects, or, at least, as being reasonably foreseeable to cause injuries to the research participants. Take, for instance, a trial that lacks equipoise as examined in chapter two; a participant in such trial who suffers injury because they received a known inferior treatment, or a placebo where an effective treatment exists, might have a cause of action in law against the investigator. Thus, in some circumstances, research participants may bring legal actions against investigators (and sponsors) with respect to injuries arising from studies in which they participated as research subjects. Accordingly, this chapter proposes to examine the causes of action that are available to research subjects in potential suits against investigators; such actions include negligence; battery; constitutional claims; unjust enrichment; breach of confidence; and compensatory claims brought in foreign jurisdictions.

### Actions in Negligence

A claim in negligence is by far the most frequently litigated cause of action in suits brought by aggrieved or injured research subjects against their researchers-investigators. Quite often, however, research subjects' allegation of negligence against their investigators turn on the adequacy or sufficiency of the informed consent process. As already examined in chapter five, any claim in negligence, including those based on lack of informed consent, must satisfy the fundamental threshold requirement of the existence of a duty of care; that analysis is relevant to this chapter, although it was made in the context of suits brought by research subjects against ethics committees and their members. Certainly, the question of whether a legal duty of care exists between an investigator and research subjects presents some significant difficulties; the challenge is compounded by the absence of clarity in the jurisprudence relevant to the issue. For instance, it is not clear from the case law whether such a legal duty actually exists. In *Greenberg v Miami Children's Hospital*, however, Moreno J tersely observed that 'in certain circumstances a medical researcher does have a duty of informed consent'.[1] In a seminal analysis, Holder opined that the informed consent requirements embodied in the US research regulations are analogous to the legal doctrine of informed consent which, in turn, evolved from the concept of fiduciary duty or relationship existing between a physician and their patient according to the US jurisprudence. In other words, the existence of a physician-patient fiduciary relationship is the theoretical basis of the legal doctrine of informed consent, at least in the US.[2] Thus, Holder implied that the well-acknowledged duty of informed consent in the research setting is, theoretically, equally attributable to the existence of a fiduciary relationship between a researcher and subject. This researcher-subject fiduciary relationship therefore gives rise to a legal duty of care imposed on the researcher for the benefit of the subject. To put it beyond cavil, Holder observed that 'a court would look with extreme disfavour on a physician who tried to excuse unfairness or injury to a subject on grounds that no fiduciary relationship existed since the subject was not a "patient"'.[3] Thus, the next section will explore this important debate to determine whether a duty relationship exists between a researcher and research subject. In the meanwhile, however, this section assumes the existence of that duty relationship in order to interrogate claims in negligence brought by research subjects against investigators and based on lack of informed consent.

More than any other jurisdiction, the US courts have wrestled with negligence claims by research participants against their investigators; thus, the US jurisprudence provides a fertile judicial ground for the analysis of claims made by research subjects against investigators-researchers. As already stated, however, most relevant US cases on this issue focus on the validity and propriety of the informed consent process. For instance, in *Stewart v Cleveland Clinic Foundation*,[4] the claimant was enrolled as a subject in a neck and head cancer

1 *Greenberg v Miami Children's Hospital*, 264 F. Supp. 2d 1064 at 1070 (S.D. Fla. 2003).

2 Angela R. Holder, 'Do Researchers and Subjects Have a Fiduciary Relationship' (1982), IRB 6.

3 Ibid., at 6.

4 *Stewart v Cleveland Clinic Foundation*, 736 N.E.2d 491 (Ct. App. Ohio, 1999).

study conducted at the defendant's hospital by the investigators. The design of the trial involved two arms; the first arm was the control, where the subjects were given the standard treatment of radiation and surgery. The second arm, however, was the experimental arm, and the subjects in that group received the experimental treatment of chemotherapy, in addition to the treatments given to the control group. As delineated by the facts of *Stewart*, although chemotherapy-combined treatment was clinically indicated for the management of the claimant's medical condition, the claimant was, however, randomly assigned to the chemotherapy-deficient control arm. Even without the randomization, it was not the practice of the defendant's hospital to apply chemotherapy-combined treatment in the management of neck and head cancer. Nonetheless, the claimant alleged that the defendant hospital and the investigators of the study were negligent by failing to inform the claimant of the efficacy of the chemotherapy-combined treatment in the investigational arm of the study; the claimant further alleged that the efficacy of chemotherapy-combined treatment was sufficiently established by substantial evidence in medical literature. Also, the claimant alleged that the defendant failed to inform the claimant of the available 'off-site' or alternative places where the claimant might have access to the investigational chemotherapy-combined treatment. In response, the defendant filed a motion to dismiss the claimant's suit for disclosing no reasonable cause of action. Sweeny J dismissed the defendant's preliminary objection to the claimant's suit, and observed that 'there exist genuine issues of material fact whether Klais (the substituted deceased claimant) gave informed consent to be a participant in the phase 111 clinical trial and received the treatment he was afforded by the Clinic'.[5]

Both *Gregg v Kane*[6] and *Burton v Brooklyn Doctors Hospital*,[7] on the other hand, exemplify the different turns a complaint on informed consent could take. In *Gregg*, the claimant sued in negligence for the injury she sustained as a result of undergoing an experimental eye operation in the form of excimer laser surgery. The claimant alleged that the investigators made significant and unauthorized deviations from the protocol, and that they failed to obtain the claimant's informed consent. Buckwalter J held that the claimant had shown sufficient evidence of negligence to warrant the case being sent to the jury. The court, therefore, rejected the defendant's motion for a summary dismissal of the claimant's suit. In contrast, however, the blind claimant in *Burton* complained that he was enrolled in a clinical trial without the consent of his parents even though he was a premature infant at the time of the trial. The assailed trial was a study on the effects of oxygen on retrolental fibroplasia (RLF), that is, blindness caused by excessive amount of oxygen administered on premature infants or by exposure to prolonged liberal application of oxygen to premature infants. In response to the claimant's allegation relating to the absence of informed consent, the defendant argued that

5 Ibid., at 501.

6 *Gregg v Kane*, 1997 WL 570909 (E.D. Pa.).

7 *Burton v Brooklyn Doctors Hospital*, 88 A.D. 2d 217 (N.Y. S. Ct., 1982).

in 1953 when the study was undertaken, there was no duty on investigators in New York State to make disclosures pertaining to the risks of a treatment. Sullivan J observed that 'in the absence of a New York case rejecting the doctrine of informed consent before 1965, or at least limiting a doctor's liability where he has received a general consent from his patients, we find that the practice at the time of plaintiff's treatment … was sufficient to establish the duty'.[8]

Not unusually, however, a research subject's suit in negligence against an investigator for failing to obtain the subject's informed consent might also raise the connected issue of voluntariness and, possibly, other causes of action that go beyond the scope of negligence. Kaufman J poignantly highlighted that possibility in *Bailey v Lally*, observing that the relevant question was 'whether conditions of incarceration … were so bad and the inducements to participate ... so great that the prisoners' participation in the medical research program was not voluntary and therefore in violation of constitutional rights to due process, privacy and protection against cruel and unusual punishment'.[9] Furthermore, the famous Canadian case of *Halushka v University of Saskatchewan* illustrates both the existence of a duty of informed consent and the standard for discharging that duty.[10] In that case, the claimant participated in a trial that tested the efficacy of a new anaesthetic agent known as Fluoromar; he suffered cardiac arrest as a result of that trial. The evidence in the case showed that information given to the claimant regarding the experiment was not sufficient and, in some instances, was misleading. Hall JA suggested that an investigator's duty of informed consent might be analogized to the duty arising from a physician-patient relationship. Thus, Hall JA observed:

> In my opinion the duty imposed upon those engaged in medical research, as were the appellants Wyant and Merriman, to those who offer themselves as subject for experimentation, as the respondent did here, is at least as great as, if not greater than, the duty owed by the ordinary physician or surgeon to his patient. There can be no exceptions to the ordinary requirements of disclosure in the case of research as there may well be in ordinary medical practice. The researcher does not have to balance the probable effect of lack of treatment against the risk involved in the treatment itself. The example of risks being properly hidden from a patient when it is important that he should not worry can have no application in the field of research. The subject of medical experimentation is entitled to a full and frank disclosure of all facts, probabilities and opinions which a reasonable man might be expected to consider before giving his consent.[11]

8 Ibid., at 226.

9 *Bailey v Lally*, 481 F. Supp. 203 at 205 (US D. Ct. ML., 1979).

10 *Halushka v University of Saskatchewan* [1965] 53 D.L.R. (2d) 436 (Sask. Ct. App.).

11 Ibid., at 443–444.

The judicial observation above was confirmed in *Zimmer v Ringrose*,[12] another Canadian case, although in *Zimmer*, the Alberta Court of Appeal emphasized that the 'full and frank' standard of disclosure required by *Halushka* was limited to the researcher-subject relationship, and, therefore, was not applicable to the doctor-patient relationship.[13] It is not clear whether the *Halushka* standard of disclosure requires the disclosure of an investigator's financial and economic interests in a proposed study. In *Moore v Regents of the University of California*, for instance, the Supreme Court of California suggested that the doctrine of informed consent entailed the disclosure of an investigator's economic and commercial interests in a proposed study or its results.[14] In contrast, the court in *Greenberg v Miami Children's Hospital* declined the invitation by the claimants to extend the duty of informed consent to the disclosure of an investigator's economic interests in a proposed research.[15] The *Greenberg* court observed that a retroactive imposition of such an extended duty would attract serious consequences. For instance, 'imposing a duty of the character that plaintiffs seek would be unworkable and would chill medical research as it would mandate that researchers constantly evaluate whether a discloseable event has occurred'.[16] Furthermore, the *Greenberg* court observed that a duty to disclose commercial interests in research results 'would give rise to a type of dead-hand control that research subjects could hold because they would be able to dictate how medical research progresses'.[17]

In England, unlike Canada, the *Halushka* standard of disclosure established for researchers must give way to the equally famous test developed by McNair J in *Bolam v Friern Hospital Management Committee*. In that case, McNair J observed that '[a medical man] is not guilty of negligence if he has acted in accordance with a practice accepted as proper by a responsible body of medical men skilled in that particular art ... merely because there is a body of opinion who would take a contrary view'.[18] The *Bolam* test was developed for those who profess skill and care (professionals) and was approved by the House of Lords in *Maynard v West Midlands Regional Health Authority*[19] and *Sidaway v Board of Governors of the Bethlem Royal Hospital and the Maudsley Hospital*.[20] In the research context, the

---

12 *Zimmer v Ringrose* [1981] 124 D.L.R. (3d) 215 (Albt. C.A.).

13 For the argument that a higher standard of disclosure should apply to researchers: Karine Morin, 'The Standard of Disclosure in Human Subject Experimentation' (1998), 19 J. Leg. Med. 157; Larry I Palmer, 'Disease management and Liability in the Human Genome Era' (2002), 47 Vill. L. Rev. 1.

14 *Moore v Regents of the University of California*, 793 P.2d 479 (Cal. S. Ct. 1990).

15 *Greenberg v Miami Children's Hospital*, 264 F. Supp. 2d 1064 at 1070 (S.D. Fla. 2003).

16 Ibid., at 1070.

17 Ibid., at 1071.

18 *Bolam v Friern Hospital Management Committee* [1957] 1 W.L.R. 582 at 587.

19 *Maynard v West Midlands Regional Health Authority* [1984] 1 W.L.R. 634.

20 *Sidaway v Board of Governors of the Bethlem Royal Hospital and the Maudsley Hospital* [1985] A.C. 871.

application of the *Bolam* test presents some significant difficulties. The *Bolam* test implies that the focus is not on the existence of a full and frank disclosure of risks by an investigator, but whether the investigator's conduct and disclosure of risks are consistent with the prevailing professional standards or, at least, could be endorsed by a responsible body of professional opinion. Thus, liability would not arise where the investigator's partial disclosure is consistent with a responsible body of professional opinion, notwithstanding that the research subject actually needed more information to make an informed consent regarding participation in a research project. In essence, *Bolam* and *Halushka* potentially lead to different outcomes, although *Halushka* is certainly a more favourable test for research subjects. Thus, a research subject would welcome any opportunity to avoid the application of *Bolam.*

It is arguable that *Bolam* contemplates only a doctor-patient relationship and, as such, is not relevant to the different context of researcher-subject relationship. Interestingly, this argument was rejected by the English Court of Appeal in *Gold v Haringey Health Authority*.[21] In *Gold*, the trial judge had avoided the application of *Bolam* by making a distinction between therapeutic and non-therapeutic procedures. The claimant's complaint was that the defendant-doctor was negligent by failing to warn the claimant of the risks inherent in a sterilization procedure undergone by the claimant. Specifically, the claimant was not informed of the risk that the procedure might not be successful. The evidence showed that a responsible body of professional medical opinion (50 per cent of doctors) would not have warned a patient of similar risks. Interestingly, the trial judge held that *Bolam* was not applicable because the sterilization procedure in question was not therapeutic but investigational in nature; in other words, the risk that the sterilization procedure would fail was something of which the claimant ought to have been warned because the procedure was not entirely therapeutic in nature. Thus, the trial court held that the defendant was liable in negligence. On appeal, however, Lloyd LJ observed that to make 'a distinction between advice given in a therapeutic context and advice given in a non-therapeutic context would be a departure from the principle on which the *Bolam* test is itself grounded'.[22] Accordingly, Lloyd LJ concluded that 'the principle (*Bolam*) does not depend on the context in which any act is performed, or any advice given. It depends on a man professing skill or competence in a field beyond that possessed by the man on the Clapham omnibus'.[23] Thus, *Gold* suggests that the *Bolam* test is as much applicable to disclosures by researchers to research subjects as disclosures by doctors to patients.

For Africa and other developing countries, however, the analysis above, and the choice between *Bolam* and *Halushka,* present interesting options. Africa's choice between the two cases is likely to be conditioned by factors affecting the

21 *Gold v Haringey Health Authority* [1988] 1 Q.B. 481.

22 Ibid., at 489.

23 Ibid., at 489-490.

conduct of international collaborative research in developing countries, such as those examined in chapters one, three and four. At the risk of repetition or oversimplification, these factors include poor regulation, poverty, disease, dilapidated health care infrastructures, abundance of research subjects, and high levels of illiteracy. Taking these factors and research scandals analysed in chapter one into consideration, it is unlikely that courts in African countries would be willing to grant investigators the immunity from negligence or informed consent suits implied by the application of *Bolam*. Put differently, African courts, for the reasons stated above, are likely to adopt the higher standard of disclosure or stricter test established in *Halushka*. In sum, therefore, it is suggested that the 'full and frank' standard of disclosure developed in *Halushka* should be the normative standard of liability applicable in African countries.

## Investigator-Research Subject Duty of Care

Before the decision in *Grimes v Kennedy Krieger Institute*,[24] it was not always clear whether a special relationship of proximity giving rise to a duty of care existed between a researcher and research subject. Probably *Grimes* is the first case to develop a comprehensive framework for analysing the researcher-subject duty of care. In *Grimes*, researchers investigating effective and low-cost procedures for lead paint dust abatement designed a protocol that contemplated the deliberate exposure of infant research subjects to lead poisoning. The infant-claimants (through their parents) argued that the defendant-investigator was negligent in failing to design a study that did not involve placing children at unnecessary risk. The investigator was not only accused of failing to inform the participants in the study of the test results in a timely manner; he also failed to give the participants complete and accurate information regarding the potential hazards and risks entailed by the study. The defendant, however, filed a motion for summary judgement against the claimant, on the basis that the defendant owed no legal duty of care to the claimants. The trial judge upheld the defendant's preliminary objection and thus dismissed the claimants' suit.

On appeal, however, the claimants asked the Maryland Court of Appeal to declare that, as a matter of law, a duty of care exists between an investigator and research subjects. For the majority, Cathell J accepted that a special relationship imposing a duty of care on a researcher for the benefit of a research subject existed between the claimants and the defendant, and that such duty could be established in one or more of five ways. First, the majority held that the consent form prepared

24 *Grimes v Kennedy Krieger Institute*, 782 A.2d 807 (Md. Ct. App., 2001). For comments on this case: Victoria Orlowski, 'Promising Protection Through Internationally Derived Duties' (2004), 36 Cornell Int'l L.J. 381; Hazel G. Beh, 'The Role of Institutional Review Boards in Protecting Human Subjects: Are We Ready to Fix a Broken System?' (2002), 26 Law & Psychol. Rev. 1.

by the investigator-defendant and signed by the claimants-research subjects, or on their behalf, embodied sufficient information that met the requirements for the constitution of a valid bilateral contract.[25] Thus, the contractual relationship implicit in the consent process gave rise to a special relationship between the parties, such that a duty of care was imposed on the defendant for the benefit the claimants.[26] Second, the majority in *Grimes* held that a special relationship of proximity giving rise to a duty of care could be established under enforceable research regulations, such as the US 45 Code of Federal Regulations (C.F.R.) Part 46 (2000);[27] this is a sort of regulation-based special relationship of duty. Of course, this second source of duty would not avail research participants in countries where the relevant research governance framework lacks a normative or legal character; for instance, chapter one suggested that research regulations in many African countries are voluntary in nature, in the sense of not being backed up by legislation. In such places, it will be difficult to assert a regulation-based special relationship giving rise to a duty of care. In anticipation of this argument, however, the majority in *Grimes* was quick to generalize this second source of duty to encompass more universally applicable regulations, such as the Nuremberg Code. Thus, the *Grimes* majority observed that the 'Nuremberg Code, intended to be applied internationally, and never expressly rejected in this country, inherently and implicitly, speaks strongly to the existence of special relationships imposing ethical duties on researchers who conduct nontherapeutic experiments on human subjects'.[28] The phrase 'ethical duties', used by the majority above, more aptly describes the content of the Nuremberg Code rather than its legal enforcement. To hold otherwise would make nonsense of the majority's conclusion that the 'breach of obligations imposed on researchers by the Nuremberg Code, might well support

25 On the controversial issue of whether a contract exists between an investigator and a research subject, Waddams suggests that 'generally speaking … a contractual relationship (exists) between an investigator and a person who agrees with him to undergo an experiment'. S.M. Waddams, 'Medical Experiments on Human Subjects' (1967), 25 U. Tor. Fac. L. Rev. 25 at 49. However, Waddams did not explain how such contracts are brought into existence or the elements that give them legal force, although he went on to discuss the applicability of exemption clauses to such contracts. See also, B. Dickens, 'Contractual Aspects of Human Medical Experimentation' (1975), 25 Uni. Tor. L. J. 406; and Alice K. Page, 'Prior Agreements in International Clinical Trials: Ensuring the benefits of research to developing countries' (2002–2003), 3 Yale J. Health Pol'y L. & Ethics 35–66.

26 Sarah Edwards recently made a case for the more explicit contractual underpinning of the researcher-subject relationship with a view to protecting investigators, and science generally, against unreasonable withdrawals by research subjects in the course of a clinical trial: Sarah J.L. Edwards, 'Assessing the Remedy: The Case for Contracts in Clinical Trials' (2011), 11 The American Journal of Bioethics 3–12. For a criticism of Edwards' proposal, see Kenneth De Ville, 'The Case Against Contract: Participant and investigator Duty in Clinical Trials' (2011), 11 The American Journal of Bioethics 16–18.

27 Grimes, supra, note 24, at 846–849.

28 Ibid., at 849.

actions sounding in negligence in cases such as those at issue here'.[29] Third, the majority argued that even international research regulations that lack any form of legal character, such as the Helsinki Declaration,[30] were capable of giving rise to a special relationship imposing a duty of care. Thus, the majority observed that since the existence of a duty relationship largely depended on policy considerations, the court was entitled to articulate a public policy in support of the researcher-subject duty of care provided there was no legislative policy to prevent it from doing so. Therefore, the majority held that it could articulate a public policy infused with the principles of the Helsinki Declaration to ground a duty relationship between an investigator and research subject. Accordingly, the majority considered some sections of the Helsinki Declaration and observed:

> In our view, otherwise healthy children should not be the subjects of nontherapeutic experimentation or research that has the potential to be harmful to the child. It is, first and foremost, the responsibility of the researcher and the research entity to see to the harmlessness of such nontherapeutic research. Consent of parents can never relieve the researcher of this duty. We do not feel that it serves proper public policy concerns to permit children to be placed in situations of potential harm, during nontherapeutic procedures, even if parents, or other surrogates, consent. Under these types of circumstances, even where consent is given, *albeit* inappropriately, policy considerations suggest that there remains a special relationship between researchers and participants to the research study, which imposes a duty of care.[31]

Four, the *Grimes* majority suggested that a special relationship of duty might also arise from the knowledge imbalance between a researcher and their research subjects. Thus, the majority observed that the 'investigators are in a better position to anticipate, discover, and understand the potential risks to the health of their subjects', and that practical 'inequalities exist between researchers, who have superior knowledge, and participants who are often poorly placed to protect themselves from risk'.[32] This informational imbalance and the dependency relationship that characterize the research context create a 'special relationship giving rise to duties, the breach of which might constitute negligence'.[33] Finally, although the majority accepted that foreseeability alone was insufficient to create a duty of care, it held that the probability and magnitude of risks in *Grimes* were so extreme that the court was justified to impose a duty of care on the defendant for the benefit of the claimants.[34] In his minority judgement, Raker J agreed with the majority's opinion

29 Ibid., at 849.
30 World Medical Association, *Declaration of Helsinki* (1964, as amended).
31 Grimes, supra, note 24, at 850.
32 Ibid., at 851.
33 Ibid.
34 Ibid., at 851–852.

that the claimants gave sufficient evidence of a special relationship between them and the defendant, and that such special relationship created a duty of care sufficient to ground an action in negligence.[35] In contrast to the majority, however, Raker J considered it 'unnecessary to reach the thorny question ... of whether the informed consent agreements in these cases constitute legally binding contracts'.[36] Thus, the dissent only challenged the factual conclusions made by the majority. Raker J held that such conclusions at the preliminary stage of the litigation were inappropriate because the case had not been heard on the merits.

Interestingly, the recent case of *Robertson v McGee* doubts the existence of a researcher-subject duty of care espoused in the second and third sources of duty outlined by *Grimes* above; unfortunately, *Robertson* did not cite *Grimes*.[37] In *Robertson*, former research subjects involved in a cancer vaccine trial sued the investigators and members of the institutional review board that approved the study for violations of the US research regulations, and one hundred and twenty-two other causes of action. Since the case was brought at a federal court, the claimants had to establish the presence of a federal jurisdiction; thus, the claimants alleged that the defendants violated the claimants' constitutional rights or a federal right emanating from the combined effects of the Declaration of Helsinki, the Nuremberg Code and the 45 C.F.R. Part 46. Cook J, however, dismissed the claimants' action for want of federal jurisdiction, observing that 'there is no private right of action for an alleged violation of international law for the protection of human research subjects under the Declaration of Helsinki and the Nuremberg Code'.[38] Furthermore, Cook J suggested that research subjects in the US do not need to rely on the Declaration of Helsinki or the Nuremberg Code because the US Code of Federal Regulations regulates comprehensively the conduct of research involving human subjects. Even at that, Cook J held that no private right of action arose from 45 C.F.R. Part 46 because the regulation developed a comprehensive enforcement mechanism that was incompatible with individual rights of enforcement. Thus, Cook J observed that within '45 C.F.R. § 46, there is a comprehensive enforcement scheme provided to the FDA, accordingly there is no private right of action enforceable under § 1983'.[39] Arguably, *Robertson* is distinguishable from *Grimes*. For instance, *Robertson* mainly engaged the question of whether the US Code of Federal Regulations, the Declaration of Helsinki and the Nuremberg Code could be used to establish an enforceable right that rose to the level of a constitutional guarantee. *Grimes*, on the other hand, addressed a different question of whether the same regulatory documents could be the basis of establishing the existence of a

35 Ibid., at 859.

36 Ibid.

37 *Robertson v McGee*, 2002 WL 535045 (N.D. Okla.).

38 Ibid., at 3. For similar decisions: *White v Paulsen*, 997 F. Supp. 1380 (E.D. Wash. 1998); *Hoover v West Virginia Department of Health and Human Services*, 129 F. 3d 1259 (11th Cir. 1997).

39 *Robertson v McGee*, supra, note 37, at 3.

special relationship of duty of care in negligence. Moreover, the recent decision of the majority of the US Court of Appeal in *Abdullahi v Pfizer* held that the principle of the Nuremberg Code has evolved into a specific, universal, and enforceable norm of customary international law.[40] Thus, although the *Abdullahi* case was decided in the context of the US Alien Tort Statute,[41] it supports the approach taken by the majority in *Grimes* by attributing a legal character to the Nuremberg Code. In sum, therefore, the analysis above suggests that a special relationship of proximity giving rise to a duty of care in negligence exists between a researcher and research subject.[42]

## Battery

In negligence actions based on lack of informed consent, the claimant's grievance is not that they failed or refused to give consent to the intervention by the defendant; rather, the complaint is that the claimant gave their consent without receiving relevant and sufficient information from the defendant; thus the consent is uninformed. In battery claims, on the other hand, the claimant's grievance is a total lack of consent to the defendant's physical contact with the claimant, or that there were factors which completely vitiated the consent initially given by the claimant. These vitiating factors include fraud, misrepresentation and undue influence.[43] Thus, where a person was the subject of a non-consensual medical experimentation they could seek the remedy of battery against the investigator.

Battery is a 'contact' tort; its function is to redress unwanted physical contacts, such as running a car intentionally over the feet of a claimant.[44] Thus, battery protects a person's interest in their physical security. In addition, battery safeguards or protects the personal autonomy of a claimant and their right to self-determination.[45] Accordingly, battery might be defined as the non-consensual, intentional and direct application of force on a claimant. Laskin CJC in *Reibl v Hughes* defined battery as an intentional tort 'consisting of an unprivileged and

---

40 *Abdullahi v Pfizer*, 562 F.3d 163 (US C.A., 2nd Cir., 2009).

41 Alien Tort Statute, 28 U.S.C. § 1350.

42 Angela R. Holder, 'Do Researchers and Subjects Have a Fiduciary Relationship?' (1982), IRB 6–7.

43 In *Chatterton v Gerson* [1981] Q.B. 432 Bristow J held that the deliberate withholding of information in bad faith would vitiate consent on the ground of fraud. Also: *Re T* [1992] 3 W.L.R. 782; D. Beyleveld and R. Brownsword, *Consent in the Law* (Oxford: Hart Publishing, 2007), 159–170; J. Montgomery, *Health Care Law, 2nd edn* (Oxford: Oxford University Press, 2003) 232–238.

44 *Fagan v Metropolitan Police Commissioner* [1969] 1 Q.B. 439.

45 *Schloendorff v Society of New York Hospital*, 211 N.Y. 125 (1914). Generally: M.M. Shultz, 'From Informed Consent to Patient Choice; a New Protected Interest'(1985), 95 Yale L.J. 219.

unconsented to invasion of one's bodily security'.[46] Battery is actionable *per se*, that is, it does not require proof of damages before liability can be imposed. In contrast, liability in negligence requires proof of damages.[47] As an element of battery, 'force' is sufficiently constituted by evidence showing physical contact between a claimant and defendant; even a slight contact would be sufficient.[48] In order for liability to arise, however, the contact need not be motivated by anger or hostility.[49] Thus, consent is critical for any claim in battery. In the medical or research context, for example, the crucial question is whether or not the research subject consented to the experimental procedure. *Halushka v University of Saskatchewan* is a case in point.[50] Recall that the claimant in that case was enrolled in a trial that tested the efficacy of a new anaesthetic agent. Information given to the claimant concerning the trial was not only scanty; it was also misleading in some respects. Hall, J.A. observed:

> Although the appellant informed the respondent that a 'new drug'was to be tried out, he did not inform him that the new drug was in fact an anaesthetic of which he had no previous knowledge, nor that there was risk involved with the use of an anaesthetic. Inasmuch as no test had been previously conducted using the anaesthetic agent 'Fluromer'to the knowledge of the appellants, the statement made to the respondent that it was a safe test which had been conducted many times before, when considered in the light of the evidence describing the characteristic of anaesthetic agents generally, was incorrect and was in reality a non-disclosure. The respondent was not informed that the catheter would be advanced to and through his heart but was admittedly given to understand that it would be merely inserted in the vein in his arm.[51]

Hall JA had to decide whether there were significant physical contacts sufficient to constitute a claim in battery; he observed that the 'attachment of the electrodes, the administration of anaesthetic and the insertion of the catheter were each an intentional application of force to the person of the respondent'.[52] On the basis that the above physical contacts were enough to ground an action in battery, the only remaining question was whether the claimant consented to the acts involved in that experimental procedure. In light of his earlier quotation (above), relating

46 *Reibl v Hughes* [1980] 114 D.L.R. (3d) 1 at 9.

47 For instance, in *Yearworth v North Bristol NHS Trust* [2010] Q.B. 1 (CA) where it was a central issue whether damage to sperm samples constituted a legally recognizable damage required for success in a negligence action.

48 *Cole v Turner* [1704] 6 Mod. 149; *Wilson v Pringle* [1987] QB 237.

49 *Re F (Mental Patient: Sterilisation)* [1990] 2 A.C. 1 (HL) *per* Lord Goff.

50 *Halushka v University of Saskatchewan* [1965] 53 D.L.R. (2d) 436 (Sask. Ct. App.).

51 Ibid., at 444.

52 Ibid., at 442.

to the deficiency of consent given by the claimant, Hall JA concluded that 'there was evidence upon which the jury could find that the respondent gave no effectual consent or release to the appellant'.[53] Thus, the appellant-defendant was held liable to the claimant in battery.

Similarly, in *Kus v Sherman Hospital*,[54] an investigator who undertook an intraocular lens implantation study modified the consent form approved by an IRB (Institutional Review Board) in order to remove references to the investigational nature of the procedure. The claimant gave consent to the study on the basis of the modified form; thus the claimant was not aware that he was involved in an experimental medical procedure. Unfortunately, the claimant suffered permanent injuries in his eyes as a result of the procedure; consequently, the claimant brought a claim in battery against the defendant. The court held that a 'claim of medical battery was found to extend to cases where the treatment given was "substantially at variance" with the consent given'.[55] Applying this principle to the case, the court observed that 'whether those modifications amounted to Kus' consent being "substantially at variance" with the treatment he actually received – that of an experimental nature – or whether Kus did or did not know of the experimental nature of the treatment are issues which necessarily belong to the jury'.[56] Thus, the defendant's motion to dismiss the claimant's action was denied.

In the past, especially in medical contexts, it was very easy to conflate claims based on nondisclosure of relevant risks associated with a medical procedure with claims in battery. But in *Chatterton v Gerson,* Bristow J warned against such conflation; he observed that in most cases patients give a general or broad consent to medical intervention or treatment and, as such, their complaints bordering on insufficient disclosure of potential risks associated with a medical procedure should give rise to negligence rather than battery.[57] For instance, the claimant in *Zimmer v Ringrose* underwent an unsuccessful sterilization procedure that involved the use of an innovative technique known as silver nitrate sterilization.[58] The claimant consented to the procedure but was not informed that the sterilization method was an innovative procedure and was yet to be generally accepted by the medical community. Also, the claimant was not told of the potential risks and benefits of the innovative method of sterilization in comparison to the traditional methods of sterilization. While the trial judge gave judgement for the claimant with respect to her claims in battery and negligence, he however awarded the claimant only nominal damages for her claim in battery, amounting to only CAN$1. On appeal, Prowse JA refuted the claim and award for battery, and observed that 'the battery theory of recovery should be restricted to situations where the practitioner performs

53 Ibid., at 445.

54 *Kus v Sherman Hospital*, 644 N.E. 2d 1214.

55 Ibid., at 1220.

56 Ibid., at 1221.

57 *Chatterton v Gerson* [1981] Q.B. 432.

58 *Zimmer v Ringrose* [1981] 124 D.L.R. (3d) 215 (Albt. Ct. App).

a totally different procedure from the one authorized or where he performs a procedure without obtaining any consent at all'.[59] Thus, Prowse JA held that the defendant was not liable in battery because the claimant gave her consent to the innovative sterilization procedure. But in the Nigerian case of *Okekearu v Tanko*, the claimant's left middle finger, which was injured in an accident, was amputated by the defendant-doctor without the consent of the claimant or that of his guardian (claimant was fourteen years old at the time of the accident); nor did the defendant inform the claimant that he was to be treated by way of amputation. The Nigerian Supreme Court held that the defendant was liable in battery for failing to obtain the claimant's consent to the amputation.[60]

The Canadian Supreme Court endorsed the principles above in the famous case of *Reibl v Hughes*.[61] The claimant in that case underwent a procedure to remove an occlusion (blockage) in his left carotid artery which allowed only fifteen per cent of claimant's blood to flow through his vessel to the brain. Unfortunately, the claimant suffered a stroke as a result of the procedure and the right side of his body was paralyzed. The claimant was, however, not warned of the potential risks of stroke and paralysis that materialized. Consequently, the claimant sued the defendant-doctor in damages for both negligence and battery; the battery claim was based on the claimant's allegation that the defendant's insufficient disclosure of potential risks associated with the procedure had vitiated the claimant's consent. The Supreme Court of Canada had to consider whether or not the claimant's claim in battery was sustainable. The lead judgement, delivered by Laskin CJC, observed that 'actions of battery in respect of surgical or other medical treatment should be confined to cases where surgery or treatment has been performed or given to which there has been no consent at all or where … surgery or treatment has been performed or given beyond that to which there was consent'.[62] Thus, Laskin CJC opined that 'unless there has been misrepresentation or fraud to secure consent to the treatment, a failure to disclose the attendant risks, however serious, should go to negligence rather than to battery'.[63]

It is suggested that the judicial observations above should apply to research involving human subjects, especially non-therapeutic research. In non-therapeutic research, such as phase 1 and 2 clinical trials, the only reason for contact between an investigator and research subject is the proposed research based on the

59 Ibid., at 220.

60 *Okekearu v Tanko* [2002] 9 S.C.N.J 1 (SCN). It is submitted that this was more properly a case of negligence, rather than battery, since there was an initial consent to treat the claimant; unless it could be argued that the treatment, by way of amputation, was beyond the treatment consented to by the claimant.

61 *Reibl v Hughes* [1980] 114 D.L.R. (3d) 1. Generally: G. Seaborne, 'The Role of the Tort of Battery in Medical Law' (1995), 24 Anglo-American L. Rev. 24; G. Robertson, 'Informed Consent to Medical Treatment' (1981), 97 L.Q.R. 102.

62 Reibl, supra, note 46, at 10.

63 Ibid., at 11.

subject's consent. This means that as Phase 1 and 2 clinical trials involve healthy participants who are not meant to gain therapeutically from the study, it is difficult to explain the contact between the investigator and subject except on the basis of the subject's consent. Thus, in such research contexts, where there exists some sort of general or broad consent, the research subject's complaint relating to non-disclosure of risks is likely to sound in negligence rather than battery. Therefore, phase 1 and 2 clinical trials offer paradigmatic examples of research contexts not amenable to battery claims. Thus, except in cases of fraud, undue influence or misrepresentation, research subjects in phase 1 and 2 clinical trials can only sue in negligence rather than battery. Battery claims are, however, more likely to arise in the context of therapeutic research; much of that is evident in the cases reviewed above. For instance, a patient might allege that their physician experimented on them without their knowledge; or that the patient thought, or was misled into thinking, that the procedure was therapy rather than research. Furthermore, a patient could allege that the treatment they actually received was at variance with the treatment to which they consented. In short, therapeutic research is much more likely than non-therapeutic research to give rise to battery claims. In sum, therefore, an action in battery is a valuable legal remedy for research participants who suffered research-related injuries.

## Constitutional Claims

In addition to tort claims examined above, a research subject may bring constitutional claims in relation to injuries (or death) suffered by them as a result of their participation in a research project. For instance, some of the research malpractices examined in chapter one might give rise to constitutional claims in national courts or international human rights tribunals. Thus, Fidler argued that the placebo-controlled short-course zidovudine (AZT) trials conducted in developing countries to test the efficacy of a short-course zidovudine in the management of perinatal or mother-to-child transmission of HIV/AIDS violated some international human right norms, including the right to life; right against non-consensual medical experimentation; and freedom from torture, inhuman, degrading and cruel treatment. Arguably, the short-course zidovudine trials also violated some social, economic and cultural rights, such as the right to health.[64] While the first three rights, outlined above by Fidler, are protected under Articles 6 and 7 of the International Covenant on Civil and Political Rights (ICCPR),[65] the right to health is protected under Article 12(1) of the International Covenant on

64 David P. Fidler, '"Geographical Morality" Revisited: International Relations, International Law, and the Controversy over Placebo-Controlled HIV Clinical Trials in Developing Countries' (2001), 42 Harv. Int'l L.J. 299–354.

65 International Covenant on Civil and Political Rights (1966), U.S.T. – 999 U.N.T.S. 171.

Economic, Social, and Cultural Rights (ICESCR).[66] Upon reflection and analysis, however, Fidler concluded that the features of the placebo-controlled HIV/AIDS study in developing countries could not satisfy the elements and requirements of the international human rights documents cited above. Similarly, Kevin King observed that the 'poor fit between human rights law and human experimentation is the result of dealing with instruments and provisions not tailored to the nuances of human experimentation'.[67] In the absence of a binding treaty provision, for instance, one critical hurdle that an international human right claim must scale is a demonstration that the asserted human right norm has acquired such a notoriety of obedience among States (that is, universal and consistent practice of obedience among States) that it ought to be recognized as a binding and peremptory rule of customary international law (*jus cogens*). In other words, proof that States obey the norm out of a sense of obligation. It may be difficult to show that international human rights guarantees relevant to a research subject's claim have attained the required status of *jus cogens*.[68] For instance, in *Abdullahi v Pfizer* the United States Court of Appeals (Second Circuit) was divided on whether the international human right norm prohibiting non-consensual medical experimentation had acquired the status of a binding rule of customary international law.[69] While the majority in that case concluded that there was a binding 'norm of customary international law prohibiting medical experimentation on human subjects without their consent',[70] the minority, however, observed that although the Nuremberg Code 'had significant import ... (as well as) evidentiary value in our inquiry, ... there is nothing to indicate that the Code establishes a norm of international law prohibiting non-consensual medical experimentation'.[71]

Despite the uncertainty that claims brought under the international human rights frameworks would succeed, it is arguable that aggrieved research subjects might be able to bring successful constitutional claims in the national courts of countries where the harm occurred.[72] Using the trovan trial examined in chapter one as an example or case study, it is possible to delineate a range of constitutional claims that might be available to the participants in the trovan trial under the

---

66 International Covenant on Economic, Social, and Cultural Rights (1966), 993 U.N.T.S. 3, 6 I.L.M. 383.

67 Kevin King, 'A Proposal for the Effective International Regulation of Biomedical Research Involving Human Subjects' (1998), 34 Stan. J. Int'l L. 163 at 178–179.

68 George J. Annas, 'Mengele's Birthmark: The Nuremberg Code in United States Courts' (1991), 7 J. Contemp. Health L. & Pol'y 17, Jonathan Todres, 'Can Research Subjects of Clinical Trials in Developing Countries Sue Physician-Investigators for Human Rights Violations' (2000), 16 N.Y.L. Sch. J. Hum. Rts. 737 and Orlowski, supra, note 24, argued that the Nuremberg Code has acquired the status of customary international law.

69 *Abdullahi v Pfizer*, 562 F.3d 163 (2009).

70 Ibid., at 187.

71 Ibid., at 201.

72 As in *US v Stanley*, 283 U.S. 669 (US S. Ct. 1987) and *White v Paulsen*, 997 F..Supp. 1380 (US Dist. Ct. 1998).

Nigerian Constitution. As the reader would recall from chapter one, the trovan trial sought to determine the efficacy of an antibiotic, Trovafloxacin, in the treatment of epidemic bacterial meningitis; unfortunately, eleven of the children involved in the trial died and others suffered different degrees of permanent injury.[73] The trial was mired in ethical and legal controversies already explored in chapter one. Thus, it is arguable that the trovan research subjects could file claims in a Nigerian court (as they actually did, but not for constitutional remedies) alleging a violation of their constitutional rights under the Nigerian Constitution; these constitutional claims might include guarantees relating to the right to life; and right to dignity of the human person, including freedom from torture, inhuman, or degrading treatment. The African Charter on Human and Peoples' Rights guarantees analogous rights.[74] The analysis below attempts to flesh out these potential constitutional claims.

## Right to Life

The author is not aware of any reported case in a national court where a research subject alleged that their participation in a research protocol amounted to a deprivation of their constitutional right to life.[75] The civil suit instituted in Nigeria by the trovan research subjects did not even allege such violation.[76] Nevertheless, a constitutional right to life could be implicated by research-related injury. The right to life is guaranteed under section 33(1) of the Nigerian Constitution: 'Every person has a right to life, and no one shall be deprived intentionally of his life, save in execution of the sentence of a court in respect of a criminal offence of which he has been found guilty in Nigeria'.[77] Under the Nigerian Constitution, the only exception to the right to life is death resulting from the use of reasonable and justifiable force in the defence of property or in the protection of any person from unlawful violence, or in order to suppress a riot, insurrection and mutiny. Similarly, it might be lawful to use reasonable and justifiable force that results to death in order to carry out a lawful arrest or to prevent the escape of a person from lawful custody.[78] Whether the trovan research subjects could successfully rely on this

73 For an excellent analysis of the background to the trovan trial, by a Nigerian official who was intimately involved in the efforts of the Nigerian government to control the spread of the epidemic (meningococcal meningitis), see Idris Mohammed, *Academics, Epidemics and Politics* (Ibadan, Nigeria: Bookcraft, 2007), 170–210.

74 African Charter on Human and Peoples' Rights, 27 June 1981, 21 I.L.M. 59; for its domestication in Nigeria: African Charter on Human and Peoples' Rights (Ratification and Enforcement) Act, Laws of the Federation of Nigerian 1990, c. 10.

75 This also involves the question of whether a Constitution operates horizontally (applicable to private actions) as well as vertically (applicable to actions against the State).

76 *A-G v Pfizer and Ors.* Suit No: FHC/ABJ/CS/309/2007 (on file with the author).

77 *The Nigerian Constitution* (1999), (Lagos: Government Printer), section 33.

78 Nigerian Constitution 1999, section 33(2). For an excellent analysis of similar provisions in the 1979 Nigerian Constitution, see B.O. Nwabueze, *The Presidential*

constitutional guarantee depends on the dynamics of the right itself. For instance, the right to life has two significant strands: first, the prohibition of intentional infliction of death, or the negative obligation to refrain from interferences that result to death. Second, the right to life also entails a positive obligation to take preventive operational measures in order to promote and protect an individual's life.[79] These elements were sharply highlighted by the court in *Osman v United Kingdom* where it was faced with the interpretation of Article 2(1) of the European Convention on Human Rights, which guarantees the right to life in a way similar to section 33(1) of the Nigerian Constitution:

> The court notes that the first sentence of article 2(1) enjoins the state not only to refrain from the intentional and unlawful taking of life, but also to take appropriate steps to safeguard the lives of those within its jurisdiction. It is common ground that the state's obligation in this respect extends beyond its primary duty to secure the right to life by putting in place effective criminal law provisions to deter the commission of offences against the person backed up by law-enforcement machinery for the prevention, suppression and sanctioning of breaches of such provisions. It is thus accepted … that article 2 of the Convention may also imply in certain well-defined circumstances a positive obligation on the authorities to take preventive operational measures to protect an individual whose life is at risk from the criminal acts of another.[80]

Unless restricted, however, it is obvious that the positive obligations of a State under the right to life guarantee would entail operational measures and resources that are beyond the reach of most States. Thus, the *Osman* court observed that 'such an obligation must be interpreted in a way which does not impose an impossible or disproportionate burden on the authorities'.[81] Accordingly, the State is not obligated to prevent every claimed risk to life from materializing. Does this mean that the positive obligation of a State under the right to life guarantee is subject to the principle of progressive realization, by analogy to economic, social and cultural rights? More recently, in *R (Pretty) v DPP*, the House of Lords suggested that the bipartite nature of the obligations imposed by the constitutional guarantee of a right to life resonates with the principles of sanctity of life.[82] For instance, the

---

*Constitution of Nigeria* (London: C. Hurst & Co., 1982), 409–418.

79 *X v Germany* [1984] 7 EHRR 152; *Keenan v United Kingdom* [2001] 33 EHRR 913. Nwabueze opined, however, that 'the limitation on power arising from a constitutional guarantee of fundamental rights and freedoms imposes no duty on the state positively to do anything to promote the material well-being of the people, but only a negative duty not to violate them': B.O. Nwabueze, *The Judiciary as the Third Estate of the Realm* (Abuja, Nigeria: Gold Press, Ltd., 2007) at 176.

80 *Osman v United Kingdom* [1998] 29 EHRR 245 at 305.

81 Ibid., at 305.

82 *R (Pretty) v DPP* [2002] 1 AC 800.

late Lord Bingham of Cornhill observed that the 'thrust of this [that is, article 2 of the European Convention] is to reflect the sanctity which, particularly in Western eyes, attaches to life'.[83] More poignantly, Lord Steyn opined that article 2 of the European Convention 'enunciates the principle of the sanctity of life and provides a guarantee that no individual "shall be deprived of life" by means of intentional human intervention'.[84] As the current Nigerian constitutional jurisprudence on right to life is mainly focused on issues relating to the constitutional validity of death sentences,[85] Nigerian courts asked to determine the scope of a constitutional right to life outside the death penalty type of cases might find the European bipartite framework above to be helpful.

It is easier to apply the analysis above to the facts of the trovan trial than those of the placebo-controlled short-course AZT trials. This hypothesis could be tested by applying the negative obligation of a State under the constitutional guarantee of a right to life to the facts of the two trials, that is, the trovan and placebo-controlled short-course AZT trials. Recall that, unlike the placebo-controlled short-course AZT trials where no death resulted from or was causally connected to the trials, some research subjects actually died in the trovan trial. Arguably, therefore, the representatives of their estates can claim that the Nigerian government violated its negative obligation under the right to life guarantee, as evidenced by the death of the research participants. In response to that argument, however, it could be argued that the death of the trovan research participants was caused by the underlying disease, that is, epidemic bacterial meningitis, and not by the experimental intervention. Fidler made similar arguments with respect to the placebo-controlled short-course AZT trials and observed that 'the trials themselves did not directly cause any deaths that have occurred or may occur in the future from perinatal HIV transmission, as HIV was already present in the pregnant women'.[86] Thus, it may be difficult for the deceased trovan claimants, through their representatives, to prove that they were intentionally deprived of their lives in violation of the constitutional guarantee of a right to life (that is, the negative obligation). However, the trovan claimants might make a more successful argument based on the State's positive obligation under the right to life guarantee. For instance, they could argue that the positive obligation of the Nigerian government extends to the regulation and effective supervision of research involving human subjects. In other words, the Nigerian government has a positive duty to eliminate unnecessary

83 Ibid., at 810.

84 Ibid., at 834. Although the House of Lords also held that Article 8(1) of the Convention, protecting the right to private and family life (not considered in this section) was not engaged, the European Court of Human Rights came to a contrary decision in *Pretty v United Kingdom* [2002] 35 EHRR 1, but held that the interference was justified under Article 8(2) of the convention. Generally, see *R (on the application of Purdy) v DPP* [2009] UKHL 45.

85 For instance, *Kalu v State* [1998] 13 NWLR (Pt. 583) 531 (SCN).

86 Fidler, supra, note 64, at 330.

and unjustifiable threats to life posed by participation in research involving human subjects. This sort of positive obligation is discharged by the development of frameworks that effectively eliminate or minimize the risks of harm to research participants. But as the analysis of the trovan trial in chapter one indicates, this positive obligation was not discharged by the Nigerian government. In the mid-1990s when the trovan trial was conducted, the Nigerian government had not established any effective regulatory or oversight mechanism for the conduct of research involving human subjects. As chapter three indicates, effective regulation and research governance in Nigeria were established more than ten years after the trovan trial. Thus, the trovan research participants could argue successfully that the Nigerian government violated their constitutional right to life by failing to discharge its positive obligation under section 33 of the Nigerian Constitution, entailing effective regulation and supervision of biomedical research in Nigeria. In contrast, the same arguments might not be available to the participants in the placebo-controlled short-course AZT trials because both the 'sponsoring and host countries reviewed the trials thoroughly before they commenced'[87] and 'no one has criticized the sponsoring or host governments of neglecting to monitor and supervise the placebo-controlled trials'.[88] This implies that the positive obligation embedded in the right to life guarantee was effectively discharged in the placebo-controlled short-course AZT trials.

However, the trovan subjects would not succeed in their (hypothetical) constitutional claim of a right to life unless they prove that the Nigerian government participated in, conducted, sponsored or endorsed the trovan trial. This directly engages the question of whether the Nigerian Constitution operates vertically or horizontally (or both ways). In the US, analysis of this question proceeds under the constitutional doctrine of 'state action', which generally means that the US Constitution is enforced against the State only or people who acted under the colour of law, that is, under State's authority.[89] It is generally accepted that a Bill of Rights or constitutional guarantees of human rights operate vertically, that is, enforceable against the State. It is not, however, clear whether the same guarantees operate horizontally, that is, enforceable against private persons. While the Nigerian Constitution revels in this controversy, as do the constitutional systems of most other countries, the debate should not detain us here as it has been explored more extensively by the author at a different forum.[90] It suffices to say that, based on the detailed analysis of the trovan trial in chapter one, even if the Nigerian Constitution were taken to apply vertically only, there is no doubt that the Nigerian government participated in or at least endorsed the trovan trial; this is sufficient to satisfy the requirement of 'state action', as employed by the

87 Ibid., at 330.

88 Ibid.

89 For instance: *Kadic v Karadzic*, 70 F.3d 232 (2nd Cir. 1996).

90 Remigius N. Nwabueze, 'Securing Widows' Sepulchral Rights Through the Nigerian Constitution (2010), 23 Harvard J. Hum. Rights 141–155.

American constitutional analytic framework. However, if the Nigerian government were held not to have played any role whatsoever in the trovan trial, then it would be open to Pfizer and its investigators to resist the constitutional claim of the trovan subjects on the basis that, being private persons, Pfizer and its investigators are not amenable to constitutional claims. Simply put, Pfizer would argue that the Nigerian Constitution does not operate horizontally. As already mentioned, however, it would be extremely difficult for the Nigerian government to deny playing a significant role in the trovan trial. Similarly, the majority of the US Court of Appeals observed in *Abdullahi v Pfizer* that the 'unlawful conduct is alleged to have occurred in a Nigerian facility with the assistance of the government and government officials and/or employees',[91] and concluded that 'these contentions meet the state action test because they adequately allege that the violations occurred as the result of concerted action between Pfizer and the Nigerian government'.[92] In sum, therefore, the trovan subjects might successfully bring claims under the Nigerian Constitution for the enforcement of their fundamental human right to life.

### Right to Human Dignity: Against Torture, Inhuman and Degrading Treatment

Another constitutional right implicated in the trovan trial is the right to dignity of the human person protected under section 34(1)(a) of the Nigerian Constitution (1999): 'Every individual is entitled to respect for the dignity of his person, and accordingly – no person shall be subjected to torture or to inhuman or degrading treatment'. A similar right is guaranteed under article 3 of the European Convention on Human Rights: 'No one shall be subjected to torture or to inhuman or degrading treatment and punishment'. Thus, in *D v United Kingdom* it was held that the proposed deportation of the applicant, a victim of HIV/AIDS, from the UK to St Kitts where there was no treatment facility, care or support for HIV/AIDS victims, in contrast to the benevolent medical environment in the UK, was tantamount to inhuman treatment by the United Kingdom in violation of article 3 of the Convention.[93]

The descriptive terms of 'torture', 'inhuman' and 'degrading' treatments contained in section 34(1)(a) of the Nigerian Constitution are not mutually exclusive but refer to varying degrees of mistreatment.[94] In the *Report of the European Commission of Human Rights on the Greek Case* it was suggested that while torture lay on the upper end of the spectrum on maltreatments, inhuman and degrading treatments lay on the lower end of that spectrum.[95] As with the

91 Abdullahi, supra, note 40, at 188.

92 Ibid., at 188–189.

93 *D v United Kingdom* [1997] 24 EHRR 423.

94 This was the approach adopted for the European Convention in the *Report of the European Commission of Human Rights on the Greek Case*, 1969 Y.B. Eur. Conv. On H.R.

95 Ibid.

right to life, the guarantee of human dignity under section 34(1)(a) of the Nigerian Constitution, entailing freedom from torture, inhuman and degrading treatment, embodies both a negative and positive obligation. For instance, the Nigerian government has a negative obligation to abstain from depriving any individual of their dignity by the infliction of torture, inhuman or degrading treatment. Correlatively, the Nigerian government has a positive obligation to take such actions that would prevent the subjection of individuals to indignity. In *R (Pretty) v DPP*, however, the House of Lords suggested that the positive obligations of States under article 3 of the European Convention were less absolute and extensive than the States' negative obligations. Thus, the House of Lords observed that 'the steps appropriate or necessary to discharge a positive obligation will be more judgemental, more prone to variation from state to state, more dependent on the opinions and beliefs of the people and less susceptible to any universal injunction'.[96] While it is not persuasive to argue that the trovan trial involved the infliction of torture on the trovan research subjects, it is possible to make a strong argument that the non-consensual nature of the trovan trial amounts to inhuman, or at least degrading, treatment of the trovan research subjects in violation of section 34(1)(a) of the Nigerian Constitution.[97] To simplify the analysis, the argument above should be bifurcated. First, on the basis that the Nigerian government was a participant in the trovan trial, it is arguable that the Nigerian government violated its negative obligation under section 34(1)(a) of the Nigerian Constitution, which requires the Nigerian government to refrain from inflicting on (the trovan) research subjects the treatment proscribed by that section. Second, even if the Nigerian government was not a participant in the trovan trial, it is still arguable that the Nigerian government violated its positive obligations under section 34(1)(a) of the Nigerian Constitution by failing to take such actions that would have prevented the exposure of the trovan research subjects to inhuman and degrading treatment. In this regard, the failure of the Nigerian government could be shown by its refusal or inability to regulate, supervise and monitor biomedical research involving human beings in Nigeria.

Furthermore, the US case of *Bailey v Lally* illustrates a claim that non-consensual medical experimentation violates the constitutional guarantee against torture, inhuman and degrading treatment.[98] Thus, *Bailey*'s case provides an additional analytical framework for assessing the putative constitutional claims by the trovan research subjects. In *Bailey*, current and former state prisoners alleged that they were used as research subjects in non-consensual medical experiments that took place at the Medical Research Unit of the Maryland House of Correction

---

96 *R (Pretty) v DPP*, supra, note 82, at 817 (Lord Bingham of Cornhill).

97 Annas observed that most 'physicians would, of course, be shocked at having anything they do to patients considered "torture or cruel, inhuman or degrading treatment"', George J. Annas, 'The Changing Landscape of Human Experimentation: Nuremberg, Helsinki, and Beyond' (1992), 2 Health Matrix 119 at 136.

98 *Bailey v Lally*, 481 F. Supp. 203 (US Dist. Ct. ML. 1979).

in violation of their (US) constitutional protection against cruel and unusual punishment.[99] Although the prisoners' informed consent was obtained for the impugned research, yet they contended that the conditions of incarceration at the Maryland House of Correction were so bad and the inducements to participate in the research at the Medical Research Unit (of the prison) so great that the prisoners' participation in the medical research experiments was not voluntary (and thus in violation of their constitutional rights). For instance, it was found as a fact that compensation for participation (by prisoners) in the research carried out at the Maryland House of Correction was higher than the average prison wage. Claimants-prisoners were, however, clearly told that participation would not have any impact on parole decision. Furthermore, in contrast to the overcrowded and dreary conditions of the prison cells, inmates who took part in the medical research programme at the Maryland House of Correction were accommodated in the live-in section of the Medical Research Unit, which was air-conditioned, adequately heated and quiet, as well as having hot water, colour television and separate bathroom facilities. Against this background, the *Bailey* claimants alleged that their consent was induced (or vitiated), and that the research (at the Medical Research Unit) was therefore non-consensual and violated their Eighth (cruel and unusual punishments) and Fourteenth Amendments (substantive due process) rights. Kaufaman J noted that the claimants' allegation of coercion did not hinge on the absence of informed consent but on the 'lack of voluntariness growing out of unconstitutional conditions such as overcrowding and other undesirable aspects of regular institutional life at the MHC'.[100] Kaufman J also observed that the standard of Eighth Amendment embodied 'broad and idealistic concepts of dignity, civilized standards, humanity, and decency … against which we must evaluate penal measure'.[101] As regards the substantive due process of the Fourteenth Amendment, Kaufman J observed that a violation occurs when an act shocks the conscience of mankind.[102] After a detailed consideration of the factual circumstances of the experiments impugned by the claimants, Kaufman J held that none of the actions of the defendants rose to the levels prohibited by the Eighth and the Fourteenth Amendments of the US Constitution. Unlike *Bailey*, where there was informed consent but its voluntariness was challenged on inherent institutional grounds, the trovan research subjects alleged that Pfizer failed to obtain their consent (through their parents); the implication is that the trovan trial was non-consensual in nature. As such, the trovan trial violates the concepts of dignity, civility, humanity and decency alluded to in *Bailey*. The point is that even if the (American) *Bailey* test

99 The experiments were mainly on known infectious diseases, including malaria, cholera, shigella, viral diarrhoea, influenza, typhoid, E. Coli, and rhinovirus.

100 Bailey, supra, note 98, at 220.

101 Ibid., at 219; quoting *Jackson v Bishop*, 404 F.2d 571 (CA, 8th Cir. 1968), *Trop v Dulles*, 356 U.S. 86 (S. Ct. 1958).

102 Bailey, supra, note 98, at 220, quoting *Rochin v California*, 342 U.S. 165 (S. Ct. 1952).

is deployed as a guide to the interpretation of section 34(1)(a) of the Nigerian Constitution, it is still arguable that the Nigerian government and Pfizer would be held liable for violating the trovan research subjects' constitutional guarantee against torture, inhuman and degrading treatment under the Nigerian Constitution.

## Unjust Enrichment

Where a research protocol involved the donation of human body tissues by the research subjects, and the tissues formed the basis of a lucrative biomedical innovation or invention by the investigator, an action for unjust enrichment might arise. *Greenberg v Miami Children's Hospital*[103] illustrates research subjects' potential claim in unjust enrichment against researchers. In that case, the claimants (parents of children suffering from Canavan disease and non-profit organizations that fund research on Canavan disease) and the defendants collaborated on a medical research that was intended to identify and develop genetic tests for Canavan disease, a rare genetic abnormality that frequently occurs in Ashkenazi Jewish families. For the research, claimants provided body tissues (blood, urine and autopsy samples) and financial support which the defendants accepted. The defendants successfully identified the gene responsible for Canavan disease and developed appropriate carrier and prenatal testing for the disorder. The Canavan gene and accompanying testing kit were patented by the defendants without the knowledge of the claimants. The claimants complained that the defendants' restrictive licensing practice limited the availability of Canavan disease testing contrary to the expectations of the claimants. They therefore sued the defendants for damages and injunction based on six causes of action: lack of informed consent; breach of fiduciary duty; unjust enrichment; fraudulent concealment; conversion; and misappropriation of trade secrets. The defendants' motion to dismiss the claimants' suit for disclosing no reasonable cause of action was allowed by Moreno J except for the action for unjust enrichment:

> The complaint has alleged more than just a donor-donee relationship for the purpose of an unjust enrichment claim. Rather, the facts paint a picture of a continuing research collaboration that involved plaintiffs also investing time and significant resources in the race to isolate the Canavan gene. Therefore, given the facts as alleged, the court finds that plaintiffs have sufficiently pled the requisite elements of an unjust enrichment claim.[104]

Since this ruling only sanctioned trial but not judgement for the unjust enrichment claim, it is still an open question whether the unjust enrichment framework is amenable to body parts donated for research. While *Washington*

103 *Greenberg v Miami Children's Hospital*, 264 F.Supp. 2d 1064 (S.D. Fla. 2003).
104 Ibid., at 1072–1073.

*University v Catalona* also involved body parts donated by research subjects in a medical research setting, the claims, however, were not as much about unjust enrichment as the research subjects' right to control the transfer and destination of their body tissues donated for research.[105] Through restitution, the law of unjust enrichment reverses enrichment or gains obtained by the defendant at the expense of the claimant. In short, unjust enrichment is mainly concerned with the recovery of money payments, for instance, money paid for a non-existent debt.[106] Birks observed that the 'law of unjust enrichment is the law of all events materially identical to the mistaken payment of a non-existent debt.'[107] With this monetary emphasis, it would appear counterintuitive to apply the law of unjust enrichment to body parts used in biomedical research. *Greenberg v Miami Children's Hospital*, therefore, accentuates the need for a closer examination of the relevance of the law of unjust enrichment to the human body and body parts.

A claimant who wishes to assert a restitutionary remedy based on unjust enrichment must establish that (a) the defendant was enriched (b) at the expense of the claimant and (c) it is unjust for the defendant to retain the benefit.[108] These elemental requirements are equally mandatory where the claimant alleges that the defendant's enrichment resulted from an interference with, or exploitation of, the claimant's body parts. This can happen in a given number of situations. *Moore v Regents of the University of California*-type of cases would be typical.[109] In *Moore*'s case a physician-researcher surreptitiously obtained Moore's bodily tissues after performing a medically needed splenectomy (removal of Moore's diseased spleen). Moore's unique tissues were subsequently applied in medical research that yielded a therapeutic product of enormous commercial value running into millions of dollars. Although *Moore*'s case concerned the body parts of a living person, the body parts of a deceased relative might also be the subject of

105 *Washington University v Catalona* 437 F.Supp. 2d 985 (Dist. Ct. Missouri, 2006). The Court of Appeal accepted the District Court's ruling that the research subjects, having voluntarily donated their body tissues to Washington University, lost any right to direct the transfer of the tissues to another university and, therefore, the tissues became the property of Washington University: Washington *University v Catalona* 490 F.3d 667 (Eight Cir., 2007). Right to appeal to the US Supreme Court was refused: *Catalona v Washington University* 128 S. Ct. 1122 (2008). For analysis of the case: Remigius N. Nwabueze, 'Donated Organs, Property Rights and the Remedial Quagmire' (2008), 16 Med. L.R. 202.

106 *Kelly v Solari* (1841) 152 ER 24. This monetary aspect of unjust enrichment was emphasized by Stoljar when comparing unjust enrichment action to tort: 'The fact remains that whereas unjust enrichment seeks the recovery of money, tort is more concerned with things. It is a very simple difference which accordingly seems minor; yet it is a most significant difference nonetheless', Samuel Stoljar, 'Unjust Enrichment and Unjust Sacrifice' (1987), M.L.R. 603 at 606.

107 Peter Birks, *Unjust Enrichment, 2nd edn* (Oxford: Oxford University Press, 2005), at 3.

108 Ibid., at 39.

109 *Moore v Regents of the University of California* 793 P.2d 479 (1990).

scientific applications, with potentials for financial gain or benefit. Even when a defendant has not applied scientific skills on the claimant's body parts, the defendant could still be unjustly enriched by those parts by selling them to DNA banks or biotechnology companies. Thus, it is no longer persuasive to argue that body parts, both of the living and the dead, have no recognizable commercial value. Modern biotechnology has enhanced both the utility and commercial value of body parts. It is doubtful that any legal system can justifiably hold that body parts obtained by a defendant at the expense of a claimant do not constitute a benefit for the purposes of the law of unjust enrichment. But this conclusion pre-empts the question that calls for analysis. Thus, the starting point is to ask whether a human body part constitutes an enrichment or benefit for the purpose of the law of unjust enrichment.

To succeed in an action for unjust enrichment, the claimant must first establish that the defendant was enriched since, according to Lord Millet in *Foskett v McKeown*, 'he (defendant) cannot have been unjustly enriched if he has not been enriched at all'.[110] But the difficulty lies in defining 'enrichment' for the purpose of an unjust enrichment action. Does it include non-money benefits? This is very crucial for body parts. Being non-monetary in nature, body parts cannot be subject to the law of unjust enrichment unless by definition they are included within the term 'enrichment'. Monetary enrichment is not problematic since money is a measure of value. Receipt of money enlarges the recipient's wealth construed as a single fund measurable in money.[111] Any doubts on enrichment, therefore, give way when the subtraction from a plaintiff sounds in money. Problem, however, arises in the case of non-money subtractions, such as pure services or benefits with no exchange value. If I give you a part of my body that enabled you to carry out an important scientific research that resulted in academic publication, you have no doubt benefited from my body part but have you been enriched? Although Beatson[112] has argued that only enrichments with exchange value suffice, Virgo thinks that it is too restrictive a definition and does not cover practical instances where enrichment might be conceded absent the possibility of market exchange.[113] Virgo suggests, therefore, that enrichment is better construed as a 'benefit' so as to cover cases of receipt of pure services. Virgo's view seems to be more acceptable and supported by cases where services[114] and non-money benefits[115] were held to

110 *Foskett v McKeown* (2000) 2 W.L.R. 1299 at 1324.

111 Birks, supra, note 107, at 71.

112 Beatson, J., *The Use and Abuse of Unjust Enrichment* (Oxford: Clarendon Press, 1991) at 29–32.

113 Graham Virgo, *The Principles of the Law of Restitution, 2nd edn* (Oxford: Oxford University Press, 2006) at 62–64.

114 *Rowe v Vale of White Horse DC* (2003) EWHC 388 (concerning the supply of sewage services).

115 *McDonald v Coys of Kesington* (2004) 1 W.L.R. 2775 (concerning a personalized registration mark).

constitute enrichment. Courts use both objective and subjective tests to determine the value of non-money benefits. Objectively, the question is whether what the defendant received is something reasonable people would value and pay for; the subjective analysis respects the defendant's autonomy and freedom to set his or her priorities by ascertaining the value placed on the receipt by the defendant. This is known as subjective devaluation.[116] Subjective devaluation is displaced by a showing of free acceptance and incontrovertible benefit.

On the analysis above, Virgo has identified four categories of enrichment which do not include body parts: money, property, services, and payment made to a third party on behalf of the defendant.[117] Some remarks could be made. First, Virgo was not concerned with problems of unjust enrichment in the unique area of body parts; and the subject as a whole, as evident from analysis of other commentators, is hardly within the contemplation of the law of unjust enrichment. Few books on restitution and unjust enrichment mention body parts. Second, although Virgo has not expressly included body parts as an example of enrichment, the categories he identified are not closed and do not conceptually exclude body parts. Third, it is arguable that body parts clearly come within the meaning of enrichment. The biotechnological contexts of body parts utilization make this argument very persuasive. It can hardly be said that no benefit is obtained from the use of a body part in a scientific research that has potentials for commercial gain. The incontrovertible benefit does not make room for subjective devaluation. The scientific researchers in *Moore* and *Greenberg*'s cases could not have argued (credibly) that they obtained no benefit from the use of claimants' tissues. Less clear, however, are cases where the research only led to academic publication, or was not successful at all. In such cases, it is difficult to see the gain or enrichment by reference to which restitution must be made. For how can you be unjustly enriched if you were not enriched at all?[118] Many cases of interference with body parts would belong to this category. Interferences like those in *Moore* and *Greenberg* capable of yielding reversible benefits are completely outweighed by the preponderant assertions of 'non-beneficial' interferences with human body parts, such as cases where no innovation or invention resulted from the execution of a research protocol. What this means is that although body parts might constitute 'enrichment' for the purpose of the law of unjust enrichment, it is only with reference to such applications of the human body that have potential for commercial gain. Thus, body parts used in pure scientific and non-commercial research may not give rise to the action for unjust enrichment. In such cases, the claimant would not be able to scale the first hurdle above.

The second element, 'at the expense' of the claimant, is also not free from difficulties when applied to the human body parts used in research. It means that the benefit must have come directly from the claimant or indirectly from him or

116 Virgo, supra, note 113, at 65–67.

117 Ibid., at 69–72.

118 *Foskett v McKeown*, supra, note 110, Lord Millet.

her if the principles of interceptive subtractions are applicable.[119] For claimants like *Moore* or *Greenberg*, the requirement is easily satisfied. Moore's physician surreptitiously obtained Moore's body parts directly from him. Greenberg and other Canavan disease families directly gave their body parts to the researchers. Complexities, however, arise in two instances. First, a human body part might be obtained by a researcher from other researchers in the course of sharing of data and materials that characterize the scientific landscape. Sharing of biological raw materials is very well known and encouraged by the scientific community. In some instances materials can be shared across regions and continents. Slices of Einstein's brain are known to have been shared and distributed among some scientists in the world.[120] It was the need not to hinder this scientific tradition that partly inspired the majority's decision in *Moore*'s case. But the tradition itself poses serious challenges to proving that a body part was subtracted from the claimant. Take a case where P's body part was taken by X and then passed through many other scientific hands until it reached D, who used it in a lucrative scientific research without knowing the provenance of the original raw material. Could D then be said to be enriched at the expense of P? It seems that policy rather than law would infuse this type of analysis; and would be dominated by the need to promote rather than inhibit scientific research. Therefore, in a case of long transactional or ambiguous chain involving a body part, a court is more likely to hold that the enrichment was not at the expense of the claimant. Second, where the body part is not directly obtained from the claimant but from the body of a deceased relative, the case for unjust enrichment is likely to be weak. In unjust enrichment, a claimant must prove that before the transfer to the defendant, the 'enrichment' belonged to him or her.[121] If you sell a car which does not belong to you and the purchase price is recovered after the transaction is terminated, you cannot sue the purchaser to recover for the use he or she made of the car in the period up to the termination of the transaction.[122] The car did not belong to you and the enrichment obtained by the purchaser was not at your expense. It was at the expense of the true owner. So also is the case of a deceased relative's body part. With the present state of the law recognizing no property interest in the dead body of a relative, a claimant would have a hard time proving that the beneficial use of a dead relative's body part was at his or her expense. The body part simply did not belong to the claimant. Although use of a decedent's body part is concededly 'at the expense' of the living relatives, such as devaluing next-of-kin's sentiments towards the dead,

119 Birks, supra, note 107, at 75–78.

120 Lori Andrews and Dorothy Nelkin, *Body Bazaar: The Market for Human Tissue in the Biotechnology Age* (New York: Crown Publishers, 2001) at 9–11.

121 Andrew Burrows, 'Proprietary Restitution: Unmasking Unjust Enrichment' (2001), 117 L.Q.R. 412 at 415.

122 *Rowland v Divall* (1923) 2 K.B. 500.

Birks argued that such broad conceptions of the phrase (at the expense of) are wrong and that its meaning is restricted to the subtractive sense.[123]

Another challenge with the element of 'at the expense' of the claimant relates to the establishment of loss. It is still a controversial matter whether the claimant is required to show that he or she suffered a loss at all or one that exactly corresponds to the defendant's gain. Birks argued strongly that 'English law appears not to insist that the claimant must have suffered one (loss)' and cited instances where benefits could be gained without a corresponding loss.[124] After analysing the contending perspectives, Virgo opined that exact correspondence should not be required though some loss must be shown. Accordingly, he preferred 'that some very limited form of the correspondence principle is recognized, but only in the sense that the defendant's gain is reflected by a loss suffered by the claimant'.[125] The case for the presence of a loss is strengthened by *Re BHT (UK) Ltd*,[126] though it decided in favour of the correspondence principle. It would appear that at the minimum, the claimant is required to demonstrate some loss. If loss is construed monetarily, as is typical of many unjust enrichment claims that involve receipt of money, or as requiring physical impact or the valuation of property, then a plaintiff complaining of interference with a human body part has a big hurdle. Apart from the probable diminishment of autonomy or privacy, what loss does a person suffer when his or her body part or that of a relative is used in a scientific research? Except the courts accept Birks' thesis on the irrelevance of the loss element, a claimant complaining of an interference with a body part can hardly prove a recognizable legal loss for the purposes of unjust enrichment.

The final element is that it must be unjust for the defendant to retain the enrichment. A defendant may be justly enriched at the expense of the claimant. It is important, however, that the unjust factor be established. English common law recognizes certain restitutionary factors. Thus, Lord Mansfield in *Moses v Macferlan* observed that an action: 'lies for money paid by mistake; or upon a consideration which happens to fail; or for money got through imposition, (express or implied) or extortion; or oppression; or an undue advantage taken of the plaintiff's situation, contrary to laws for the protection of persons under those circumstances'.[127] Though Lord Mansfield's formulation of restitutionary grounds apparently relate to money enrichment, they are equally applicable to non-money benefits. For, as Virgo has observed, there is 'no reason why the application of any of the grounds of restitution should depend on the nature of the enrichment which the defendant has received'.[128] Examining these factors from the claimant's perspective means that there would be restitution whenever it is

123 Birks, supra, note 107, at 74.

124 Ibid., at 78.

125 Virgo, supra, note 113, at 114.

126 *Re BHT (UK) Ltd* (2004) EWHC 201 (Ch).

127 *Moses v Macferlan* (1760) 97 ER 676 at 681.

128 Virgo, supra, note 113, at 126.

established that the claimant's intention was impaired. This impairment was raised by the *Greenberg* claimants who argued that they would not have provided the defendants with their body parts if they had known that the defendants would commercialize their genetic materials through patenting and restrictive licensing. In other circumstances involving an interference with dead bodies and body parts, it is relatively easy for a claimant to prove the absence of consent, undue influence or exploitation. For instance, in *AB v Leeds*, the claimants were able to prove that the retention of their children's body parts after autopsy was done without their consent; and in *Moore v Regents of the University of California*, the court held that the harvesting of the claimant's bodily tissues infringed the rules of informed consent. It is difficult to see how an abuse, mutilation, or exploitation of the human body or body parts would not come within one of the recognized grounds of restitution. Provided a claimant is able to scale the first two elements of an action for unjust enrichment, the third element of an unjust ground is relatively easy to establish.

## Breach of Confidence

In research consent forms generally, investigators promise to keep confidential not only the information and materials supplied by the research subject, but also the fact that the research subject participated in that research; in other words, the identity of the research subject is equally kept confidential.[129] Thus, Biggs observed that research involving human beings 'raises issues about confidentiality in relation to the recruitment of participants, protection of their data during the research process, and protection of their identities when the research findings are being disseminated'.[130] The duty of confidence is a fundamental ethical and legal obligation owed by investigators to research subjects. Guideline 18 of the CIOMS guidelines, for instance, provides that the 'investigator must establish secure safeguards of the confidentiality of subjects' research data';[131] similarly, Guidance Point 18 of the UNAIDS/WHO Guidance Document requires that '[r]esearchers and research staff must ensure full respect for the entitlement of potential and enrolled participants to confidentiality of information disclosed or discovered in the recruitment and informed consent process, and during conduct

129 Generally: Deryck Beyleveld, 'Conceptualising Privacy in Relation to Medical Research Values', in Sheila McLean (ed.), *First Do No Harm: Law, Ethics and Healthcare* (Aldershot: Ashgate Publishing Ltd, 2006), 151–163.

130 Hazel Biggs, *Healthcare Research Ethics and Law: Regulation, Review and Responsibility* (London: Routledge-Cavendish, 2010), at 95.

131 CIOMS, *International Ethical Guidelines for Biomedical Research Involving Human Subjects* (Geneva: CIOMS, 2002), Guideline 18.

of the trial'.[132] In addition to these ethical and policy documents underpinning the duty of confidence, it is, as a matter of law, firmly entrenched in the equitable jurisdiction of common-law based courts.[133] In *Stephens v Avery*, for instance, Sir Nicholas Browne-Wilkinson V-C (as he then was) observed that 'the basis of equitable intervention to protect confidentiality is that it is unconscionable for a person who has received information on the basis that it is confidential subsequently to reveal that information'.[134] The duty of confidence is, however, not absolute and must yield to overriding public interests, such as disclosures in the interest of public health or personal security.[135] Thus, the CIOMS guidelines require investigators to tell subjects 'the limits, legal or other, to the investigators' ability to safeguard confidentiality and the possible consequences of breaches of confidentiality'.[136] Similarly, in HIV/AIDS vaccine trials, the investigators must explain to participants 'what limitations may exist on their ability to do so (that is, ability to protect the subjects' confidentiality)'.[137] A detailed exploration of the equitable, ethical, constitutional and human rights bases of the duty of confidence is not possible in a subsection of a chapter, as is the case here; but such extended analysis has been done elsewhere by the author and other commentators.[138] This subsection, however, intends to deploy the protection of research subjects' identity to illustrate the fundamental nature of the duty of confidence in relation to research in Africa, and the potential legal liability issues that might arise where an investigator breached their duty of confidence.

Keeping confidential the very fact of participation in a research project is very important for the protection of research subjects, especially in relation to research protocols like HIV/AIDS which raise significant potential for stigmatization, discrimination and violence. The UNAIDS/WHO Guidance Document captures this potential risk in its observation that, for HIV vaccine and prevention research, 'even association with the trial could be highly stigmatizing and might be socially harmful if other people wrongly discover it'.[139] Similarly, the CIOMS guidelines observe that participation in 'HIV/AIDS drug and vaccine trials may impose

132 UNAIDS/WHO, *Ethical Considerations in Biomedical HIV Prevention Trials: UNAIDS/WHO Guidance Document* (Geneva: UNAIDS, 2007), Guidance Point 18.

133 *Fraser v Evans* [1969] QB 349; G. Hammond, 'The Origins of the Equitable Duty of Confidence' (1979), 8 Anglo-American Law Review 71.

134 *Stephens v Avery* [1988] Ch. 449 at 456.

135 *Tarasoff v The Regents of the University of California*, 551 P.2d 334 (Cal. Sup. Ct., 1976); *W v Egdell* [1889] 2 WLR 689 (CA).

136 CIOMS, supra, note 131, Guideline 18.

137 *UNAIDS/WHO Guidance Document*, supra, note 132, commentary to Guidance Point 18.

138 For instance, Remigius N. Nwabueze, *Biotechnology and the Challenge of Property: Property Rights in Dead Bodies, Body Parts,and Genetic Information* (Aldershot: Ashgate Publishing Ltd, 2007), at 180–184 and 204–210; Biggs, supra, note 130, at 95–113.

139 *UNAIDS/WHO Guidance Document*, supra, note 132, commentary to Guidance Point 18.

upon the research subjects significant associated risks of social discrimination or harm'.[140] In Africa, attitudes towards people living with HIV/AIDS are generally negative. For instance, HIV positive women in Africa are reluctant to disclose their sero-status to their husbands or sexual partners because of the potential for violence against them. Interestingly, the IRIN PlusNews reported that at least three Ugandan women were killed by their husbands in 2008 for testing HIV positive.[141] HIV/AIDS- related violence against women is not, however, restricted to Africa. In the US, for instance, North and Rothenberg acknowledged cases of 'two women who were shot and many others who were injured or abandoned after revealing to their partners that they were infected with HIV'.[142] Abandonment is the common fate of most HIV positive women in Africa who were lucky enough to escape death or physical abuse following the disclosure of their HIV status to their partners.[143] As a UNAIDS report observed: 'Women with AIDS are commonly sent back to their natal families to be looked after by female relatives'.[144] Spousal abandonment, following the disclosure of HIV status, carries enormous economic consequences for most women in Africa, who have no independent means of economic existence. Thus, Medley and colleagues observed that women's fear of abandonment was closely tied to the 'fear of loss of economic support from a partner. In these settings where … women's access to resources independent of their partner is uncommon, it is not surprising that fear of losing this instrumental support from a partner is a major consideration when deciding whether to share HIV test results or not'.[145] This anecdotal account of HIV/AIDS-related violence illustrates the need to protect the

---

140 CIOMS, supra, note 131, commentary to Guideline 18.

141 IRIN PlusNews, 'Uganda: A Draft HIV Bill's Good Intentions Could Backfire', 24 November 2008: http://www.plusnews.org/PrintReport.aspx?Report1d=81636 (Last accessed on 5 January 2011).

142 R.L. North and K.H. Rothenberg, 'Partner Notification and the Threat of Domestic Violence against Women with HIV' (1993), 329 New Eng. J. Med. 1194. Also: El-Bassel, et al., 'Intimate Partner Violence Prevalence and HIV Risks among Women Receiving Care in Emergency Departments: Implications for IPV and HIV Screening' (2007), 24 Emerg. Med. J. 255; L.J. Koenig, et al., 'Violence During Pregnancy Among Women with or at Risk for HIV Infection' (2002), 92 AJPH 367; Andrea Carlson Gielen, Karen A. McDonnell, Jessica G. Burke, et al., 'Women's Lives After an HIV-Positive Diagnosis: Disclosure and Violence' (2000), 4(2) Maternal & Child Health Journal 111.

143 This phenomenon is also evident in industrialized countries. For instance, in a 1995 study, 20 per cent of the women surveyed reported being left by their partners following disclosure of their seropositive status. See Jane M. Simoni, Hyacinth R.C. Mason, Gary Marks, et al., 'Women's Self-Disclosure of HIV Infection: Rates, Reasons, and Reactions' (1995), 63 (3) Journal of Consulting and Clinical Psychology 474–478.

144 UNAIDS, *Facing the Future Together: Report of the Secretary General's Task Force on Women, Girls and HIV/AIDS in Southern Africa* (Geneva: UNAIDS, 2004), at 18.

145 A. Medley, et al., 'Rates, Barriers and Outcomes of HIV Serostatus disclosure among Women in Developing Countries: Implications for Prevention of Mother-to-Child Transmission Programmes' (2004), 82 Bulletin of the World Health Organisation 299 at 300.

identity and data of participants in HIV/AIDS research in Africa, especially African women who participate in research but are already victims of HIV/AIDS. Most likely, the mere (and unauthorized) disclosure that a particular African woman participated (as a research subject) in a research project on HIV/AIDS is likely to incentivize the husband or sexual partner to abandonment, violence, discrimination or stigmatization against the woman. However, it is arguable that an investigator can lawfully disclose data concerning a subject's participation in research provided the data is effectively anonymized. In *R v Dept. of Health, ex parte Source Informatics Ltd.*, the English Court of Appeal gave the weight of its authority to that approach; it held that anonymized prescription data sourced from doctors and pharmacists, and of use to pharmaceutical industries for the effective marketing of their products, could be lawfully used without the consent of the patients involved; nor did such use breach their privacy or confidentiality.[146] Beyleveld has criticized the Court of Appeal's decision in the above case, arguing that it entrenched a narrow construction of the right of privacy contrary to s. 8 of the Human Rights Act 1998; thus, he suggested a broad conception and interpretation of privacy that is consistent with the values of medical research.[147] The point, in essence, is that anonymization might not always be an effective safeguard for the protection of research subjects' identities and data.

Where, therefore, an unauthorized disclosure (as in the HIV/AIDS example above) occurs, the aggrieved research subject might sue the investigator for breach of confidence. Unfortunately, the action for breach of confidence is not well developed in Nigeria and other common law African countries. Common law African countries might, therefore, have recourse to England where, recently, the House of Lords held that the cause of action for breach of confidence is expansive enough to include complaints relating to the invasion of privacy under section 8 of the Human Rights Act 1998.[148] However, *Coco v Clark* remains the leading or foundational English authority for the action for breach of confidence.[149] In *Coco v Clark*, the court identified three elements which a claimant must establish in order to succeed in an action for breach of confidence: (a) the information is capable of being protected; (b) the defendant owes the claimant an obligation to keep the information confidential. In *Attorney General v Guardian Newspapers (No 2)*,[150] however, the House of Lords held that a duty of confidence need not be dependent on the existence of a prior relationship of confidence between the parties; it is sufficient if the defendant received the information knowing that it was confidential, or ought to be kept confidential; and (c) the defendant used the

146 *R v Dept. of Health, ex parte Source Informatics Ltd.* [2000] 1 All ER 786 (CA).

147 Beyleveld, in McLean, supra, note 129.

148 *Campbell v MGN Ltd* (2004) 2 A.C. 457; *Attorney General v Guardian Newspapers Ltd. (No 2)* (1990), 1 A.C. 109; *Attorney General v Guardian Newspapers Ltd. (No 2)* [1990] 1 A.C. 109.

149 *Coco v A.N. Clark (Engineers) Ltd.* (1969) RPC 41.

150 *Attorney General v Guardian Newspapers (No 2)* [1990] 1 A.C. 109 (HL).

information in a way that breached that duty. In view of the analysis above, it is obvious that information identifying a person as a participant in a research protocol is not a trivial, but an important piece of information which ought to be protected; this is especially so when the information relates to a subject's participation in an HIV/AIDS research in Africa. Also, the researcher-subject duty of care established at the beginning of this chapter, coupled with the express obligation of confidence usually undertaken by researchers in consent forms, clearly shows that an investigator is under a duty to keep the subject's identity and other research information strictly confidential. Thus, an unauthorized disclosure of a claimant's participation in research is likely to meet the criteria for breach of confidence developed in *Coco v Clark*.[151]

## Foreign Suits by African Research Subjects: Procedural and Substantive Problems

While the legal categories of action examined above typify claims that injured research subjects might wish to litigate in local or national courts of the territory where the research took place, *Abdullahi v Pfizer*,[152] however, illustrates the preference for foreign suits by research subjects injured in international collaborative research undertaken in Africa. Recall that *Abdullahi v Pfizer* was a civil suit instituted in a US District court by Nigerian research subjects injured in the trovan trial discussed in chapter one.

At first glance, it is a bit surprising that injured research subjects in Africa prioritize extraterritorial suits (in foreign jurisdictions) over litigation in local or national courts, especially where the foreign jurisdictions operate legal systems similar to those received in most parts of Africa. For instance, the English common law applicable in England, Canada, Australia, New Zealand and, to a large extent, the US was received into Nigeria in the nineteenth century and other African countries colonized by the Great Britain. It is possible to unpack the factors that incentivize injured research subjects in Africa to bring compensatory claims in foreign courts of territories where their investigators reside or have their permanent residence. The first factor is that investigators (and sponsors) of international collaborative research undertaken in Africa are likely to have more presence in their home countries in terms of money and property. This makes it easier for a research subject-claimant to levy execution on any judgement obtained against an investigator and sponsor for injuries arising from international collaborative research conducted in a developing country. If such favourable judgement were to be obtained in a developing or African country where the research took place,

151 For detailed assessment of the individual elements of the action for breach of confidence: Lionel Bently and Brad Sherman, *Intellectual Property Law, 3rd edn* (Oxford: Oxford University Press, 2009) 1007–1046.

152 *Abdullahi v Pfizer*, supra, note 40.

the successful research subject-claimant would have to go through the tedious and complicated procedure for the enforcement of foreign judgements before they could access the money or property of the investigator and sponsor located in a foreign country. Though there have been recent attempts at harmonization, enforcement of foreign judgements is subject to complex rules that vary from country to country, and some countries are instinctively averse to the enforcement of judgements other than those of their courts.[153] Thus, an African research subject injured in the conducting of international collaborative research might consider it advantageous to bring an action in the foreign country where the investigator or sponsor resides rather than the court of the African country where the research took place. Second, courts in Nigeria and many other African countries are notorious for the award of compensatory damages that are meagre in amount. This problem has been examined elsewhere and should not detain us here.[154] In contrast, US courts are known for awarding sizeable amounts of compensatory damages. Thus, an action in a developed country's court, like the US courts for instance, offers an African research subject injured in international collaborative research the greatest opportunity of getting an award of a substantial sum of money as compensatory damages. Third, courts in Nigeria and many other African countries are notoriously congested; it might take many years before final judgement is given in a case by the court of first instance. As the saying goes, justice delayed is justice denied. African research subjects injured in international collaborative research might, therefore, prefer to institute their claims in foreign jurisdictions where their action is likely to be adjudicated expeditiously. The fourth, and most important factor that influences the commencement of foreign litigation by African subjects injured in international collaborative research, is the prevalence of judicial corruption in some African countries. In Nigeria, for instance, the malaise of judicial corruption is so entrenched that a retired justice of the Supreme Court of Nigeria recently had to speak openly about the problem.[155] No doubt, judicial corruption in Nigeria was one of the important factors that influenced the trovan research subjects' decision to look for justice in the US courts.

*Abdullahi v Pfizer* (*Abdullahi No. 1*),[156] for instance, illustrates the problem of judicial corruption identified above; it was the first of the series of suits filed by the trovan research subjects in the US. The defendant filed a motion to dismiss the claimants' suit on the ground that it failed to disclose a reasonable cause of action; the defendant also objected to the claimants' suit on the ground of *forum*

153 For detailed analysis: David McClean and Kisch Beevers, *Morris: Conflict of Laws, 7th edn* (London: Sweet and Maxwell, 2009) 157–188.

154 Remigius N. Nwabueze and Polycarp C. Okorie, 'Flexibility of Damages for Conversion and Detinue' (2009), 17 African Journal of International & Comparative Law 102.

155 For instance, the valedictory speech of Uwaifo, JSC (as he then was) on 24 January 2005, excerpted in B.O. Nwabueze, *The Judiciary as the Third Estate of the Realm* (Abuja, Nigeria: Gold Press, Ltd., 2007) at 168.

156 *Abdullahi v Pfizer*, 2002 WL 31082956 (S.D.N.Y).

*non conveniens*. Pauley J held that the claimants pleaded enough violation of international law to justify a trial on the merits. As regards the *forum non conveniens* objection, however, Pauley J held that the claimants would need to show that Kano High Court, that is, the court with jurisdiction in Nigeria over the trovan trial, was not an adequate alternative forum, and that the balance of private and public factors was in favour of maintaining the suit in the US. In order to satisfy that condition, the claimants alleged that Kano High Court was corrupt, and was also the product of a corrupt but democratically elected government. Furthermore, the claimants alleged that 'the Nigerian judicial system is subject to influence from powerful entities, such as the executive and legislative branches of the government, and the wealthy, and consists of safeguards that are generally by-passed in favour of powerful and influential parties'.[157] Regarding these allegations, the *Abdullahi No. 1* court warned itself of the need to exercise restraint in assessing the sufficiency of the courts and legal systems of other countries. Thus, it held that the claimants' allegations of judicial corruption in Nigeria were mere general characterizations, and that 'conclusory allegations of corruption or bias on the part of the foreign forum will not prevent a dismissal on *forum non conveniens* grounds'.[158] At the time *Abdullahi No. 1* was on appeal (*Abdullahi v Pfizer, No. 2*),[159] the Kano High Court of Nigeria dismissed, in questionable and controversial circumstances, a parallel action instituted in Nigeria by a different set of trovan subjects.[160] This provided evidence for the complaint of *Abdullahi No. 1* claimants that judicial corruption was rife in Nigeria. Thus, the claimants asked the Court of Appeal in *Abdullahi No. 2* to take judicial notice of the dismissal of the *Zango v Pfizer* suit in Nigeria, and to use the fact of dismissal and reasons underlying dismissal of the parallel Nigerian suit as specific evidence of judicial corruption in Nigeria.[161] Pfizer, however, placed a different interpretation on the reasons for the dismissal of the *Zango* case in Nigeria; because of this conflict in the interpretations of the *Zango* case, *Abdullahi No. 2* was unable to take judicial notice of it. *Abdullahi No. 2* held that the *Zango* 'facts, however, would seem to be relevant to the *forum non conveniens* analysis – perhaps providing just the type of specific information that the District Court found lacking'.[162] In the end, *Abdullahi No. 2* had to 'remand the case to the District Court for proceedings to determine what precipitated the dismissal in *Zango* and to evaluate whether that impacts the District Court's *forum non conveniens* analysis'.[163] Upon remand, in *Abdullahi v Pfizer No. 3*,[164] the District Court held that the dismissal of *Zango* did not impact on the *forum non conveniens*

157 Ibid., at 8.

158 Ibid., at 9.

159 *Abdullahi v Pfizer*, 77 Fed. Appx. 28 (C.A. 2nd Cir, 2003) – *Abdullahi No. 2*.

160 *Zango v Pfizer*, No. FHC/K/CS/204/2001 (Kano Federal High Court, Nigeria).

161 Abdullahi No. 2, supra, note 159, at 52.

162 Ibid., at 53.

163 Ibid.

164 *Abdullahi v Pfizer*, 2005 WL 1870811 (*Abdullahi No. 3*).

analysis, and that Nigeria was an available and adequate alternative forum for the claimants' litigation. In addition, *Abdullahi v Pfizer No. 3* granted Pfizer's motion to dismiss the suit for failing to state a reasonable cause of action under the Alien Tort Statute. In *Abdullahi v Pfizer No. 4*, the District Court reached the same conclusion in another action brought in the US by some of the *Zango* claimants after their Nigerian claim was dismissed.[165] On appeal to the US Court of Appeals, Second Circuit, the majority set aside the District Courts' decisions above and held that the trovan claimants stated a good cause of action under the Alien Tort Act.[166] As noted in chapter one, an appeal by Pfizer to the US Supreme Court against the decision of the majority of the Court of Appeals in *Abdullahi* was dismissed in June 2010. In sum, therefore, the *Abdullahi* procedural history provides evidence that judicial corruption in Africa undergirds the decision of research subjects injured in international collaborative research to pursue extraterritorial compensatory claims abroad. Having examined the factors that influence the institution of foreign suits by African research subjects injured in international collaborative research, the next section proposes to adumbrate the procedural and substantive requirements which a foreign suit by an African research subject must satisfy; the US and English jurisdictions are used as examples.

## USA

A suit proposed in the US by an injured African research subject is most likely to be brought, as in *Abdullahi,* under the Alien Tort Statute (ATS, 1789).[167]

ATS confers original jurisdiction on (Federal) District Courts in the US over 'any civil action by an alien for a tort only, committed in violation of the law of nations or a treaty of the United States'.[168] Among the tripartite requirements of 'alien', 'tort' and 'violation of the law of nations', the last requirement has proven to be the most problematic for many claimants under the ATS. In *Filartiga v Pena-Irala*, one of the most cited cases under the ATS, Kaufman J alluded to this difficulty in his observation that the 'paucity of suits successfully maintained under the section is readily attributable to the statute's requirement of alleging a "violation of the law of nations" at the jurisdictional threshold'.[169] The ATS entails a more searching review of the merits of a claimant's case even at the pre-trial

165 *Abdullahi v Pfizer*, 399 F. Supp. 2d 495 (2005) (No. 4).

166 *Abdullahi v Pfizer (No. 5)*, 562 F.3d 163 (2009).

167 For an excellent overview of litigation under the ATS: M. Swan, 'International Human Rights Tort Claims and the Experience of United States Courts: An Introduction to the US Case Law, Key Statutes and Doctrines', in C. Scott, *Torture as Tort: Comparative Perspectives on the Development of Transnational Human Rights Litigation* (Portland, Oregon: Hart Publishing, 2001), 65–107.

168 Alien Tort Statute, 28 U.S.C. s1350.

169 *Filartiga v Pena-Irala*, 630 F.2d 876 at 887 (2nd Cir., 1980).

stage where subject-matter jurisdiction is likely to be contested. Aggrieved African research subjects can easily establish that they are aliens and that their cause of action relates to tort only under the ATS. But in the absence of a claim under the treaty of the United States (and there is currently no such treaty on research involving human subjects), research subjects from developing countries would have a hard time proving that their cause of action rises to the normative level of the 'law of nations'. *Filartiga*, for instance, involved the question of whether torture by a state official (Inspector-General of Police in Asuncion, Paraguay), leading to the death of one of the claimants' son, amounted to a violation of an obligatory norm of international law. Recognizing that the prohibition of torture was universally accepted as binding by all civilized nations and reflected in numerous international agreements and declarations, the *Filartiga* Court observed that 'an act of torture committed by a state official against one held in detention violates established norms of the international law of human rights, and hence the law of nations'.[170] Consequently, it concluded that the 'prohibition (of torture) has become part of customary international law'.[171] In the nature of things, however, torture in the context of research involving human subjects is likely to be a rare occurrence. Of course, the atrocities committed by Nazi physicians in the name of research, which were the subject of the Nuremberg trial in the 1940s, provide a remarkable example of research-related tortures. By definition, torture is the intentional infliction of severe physical or mental pain and suffering.[172] Apart from the constitutional proscription of this type of treatment, as examined above, the institutionalization and increasing globalization of the framework of ethics review (explored in chapter four) are most likely to ensure that torturous protocols would not see the light of the day. In other words, the brutal facts of *Filartiga*, which justified jurisdiction under the ATS, might not be easily replicated in the research setting; of course, with due exception to the horrors of the Nazi medical experiments which formed the basis of the Nuremberg trial and led to the promulgation of the Nuremberg Code (analysed in chapter one).

While *Kadic v Karadzi*, like *Filartiga*, involved torture, the claim also raised other causes of action including genocide, rape, forced prostitution and impregnation, assault and battery, sex and ethnic inequality, summary execution, and wrongful death.[173] The facts of *Kadic* were set against the background of the crisis in Bosnia-Herzegovina in the 1990s where the defendant was the president of a self-proclaimed Bosnian-Serb republic (Srpska). *Kadic* action raised the issue of whether a non-state actor (private person) could be liable for claims made under the ATS. The *Kadic* Court refused to accept 'that the law of nations, as understood in the modern era, confines its reach to state action. Instead, we hold that certain forms of conduct violate the law of nations whether undertaken by those acting

170 Ibid., at 880.

171 Ibid., at 882.

172 *Ireland v UK* [1978] 2 EHRR 25 (ECtHR).

173 *Kadic v Karadzi*, 70 F.3d 232 (2nd Cir. 1996).

under the auspices of a state or only as private individuals'.[174] Thus, *Kadic* gave examples of universal liability under international law which includes piracy, war crimes and genocide. Torture, however, requires state-action, except it was alleged as part of war crimes or genocide. In any event, *Kadic* held that the claimant's allegation of torture satisfied state-action requirement because of the assistance received by the defendant from the former state of Yugoslavia.

In contrast to *Kadic* and *Filartiga* above, *Abdullahi* squarely raised the issue of whether claims arising from biomedical research in a developing country (Nigeria) could be brought under the ATS. More specifically, in *Abdullahi No. 5*, the Second Circuit addressed the question of whether the prohibition of non-consensual medical experimentation on humans has become an obligatory norm of international law.[175] Writing for the majority, Parker J set out three criteria which a norm must satisfy in order to acquire an obligatory character under international law.[176] First, the norm must be of an international character which States universally abide by, or accede to, out of a sense of obligation. For this criterion, Parker J observed that the prohibition of non-consensual medical experimentation on humans is generally recognized in numerous international instruments and agreements, including the Nuremberg Code; the World Medical Association's Declaration of Helsinki; the guideline of the Council for International Organisation of Medical Services; and Article 7 of the International Covenant on Civil and Political Rights. Parker J further observed that the prohibition above meets the standards of specificity and precision, in addition to being universally subscribed to by all nations in the world without significant exception.[177] Accordingly, the majority concluded that the history of the international instruments above illustrates that from 'its origins with the trial of the Nazi doctors at Nuremberg through its evolution in international conventions, agreements, declarations, and domestic laws and regulation, the norm prohibiting non-consensual medical experimentation on human subjects has become firmly embedded and has secured universal acceptance'.[178] Second, an obligatory norm of international law must be defined with specificity comparable to the 18th century paradigms relating to the offences against ambassadors, violations of the right to safe passage, and individual actions arising out of piracy. The majority held that the prohibition of non-consensual medical experiment on humans met this high standard of specification. Finally, an obligatory norm of international law, for purposes of ATS litigation, must relate to transgressions that are of mutual concern to states. This criterion requires 'a showing that the conduct in question is capable of impairing international peace and security'.[179]

174 Ibid., at 239.

175 *Abdullahi v Pfizer (No. 5)*, 562 F.3d 163.

176 These were developed from the US Supreme Court decision in *Sosa v Alvarez-Machin*, 542 U.S. 692 (2004).

177 Abduallahi, *No. 5*, supra, note 166, at 177.

178 Ibid., at 183–184.

179 Ibid., at 187.

The majority observed that non-consensual medical research of the trovan genre was capable of threatening international peace and security: 'The administration of drug trials without informed consent … poses threats to national security by impairing our relations with other countries'.[180] Accordingly, the majority concluded that the prohibition of non-consensual research on humans has risen to a binding norm of customary international law, and that its violation could ground substantive jurisdiction under the ATS. In sum, *Abdullahi No. 5* provides a beneficent analytical framework for adjudicating extraterritorial claims brought in the US by African research subjects injured in international collaborative research undertaken in their countries.

## England and Wales

Apart from issues of *forum non conveniens* which might arise from extraterritorial tort actions commenced in England by African research subjects injured in international collaborative research undertaken in Africa,[181] extraterritorial or foreign tort actions are likely to be analysed in England under the rule in *Phillips v Eyre*,[182] except to the extent that the Rome 11 Regulation, which seeks to harmonize the conflict of law rules in the European Union, applies to the case.[183] Against the defendant in *Phillips v Eyre*, who was the Governor of the then colony of the Island of Jamaica, the claimant alleged that he was falsely imprisoned as a result of emergency measures adopted by the government of the colony to quell a rebellion in that territory. The offending executive acts were later ratified by an Act of the colony's legislature (Act of Indemnity) and the question was whether, in a suit commenced in England, the (colony's) Act applied to immunize the

180 Ibid.

181 The applicable principles were restated by Lord Bingham of Cornhill in *Lubbe v Cape Plc* [2000] 1 W.L.R. 1545 at 1554: '[t]he court's first task is to consider whether the defendant who seeks a stay is able to discharge the burden resting upon him not just to show that England is not the natural or appropriate forum for the trial but to establish that there is another available forum which is clearly or distinctly more appropriate than the English forum …. At this first stage of the inquiry the court will consider what factors there are which point in the direction of another forum …. If the court concludes at that stage that there is another available forum which is clearly more appropriate for the trial of the action, that is likely to be the end of the matter. But if the court concludes at that stage that there is some other available forum which prima facie is more appropriate for the trial of the action it will ordinarily grant a stay unless the plaintiff can show that there are circumstances by reason of which justice requires that a stay should nevertheless not be granted. In this second stage the court will concentrate its attention … on whether the plaintiff will obtain justice in the foreign jurisdiction'.

182 *Phillips v Eyre* [1870] 6 L.R.Q.B. 1.

183 Regulation (EC) No. 864/2007 of the European Parliament and of the Council of 11 July 2007 on the law applicable to non-contractual obligations (Rome II).

defendant-governor from civil liability. In the course of his judgement, Willes J, after noting that English 'courts are said to be more open to admit actions founded upon foreign transactions than those of any other European country',[184] famously observed:

> As a general rule, in order to found a suit in England for a wrong alleged to have been committed abroad, two conditions must be fulfilled. First, the wrong must be of such a character that it would have been actionable if committed in England .... Secondly, the act must not have been justifiable by the law of the place where it was done.[185]

The formulation above is generally characterized as the rule of double actionability.[186]

A century later ,in *Boys v Chaplin*,[187] the House of Lords was divided as to the meaning of Willes J's formulation above. In *Boys*, the claimant and defendant were both members of British military personnel temporarily stationed in Malta but ordinarily resident in England. Due to the admitted negligence of the defendant, the claimant suffered serious injuries in a road accident in Malta. By the law of Malta, damages were only recoverable for direct financial loss (assessed by the trial judge as £53), but would not include damages for pain and suffering under English law (equally assessed as £2,250). The court was, therefore, asked to determine which law, Maltese or English, would provide the rule of decision. While all the members of the House of Lords held that English law was applicable, they diverged on the reasons for their judgements, and the appropriate interpretation for *Phillips v Eyre*. For instance, while Lord Hodson held that the rule in *Phillips v Eyre* was jurisdictional in nature,[188] Lord Wilberforce held that it established a choice of law rule favouring English law as the law of the forum.[189] In contrast, Lord Pearson held that the rule in *Phillips v Eyre* entailed a combination of both the law of the place of wrong and the law of the forum, with the latter playing a dominant role.[190] These differences notwithstanding, all the members of the House of Lords accepted that a flexible approach to the interpretation of the rule in *Phillips v Eyre* was necessary in order to avoid injustice in individual cases. The double actionability rule in *Phillips v Eyre* was, however, practically abrogated by section 11(1) of the Private International Law (Miscellaneous Provisions) Act 1995,

---

184 Phillips, supra, note 182, at 28.

185 Ibid., at 28–29.

186 David McClean and Kisch Beevers, *Morris: The Conflict of Laws, 7th edn* (London: Sweet and Maxwell, 2009), at 398.

187 *Boys v Chaplin* [1971] A.C. 356.

188 Ibid., at 381.

189 Ibid., at 385.

190 Ibid., at 397–398.

which prefers the law of the place of wrong as a general rule.[191] Section 12 of the same Act creates an exception that incorporates the flexible approach enunciated in *Boys v Chaplin*. At the European level, article 4(1) of the Rome 11 Regulation makes provisions that are similar to the English 1995 Act above.[192] Respectively, articles 4(2) and 4(3) of the Rome 11 Regulation provide for exceptions based on the common habitual residence of the parties and the country with which the tort is more closely connected. In sum, therefore, if the trovan research subjects, and others in similar circumstances, were to sue in England, they would most likely have to rely (successfully) on the rule in *Phillips v Eyre*, as interpreted in *Boys v Chaplin* and modified by the 1995 Act and the Rome 11 Regulation.

## Conclusion

While it is not desirable that, for fear of legal liability, an investigator should be looking constantly over their shoulders in the course of their scientific enterprise, this chapter suggested that the conduct of research involving human subjects might expose an investigator to a range of potential legal liabilities. The potential legal liability arising from research involving human subjects serves as a warning (against unethical conduct) to investigators, especially those involved in international collaborative research undertaken in developing countries, who construe the abundance of research subjects and low level of regulations in developing countries as an opportunity to do mischief or execute a research protocol that is legally and ethically questionable. As suggested in this chapter, such unlawful actions by investigators are likely to be challenged by aggrieved research subjects in the national court of the territory where the research took place, or in a foreign court of the territory where the investigator resides. Thus, an injured research subject may sue an investigator in negligence if the consent process was deficient in any respect or the trial design failed to meet the criterion of equipoise; for actions in negligence, the research subject needs to establish a relationship of proximity between them and the investigator. Happily, this chapter suggested that the law imposes a legal duty of care on an investigator for the benefit of a research subject. The chapter also suggested that there are other private and public law causes of action which an aggrieved subject could bring against an investigator; these include an action in battery; constitutional law claims, such as the right to life guarantee, and freedom from torture, inhuman and degrading treatment; an action for unjust enrichment; and breach of confidence. Finally, this chapter explored

191 *Harding v Wealands* [2005] 1 W.L.R. 1539 illustrates some of the interpretative difficulties that can arise with the application of the general rule.

192 'the law applicable to a non-contractual obligation arising out of a tort shall be the law of the country in which the damage occurs irrespective of the country in which the event giving rise to the damage occurred and irrespective of the country or countries in which the indirect consequences of that event occur', article 4(1) of the Rome 11 Regulation.

the reasons why extraterritorial compensatory claims are attractive to research subjects injured in international collaborative research undertaken in Africa, and used the examples of US and England to illustrate some of the procedural and substantive requirements of such foreign claims.

# Conclusion – Themes, Suggestions and Ruminations

## Research Involving Human Subjects in Africa: the Need for both Ethical and Legal Analyses

One of the themes underpinning this book, reflected in the distribution and structure of the chapters, is the necessity for both ethical and legal analyses of research involving human subjects in Africa. Although international collaborative research in Africa engages both legal and ethical issues, as illustrated by the research scandals examined in chapter one, most commentators on the topic have, however, focused on the ethical aspects, leaving the legal liability issues largely unanalysed. While the ethical analysis of research involving human subjects in developing countries is important, and should remain the preoccupation of commentators, it is also critical that equal (analytical) attention should be devoted to the legal aspects of biomedical research in Africa and other developing countries. The author has begun the process of closing this analytical gap, by examining not only the ethical issues that arise from research involving human subjects in Africa, but also the legal issues. Thus, while the chapters of this book are not formally divided into two parts, that is, ethical and legal, they can be read as such. For instance, chapters one, two, three and four focused on some of the important ethical issues that arise from international collaborative research in Africa; chapters five, six and seven, on the other hand, examined some of the legal liability issues that are engaged by such research. However, to ensure the continuity of the chapters, and thus minimize the risk of their dissonance, the legal analysis in the last three chapters of this book is inspired by the ethical discussion in the first four chapters. For instance, the trovan and short-course zidovudine clinical research scandals (examined more fully in chapter one) not only formed the bases of ethical discussions relating to issues, such as equipoise, the consent of research subjects, placebo-controlled designs and standard of care; they also underpinned the legal analysis undertaken in chapter seven, regarding the legal liability of investigators and sponsors in actions instituted by research subjects. Similarly, while chapter four explored some of the most important ethical functions of research ethics committees, chapters five and six analysed the legal liability issues that might confront an ethics committee in the performance of those ethical duties. In this way, a sort of synergy is maintained across the chapters of this book. The point, however, is that research involving human subjects in developing countries raise significant legal liability issues that need to be addressed alongside the ethical issues.

**African Charter on Human and Peoples' Rights – Protocol on Research Involving Human Subjects and Embedment of Equipoise**

As highlighted in the introduction to this book, the African Union, through the African Charter on Human and Peoples' Rights, can play a potentially significant role in the regulation of research involving human subjects in Africa. It is a bit surprising that despite the urgency of the need for a national and regional debate on the regulation of research in Africa, as underscored by the various research scandals examined in chapters one and three, the African Union (formerly, the Organisation of African Unity) has not yet initiated a debate on the topic of research subjects' protection in Africa. The impression of low priority assigned to the subject matter by the African Union contrasts sharply with the regulatory experiences of other regional bodies (for instance, the European Union) where regional oversight mechanisms have been imposed on biomedical research interventions, including the promulgation of the Directive 2001/20/EC of the European Parliament and of the Council of 2 April 2001 (Directive on Clinical Trials). Interestingly, the African Commission, established under Art. 30 of the African Charter to promote and protect human rights in Africa, is empowered to 'collect documents, undertake studies and researches on African problems in the field of human and peoples' rights, organize seminars, symposia and conferences, disseminate information, encourage national and local institutions concerned with human and peoples' rights and, should the case arise, give its views or make recommendations to Governments'.[1]

The time has come for the African Commission to take advantage of the provision above and lead a debate on the regulation of research involving human subjects in Africa. Clearly, the protection of human subjects of biomedical or other research interventions involves issues of human rights as envisaged by Art. 45(1)(a) the African Charter; this linkage is further underscored by the analysis in chapters six and seven relating to important human rights' issues involved in the conduct of research involving human subjects. The embarrassing silence of the African Commission (and the African Union) on the matter can no longer be tolerated in view of the accelerating developments in biology and medicine. Even if it could be argued that these developments have not been remarkable in the African milieu or substantial enough to warrant some concern, yet the globalization of biomedical research and the increasing conduct of offshored clinical trials in Africa would certainly ensure that Africa is not isolated from the effects of modern innovations in science and technology; therefore, African countries cannot afford a weak regulatory climate that potentially exposes their citizens to avoidable or unnecessary research injuries. While the African Charter itself does not have a specific provision on the protection of human subjects of biomedical or other research interventions, Art. 66 of the African Charter, however, empowers the promulgation of '[S]pecial protocols or agreements [which] may, if necessary, supplement the provisions of the present Charter'. As a matter of

1 African Charter on Human and Peoples' Rights, 21 I.L.M. 58 (1982), Art. 45(1)(a).

urgency, therefore, it is suggested that the African Union should begin the process of developing a special protocol to the African Charter concerning research involving human subjects.

Perhaps, one advantage that might come from a late consideration of this topic (research involving human subjects) by the African Union is that it provides the African Union with an opportunity for developing a regulatory model of research that would be required to be legally enforceable in the member states of the African Union. Most countries and organizations that initially considered the topic of biomedical research adopted voluntary, non-legally enforceable, regulations, but as indicated in this book, the modern trend is towards a legally enforceable regulation. Since the African Union does not yet have any research guideline of its own, it can cash in on this modern trend by developing or prescribing an enforceable regulatory framework for its member states. This book, especially the introduction and chapters one and three, has emphasized the advantages of a legally enforceable regulatory framework and its special importance for most African countries. While a few countries in Africa, including Nigeria and South Africa, have (happily) developed legally enforceable research guidelines, the protocol suggested for the African Union above would help to generalize and extend the legal model of research regulation to other African countries. Interestingly, the African Union will not lack useful precedents to help it develop a protocol on research involving human subjects in Africa.

One of such precedents is the Additional Protocol to the Convention on Human Rights and Biomedicine.[2] This is a protocol to the Convention for the Protection of Human Rights and Dignity of the Human Being with regard to the Application of Biology and Medicine: Convention on Human Rights and Biomedicine (the Convention on Human Rights and Biomedicine).[3] The Convention on Human Rights and Biomedicine was promulgated to deal with difficult issues arising from the application of modern developments in biology and medicine, and revolves around the concept of dignity as its philosophical framework of protection. Because the Convention's scope was intended to be expansive, covering most areas of biology and medicine, including the conduct of scientific research,[4] there was limited opportunity for detailed provisions on research involving human subjects. This was left to be fleshed out in a Protocol, which materialized with the Additional Protocol to the Convention on Human Rights and Biomedicine (promulgated in 2005). While both the Convention and Protocol bear titles suggesting a restriction of their scope to biomedical research, and presumably excluding other research involving human subjects, such as anthropological research, it was, however,

2 Additional Protocol to the Convention on Human Rights and Biomedicine (Strasbourg, 2005).

3 Convention for the Protection of Human Rights and Dignity of the Human Being with regard to the Application of Biology and Medicine: Convention on Human Rights and Biomedicine (Oviedo, 4.IV. 1997).

4 Convention on Human Rights and Biomedicine, chapter v.

suggested in chapter one of this book that the nomenclature of 'health' or 'biomedical' research has the potential to cover most aspects or categories of research involving human beings. The Additional Protocol to the Convention on Human Rights and Biomedicine is reasonably comprehensive and covers most issues that arise from the conduct of research involving human beings, including analysis of risks and benefits, scientific validity, prior ethical review by competent and independent ethical review committees, sufficient information to and consent of subjects, confidentiality, and protection of vulnerable groups. However, Art. 33 of the Additional Protocol to the Convention on Human Rights and Biomedicine regards most of the Articles of the Protocol as additional articles to the Convention on Human Rights and Biomedicine which, as explained in the introduction to this book, is not enforceable by private action. For instance, Art. 29 of the Convention on Human Rights and Biomedicine provides that:

> The European Court of Human Rights may give, without direct reference to any specific proceedings pending in a court, advisory opinions on legal questions concerning the interpretation of the present Convention at the request of:
>
> - the Government of a Party, after having informed the other Parties;
> - the committee set up by Article 32, with membership restricted to the Representatives of the Parties to this Convention, by a decision adopted by a two-thirds majority votes cast.

Thus, only signatory states can enforce the provisions of the Conventions, and even then, it is only through the delivery of advisory opinions by the European Court of Human Rights. However, the provisions of the Convention on Human Rights and Biomedicine could be used to expound the provisions of the European Convention on Human Rights in cases before the European Court of Human Rights. The non-availability of private actions under the Convention and Protocol above limits their relevance and applicability in Africa where, as suggested in this book, a legal regulatory framework enforceable by private actions is needed. Thus, should the African Union consider the adoption of the Convention on Human Rights and Biomedicine and its additional protocol on biomedical research, it is suggested that the African Union should dispense with a provision similar to Art. 29 of the Convention on Human Rights and Biomedicine. The African Union should also emphasize that any measure it adopts for the regulation of biomedical or other research involving human beings in Africa is enforceable by private actions in the courts of member states of the African Union.

Another regulatory precedent that could inspire the development of a regional guideline in Africa is the Directive 2001/20/EC of the European Parliament and of the Council of 4 April 2001 (the Directive on Clinical Trials). Unlike the Convention on Human Rights and Biomedicine and the Protocol above, the provisions of the Directive on Clinical Trials are solely concerned with the 'conduct of clinical trials, including multi-centre trials, on human subjects involving medicinal products (and) does not apply to non-interventional trials'.[5] In further contrast to the Convention on Human Rights and Biomedicine, and its additional Protocol, the Directive on Clinical Trials was meant to be legally enforceable by private action in signatory states, and 'without prejudice to the civil and criminal liability of the sponsor or the investigator' already existing under a signatory state's domestic legal system.[6] To ensure speedy domestication of the Directive, Art. 22(1) gave member states only two years, from the date of the Directive, to adopt and publish 'the laws, regulations and administrative provisions necessary to comply with this Directive'. Similarly, member states 'shall apply these provisions at the latest with effect from 1 May 2004'.[7] In essence, within three years of the promulgation of the Directive on Clinical Trials, member states were required to make the Directive legally enforceable in their territories. This sort of timeline is direly needed in Africa and should be seriously considered by the African Union while reflecting on the regulation of research involving human subjects in Africa. A timeline of two to three years, as in the Directive on Clinical Trials above, emphasizes the urgency of the subject-matter and avoids unnecessary bureaucratic delays.

Furthermore, any future regulation on research involving human subjects, developed by the African Union as suggested above, should contain provisions clarifying that the existence, or presence, of equipoise is a fundamental ethical requirement for the conduct of clinical research in Africa. This approach has become important in view of the scanty reference to equipoise in existing African research guidelines. Yet, as chapters one, two and three illustrated, various research scandals in Africa could be explained on the basis of non-compliance with the requirements of equipoise. The importance of equipoise also follows from the fact that legal liability could ensue if an investigator conducted a trial that was not underpinned by equipoise; such instances of legal liability are evident in chapters six and seven.

Compliance with equipoise, implying the provision of proven treatments to research subjects and prohibition of placebo-controlled trials, might, however, potentially limit the number of international collaborative researches conducted in Africa, a region characterized by scarcity of resources, inadequate health infrastructures and much-needed medicines. Among the African guidelines considered in this book, it is only the Nigerian guideline that clearly and specifically made reference to equipoise. It provides that the '[T]he therapeutic procedures must fulfil requirements of clinical equipoise – there must be genuine uncertainty, among at least a significant minority of unbiased acknowledged experts who are not associated with the study under consideration, about preferred treatment'.[8] However, as chapter two highlighted, the concept of equipoise is not

5 Directive 2001/20/EC of the European Parliament and of the Council of 4 April 2001, Art. 1.

6 Ibid. (Directive) Art. 19.

7 Ibid. (Directive) Art. 22(1).

8 Federal Ministry of Health (Nigeria), National Code of Health Research Ethics (Abuja, Nigeria: Federal Ministry of Health, 2007), at 36.

free from controversy. For instance, there is a controversy regarding its meaning, nomenclature and effects; with regards to Africa, it is also not clear which version of equipoise, clinical or theoretical, is applicable to the countries in the continent; the Nigerian guideline, however, avoids that dispute by clarifying that *clinical* equipoise applies in Nigeria. Moreover, equipoise implies duties that are not generally acknowledged, such as the duty not to provide inferior treatments to research participants, and the prohibition of a placebo-controlled trial when an effective treatment exists for the condition being studied. Despite these difficulties, and for reasons already articulated in chapter two, it is suggested that the concept of equipoise should be the fundamental ethical criterion for clinical research in Africa. By making equipoise a condition precedent to the conduct of clinical trials in Nigeria, the Nigerian guideline has blazed a trail that other African countries are encouraged to traverse. Also, as mentioned above, the Nigerian approach should be adopted by any future regulation developed by the African Union relating to the conduct of clinical research in Africa.

In sum, therefore, it is suggested that the African Union should develop a Protocol to the African Charter on Human and Peoples' Rights, which should be based on the Additional Protocol to the Convention on Human Rights and Biomedicine, and the Directive on Clinical Trials. Thus, the protocol suggested for the African Union should be able to contain general provisions on the conduct of research involving human beings, as well as special or specific provisions to regulate the conduct of clinical trials, including the establishment of equipoise as a fundamental ethical criterion for the conduct of clinical research in Africa. The suggested Protocol should be legally enforceable by private actions in the member states of the African Union, and members of the African Union should be given just a few years to domesticate the Protocol in their respective states.

## Establishment of a Clinical Trials Registry in African Countries

Transparency in the ethics of biomedical research in Africa would be significantly improved by the establishment of a Clinical Trials Registry in every African country. As the analysis in this book shows, research scandals in Africa took place under a climate of low-regulatory visibility. The trovan trial analysed in chapter one, where the authority of senior public officials (in Nigeria) who ought to have controlled the approval process was circumvented, and they were kept in the dark regarding the trial by 'higher' authorities who surreptitiously granted permission for the trovan research, exemplifies the lack of transparency that characterizes international collaborative research in African countries. Such problems would be significantly assuaged by the adoption of a regulatory process which compels the registration of clinical trials conducted in a country. The World Health Organisation (WHO) has shown commendable leadership in this direction by promoting the development of Clinical Trials Registry in all countries through its

International Clinical Trials Registry Platform (ICTRP).[9] The ICTRP is a 'global initiative that aims to make information about all clinical trials involving humans publicly available'.[10] Particularly, the ICTRP aims to:

- improve the comprehensiveness, completeness and accuracy of registered trial data;
- communicate and raise awareness of the need to register clinical trials;
- ensure the accessibility of registered data;
- build capacity for clinical trial registration;
- encourage the utilization of registered data; and
- ensure the sustainability of the ICTRP.[11]

The registration of clinical trials enhances transparency in the clinical research process, and through that, contributes to strengthening the validity and value of the scientific evidence base. The ICTRP has identified other important reasons that justify the registration of clinical trials:

- There is a need to ensure that decisions about health care are informed by all of the available evidence;
- It is difficult to make informed decisions if publication bias and selective reporting are present;
- The Declaration of Helsinki requires that every clinical trial must be registered in a publicly accessible database before recruitment of the first subject;
- Improving awareness of similar or identical trials will make it possible for researchers and funding agencies to avoid unnecessary duplication;
- Describing clinical trials in progress can make it easier to identify gaps in clinical trials research;
- Making researchers and potential participants aware of recruiting trials may facilitate recruitment;
- Enabling researchers and health care practitioners to identify trials in which they may have an interest could result in more effective collaboration among researchers. The type of collaboration may include prospective meta-analysis;
- Registries checking data as part of the registration process may lead to improvements in the quality of clinical trials by making it possible to identify potential problems, such as problematic randomization methods, early in the research process.[12]

---

9 http://www.who.int/ictrp/en/.

10 http://www.who.int/ictrp/faq/en/index.html (last visited on 24 August 2012).

11 Ibid.

12 http://www.who.int/ictrp/trial_reg/en/index.html (last accessed on 24 August 2012).

India, as the introduction to this book highlighted, imbibed these insights by developing a Clinical Trials Registry, which was initially voluntary in approach, but registration of clinical trials was later made compulsory by law.[13] India, like most other countries with a clinical trial registry, requires an applicant seeking to register a clinical trial to declare numerous items of registration data set, all geared towards enhancing the transparency and ethics of clinical research.

The data required for registration includes, the full title of the study, as well as its scientific name in the format of the Participant-Intervention-Comparator-Outcome – PICO; the health condition or problem being studied; the names and description of the interventions being studied; the specific name and description of the comparator or control treatment being studied (could be active control or placebo-control); the primary outcome and time-point of the intervention (that is, the basis for determining whether or not the intervention was effective); the eligibility criteria for patients' participation in the study (that is, inclusion criteria); whether or not the study includes healthy volunteers; the type of study involved, that is, whether interventional or observational; the purpose of the study, whether it is for treatment, prevention, diagnosis or education; the method of allocation to intervention, that is, whether or not by randomization; the phase of the trial (drug trials are phased from one to four); the date of first participant enrolment; the expected total number of research participants to be enrolled; particulars of the source of funding for the study; particulars of the sponsor or investigator for the study; whether or not the study has received approval from at least one ethics committee; and the person to contact for public and scientific queries.[14]

While the development of Clinical Trials Registry in African countries would not guarantee the absence of unethical research in Africa, it would at least ensure that both local and international collaborative research in Africa is conducted under the searchlight of scientists and the public. For instance, if the Nigerian law had mandated the provision of the registration data set above, as a condition for the conduct of the trovan trial, it is most likely that the investigators would have been more compliant with the ethical requirements of the trial; or at least, it would have been difficult to maintain the secrecy that shrouded the trovan trial. As a matter of urgency, therefore, it is suggested that every African country should establish a Clinical Trials Registry in its territory; registration of a trial in the Registry should be made legally compulsory.

13 Sachin Nikarge, 'The contours of clinical research in India' (2010), 7 Indian Journal of Medical Ethics 178–179.

14 Australian New Zealand Clinical Trials Registry, Data Item Definition/Explanation (posted on http://www.anzctr.or.au).

**Legal Liability: the 'Judicialization' of Research Involving Human Subjects**

As mentioned above, one of the aims of this book is to show that while the current discourse on research involving human beings has been dominated by ethical analysis and, for good reasons, will remain so in the years to come, analytical attention needs to be bestowed on the equally important theme of legal regulation; this new frontier of analysis should include the socio-legal impacts of the increasing resort to courts for compensation by injured research subjects.

The Pfizer line of cases (concerning the trovan trial) analysed in chapters one and seven, and some of the unreported cases in the USA involving ethics committees, analysed in chapter five, suggest that the future is likely to witness an increasing judicialization of biomedical research. Judicial intervention, as a regulatory tool for research involving human subjects, raises interesting questions for commentators; the concept of judicialization is, however, yet to be comprehensively analysed.[15] Judicial intervention in the research process may take several forms. Apart from judicial review of research ethics committees' decisions, judicial control may be exercised through a series of private law actions, such as those analysed in chapters five, six and seven of this book. Judicialization of biomedical research raises some interesting questions, such as the policy arguments for and against judicial intervention? Could the special problems of research and access to justice in developing countries justify judicial intervention? Can it be said that recent court actions against researchers and ethics committees have impacted negatively on the research enterprise?

In Africa, however, the judicialization of research involving human beings is unlikely to lead to a flood of litigation because of the material poverty of most potential litigants, and the absence of a system of public interest litigation in most African countries. Unsurprisingly, some African claimants involved in litigation arising from international collaborative research conducted in Africa (such as claimants in the suit concerning the trovan trial) have resorted to the courts of some foreign jurisdictions (for instance, the USA) where some sort of legal fee arrangement could be made lawfully. In addition, however, the trovan claimants (as explained in chapter seven) opted for a foreign (USA) jurisdiction because of the perceived corruption of the Nigerian judiciary. In any event, the small number of reported cases on research involving human subjects does not lend to any quantitative or qualitative analysis on whether increased litigation over research-related injuries would be a positive or negative thing for Africa. In other words, it is not clear whether litigation would lead to the conduct of more ethically justifiable research in Africa, or would simply create a sort of risk-averseness on the part of foreign investigators, which could discourage them from conducting potentially useful research in Africa. If researchers were to continually look over

15 Generally: Christine Rothmayr, 'Towards the judicialisation of Swiss politics? (2001), 24 Western European Politics 77–94, noting that the 'concept of judicialization is often used to describe the process whereby courts have broadened their influence at the expense of parliament and government', at 77.

their shoulders, or become unduly sensitive to legal liability, then that could cause a drop in the number of research conducted in Africa. This, however, points to the need for independent and competent ethics committees in Africa. A protocol that is competently reviewed by an ethics committee, and equally executed by a competent researcher, will hardly give rise to any legal liability issues; this probably accounts for the sparse litigation involving researchers and ethics committees in most industrialized countries

Whatever view one takes on the judicialization of biomedical research, it is likely that the current trend of litigation would continue. As suggested in the introduction to this book, and more fully fleshed out in chapters five, six and seven, the law of torts is likely to play a significant role in suits brought to demand judicial compensations for research-related injuries; other legal categories would equally be useful. Furthermore, the perceived corruption in most African legal systems would ensure that more, rather than fewer, cases of research-related injuries are litigated extraterritorially, especially in jurisdictions like the USA where the judiciary is famous for giving exemplary or heavy award of damages as compensation in civil cases.

## Value of Extraterritorial Litigation

Just to emphasise the point made in the last paragraph above, the *Abdullahi* line of cases, fully examined in chapter seven (eventually resulting to USA$70m compensation for the trovan research subjects by way of out-of-court settlement), has shown that extraterritorial litigation could significantly compensate African research subjects for research-related injuries arising from international collaborative research conducted in Africa. Apart from the monetary rewards from such international litigation, there are other dividends, such as the relative absence of judicial corruption, quick dispensation of cases, availability of 'no-win-no-fee' type of professional fee structure or contracts, and the relative ease of executing judgement against the defendants-investigators-sponsors in their own countries where the litigation was instituted. Considering that there has been no equivalent case in any of the African countries examined in this book where judicially related compensation was awarded to claimants for research-related injuries, the resort of African research subjects to the courts of foreign countries (where the investigators and sponsors of research conducted in Africa are habitually resident) is likely to continue. In addition, while the *Abdullahi* line of extraterritorial litigation (in the US) shows that the legal and ethical problems arising from international collaborative research conducted in Africa are not just matters of African law but, rather, a potentially critical subject for international law, it also suggests that the framework of international litigation (for instance, in the US or the UK) might be a better or more effective means of addressing the problems of access to justice encountered by research subjects in most African countries, as analysed in chapter seven.

# Bibliography


Abuh, Adamu, 'The Trovan debacle comes to a close', The Guardian (Nigeria), 20 May 2010, 13.

Allott, A. N., *Judicial and Legal Systems in Africa, 2nd edn* (London: Butterworths African Law Series, 1970).

——, A *New Essays in African Law* (London: Butterworths – African Law Series, No. 13, 1970).

Andanda, P.A., 'Human-tissue-related inventions: ownership and intellectual property rights in international collaborative research in developing countries' (2008), 34 J. Med. Ethics 171.

Anderlik, Mary R. and Elster, Nanette, 'Lawsuits Against IRBs; Accountability or Incongruity? (2001), 29 Journal of Law, Medicine & Ethics 220.

Andrews, Lori and Nelkin, Dorothy, *Body Bazaar: The Market for Human Tissue in the Biotechnology Age* (New York: Crown Publishers, 2001).

Angell, M., 'Ethical Imperialism? Ethics in International Collaborative Clinical Research' (1988), 319 New England Journal of Medicine 1081.

——, 'Investigators' Responsibilities for Human Subjects in Developing Countries' (2000), 342 New Eng. J. Med. 324.

——, 'The Ethics of Clinical Research in the Third World,' (1997), 337 New Eng. J. Med. 847.

——, *The Truth About the Drug Companies* (New York: Random House, 2005).

Annas, G.J. and Grodin, M.A., 'Treating the Troops: Commentary' (1991), 21 Hastings Center Report 24.

——, 'Medical Ethics and Human Rights: Legacies of Nuremberg' (1999), 3 Hofstra L. & Pol'y Symp. 111.

——, 'Research Forum: Ethics and Studies of HIV; Human Rights and Maternal-Fetal HIV Transmission Prevention Trials in Africa' (1998), 88(4) American Journal of Public Health 560.

Annas, G. J. and Grodin, M. (eds), *The Nazi Doctors and the Nuremberg Code: Human Rights in Human Experimentation* (New York: Oxford University Press, 1992).

Annas, G.J., 'The Changing Landscape of Human Experimentation: Nuremberg, Helsinki, and Beyond' (1992), 2 Health Matrix 119.

——, 'The Man on the Moon, Immortality, and other Millenial Myths: The Prospects and Perils of Human Genetic Engineering' (2000), 49 Emory L.J. 753.

——, 'Mengele's Birthmark: The Nuremberg Code in United States Courts' (1991), 7 J. Contemp. Health L. & Pol'y 17.

——, *Some Choice: Law Medicine, and the Market* (New York: Oxford University Press, 1998).

——, 'Changing the Consent Rules for Desert Storm' (1992), 326 New England Journal of Medicine 770.

Aptheker, Herbert, 'Racism and Human Experimentation' (1974) 53 Political Affairs 27.

Arvind Pandey, et al., 'The upgraded Clinical Trials Registry India: a summary of changes' (2011), 8 Ind. J. Med. Ethics 186.

Ashcroft, R. and Pfeffer, N., 'Ethics behind closed doors: do research ethics committees need secrecy?' (2001), 322 BMJ 1294.

Ashcroft, R., 'Equipoise, Knowledge and Ethics in Clinical Research and Practice' (1999), 13 Bioethics 314.

Baker, R., 'A Theory of International Bioethics: Multi-Culturalism, Postmodernism, and the Bankruptcy of Fundamentalism' (1998), 8 Kennedy Institute of Ethics Journal 2001.

——, 'A Theory of International Bioethics: The Negotiable and the Non-Negotiable' (1998), 8 Kennedy Institute of Ethics Journal 233.

Ballantyne, Angela, 'Benefits to Research Subjects in International Trials: Do They Reduce Exploitation or Increase Undue Inducement?' (2008), 8 Developing World Bioethics 178.

Baraza, Richard, 'Kenyan Statutory Body was Unaware of Study' (2001), 1 BMJ 625.

Barendt, Eric, *Academic Freedom and the Law: A Comparative Study* (Oxford: Hart Publishing, 2010).

Barry, Michele, 'Ethical Considerations of Human Investigation in Developing Countries: The AIDS Dilemma' (1988), 319 New Eng. J. Med. 1083.

Bassiouni, M.C. et al., 'An Appraisal of Human Experimentation in International Law and Practice' (1981), 72 J. Crim. Law and Criminology 1597.

Bayer, Ronald, 'The Debate Over Maternal-Fetal HIV Transmission Prevention Trials in Africa, Asia, and the Caribbean: Racist Exploitation or Exploitation of Racism?' (1998), 88 Am. J. Pub. Health 567.

Beatson, J., *The Use and Abuse of Unjust Enrichment* (Oxford: Clarendon Press, 1991).

Beauchamp, T.L. and Walters, L. (eds), *Contemporary Issues in Bioethics* (Encino, C.A.: Dickenson, 1978).

Beauchamp, T.L., 'Methods and principles in biomedical ethics' (2003), 29 J. Med. Ethics 269–274.

Beauchamp, T.L. and Childress, J.F., *Principles of Biomedical Ethics, 6th edn* (New York: Oxford University Press, 2009).

——, *Principles of Biomedical Ethics, 5th edn* (Oxford: Oxford University Press, 2001).

Bechtler, T.W. (ed.) *Law in a Social Context: Liber Amicorum Honouring Professor Lon L. Fuller* (The Netherlands: Kluwer, 1987).

Beecher, H., 'Ethics and Clinical Research' (1966), New Eng. J. Med. 1354.

Beh, Hazel G., 'The Role of Institutional Review Boards in Protecting Human Subjects: Are We Ready to Fix a Broken System?' (2002), 26 Law & Psychol. Rev. 1.

Benatar, S.A. and Singer, P.A., 'Responsibilities in International Research: A New Look Revisited' (2010), 36 J. Med. Ethics 194–197.

——, 'A New Look at International Research Ethics' (2000), 321 BMJ 824.

Bently, L. and Sherman, B., *Intellectual Property Law, 3rd edn* (Oxford: Oxford University Press, 2009).

Beyleveld, D. and Brownsword, R., *Consent in the Law* (Oxford: Hart Publishing, 2007) 159.

Beyleveld, D., 'Law, Ethics, and Research Ethics Committees' (2002), 21 Medicine and Law 57.

Beyleveld, D., et al., *Research Ethics Committees, Data Protection and Medical Research in European Countries* (Aldershot, Ashgate Publishing, 2005).

Bhan, A., Majd, M. and Adejumo, A., 'Informed Consent in International Research: Perspectives from India, Iran and Nigeria' (2006), 3 McMaster University Medical Journal 36.

Biggs, Hazel, *Healthcare Research Ethics and Law: Regulation, Review and Responsibility* (London: Routledge-Cavendish, 2010).

Birks, Peter, *Unjust Enrichment, 2nd edn* (Oxford: Oxford University Press, 2005).

Bledsoe, Caroline H., et al., 'Regulating Creativity. Research and Survival in the IRB Iron Cage' (2007), 101 Northwestern University Law Review 593.

Blumenthal, David, 'Conflict of interest in Biomedical Research' [2002], 12 Health Matrix: Journal of Law-Medicine 377.

Bordas, Linda M., 'Tort Liability of Institutional Review Boards' (1984–85), 87 W. Va. L. Rev. 137.

Boseley, Sarah, 'Ailing Ethics: A clinical trial raises disturbing questions about drug companies' activities in Africa', the Guardian (UK), 20 January 2001, page unknown.

Brandt, Allan M., 'Racism and Research: The Case of the Tuskegee Syphilis Study' [1978], Hastings Center Report 21.

Brazier, M. and Cave, E., *Medicine, Patients and the Law, 4th edn* (London: Penguin Books, 2007).

Brazier, Margaret, 'Liability of ethics committees and their members' (1990), Professional negligence 186.

——, 'Retained organs: ethics and humanity' (2002), 22 Legal Stud. 550.

Brody, B.A., McCullough, L.P. and Sharp, R.R., 'Consensus and Controversy in Clinical Research Ethics' (2005), 294 Journal of the American Medical Association 1411.

Brody, Baruch A., 'When are Placebo-Controlled Trials No Longer Appropriate?' (1997), 18 Control Clinical Trials 602.

Burrows, Andrew, 'Proprietary Restitution: Unmasking Unjust Enrichment' (2001), 117 L.Q.R. 412.

Bussani, Mauro, 'Tort Law and Development: Insights Into The Case of Ethiopia and Eritrea' (1996), 40 J. Afri. L. 43.
Calabresi, Guido, *The Costs of Accidents: A Legal and Economic Analysis, 2nd edn* (New Haven: Yale University Press, 1970).
Campbell, A.V., 'The virtues (and vices) of the four principles' (2003), 29 J. Med. Ethics 292.
Campbell, Angela and Glass, Kathleen C., 'The Legal Status of Clinical and Ethics Policies, Codes, and Guidelines in Medical Practice and Research' (2000–2001), 46 McGill L.J. 473.
Campbell, Denis, 'I told the truth all along, says doctor at the heart of autism row', the Observer, Sunday 8 July 2007 (page unknown).
Carnall, Douglas, 'Doctor Struck Off for Scientific Fraud' (1996), 312 BMJ 399.
Carol, Levine, 'Placebos and HIV: Lessons Learned', (November – December 1998) Hastings Center Report 43.
Caulfied, T. and Williams-Jones, B. (eds), *The Commercialization of Genetic Research: Ethical, Legal and Policy Issues* (New York: Kluwer, 1999).
Caulfield, Timothy, et al., 'Research Ethics and the Role of the Professional Bodies: A View From Canada' (2004), 32 J.L. Med. & Ethics 365.
Cha, Ariana E., 'AIDS Drug Trial Turned Away: Protests by Prostitutes in Cambodia Ended Tenofovir Testing', The Washington Post, 23 May 2006, page unknown.
Chalmers, T.C., 'Invited Remarks' (1979), 25 Clinical and Pharmacological Therapy 649.
Charrow, Robert, 'Protection of Human Subjects: Is Expansive Regulation Counter-Productive?' (2007), 101 Northwestern University Law Review 707.
Chatterjee, Patralekha, 'Clinical Trials in India: Ethical Concerns' (2008), 86 Bulletin of the World Health Organisation 581.
Chima, Sylvester C., 'Regulation of biomedical research in Africa' (2006), 332 BMJ 848.
Chiong, Winston, 'The Real Problem with Equipoise' (2006),6 American Journal of Bioethics 37.
Christakis, A.A. and Panner, J., 'Existing International Ethical Guidelines for Human Subjects Research: Some Open Questions' (1991), 19 Law, Medicine, & Health Care 214.
Chua, Arlene, et al., 'The Tenofovir Pre-Exposure Prophylaxis Trial in Thailand: Researchers Should Show More Openness in Their Engagement with the Community' (2005), 2 PLoS Medicine 1044.
Cook, K., Mbori-Ngacha, D. and Marum, E., 'Shadow on the Continent: Public Health and HIV/AIDS in Africa' (2002), 360 Lancet 67.
Costello A. and Zumla, A., 'Moving to research partnerships in developing countries' (2000), 321 BMJ 827.
Cottrell, Jill, 'The Functions of the Law of Torts in Africa' (1987), 31 J. Afr. L. 161
——, 'The Tort of Negligence in Nigeria' (1973), 17 J. Afr. L. 30.

Council for International Organisations of Medical Sciences (CIOMS), *International Ethical Guidelines for Biomedical Research Involving Human Subjects* (Geneva: CIOMS, 2002).

Council of Europe, Convention on Human Rights and Biomedicine, Oviedo, 4. IV. 1997.

Craig, Paul, *Administrative Law 6th edn* (London: Sweet & Maxwell, 2008).

Crouch, Robert A. and Arras, John D., 'AZT Trials and Tribulations' (November – December 1998), Hastings Center Report 26.

Curran, W.J., 'Governmental regulation of the use of human subjects in medical research: The approach of two federal agencies' (1969), 98 Daedalus 409.

Davies, Richard B., 'The Principlism Debate: A Critical Overview' (1995), 20 Journal of Medicine and Philosophy 85.

Davis, Dena S., 'Case Study "Dear Mrs. X …"' (1983), IRB November/December 6.

Dawson, A.J. and Yentis, S.M., 'Contesting the science/ethics distinction in the review of clinical research' (2007), 33 J. Med. Ethics 165.

De Ville, Kenneth, 'The Case Against Contract: Participant and investigator Duty in Clinical Trials' (2011), 11 The American Journal of Bioethics 16.

——, 'The Role of Litigation in Human Research Accountability' (2002) 9 Accountability in Research 17.

Denny, Colleen C. and Grady, Christine, 'Clinical research with economically disadvantaged populations' (2007), 33 J. Med. Ethics 382.

Department of Health and Human Services, Office of the Inspector General, *The Globalization of Clinical Trials: A Growing Challenge in Protecting Human Subjects* (DHHS, 2001).

Department of Health, Education, and Welfare, *Final Report of the Tuskegee Syphilis Study Ad Hoc Advisory Panel* [Washington, D.C.: GPO, 1973].

Department of Health, *Ethics in Health Research: Principles, Structures and Processes* (Pretoria, DoH, 2004).

Department of Health, *Governance Arrangements for NHS Research Ethics Committees* (2001).

Department of Health, *Guidelines for Good Clinical Practice in the Conduct of Clinical Trials in Human Participants in South Africa* (Pretoria, DOH, 2000).

Department of Health, *Research Governance Framework for Health and Social Care* (2005).

Dhai, Ames, et al., 'A pilot study evaluating an intervention designed to raise awareness of clinical trials among potential participants in the developing world' (2010), 36 J. Med. Ethics 238.

Diallo, D.A., et al.. 'Community Permission for medical Research in Developing Countries' (2005), 41 Clinical Infectious Diseases 255.

Dickens, B.M., 'Conflicts of Interest in Canadian Health Care Law' (1995), 21 American Journal of Law & Medicine 259.

——, 'Contractual Aspects of Human Medical Experimentation' (1975), 25 Uni. Tor. L. J. 406.

——, 'Research Ethics and HIV/AIDS' (1997), 16 Med. Law 187.

Dickens, Bernard, et al., 'Research on Human Populations: National and Internal Ethical Guidelines' (1991), 19 Law, Medicine & Health Care 157.

Ditmore, Melissa, 'Response to Joep M.A. Lange' (2005), 2 PLoS Medicine 1045.

Dodge, C.P. and Wiebe, P.D. (eds), *Crisis in Uganda: The Breakdown of Health Services* (Oxford: Oxford University Press, 1985).

Dominique Sprumont, 'Legal Protection of Human Research Subjects in Europe' (1999), 6 European Journal of Health Law 25.

Douglas, T.M., 'Ethics committees and the legality of research' (2007), 33 J. Med. Ethics 732.

Dowdy, D.W., 'Partnership as an ethical model for medical research in developing countries: the example of the "implementation trial"' (2006), 32 J. Med. Ethics 357.

Downie, J. et al. (eds), *Canadian Health Law and Policy* (Markham: Butterworths, 2002, 2nd edn).

Du Bois, F. (ed.), *Wille's Principles of South African Law, 9th edn* (Cape Town: Juta & Co., 2007).

Edejer, Tessa Tan-Torres, 'North-South research partnership: the ethics of carrying out research in developing countries' (1999), 319 BMJ 438.

Edwards, J.L., 'Assessing the Remedy: The Case for Contracts in Clinical Trials' (2011), 11 The American Journal of Bioethics 3.

Eferaro, Sam, 'NAFDAC Okayed Pfizer's Trovan Trials', Vanguard (Lagos) 8 January 2001, page unknown.

Ehni, H-G. and Wiesing, U., 'International ethical regulations on placebo-use in clinical trials: a comparative analysis' (2008), 22 Bioethics 64.

El-Bassel, et al., 'Intimate Partner Violence Prevalence and HIV Risks among Women Receiving Care in Emergency Departments: Implications for IPV and HIV Screening' (2007), 24 Emerg. Med. J. 255.

Elsayed, D.E. and Kass, N.E., 'Assessment of Ethical Review Process in Sudan' (2007), 7 Developing World Bioethics 143.

Emanuel, E.J. et al., 'What Makes Clinical Research in Developing Countries Ethical? The Benchmarks of Ethical Research' (2004), 189 Journal of Infectious Diseases 930.

——, 'What Makes Clinical Research Ethical?' (2000), 283 Jama 2701.

Emmanuel, E.J. and Steiner, D., 'Institutional Conflict of Interest' (1995), 332 N. Eng. J. Med. 262.

Emmanuel, Ezekiel J. and Miller, Franklin G., 'The Ethics of Placebo Controlled Trials – A Middle Ground' (2001), 345 New England Journal of Medicine 915.

Enkin, Murray E., 'For and against: clinical equipoise and not the uncertainty principle is the moral underpinning of the randomised controlled trial' (2000), 321 BMJ 756.

ENRECA Health Research Network, *Ethics and Health Research in Low Income Societies: Ethical Capacity Building – Obstacles and Challenges* (Copenhagen: ENRECA, 2003).

Epstein, M. and Wingate, D.L., 'Is the NHS Research Ethics Committees System to be Outsourced to a Low-Cost Offshore Call Centre? Reflections on Human Research Ethics After the Warner Report' (2007), 33 J. Med. Ethics 45.

Erinosho, Olayiwola, *Ethics for Public Health Research in Africa* (Ago-Iwoye, Ogun State, Nigeria: Olabisi Onabanjo University Press, 2008).

Esther Chang, 'Fitting a Square Peg into a Round Hole?: Imposing Informed Consent and Post-Trial Obligations on United States Sponsored Clinical Trials in Developing Countries' (2002), 11 S. Cal. Interdisc. L.J. 339.

Ethiopian Science and Technology Commission, National Health Research Ethics (Addis Ababa, 2005).

Ethiopian Science and Technology Commission, *National Health Research Ethics Review Guideline* (Addis Ababa, 2005).

European Commission, *Ethics, Research and Globalisation: Europe and its Partners Building Capacity in Research Ethics* (European Commission: Directorate-General for Research, 2007).

Ezeome, Emmanuel R. and Simon, Christian, 'Ethical Problems in Conducting Research in Acute Epidemics: The Pfizer Meningitis Study in Nigeria as an Illustration' (2010), 10 Developing World Bioethics 1.

Fadare, Joseph O., 'Informed Consent in Human Subject Research: A Comparison of Current International and Nigerian Guidelines' (2010), 5(1) Journal of Empirical Research on Human Research Ethics 67.

Fairchild, Amy L. and Bayer, Ronald, 'Uses and Abuses of Tuskegee' [1999], 284 Science 919.

Fan R. and Holliday, I., 'Which Medicine? Whose Standard? Critical Reflections on Medical Integration in China' (2007), 33 J. Med. Ethics 454.

Farmer, P. and Campos, N.G., 'New malaise: Bioethics and Human Rights in the Global Era' (2004), 32 J.L. Med. & Ethics 243.

Federal Ministry of Health (Nigeria), *National Code of Health Research Ethics* (Abuja, Nigeria: Federal Ministry of Health, 2007).

Feldthusen, Bruce, *Economic Negligence, 4th edn* (Toronto: Carswell, 2000).

Ferguson, P., 'Do Researchers Feel an LREC Hinders Research?' (2001), 165 Bull. of Med. Ethics 17.

Ferguson, Pamela R., 'Clinical Trials and Healthy Volunteers' (2008), 16 Med. L. R. 23.

Fidler, Eavid P., '"Geographical Morality" Revisited: International Relations, International Law, and the Controversy over Placebo-Controlled HIV Clinical Trials in Developing Countries' (2001), 42 Harv. Int'l L.J. 299.

Flaherty, Mary Pat and Stephens, Joe, 'Pa. Firm Asks FDA To Back Experiment Forbidden in U.S.', Wash. Post, 23 February 2001, A3.

Fleck, Fiona, 'Nigerian president holds key to global polio eradication' (2004) 328 BMJ 544.

Fleming, John G., *The Law of Torts, 9th edn* (Sydney: LBC Information Services, 1998).

Forgarty AIDS International Training Program, *A Survival Guide for Conducting International Collaborative Research in Uganda* (San Francisco: Fogarty AITRP, University of California, 2004).

Foster, C. Gilbert (ed.), *Manual for Research Ethics Committees* (Centre of Medical Law and Ethics, Kings College, London, 1991).

Foster, Charles, *Human Dignity in Bioethics and Law* (Oxford: Hart Publishing, 2011).

Foster, Claire, *The Ethics of Medical Research on Humans* (Cambridge: Cambridge University Press, 2001).

Freedman, Benjamin, 'Equipoise and the Ethics of Clinical Research' (1987), 317 New England Journal of Medicine 141.

——, 'Placebo Controlled Trials and the Logic of Clinical Purpose' (1990), 1 IRB: A Review of Human Subjects Research 1.

Freedman, B. and Glass, K.C., 'Weiss v Solomon: A Case Study in Institutional Responsibility for Clinical Research' (1990), 88 Law, Medicine & Health Care 395.

Freedman, B., Glass, K. and Weijer, C., 'Placebo Orthodoxy in Clinical Research 11: Ethical, Legal, and Regulatory Myths' (1996), 24 J.L. Med. & Ethics 252.

——, 'Placebo Orthodoxy in Clinical Research 1: Empirical and Methodological Myths' (1996), 42 J.L. Med. & Ethics 243.

Fried, C., *Medical Experimentation, Personal Integrity and Social Policy* (Amsterdam: North-Holland Publishing, 1974).

Friele, Minou B., 'Do Committees Ru(i)n the Bio-Political Culture? On the Democratic Legitimacy of Bioethical Committees' (2003), 17 Bioethics 301.

Garrafa, V. et al., 'Between the needy and the greedy: the quest for a just and fair ethics of clinical research' (2010), 36 J. Med. Ethics 500.

Garwood-Gowers, A *Healthcare Law: The Impact of the Human Rights Act 1998* (London: Cavendish Publishing, 2001).

Gibson, E., Baylis, F., Lewis, S., 'Dances with the Pharmaceutical Industry' (2002), 166 Canadian Medical Association Journal 448.

Gielen, Andrea Carlson, McDonnell, Karen A., Burke, Jessica G., et al., 'Women's Lives After an HIV-Positive Diagnosis: Disclosure and Violence' (2000), 4(2) Maternal & Child Health Journal 111.

Gifford, F., 'Community Equipoise and the Ethics of Randomized Clinical Trials' (1995), 9 Bioethics 127.

——, 'Freedman's "Clinical Equipoise" and "Sliding-Scale All-Dimensions-Considered Equipoise"' (2000), 25 Journal of Medicine and Philosophy 399.

——, 'Pulling the Plug on Clinical Equipoise: A Critique of Miller and Weijer' (2007), 17 Kennedy Institute of Ethics Journal 203.

——, 'So-Called "Clinical Equipoise" and the Argument from Design' (2007), 32 Journal of Medicine and Philosophy 135.

Gilbert, Susan, 'Trials and Tribulations' (2008), 38 Hastings Centre Report 14.

Gillis, Charlie, 'Doctor Left Autopsies Unfinished in Halifax: Children's Organs Found in Warehouse', National Post, 3 October 2000, A8.

Gillon, R., 'Four Scenarios' (2003), 29 J. Med. Ethics 267.
Giussani, Elizabeth, *Constitutional and Administrative Law* (London: Sweet & Maxwell, 2008).
Global Forum for Health Research, *Monitoring Financial Flows for Health Research* (Geneva: Global Forum for Health Research, 2001).
Gold, Jennifer L., 'Watching the Watchdogs: Negligence, Liability, and Research Ethics Boards' (2003), 11 Health L.J. 153.
Goldner, J.A., 'An Overview of Legal Controls on Human Experimentation and the Regulatory Implications of Taking Professor Katz Seriously' (1993), 38 St Louis University L. J. 63.
——, 'Dealing with Conflicts of Interest in Biomedical Research: IRB Oversight as the Next Best Solution to the Abolitionist Approach' (2000), 28 J.L. Med. & Ethics 379.
Gorner, Peter, 'Parents Suing Over Patenting of Genetic Test: They Say Researchers They Assisted are Trying to Profit From a Test for a Rare Disease', Chicago Tribune, 19 November 2000, A1.
Gostin, Larry, 'Ethical Principles for the Conduct of Human Subject Research: Population-Based Research and Ethics' (1991), 19 Law, Medicine & Health Care 191.
Gray, K., 'Interlocutory Injunctions Since American Cyanamid' (1981), 40 CLJ 307.
Hadskis M. and Carver, P., 'The Long Arm of Administrative Law: Applying Administrative Law Principles to Research Ethics Boards' (2005), 13 Health Law Review 19.
Halpern, D., et al., 'Informing Patients of Uncertainty in Clinical Trials' (2001), 285 Jama 2713.
Hamburger, P.,'Getting Permission' (2007), 101 Northwestern University law Review 405.
Hammond, G., 'The Origins of the Equitable Duty of Confidence' (1979), 8 Anglo-American Law Review 71.
Harris, J., 'In praise of unprincipled ethics' (2003), 29 J. Med. Ethics 303.
——, 'Scientific Research is a Moral Duty' (2005), 31 J. Med. Ethics 242.
Health Research and Development Committee (Bostwana), *Guidelines for the Review of Research Proposals* (Ministry of Health, Bostwana, 2005).
Hellsten, Sirkku K., 'Bioethics in Tanzania: Legal and Ethical Concerns in Medical Care and Research in Relation to the HIV/AIDS Epidemic' (2005), 14 Cambridge Quarterly of Healthcare Ethics 256.
Hershey, Nathan and Miller, Robert D., *Human Experimentation and the Law* (Maryland: Aspen Systems Corporation, 1976).
Hill, Z., et al., 'Informed consent in Ghana: what do participants really understand?' (2008), 34 J. Med. Ethics 48.
Hirtle, Marie, Lemmens, Trudo and Sprumont, Dominique, 'A Comparative Analysis of Research Ethics Review Mechanisms and the ICH Good Clinical Practice Guideline' [2000], 7 European Journal of Health Law 267.

Hohfeld, W.N., 'Fundamental Legal Conceptions as Applied in Judicial Reasoning' (1917), 26 Yale Law Journal 710.

——, 'Some Fundamental Legal Conceptions as Applied in Judicial Reasoning' (1911) 23 Yale Law Journal 16.

Holder, Angela R., 'Do Researchers and Subjects Have a Fiduciary Relationship' (1982), IRB 6.

Holm, S., 'Not just autonomy – the principles of American biomedical ethics' (1995), 21 J. Med. Ethics 332.

Hosford, Bowen, *Bioethics Committees: The Health Care Provider's Guide* (Maryland: An Aspen Publication, 1986).

House of Commons, *The Royal Liverpool Children's Inquiry* (London: House of Commons, 2001).

Huijstee, M. and Schipper, I. (eds), *Putting Contract Research Organisations on the Radar* (Amsterdam: SOMO, 2011).

Human Radiation Experiments, *Final Report of the President's Advisory Committee* (New York: Oxford University Press, 1996).

Hyder, A.A., 'Ethical Review of Health Research: A Perspective from Developing Country Researchers' (2004), 30 J. Med. Ethics 68.

Ikingura, Joyce K., 'Health Research Ethics Review and Needs of Institutional Ethics Committees in Tanzania' (2007), 9 Tanzania Health Research Bulletin 154.

Ilcana Dominguez-Urban, 'Harmonization in the Regulation of Pharmaceutical Research and Human Rights: The Need to Think Globally' (1997), 30 Cornell Int'l L.J. 245.

Indian Council of Medical Research, *Ethical Guidelines for Biomedical Research on Human Subjects* (New Delhi: Indian Council of Medical Research, 2006).

International Conference on Harmonisation of Technical Requirements for Registration of Pharmaceuticals for Human Use, *ICH Harmonised Tripartite Guideline: Guideline for Good Clinical Practice* (1996).

Irwin, Dana R., 'Freedom of Thought: The First Amendment and the Scientific Method' (2005), Wis. L. Rev. 1479.

Jafarey, A.M. and Farooqui, A., 'Informed consent in the Pakistani milieu: the physician's perspective' (2005), 31 J. Med. Ethics 93.

Jecker, Nancy S., et al. (eds), *Bioethics: An Introduction to the History, Methods, and Practice* (Boston: Jones and Bartlett Publishers, 1997).

Jeremy Sugarman, et al., 'Ethical oversight of multinational collaborative research: lessons from Africa for building capacity and for policy' (2007), 3 Research Ethics Review 84.

Joint United Nations Programme on HIV/AIDS and World Health Organisation, *Ethical Considerations in Biomedical HIV Prevention Trials: UNAIDS/WHO Guidance Document* (Geneva: UNAIDS/WHO, 2007).

Jones, James H., *Bad Blood: The Tuskegee Syphilis Experiment* (New York: Free Press, 1993)

Kanyeihamba, G.W., *Constitutional and Political History of Uganda: From 1894 to the Present* (Kampala, Uganda: Centenary Publishing House Ltd., 2002).

Karbwang, Juntra, et al., 'Ethical Review and the Globalisation of Clinical Trials' (2002), Applied Clinical Trials 90.

Karlawish, J.H.T. and Lantos, J., 'Community Equipoise and the Architecture of Clinical Research (1997), 6 Cambridge Quarterly of Healthcare Ethics 385.

Kass, Nancy, et al., 'The Structure and Function of Research Ethics Committees in Africa: A Case Study' (2007), 4 PLoS Medicine 26.

Katz, Doleres, 'Why 430 Blacks with Syphilis Went Uncured for 40 Years', Detroit Free Press, 5 November 1972.

Katz, J., 'Human Experimentation and Human Rights' (1993), 38 Saint Louis University L.J. 7.

——, *Experimentation with Human Beings: The Authority of the Investigator, Subject, Professions, and State in the Human Experimentation Process* (New York: Russell Sage Foundation, 1972).

Kavanagh, John A., *A Guide to Judicial Review* (Toronto: Carswell Co. Ltd., 1978).

Kefalides, P.T., 'Research on Humans Faces Scrutiny: New Policies Adopted' (2000), 132 Annals of Internal Medicine 513.

Kennedy, Ian, *Treat Me Right: Essays in Medical Law and Ethics* (Oxford: Oxford University Press, 1988).

Kevin King, 'A Proposal for the Effective International Regulation of Biomedical Research Involving Human Subjects' (1998), 34 Stan. J. Int'l L. 163.

Kiriga, Joses M. and Wambebe, Charles, 'Status of National Health Research Systems in Ten Countries of the WHO African Region' (2006), 6 BMC Health Services Research 135.

Kishore, R.R., 'Biomedical Research and Mining of the Poor: The Need for their Exclusion' (2006), 12 Science and Engineering Ethics 175.

Kitua, Andrew, et al., 'The use of placebo in a trial of rectal artesunate as initial treatment for severe malaria patients en route to referral clinics: ethical issues' (2010), 36 J. Med. Ethics 116.

Kitua, Andrew Y., 'Coordinating health research to promote action: the Tanzania experience' (2000), 321 BMJ 821.

Klar, L.N., 'Judicial Activism in Private Law' (2001), 80 Can. Bar. Rev. 215.

Kodilinye, G., *The Nigerian Law of Torts* (London: Sweet and Maxwell, 1982).

Koenig, L.J., et al., 'Violence During Pregnancy Among Women with or at Risk for HIV Infection' (2002), 92 AJPH 367.

Kopelman, L., 'Estimating Risk in Human Research' (1981), 29 Clinical Research 1.

Kuhse, Helga and Singer, Peter, *Bioethics: An Anthology* (Oxford: Blackwell Publishing, 2006).

Ladimer, Irving and Newman, Roger W. (eds), *Clinical Investigation in Medicine: Legal, Ethical, and Moral Aspects* (Boston: Law-Medicine Research Institute, Boston University, 1963).

Lancet (Editorial), 'A Curious Stopping Rule from Hoechst Marion Roussel' (1997), 350 Lancet 155.

——, 'The Economics of HIV in Africa' (2002), 360 Lancet 1.
——, 'The Trials of Tenofovir Trials' (2005), 365 Lancet 1111.
——, 'Good Manners for the Pharmaceutical Industry,' (1997), 349 Lancet 1635.
Langat, Simon K., 'Reuse of Samples; Ethical Issues Encountered by Two Institutional Ethics Review Committees in Kenya' (2005), 19 Bioethics 537.
Lange, J., 'We must not let protestors derail trials of pre-exposure prophylaxis for HIV' (2005), 2 PLoS Medicine e248.
Laurence, Desmond R., 'Research ethics committees and the law: indemnity and independence' (2006), 2 Research Ethics Review 140.
Laurie, P. and Greco, D.B., 'US exceptionalism comes to research ethics' (2005), 365 Lancet 1111.
Lee, Marvin J.H., 'The problem of "thick in status, thin in content" in Beauchamp and Childress' principlism' (2010), 36 J. Med. Ethics 525.
Lemmens, T. and Archibald, T. (eds), *The Regulation and Organization of Research Ethics Review* (Toronto: Brown Book Co., 2006).
Lemmens, T. and Freedman, B., 'Ethics Review for Sale? Conflict of Interest and Commercial Research Review Boards' (2000), 78 Millbank Quarterly 547.
Lemmens, Trudo and Thompson, Alison, 'Noninstitutional Commercial Review Boards in North America' (2001), 23 IRB: Ethics & Human Research 1.
Lemmens, Trudo and Warring, Duff (eds), *Law and Ethics in Biomedical Research: Regulation, Conflict of Interests, and Liability* (Toronto: University of Toronto Press, 2006).
Lemmens, Trudo, 'Federal Regulation of REB Review of Clinical Trials: A Modest But Easy Step Towards An Accountable REB Review Structure in Canada' (2005), 13 Health Law Review 39.
——, 'In the Name of National Security: Lessons from the Final Report on the Human Radiation Experiments' (1999), 6 European Journal of Health Law 7.
Leonard H. Glantz, et al., 'Research in Developing Countries: Taking "Benefit" Seriously' (1998), Hastings Center Rep., Nov–Dec. 1998, 38.
Leubsdorf, J., 'The Standard for Preliminary Injunctions' (1978), 91 Harvard L. Rev. 525.
Levine, Robert, 'International Codes of Research Ethics: Current Controversies and the Future' (2002), 35 Indiana L. Rev. 557.
——, 'Uncertainty in Clinical Research' (1988), 16 Law, Medicine & Health Care174.
——, 'International Codes of Research Ethics: Current Controversies and the Future' (2002), 35 Ind. L. Rev. 557.
Linden, Allen M., *Canadian Tort Law, 7th edn* (Markham, Ontario: Butterworths, 2001).
Lippman, Matthew, 'The Nazi Doctors Trial and the International Prohibition on Medical Involvement in Torture' [1993 ], 15 Loy. L.A. Int'l Comp. L.J. 410.
Little, M., 'Research, Ethics and Conflicts of Interest' (1999), 25 J. Med. Ethics 259.

Litton, P. and Miller, F.G., 'A normative justification for distinguishing the ethics of clinical research from the ethics of medical care' (2005), 33 J.L. Med. & Ethics 566.

Liu, B.R., 'Legal Regulations of AIDS Detection and Administration in P.R. China' (1992), 3 International Journal of Bioethics 25.

London, Alex J., 'Equipoise and International Human-Subjects Research' (2001), 15 Bioethics 312.

——, 'Two Dogmas of Research Ethics and the Integrative Approach to Human-Subjects Research' (2007), 32 Journal of Medicine and Philosophy 99.

——, 'Justice and the Human Development Approach to International Research' (2005), 35 Hastings Centre Report 37.

Loue, Sana and Okello, David, 'Research Bioethics in the Ugandan Context 11: Procedural and Substantive Reform' (2000), 28 Journal of Law, Medicine & Ethics 165.

Loue, Sana, et al., 'Research Bioethics in the Ugandan Context: A Program Summary' (1996), Journal of Law, Medicine & Ethics 47.

Lurie, Peter and Wolfe, Sidney M., 'Unethical Trials of Interventions to Reduce Perinatal Transmission of the Human Immunodeficiency Virus in Developing Countries' (1997), 337 New Eng. J. Med. 853.

Lynch, John A., '"Through a Glass Darkly": Researcher Ethnocentrism and the Demonization of Research Participants' (2011), 11 The American Journal of Bioethics 22.

Macklin, Ruth, *Double Standards in Medical Research in Developing Countries* (Cambridge: Cambridge University Press, 2004).

——, 'Applying the four principles' (2003), 29 J. Med. Ethics 275.

Madhiwalla, N., 'The NBC and the Bioethics Movement in India' (2011), 8 Ind. J. Med. Ethics 3.

Maina-Ahlberg, B., et al., 'North-South health research collaboration: Challenges in institutional interaction' (1997), 44 Soc. Sci. Med. 1229.

Marshall, P., et al., 'Voluntary Participation and Informed Consent to International Genetic Research' (2006), 96 American Journal of Public Health 1989.

Marshall, Patricia A., 'Human Rights, Cultural Pluralism, and International Health Research' (2005), 25 Theoretical Medicine and Bioethics 529.

Mbidde, Edward, 'Bioethics and Local Circumstances' (1998), 279 Science 155.

McCall, M.L., 'AIDS Quarantine Law in the International Community: Health and Safety Measures or Human Rights Violations?' (1993), 15 Loyola of Los Angeles International and Comparative Law Annual 1001.

McClean, David and Beevers, Kisch, *Morris: Conflict of Laws, 7th edn* (London: Sweet and Maxwell, 2009).

McDonald, Michael, *The Governance of Health Research Involving Human Subjects* (Ottawa: Law Commission of Canada, 2000).

McDonald, P.B., 'Government regulation or other "abridgements" of scientific research: the proper scope of judicial review under the First Amendment' (2005), 54 Emory L. Rev. 979.

McGuinness, S., 'Research ethics committees: the role of ethics in a regulatory authority' (2008), 34 J. Med. Ethics 695.
McHale, J.V., 'Guidelines for Medical Research – Some Ethical and Legal Problems' (1993), 1 Med. L. Rev. 160.
——, 'Liability in the law of tort of research ethics committees and their members' (2005), 1 Research Ethics Review 53.
McLean, Sheila (ed.), *First Do No Harm: Law, Ethics and Healthcare* (Aldershot: Ashgate Publishing Ltd, 2006).
McNeill, P.M., 'The Implications for Australia of the New Zealand Report of the Cervical Cancer Inquiry: No Cause for Complacency' (1989), 150 Medical Journal of Australia 264.
Mduluza, T. (ed.), *A Gateway to Biomedical Research in Africa* (New York: Nova Science Publishers, Inc., 2007).
Medical Research Council (South Africa), *Guidelines on Ethics for Medical Research* (2001–2002).
Medical Research Council (Zimbabwe), *Guidelines for Researchers and Ethics Review Committees in Zimbabwe* (MRC, 2004).
Medley, A., et al., 'Rates, Barriers and Outcomes of HIV Serostatus disclosure among Women in Developing Countries: Implications for Prevention of Mother-to-Child Transmission Programmes' (2004), 82 Bulletin of the World Health Organisation 299.
Menikoff, Jerry, 'Where's The Law? Uncovering The Truth About IRBs And Censorship' (2007), 101 Northwestern University Law Review 791.
Merritt, Andrew L., 'The Tort Liability of Hospital Ethics Committees' (1987), 60 Southern Cal. L. Rev. 1239.
Meslin, E., et al., 'Principlism and the ethical appraisal of clinical trials' (1995), 9 Bioethics 399.
Metz, Thaddeus, 'African and Western Moral Theories in a Bioethical Context' (2010), 10 Developing World Bioethics 49.
Mfutso-Bengu, Joseph M. and Taylor, T.E., 'Ethical Jurisdictions in Biomedical Research' (2002), 18 Trends in Parasitology 231.
Michael H. Cohen, *Future Medicine* (Ann Arbor, Michigan: The University of Michigan Press, 2003).
Mill, John S., *Utilitarianism* (Indianapolis: Hackett Publishing Co., 1979. Edited by G. Sher and originally published in 1861).
Miller, Dawn Joyce, 'Research and Accountability: The Need for Uniform Regulation of International Pharmaceutical Drug Testing' (2001), 13 Pace Int'l L. Rev. 197.
Miller, F., 'Trusting Doctors: Tricky Business When It Comes to Clinical Research' (2001), 81 Boston University Law Review 423.
Miller, Franklin G. and Brody, Howard, 'A Critique of Clinical Equipoise' (2003), 33 The Hastings Center Report 19.
——, 'Clinical Equipoise and the Incoherence of Research Ethics' (2007), 32 Journal of Medicine and Philosophy 151.

——, 'What Makes Placebo Controlled Trials Unethical?' (2002), 2 American Journal of Bioethics 3.

Miller, Franklin G. and Veatch, Robert M., 'Symposium on Equipoise and the Ethics of Clinical Trials' (2007), 32 Journal of Medicine and Philosophy 77.

Miller, Paul B. and Weijer, Charles, 'Equipoise and the Duty of Care in Clinical Research: A Philosophical Response to Our Critics' (2007), 32 Journal of Medicine and Philosophy 117.

——, 'Rehabilitating Equipoise' (2003), 13 Kennedy Institute of Ethics Journal 93.

Ministry of Health (Kenya), *National Guidelines for Research and Development of HIV/AIDS Vaccines* (MoH, 2005).

Ministry of Public Health (Cameroon), *Ministerial Decree No. 079 on the Creation and Organisation of an Ethics Committee Regulating all Research Involving Human Beings* (22 October 1987).

Mittendorf 11, Robert, 'Primum Non Nocere: Implications for the Globalisation of Biomedical Research Trials' (2001), 25 Fletcher F., World Aff. 239.

Mohammed, Idris, *Academics, Epidemics & Politics* (Ibadan, Nigeria: Bookcraft, 2007).

Monnye, Segoane L., 'Protection of Human Participants from Risks in Biomedical Research: An Analysis of the Law of South Africa and International Ethical Guidelines' (2003), 22 Med. Law 73.

Montgomery, J., 'Time for a Paradigm Shift? Medical Law in Transition' (2000), 53 Current Legal Problems 363.

——, *Health Care Law, 2nd edn* (Oxford: Oxford University Press, 2003).

Moodley, K., et al., 'Informed consent and participant perceptions of influenza vaccine trials in South Africa' (2005), 31 J. Med. Ethics 727.

——, 'Health Research Ethics Committees in South Africa 12 Years into Democracy' (2007), 8 BMC Medical Ethics.

Morin, Karine, 'The Standard of Disclosure in Human Subject Experimentation' (1998), 19 J. Leg. Med. 157.

Moss, J., 'If Institutional Review Boards Were Declared Unconstitutional, They Would Have To Be Reinvented' (2007), 101 Northwestern University Law Review 801.

Mtunthama, N., et al., 'Malawians permit research bronchoscopy due to perceived need for healthcare' (2008), 34 J. Med. Ethics 303.

Mugerwa, R.D., et al., 'First Trial of the HIV-1 Vaccine in Africa: Ugandan Experience' (2002), 324 BMJ 226.

Mukama, Benedict C. and Yongolo, Charles S., *Development of S & T System and Experience of Tanzania on S & T Data Collection* (Presentation at the Regional Workshop on Science and Technology Statistics at Entebbe, Uganda, 17–22 September 2005).

Murray, R.A. and Malcolm, D. (eds), *African Charter on Human and Peoples' Rights: The System in Practice, 1986-2000* (Cambridge: Cambridge University Press, 2002).

Nadig, Pratibha, et al., 'Competence of ethics committees in patient protection in clinical research' (2011), 8 Ind. J. Med. Ethics 151.

Nagral, Sanjay, 'Ethics, equity and justice: a view from the belly of the beast' (2011), 8 Ind. J. Med. Ethics 9.

Nair, V.M. and Martin, D.K., 'Concerns about ethical review of health research in India' (2004), 1 Ind. J. Med. Ethics 119.

Nathan, D.G. and Weatherall, D.J. 'Academic Freedom in Clinical Research' (2002), 347 New England Journal of Medicine 1368.

National Bioethics Advisory Commission, *Ethical and Policy Issues in International Research: Clinical Trials in Developing Countries, vols. 1 and 2* (Bethesda, Maryland: NBAC, 2001).

National Commission, *Belmont Report: Ethical Principles and Guidelines for the Protection of Human Subjects of Research* (National Commission, 1979).

National Council for Science and Technology (Kenya), *Guidelines for Ethical Conduct of Biomedical Research Involving Human Subjects in Kenya* (NCST, 2004).

National Health and Medical Research Council, Australian Research Council, Australian Vice-Chancellors' Committee, National Health and Medical Research Council, *National Statement on Ethical Conduct in Human Research* (Canberra; Commonwealth of Australia, 2007).

Newton, L., 'Ethical Imperialism and Informed Consent' (1990), 12 IRB: A Review of Human Subjects Research 10.

Nikarge, S., 'The Clinical Contours of Clinical Research in India' (2010), 7 Ind. J. Med. Ethics 178.

Nikarge, S. and Pamnani, D., 'Clinical Trials Watch' (2009), 6 Ind. J. Med. Ethics 228.

NIMR, *Tanzania Essential National Health Research, & Priority Setting* (Dar es Salaam, Tanzania: NIMR, 1999).

Nkkash, R., Makhoul J. and Afifi, R., 'Obtaining informed consent: observations from community research with refugee and impoverished youth' (2009), 35 J. Med. Ethics 638.

North, R.L. and Rothenberg, K.H., 'Partner Notification and the Threat of Domestic Violence against Women with HIV' (1993), 329 New Eng. J. Med. 1194.

NRCM, *Procedures and Guidelines for the Conduct of Research in Malawi* (NRCM, Office of the President and Cabinet, 2002).

Nuffield Council on Bioethics, *The Ethics of Research Related to Healthcare in Developing Countries* (London, NCB, 2002).

Nuffield Council on Bioethics, *The Ethics of Research Related to Healthcare in Developing Countries* (London: NCB, 2005).

Nundy, Samiran, et al., 'A New Colonialism? – Conducting Clinical Trials in India' (2005), 352 New England Journal of Medicine 1633.

Nwabueze, B.O., *The Judiciary as the Third Estate of the Realm* (Abuja, Nigeria: Gold Press, Ltd., 2007).

——, *The Machinery of Justice in Nigeria* (London: Butterworths – African Law Series, 1963).
——, *The Presidential Constitution of Nigeria* (London: C. Hurst & Co., 1982).
Nwabueze, Remigius N., *Biotechnology and the Challenge of Property: Property Rights in Dead Bodies, Body Parts,and Genetic Information* (Aldershot: Ashgate Publishing Ltd., 2007).
——, 'A Widow's Sepulchral Right as a Human Right' (2010), 23 Harvard J. Hum. Rights 141.
——, 'Biotechnology and the New Property Regime in Human Bodies and Body Parts' (2002), 24 Loy. L.A. Int'l & Comp. L. Rev.19.
——, 'Breach of Trust as a Professional Misconduct' (2009), 7 Commonwealth Journal of Law & Legal Education 17.
——, 'Donated Organs, Property Rights and the Remedial Quagmire' (2008), 16 Med. L.R. 202.
——, 'The Dynamics and Genius of Nigeria's Indigenous Legal Order' (2002), 1 Indigenous Law Journal 153.
——, 'What Can Genomics and Health Biotechnology Do for Developing Countries' (2005), 15 Albany Law Journal of Science and Technology 369.
Nwabueze, Remigius N. and Okorie, Polycarp, 'Flexibility of Damages for Conversion and Detinue' (2009), 17 African Journal of International and Comparative Law 102.
Nwankwo, Joe, 'Pfizer compensates Trovan victims with N26m each', Daily Independent, 26 January 2010, page unknown.
Nyika, A., et al., 'Composition, training needs and independence of ethics review committees across Africa: are the gate-keepers rising to the emerging challenges?' (2009), 35 J. Med. Ethics 189.
Obilade, A.O., *The Nigerian Legal System* (London: Sweet and Maxwell, 1979).
Oboh, Mike, 'Nigerian state files criminal suit against Pfizer', Reuters, 30 May 2007.
Office of Inspector General, *Institutional Review Boards: The Emergence of Independent Boards* (Washington, D.C.: U.S. Department of Health and Human Services, 1998).
Ogundiran, T.O. and Adebamowo, C.A., 'Surgeons' opinions and practice of informed consent in Nigeria' (2010), 36 J. Med. Ethics 741.
Ogundiran, Temidayo O., 'Enhancing the African Bioethics Initiative' (2004), 4 BMC Medical Education 21.
Ohia, Paul, 'More Woes for Pfizer, Loses Appeal in US Supreme Court', THIS DAY, 30 June 2010, page unknown.
Onyemelukwe, Cheluchi, 'Regulating Research Involving Humans in Nigeria: Some Recent Improvements' (2008), 16 Health Law Review 36.
——, 'Research Involving Humans in African Countries: A Case for Domestic Legal Frameworks' (2008), 16 Afr. J. Int'l & Comp. L. 152.
Orentlicher, David, 'Universality and its Limits: When Research Ethics can Reflect Local Circumstances' [2002], 30 J.L. Med. & Ethics 403.

Oricha, Bello S. and Yauri, Muhammad B., 'Uncertainty Principle Versus Clinical Equipoise in Clinical Trials in Sub-Saharan Africa: Are They Really Tenable? (2003), 2 Annals of African Medicine 99.

Orlowski, Victoria, 'Promising Protection Through Internationally Derived Duties' (2004), 36 Cornell Int'l L.J. 381.

Page, Alice K., 'Prior Agreements in International Clinical Trials: Ensuring the benefits of research to developing countries' (2002–2003), 3 Yale J. Health Pol'y L. & Ethics 35.

Page, W., et al., (eds), Prosser and Keeton on the Law of Torts, 5th edn (St Paul, MN.: West Publishing Co., 1984).

Pagnattaro, Marisa Anne, 'International Legal and Ethical Consideration at Pfizer, Inc.' (2005), 22 J. Legal Stud. 169.

Palmer, Larry I., 'Disease management and Liability in the Human Genome Era' (2002), 47 Vill. L. Rev. 1.

Pande, B.B., 'Protecting the Individual Against the State Through False Imprisonment Actions: The Tanzanian Experience' (1983), 32 Int'l & Com. L. Q. 506.

Pandeya, Radhieka, 'New Code for Inspecting Human Drug Trials Mint', New Delhi, 10 November 2010.

Parry, Eldryd, 'The Ethics of Clinical Research in Developing Countries' (2000), 34 J. Royal C. Physicians Lon. 328.

Perry, Michael, '"Body-Parts Supermarket" Causes Uproar in Australia: No consent for Research', National Post, 20 March 2001, A13.

Peto, Richard and Baigent, Colin, 'Trials: the next 50 years: Large scale randomised evidence of moderate benefits' (1998), 317 BMJ 1170.

Phillips, R.A. and Hoey, J., 'Constraints of Interest: Lessons at the Hospital for Sick Children' (1998), 159 C.M.A.J. 955.

Phoenix, Janet A., 'Ethical considerations of research involving minorities, the poorly educated and/or low-income populations' (2002), 24 Neurotoxicology and Teratology 475.

Plomer, Aurora, *The Law and Ethics of Medical Research: International Bioethics and Human Rights* (London: Cavendish Publishing Ltd., 2005).

Quinn, T.C., et al., 'Viral Load and Heterosexual Transmission of Human Immunodeficiency Virus Type 1' (2000), 342 New Eng. J. Med. 921.

Rathod, Sujit D., 'Commentary on HPV screening for cervical cancer in rural India' (2011), 8 Ind. J. Med. Ethics 180.

Raufu, Abiodun, 'Nigeria postpones programme of polio immunisation' (2004), 328 BMJ 1278.

——, 'Traditional rulers in northern Nigeria call for halt to polio vaccination' (2004), 328 BMJ 306.

Richardson, Henry S. and Belsky, Leah, 'The Ancillary-care Responsibilities of Medical Researchers: An Ethical Framework for Thinking about the Clinical Care That Researchers Owe their Subjects' (2004), 34 The Hastings Center Report 25.

Richardson, Henry S., 'Incidental Findings and Ancillary-Care Obligations' (2008), 36 Journal of Law, Medicine and Ethics 256.

Robertson, G., 'Informed Consent to Medical Treatment' (1981), 97 L.Q.R. 102.

Robertson, John A., 'The Law of Institutional Review Boards' (1979), 26 UCLA L. Rev. 484.

——, 'The Scientist's Right To Research: A Constitutional Analysis' [1977]. 51 Southern California L. Rev. 1203.

Rogers, W.V.H., *Winfield & Jolowicz on Tort, 18th edn* (London: Sweet and Maxwell, 2010).

——, *Winfield & Jolowicz on Tort, 16th edn* (London: Sweet and Maxwell, 2002).

Roman, Joanne, 'U.S. Medical Research in the Developing World: Ignoring Nuremberg' (2002), 11 Cornell J.L. & Pub. Pol'y 441.

Rothman, D.J., 'Ethical and Social Issues in the Development of New Drugs' (1987), 63 Bull. N.Y. Acad. Med. 557.

Rothmayr, C., 'Towards the judicialisation of Swiss politics? (2001), 24 Western European Politics 77.

Roy D. Mugerwa, et al., 'First Trial of the HIV-1 Vaccine in Africa: Ugandan Experience' (2002), 324 BMJ 226.

Roy-Toole, Christopher, 'Illegality in the research protocol: the duty of research ethics committees under the 2001 Clinical Trials Directive' (2008), 4 Research Ethics Review 111.

Rwabihama, Jean-Paul, et al., 'Ethics committees for biomedical research in some African emerging countries , which establishment for which independence? A comparison with the USA and Canada' (2010), 36 J. Med. Ethics 243.

Samuels, Alec, 'Serious Professional Misconduct' (2005), 73 Medico-Legal Journal 166.

Sankaranarayanan, R., et al., 'Reply to S.D. Rathod's Commentary on HPV screening for cervical cancer in rural India' (2011), 8 Ind. J. Med. Ethics 182.

Santoro, M.A. and Gorrie, T.M. (eds), *Ethics and the Pharmaceutical Industry* (Cambridge: Cambridge University Press, 2005).

Santosuosso, Amedeo, et al., 'What constitutional protection for freedom of scientific research?' (2007), 33 J. Med. Ethics 342.

Saunders, John, 'More Guidelines on Research Ethics?' (2007), 33 J. Med. Ethics 683.

Savulescu, J. and Spriggs, M., 'The Hexamethonium Asthma Study and the Death of a Normal Volunteer in Research' (2002), 28 J. Med. Ethics 3.

Savulescu, J., 'Two Deaths and Two Lessons: Is it Time to Review the Structure and Function of Research Ethics Committees?' (2002), 28 J. Med. Ethics 1.

——, 'Does setting good practice standards for research ethics committees increase their legal liability?' (1997), 314 BMJ 1833.

Schafer, A., 'The Randomized Clinical Trial: For Whose Benefit? (1985), 7 IRB: A Review of Human Subjects Research 4.

Schaffer, D.N., et al., 'Equitable treatment for HIV/AIDS clinical trial participants: a focus group study of patients, clinician researchers, and administrators in western Kenya' (2006), 32 J. Med. Ethics 55.

Schipper, Irene and Weyzig, Francis, *Ethics for Drug Testing in Low and Middle Income Countries: Considerations for European Market Authorisation* (Amsterdam: SOMO, 2008).

Schuchardt, E.J., 'Walking a Thin Line: Distinguishing Between Research and Medical Practice During Operation Desert Storm' (1992), 26 Columbia J. Law Soc. Prob. 77.

Schuklenk, U., 'For-Profit Clinical Trials in Developing Countries – Those Troublesome Patient Benefits' (2010), 10 The American Journal of Bioethics 52.

Scott, C., *Torture as Tort: Comparative Perspectives on the Development of Transnational Human Rights Litigation* (Portland, Oregon: Hart Publishing, 2001).

Seaborne, G., 'The Role of the Tort of Battery in Medical Law' (1995), 24 Anglo-American L. Rev. 24.

Setouhy, M. El, et al., 'Fair Benefits for Research in Developing Countries' (2002), 298 Science 2133.

Shalala, D., 'Protecting Research Subjects – What Must be Done' (2000), 343 N. Eng. J. Med. 808–810.

Shamoo, Adil E., 'Institutional Review Boards (IRBs) and Conflict of Interest' (1999), 7 Accountability In Research 201.

Shapiro, K. and Benatar, S.R., 'HIV Prevention Research and Global Inequality: Steps Towards Improved Standards of Care' (2005), 1 J. Med. Ethics 39.

Shapshay, Sandra and Dimple, Kenneth D., 'Participation in Biomedical Research is an Imperfect Moral Duty: A Response to John Harris' (2007), 33 J. Med. Ethics 414.

Shaul, Randi Z., et al., 'Legal liabilities in research: early lessons from North America' (2005), 6 BMC Medical Ethics 4.

Shaw, Sonia, 'Globalizing Clinical Research: Big Pharma Tries Out First World Drugs on Unsuspecting Third World Patients', The Nation, 1 July 2002, at 1.

Shultz, M.M., 'From Informed Consent to Patient Choice; a New Protected Interest' (1985), 95 Yale L.J. 219.

Simmerling, Mary, et al., 'Introducing A New Paradigm For Ethical Research In The Social Sciences: Part 1' (2007), 101 Northwestern University Law Review 837.

Simoni, Jane M., Mason, Hyacinth R.C., Marks, Gary, et al., 'Women's Self-Disclosure of HIV Infection: Rates, Reasons, and Reactions' (1995), 63 (3) Journal of Consulting and Clinical Psychology 474.

Singh, J.A. and Mills, E.J., 'The Abandoned Trials of Pre-Exposure Prophylaxis for HIV: What Went Wrong' (2005), 2 PLoS Medicine 824.

Singh, Jerome A., 'Health Research and Human Rights in South Africa' (2004) 363 The Lancet 1393.

Sokol, D., 'Sweetening the scent: commentary on "What principlism misses"' (2009), 35 J. Med. Ethics 232.

Spece, R.G., et al. (eds), *Conflicts of Interest in Clinical Practice and Research* (New York: Oxford University Press, 1996).

——, 'First Amendment Protection of Experimentation: A Critical Review and Tentative Synthesis/Reconstruction of the Literature'(1998), 8 S. Cal. Interdisc. L.J. 185.

Ssemigavu, Mpanga S., *Protection of Human Subjects of Biomedical Research and Medical Interventions: The Legal and Ethical Concerns* (Dissertation submitted in 1997 to the Faculty of Law, Makerere University, Uganda, in partial fulfilment of the requirement for the grant of Bachelors of Law).

Stead, M., et al., 'Hello, hello – it's English I speak!: a qualitative exploration of patients' understanding of the science of clinical trials' (2005), 31 J. Med. Ethics 664.

Stephens, Joe, 'Doctors Say Trial's Approval Was Backdated', Washington Post, 16 January 2001, page A01.

Stolberg, Sheryl Gay, 'Placebo Use Is Suspended in Overseas AIDS Trials', New York Times, 19 February 1998, A16.

Stoljar, Samuel, 'Unjust Enrichment and Unjust Sacrifice' (1987), M.L.R. 603.

Sudha, Sree P., 'How Ethical are Clinical Trials in India' (2007), Indian L.J. 9.

Tabor, E, et al., 'Did HIV and HTLV Originate in Africa?' (1990), 264 JAMA 691.

Tangwa, G.B., 'Between universalism and relativism: a conceptual exploration of problems in formulating and applying international biomedical ethical guidelines' (2004), 30 J. Med. Ethics 63.

TANHER and NHREC, Guidelines on Ethics for Health Research in Tanzania (2001).

Tännsjö, Torbjörn, 'The Morality of Clinical Research: A Case Study' (1994), 19 Journal of Medicine and Philosophy 7.

Taylor, Allyn L., 'Globalisation and Biotechnology: UNESCO and an International Strategy to Advance Human Rights and Public Health' (1999), 25 American Journal of Law & Medicine 479.

Taylor, K.M., et al., 'Physicians' Reasons For Not Entering Eligible Patients in a Randomised Clinical Trial of Surgery for Breast Cancer' (1984), 310 New England Journal of Medicine 1363.

Thompson, J., Baird, P. and Downie, J., *Report of the Committee of Inquiry on the Case Involving Dr Nancy Olivieri, the Hospital for Sick Children, the University of Toronto, and Apotex Inc.* (Toronto: Canadian Association of University Teachers, 2001).

Todres, Jonathan, 'Can Research Subjects of Clinical Trials In Developing Countries Sue Physician-Investigators For Human Rights Violations?' (2000), 16 N.Y.L Sch. J. Hum. Rts 737.

Tomossy, George and Weisstub, David N., *Human Experimentation and Research* (Aldershot, Ashgate Publishing, 2003).

Tröhler, Ulrich and Reiter-Theil, Stella (eds), *Ethics Codes in Medicine: Foundations and Achievements of Codification Since 1947* (Sydney: Ashgate Publishing Co., 1998).

Uganda AIDS Commission, *Uganda Guidelines for AIDS Vaccine Research* (UAC, 2006).

Uganda National Health Research Organisation, *Guidelines for the Conduct of Health Research Involving Human Subjects in Uganda* (Entebbe, Uganda: Ministry of Health, 2000).

Ugandan National Council for Science and Technology, *National Guidelines for Research Involving Humans as Research Participants* (Kampala: UNCST, 2007).

Umerah, B.C. (ed.), *Medical Practice and the Law in Nigeria* (Ibadan, Nigeria: Longman Nig. Ltd., 1989).

Umozurike, U.O., *The African Charter on Human and Peoples' Rights* (The Hague: Martins Nijhoff, 1997).

UNAIDS, *Ethical Considerations in Biomedical HIV Prevention Trials: UNAIDS/WHO Guidance Document* (Geneva: UNAIDS, 2007).

——, *Ethical Considerations in HIV Preventive Vaccine Research – UNAIDS Guidance Document* (Geneva: UNAIDS, 2000).

Valiathan, M.S., 'Clinical Trials Should Promote Health Care', The Hindu (vol. 18), 18–31 August 2001 (page unknown).

Varmer, Harold and Satcher, David, 'Ethical Complexities of Conducting Research in Developing Countries' (1997), 337 New Eng. J. Med. 1003.

Veatch, Robert, 'The Irrelevance of Equipoise' (2007), 32 Journal of Medicine and Philosophy 167.

——, *Medical Ethics* (Boston: Jones & Bartlett Publishers, 1997, 2nd edn).

——, 'Indifference of Subjects: An alternative to equipoise in randomized clinical trials' (2002), 19 Social Philosophy and Policy 295.

Veitch, E., *East African Cases on the Law of Tort* (London: Sweet and Maxwell, 1972).

Verdun-Jones, Simon and Weisstub, David N., 'The Regulation of Biomedical Research Experimentation in Canada: Developing an Effective Apparatus for the Implementation of Ethical Principles in a Scientific Milieu' (996–997) 28 Ottawa Law Review 297.

Vikenty Veressayev, *The Memoirs of a Physician* (New York: Alfred A. Knopf, 1916; translated from Russian by Simeon Linden).

Virgo, Graham, *The Principles of the Law of Restitution, 2nd edn* (Oxford: Oxford University Press, 2006).

Vogel, Gretchen, 'Study of HIV Transmission Sparks Ethics Debate' (2000), 288 Science 22.

Waddams, S., 'Johanna Wagner and the Rival Opera Houses' (2001), 117 L.Q.R. 431.

——, 'Medical Experiments on Human Subjects' (1967), 25 U. Tor. Fac. L. Rev. 25.

Wade, H.W.R. and Forsyth, C., *Administrative Law, 9th edn* (Oxford; OUP, 2004).

Wade, John W., 'Tort Law as Ombudsman' (1986), 65 Or. L. Rev. 309–325.

Walker, Tom, 'What principlism misses' (2009), 35 J. Med. Ethics 229–231.

Wang, Y.G., 'AIDS Policy and Bioethics: Ethical Dilemmas Facing China in HIV Prevention' (1997), 11 Bioethics 323.

Warring, D.R. and Lemmens, T., 'Integrating Values in Risk Analysis of Biomedical Research: The Case for Regulatory and Law Reform' (2004), University of Toronto Law Journal 249.

Warlow, Charles, 'Should research ethics committees be observing the law or working by ethical principles?' (2005), 1 Research Ethics Review 23.

Wasuna, Angela, 'Researchers Abroad' (2005), Hastings Centre Report 3.

Weijer, C. and Miller, P.B., 'When are research risks reasonable in relation to anticipated benefits?' (2004), 10 Nature Medicine 570.

Weijer, C., Shapiro S., and K. Glass, 'For and against: clinical equipoise and not the uncertainty principle is the moral underpinning of the randomised controlled trial' (2000), 321 BMJ 756.

Weinrib, Ernest, 'Understanding Tort Law' (1989), 23 Valp. L. J. 485.

Weinstein, James, 'Institutional Review Boards and the Constitution' (2007), 101 Northwestern University Law Review 493.

Weisstub, D.N., *Research on Human Subjects: Ethics, Law and Social Policy* (Oxford, Elsevier Science Ltd., 1998).

Welsome, E., 'The Plutonium Experiment', Albuquerque Tribune, 15, 16 and 17 November 1993.

Westen, Peter, 'The Empty Idea of Equality' (1982), 95 Harv. L Rev. 537.

White, Mary T., 'Guidelines for IRB Review of International Collaborative Medical Research: A Proposal' (1999), 27 Law, Medicine & Ethics 87.

White, Stephen, 'The Law Relating to Dealing with Dead Bodies' (2000), 4 Medical Law International 145.

Wildie, Paul, 'Husband Sues After Brain Tissue Taken From Dead Wife,' National Post, 29 January 2000, A13.

Williams, C.J. (ed.), *Introducing New Treatments for Cancer: Practical, Ethical and Legal Problems* (Chichester, England: John Wiley & Sons, 1992).

Wilson, Robin F., 'Rethinking the Shield of Immunity: Should Ethics Committees be Accountable for their Mistakes' (2002), 14 HealthCare Ethics Committee Forum 172.

Winfield, P.H., 'The History of Negligence in the Law of Torts' (1926), 42 L.Q.R. 184.

Winter, Jane E. and Baguley, Jane (eds), *Outsourcing Clinical Development: Strategies for Working with CROs and Other Partners* (Aldershot: Gower Publishing Ltd., 2006).

Woetzel, Robert K., *The Nuremberg Trials in International Law* (London: Stevens & Sons Ltd., 1962).

World Health Organisation, Press Release: WHO Launches the First Global Strategy on Traditional and Alternative Medicine, WHO/38/16 May 2002.

——, *Operational Guidelines for Ethics Committees that Review Biomedical Research* (Geneva: WHO, 2000).

World Medical Association, *Declaration of Helsinki, Ethical Principles for Medical Research Involving Human Subjects* (59th WMA General Assembly, Seoul, 2008).

——, *Declaration of Helsinki – Ethical Principles for Medical Research Involving Human Subjects* (48th World Medical Assembly, Somerset West, Republic of South Africa, 1996).

——, *Declaration of Helsinki – Recommendations Guiding Physicians in Biomedical Research Involving Human Subjects* (41st World Medical Assembly, Hong Kong, September 1989).

Wyngaert, Christine V.D. and Stessens, Guy, *International Criminal Law: A Collection of International and European Instruments* (The Hague: Kluwer Law International, 1996).

Zarembo, A., 'Guatemala: life-or-death lottery – the medicine is scarce; it must be allotted somehow', Newsweek, 5 July 1999, 25.

Zimmerman, Susan V., 'Translating Ethics into Law: Duties of Care in Health Research Involving Humans' (2005), 13 Health Law Review 13.

Zong, Zhiyong, 'Should post-trial provision of beneficial experimental interventions be mandatory in developing countries' (2008), 34 J. Med. Ethics 188.

# Index

For Product Safety Concerns and Information please contact our EU
representative GPSR@taylorandfrancis.com
Taylor & Francis Verlag GmbH, Kaufingerstraße 24, 80331 München, Germany

www.ingramcontent.com/pod-product-compliance
Ingram Content Group UK Ltd.
Pitfield, Milton Keynes, MK11 3LW, UK
UKHW020019200926
475702UK00014B/1967
* 9 7 8 1 1 3 8 2 7 9 3 0 8 *